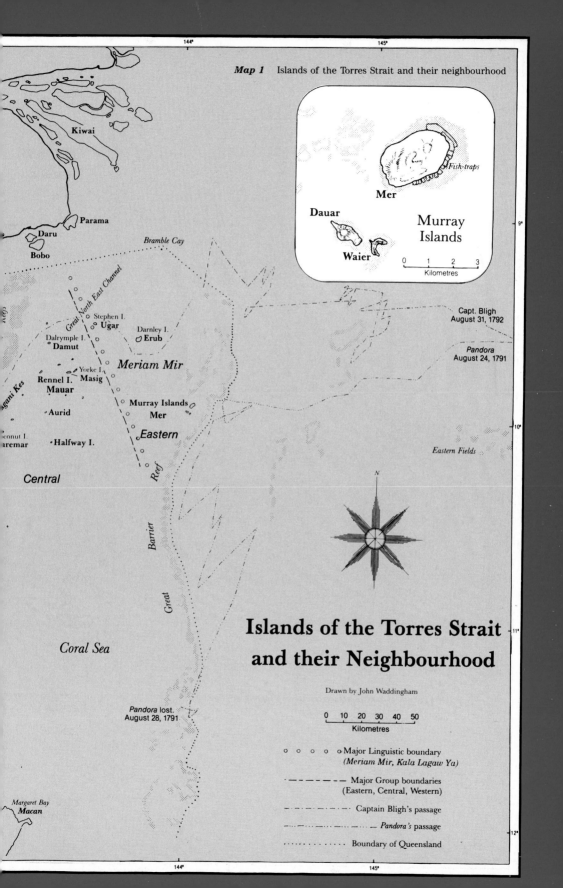

Map 1 Islands of the Torres Strait and their neighbourhood

Kiwai

Parama

Daru

Bobo

Bramble Cay

Fish-traps

Mer

Dauar

**Murray
Islands**

Waier

0 1 2 3
Kilometres

Great North East Channel

Stephen I.

Ugar

Darnley I.

Dalrymple I.

Damut

Erub

Meriam Mir

Yorke I.

Rennel I. **Masig**

Mauar

Aurid

Coconut I.

aremar

Halfway I.

Murray Islands

Mer

Eastern

Reef

Central

Barrier

Capt. Bligh
August 31, 1792

Pandora
August 24, 1791

Eastern Fields

N

Great

Islands of the Torres Strait
and their Neighbourhood

Drawn by John Waddingham

0 10 20 30 40 50
Kilometres

Coral Sea

Pandora lost.
August 28, 1791

o o o o o Major Linguistic boundary
        (Meriam Mir, Kala Lagaw Ya)

– – – – – Major Group boundaries
        (Eastern, Central, Western)

–·–·–·– Captain Bligh's passage

–··–··– *Pandora's* passage

·········· Boundary of Queensland

Margaret Bay
Macan

STARS OF TAGAI

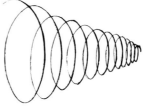

nor can the Sunne
Perfit a Circle, or maintaine his way
One inch direct; but where he rose to-day
He comes no more, but with a couzening line,
Steales by that point, and so is Serpentine:
And seeming weary with his reeling thus,
He meanes to sleepe, being now falne nearer us.
So, of the Starres which boast that they doe runne
In Circle still, none ends where he begun.

John Donne, The First Anniversary

Plate 1 Tombstone unveiling, Crossfield Ahmat, Badu Island, 1987

NONIE SHARP

STARS OF TAGAI
The Torres Strait Islanders

ABORIGINAL
STUDIES
PRESS
Canberra 1993

FIRST PUBLISHED IN 1993 BY

Aboriginal Studies Press

for the Australian Institute of Aboriginal and Torres Strait Islander Studies

GPO Box 553, Canberra ACT 2601

The views expressed in this publication are those of the author and not necessarily those of the Australian Institute of Aboriginal and Torres Strait Islander Studies.

NATIONAL LIBRARY OF AUSTRALIA CATALOGUING-IN-PUBLICATION DATA:

Sharp, Nonie.

Stars of Tagai: The Torres Strait Islanders.

Bibliography.

Includes index.

ISBN 0 85575 238 6.

1. Torres Strait Islands (Qld.) — History. 2. Torres Strait Islands (Qld.) — Colonial influence. 3. Torres Strait Islands (Qld.) — Social life and customs. 4. Torres Strait Islands (Qld.) — Politics and government. 5. Murray Islands (Qld.) — Social life and customs. I. Title.

994.38

COVER based upon a watercolour by Lieutenant George Tobin;colour negative ZPXA 563 f76 courtesy Mitchell Library, State Library of New South Wales, and drawings of the Tagai constellation by Gizu and Mariget of Mabuiag (Haddon 1908,4).

 COVER DESIGN by Paul James, *Arena.*

TYPESET in 9/14 Compugraphic Century Schoolbook by Jackie Covington, Aboriginal Studies Press.

DESIGNED by Denis French, Aboriginal Studies Press.

PRINTED on 115gsm semi matt by Southwood Press, Marrickville, NSW.

3000 02 93

For the children of the Torres Strait Islands in the memory of Kitty
Ware, Harry Captain, Wees Nawia, Crossfield Ahmat, Sam Passi, Eddie
Koiki Mabo.

CONTENTS

ILLUSTRATIONS

PLATES

FIGURES

MAPS

CALENDAR

PREFACE

Stars of Tagai is about life among the blue-water people of the Torres Strait Islands. The title is drawn from the myth of Tagai which belongs to all Torres Strait Islanders. The rhythm of Islanders' lives follows the movement of the constellation Tagai, a man standing in a canoe; his left hand, the Southern Cross, holds a fish spear. The stars of Tagai usher in seasonal changes and are a guide to voyaging and cultivating. The book explores the changing life of a sea people in the period of sustained encroachment and invasion from the mid-nineteenth century until today. It discusses the patterns and the consequences of interrelationships between cultures with deeply contrasting ways of living and meaning systems which came face to face in the Islands.

The central theme concerns the creation and re-creation of a Torres Strait Islander identity and its expression in self-awareness as a unique sea culture.

In the years since major contact, the forces of change, together with the power of social processes inherent within the pre-existing culture, led to the creation of modern Torres Strait Islander identity continuous with, yet different from, the old. Today, a sense of Islander identity is growing. The book explores the way in which this identity is grounded and gains its strength from the diversity of small Islander communities which together make up the whole.

Stars of Tagai consists of four parts. The first part introduces the main themes of encounter: special emphasis is placed upon gift exchange or reciprocity as the key principle in the creation and re-creation of identities as diversities-in-unity. The second part focuses upon the ordering of the world of the Meriam people of Mer, Dauar and Waier within the movement of cosmic cycles, as a living example of the unity of separate identities created by the principle of reciprocity. Part III explores the forces for change and renewal and Part IV depicts the expressions of contemporary Torres Strait Islander identity and the quest for autonomy in the context of five key events,[1] beginning with a comprehensive study of the maritime strike against Protection in 1936, which draws upon hitherto silent or unavailable primary sources, namely Islander participants and correspondence within the Aboriginals Department in 1936 and 1937. The other four events are the Second World War; the attempt to move the maritime boundaries with Papua New Guinea and so divide the Torres Strait, known as the 'border issue' in the 1970s; a move by Islanders for political sovereignty in the 1980s; and the *Murray Island Land/Mabo* case (1982–92).

The original work for *Stars of Tagai* comes from a PhD thesis completed in 1984, titled 'Springs of Originality among the Torres Strait Islanders: After the Storm-Winds the Leafing of the Wongai Tree'. The Storm-Winds is a metaphor for the singular or non-reciprocal invading forces, the powers of destruction carried especially by Kole. 'Kole', a word in Meriam Mir, means both master and white man.

The thesis arose from a longstanding interest in the meanings and the possibilities of the cultural stirrings of people on the other side of the Great Divide between cultures in the period of the 1960s and 1970s, which combined primordial sentiments with cultural renewal. This interest affects the way the study was conceived and carried out. I arrived at a time when the seeds of cultural ferment were taking root within the Islands — later than in the lands to the north and the south. In the next ten years they were to sprout and begin to flower.

In 1978, the time of my first visit to the Torres Strait Islands, I was, like another scholar had been eight years before me, met by the 'constant argument...that the traditional culture of the Torres Strait Islanders had long since faded' (Laade 1971, ix). Dr Haddon and his colleagues of the Cambridge Anthropological Expedition in 1898 saw themselves as 'just in time to record the memory of a vanished past' (1904, vi). In his fieldwork of twenty-four months from 1958 to 1961, Jeremy Beckett, an almost lone scholar of the Torres Strait for nearly twenty years, had found a fading and fragmenting culture (1963; 1972, 307–26). My mind had been kept open on the question by the work of Dr Hironobu Kitaoji, who had concluded from his fieldwork in the period from 1975 to 1977, that the work of Dr Haddon and his colleagues had underestimated 'the unity, cohesiveness and integrity of the Torres Strait Islanders and their culture', and that such thinking had persisted in Beckett's work (1978, 55). Understandably, given the magnitude and many-sidedness of the forces for change, Beckett had set himself the task of showing 'the magnitude of the changes which have taken place' through the profound transformation wrought over ninety years (1963, 2). Did these differing emphases stem, at least in part, from the different historical circumstances in which the respective field workers carried out their studies? Beckett himself suggests a positive answer to this question in his book about the Islanders published in 1987: the 'centre of gravity' of his study lay in the transitional period when the tide was about to turn on the 'old colonial regime' (1987, 21). In his book he conveys an understanding of a collective identity among Islanders centred around 'Island custom', while retaining his original belief in a basic cultural discontinuity between latter-day Islanders and the pre-colonial people of the Torres Strait (1987, 12).

Since the study I began towards the end of 1978 departs from the mainstream of cross-cultural studies in both its substance and its form, I shall explain the various strands which came to compose it.

In 1978, I found a church-going people who lived in European-style houses and spoke English as well as the *lingua franca*, an indigenous pidgin language, Torres Strait Creole (Shnukal 1983a; 1983b; 1985; 1989), or Broken, Blaikman, Big Thap or Pizin, and as far as I could gather then, their original languages, Meriam Mir (MM) in the Eastern Islands and Kala Lagaw Ya (KLY) in the Western and Central Islands (Ray 1907; Rigsby in Reynolds (ed) 1992). I soon saw for myself that most of the sacred shrines and outward symbols of the old culture had been destroyed or removed.[2] I also noted that in each Islander household a lamp burned at night to ward off the powers of evil.

I was appalled and indignant at what I heard and observed. 'Killing them softly' were the words that came to mind as I watched many Islander people who had lost the will to struggle or do things for themselves. Although I was largely unaware then, I was entering upon the end of an era created seventy-four years before in 1903-04, when Islanders were brought under the Aboriginals Protection and Restriction of the Sale of Opium Act 1897. Up to the 1940s children were actively prevented from going beyond third-grade standard. At the same time, in some islands, they were punished for speaking their own language even in the school grounds (Shnukal 1985, 230).

In November 1978, I found myself standing in the office of the Department of Aboriginal and Islanders Advancement (DAIA), Thursday Island, seeking a passage on a DAIA cargo-passenger boat. Each of the fourteen Island communities lived on land reserved for them under the Torres Strait Islanders Act, in most cases on their own islands, and each elected its own community council. Island Councils had the power to give permission to intending visitors to visit the reserves, but to be sure of a reply, in many cases it was necessary to rely on the Department's radio telephone system, there being no public telephones on the islands until the end of 1980. The only way to reach most of the islands without the exorbitant expense of chartering a helicopter was on a DAIA boat. Commonly, there were agonising delays in securing the necessary Council permission.

To my surprise I was offered a free passage on the *Melbidir*, bringer of glad tidings, the Department's main cargo-passenger boat. 'You're okay', said the stand-in for the local manager (known as 'Mr Brisbane' by Islanders), 'We just want to keep out Southern trouble-makers'. Holding my peace and my breath, with a pale chuckle I boarded the *Melbidir*, only to discover that I was travelling 'white'; the Islanders were 'housed' on deck.

At the beginning of this visit I met Flo Kennedy, who was to become sister, friend, adviser and source of strength, a central figure of the *Stars of Tagai* (see Kennedy 1991). On the *Melbidir* voyage, Etta Passi from Mer, adopted me as her sister. Out at Mer I met Au Bala, whose wisdom on the depth and the durability of Meriam culture inspired the central theme of this book. During this visit, the

Chairman of Kubin Council, Moa Island, a descendant of the Kaurareg of the islands close to Cape York — known as Uncle here — gave me the beginnings of the story that went behind the invisible net which tightly secured the Islanders to Queensland. I soon discovered that the DAIA's ultimate control of access to Island reserves was consistent with a more general situation of paternalist dependence and isolation which still existed in the late 1970s, and as I was to discover, continued well into the 1980s.

In 1980, there was only one qualified Islander primary teacher. Self-initiated, Islander-controlled economic ventures also remained the exception. One rare example, the housing cooperative known as MAW, which stands for Moa Island, Adai (Northern Peninsula Area), Waiben (Thursday Island), was subjected to Departmental veto even though amendments to the Torres Strait Islanders Act 1971 in April 1979 had made Island Councils corporate bodies. Regulation 19 of the Act required that all moneys raised in reserve communities be paid into an Island fund which was subject to the ultimate control of the DAIA manager. In 1980 this regulation was used by the Director of the Department of Aboriginal and Islanders Advancement, PJ Killoran, to prevent MAW from collecting house rents, because it was a self-managing body outside the Act.

As a result of my first two visits in 1978 and 1979, I felt an intense desire to help change the existing state of affairs through my writing. It became important to me to establish my relationships with Islanders on the basis of equality and mutual respect for cultural difference: I was not attempting to study Islanders as a one-way activity; I saw my research activities as a partnership. My critical attitudes were reflected in my writing and media work (*National Times*, 29 December 1979; Sharp 1980c, 1–16, a submission to Island Councils). In July 1980, I went from island to island with a tape-recorder hanging a little awkwardly from my shoulder, preparing an all-Islander program, Torres Strait Islanders: Their Quest for a Future (Broadband, ABC Radio, 1 October 1980). Much later, in 1988–89 I acted as script adviser to Yarra Bank Films in the making of the documentary film, *Land Bilong Islanders* (1990).

When I returned to the Islands at the end of 1979 I carried from reserve to reserve a file of Protectors' once-secret letters unearthed from Queensland's public state archives. They told the inside story of the alarm and concern the Islanders caused the government when they had refused to work the 'Company boats' in 1936; how the 'discontented natives' had been got back to work; how the Islanders I was meeting, whom the Protector believed would 'never be the same again', were schooled to forget about the strike. Islanders' interest in the letters truly astonished me. The file passed from hand to hand. All fourteen Island Councils received a preliminary paper I had written on the strike together with the documentation of the Aboriginals' Department (see Sharp 1980a; and also 1982b).

In 1980, I published *Torres Strait Islands 1879–1979: Theme for an Overview*. Three phases of Islanders' relationship to the dominant society provided a context for their responses. The central theme which emerged was the continuing existence of Islander communities within a larger cultural whole — the Torres Strait Islanders.

In October 1979, I was awarded a La Trobe University post-graduate research scholarship and I began full-time research on the theme of cultural continuity and change in the Torres Strait Islands. Many of the external features of Island culture had disappeared; Islanders had been taught to regard traditional beliefs and many practices as 'savage' and 'heathen'; and many customs which continued were simply taken for granted and not talked about by Islanders. A reflection upon these facts led me to take a broad approach which combined oral history in the form of conversational narratives by Islanders with a strong sense of their own culture, with a discussion which situated their life stories within a social–historical context. Islanders became the central primary source of the thesis, and the stories of their lives and experiences, their songs and dances, were supplemented by the written accounts of a variety of other participants in and observers of the era.

When the Cambridge anthropologists visited Mer in 1898 they found Murray Islanders reluctant to talk about certain subjects, partly because they 'were originally of a secret or sacred character', and partly because they believed that white men expected that they 'ought to be ashamed of the past' (1908, xix). In 1978, I found a similar reticence.

In mid-1980, in beginning to record Islanders' narratives, I found a readiness to talk about the past in the present. I began to observe an important continuity in which the sacred power or *zogo* of the Meriam culture heroes, Malo-Bomai had been handed down into the present life of Murray Islanders. In particular, I noted the way it was embedded within the tradition of Christianity at Murray Island. I was struck by the manner in which the everyday activities of Murray Islanders were framed and guided by the sacred law known as Malo's Law. 'Before he did anything he thought about his *zogo*', an Islander observed to me about the person I call First Meriam Man here, perhaps the most outspoken and politically radical leader Murray Island has produced. I was told how Malo's Law helped people to live together; its rules were like the Ten Commandments; so on Murray Island Christianity was readily accepted. I was guided by several Islanders in the search for a story of survival made possible by an inner spiritual strengthening, an untold story with its own uniqueness.

Stars of Tagai is about the best of Torres Strait Islander culture as it has evolved to the present day. It is deliberately and explicitly highly selective: the ten main Islander narrators, whose life stories reveal a strong sense of their culture, are people who have attempted to find an integrative balance between the old and the new under conditions of rapid and enforced culture change. In a real sense too the stars of Tagai are the people of the Torres Strait, those living today and in past times. Countless Islanders contributed to the book.

September 1992   *Nonie Sharp*

ACKNOWLEDGEMENTS

Many people have assisted in creating this book: in the Islands, in university circles, and in my own family. I express my gratitude to them all.

Some Islanders appear by name, or by pen-name; others gave intellectual, practical and moral support. To Lizzie Nawia, Rotannah Passi, Etta Passi, the late Lena Passi, Telei Ahmat, Dolly and the late Oscar Nasslander, Pauline and Alan Mills, Betty and Noel Loos, Maudie Salam, Robert Salam, Sissy Lee, Anna Shnukal, Kathe and Gil Boehringer, Lyndall Ryan, who made me one of their families and drew me into their homes; for their many acts of kindness and for their wisdom and advice, I am especially grateful. To Flo for all these too and for her deep friendship and guidance.

The following people and families have a special place in the book: Marou Mimi of Mer and his family, Harry Captain, Kitty Ware, Wees Nawia, Sam Passi and his family, Iopelli Panuel, Flo Kennedy and her father, mother and her father's father, George Mye, Rev Dave Passi and Eddie Koiki Mabo.

I am grateful to Freddie Ware, Jacob Abednego, Ben Nona, Newcamp Wasaga, Abigail Bann, James Rice, Olive Morseo, Lui Bon and Mau Bon, Sister Peta Warusam, for their stories and recollections, as well as countless other Torres Strait Islanders. Reverend Alf Clint, Stan Tapper and Charlie Matters provided important accounts and helpful advice. James Akee and Carlemo Wacando provided me with verbal information and correspondence on the Torres United Party. Island Councils and the members of Island communities offered me hospitality and friendly assistance over many years. I would specially like to thank the late chairmen of Badu and Kubin councils, Crossfield Ahmat and Wees Nawia.

The original work for this book began in October 1979 when I was awarded a La Trobe University research scholarship. The study was made possible through the support of my family and by financial assistance from the Research Committee, School of Social Sciences and Economics, the Centre for South West Pacific Studies at La Trobe University and the Australian Institute of Aboriginal Studies. It is continuous with work on millenarian movements and cultural nationalism in Melanesia carried out in the 1970s as an Honorary Research Fellow in the Department of Sociology, La Trobe University. At that time Dr Heinz Schütte helped me begin a fresh course and used his good offices to make this course possible; Dr Hironobu Kitaoji suggested I go to the Torres Strait in 1978; he put me in touch with Islanders, gave me the understanding and the confidence to make Islanders the primary source of the PhD thesis, readily shared with me his insights into Islanders' culture, and generously gave me access to his field records on Meriam lexicons. Since August 1981, Professor Noel Loos of James Cook University has made helpful suggestions, and has given me encouragement and advice during the thesis work and critical comments on the manuscript of the book. I would like to thank Professor Kenelm Burridge, University of British Columbia, the late Professor Stanley Diamond, New School for Social Research and Emeritus Professor Kurt Wolff, Brandeis University, whose critical comments in examining the PhD thesis greatly helped in plans for this book. Professor Bruce Rigsby made helpful comments on the manuscript of the book.

Dr Fiona Mackie was supervisor of the thesis. Her intellectual and moral support and her friendship sustained me in my effort to join the circle of my experience of the Islanders and ourselves; her strength with me made its completion possible.

I would like to thank the secretarial staff of the Sociology Department for their help over many years. Barbara Matthews, Beth Robertson, Therese Lennox and Elaine Young, not only typed the book; they did so with patience, good humour and competence. I am also indebted to Ros Giddings, who typed the original thesis, for her forbearance and personal concern. Jill Gooch, Administrative Officer of the Sociology Department during the course of the thesis, always went out of her way to help as did Judy Carr, also of the Sociology Department. Margot Hislop, reference librarian, Pat Bate, and the staff of La Trobe University Library, and the staff of the Queensland State Archives provided valuable assistance. The Anglican Diocese of Carpentaria provided advice and access to their records; John Scott, DAA, Thursday Island, provided assistance in the early years of the study. John Waddingham drew the map of the Torres Strait area with care and attention. Lindsay Howe and Russel Baader at La Trobe University made the plates. Deanne Gill, granddaughter of Rev John Done, drew the illustrations and took a general interest in the book. Christopher Pound, Language Centre, La Trobe University, helped with cassettes of oral history. I am grateful to the staff of the Australian Institute of Aboriginal and Torres Strait Islander Studies and Aboriginal Studies Press for their care, consideration and technical expertise.

Bob Scott kindly provided the photographs for the Frontispiece and Plate 18; I wish to thank the Mitchell Library, State Library of New South Wales, for Plate 2 (ZPXA 563 f 76), from a watercolour by Lieutenant George Tobin; Bonny Sabatino for the photograph for Plate 7; Department of the Premier, Economic and Trade Development, Queensland, for Plate 8 (EDU/Z1993); Sissy Lee for Plates 9 and 16; John Oxley Library for Plate 11; Elma and Maurice Nona for Plates 12 and 13; Gaul Marou for Plate 15; and Yarra Bank Films for Plates 6, 19, 20 and 21. Permission to present the *seuriseuri* was given by the Meriam; permission to include the Frontispiece and plates 10, 15, 19, 20 and 21 was given by respective families.

My gratitude goes to Geoff who for many years has shared with me the perspectives from which this study arises and whose inspiration, judgement and detailed concern have always been a guide to uncharted courses. The study brought to completion here has been worked through in a context formed by those associated with the journal *Arena*: a group of people who for many years have been concerned with the cultural identity and the social and political rights of indigenous peoples of Australia and its neighbourhood.

ABBREVIATIONS

'the Act'	Aboriginals Protection and Restriction of the Sale of Opium Act, Torres Strait Islanders Act
ADC	Aboriginal Development Commission
AIATSIS	Australian Institute of Aboriginal and Torres Strait Islander Studies
AITEP	Aboriginal and Islander Teacher Education Program
ATSIC	Aboriginal and Torres Strait Islander Commission
DAA	Department of Aboriginal Affairs, Canberra
DAIA	Department of Aboriginal and Island Affairs; Department of Aboriginal and Islanders Advancement, Brisbane
DCS	Department of Community Services, Brisbane
'the Department'	DAIA, DNA, the Aboriginals(s) Department, Brisbane
DL	Dixson Library, Sydney
DNA	Department of Native Affairs, Brisbane
HCA	High Court of Australia
ICC	Island Coordinating Council
IIB	Island Industries Board
KLY	Kala Lagaw Ya: original language of the Western and Central Islands
LMS	London Missionary Society
MILC	*Murray Island Land* Case
ML	Mitchell Library, Sydney
MM	Meriam Mir: original language of the Eastern Islands
'the 1985 Act'	Queensland Coast Islands Declaratory Act 1985
PIL	Papuan Industries Limited
QPP	Queensland Parliamentary Papers
QSA	Queensland State Archives
QV&P	Queensland Votes and Proceedings
SCQ	Supreme Court of Queensland
TI	Thursday Island
TSC	Torres Strait Creole
TSLIB	Torres Strait Light Infantry Battalion
TUP	Torres United Party
TUPOW	Torres United Party Prince of Wales
VDC	Volunteer Defence Corps

The Torres Strait Islands are the homelands of as many as 30,000 people today. They are bounded by the Great Barrier Reef in the east and by longitude 142⁰ in the west. Two long-existing languages spoken by Torres Strait Islanders are Meriam Mir, a Papuan language spoken in the Eastern Islands and Kala Lagaw Ya, a language belonging to the Pama-Nyungan group of the Australian mainland, spoken in the Western and Central Islands. Kala Lagaw Ya is referred to as Mabuiag by the Cambridge anthropological expedition of 1898; it is often known as Yagar Yagar among Islanders. A third indigenous language known as Broken, Pizin, Big Thap and Blaikman, among Islanders, and also termed Torres Strait Creole, has become the *lingua franca* of Torres Strait Islanders.

The Torres Strait Islands are frequently referred to as 'the Islands' and the people as 'the Islanders' or *'Ailanman'* in Broken.

The Storm-Winds is a metaphor for the singular or non-reciprocal invading forces; the powers of destruction carried especially by *Kole*. *Kole* means both master and white man — from Meriam Mir, *kole*, master.

Em is a Torres Strait Creole word used by Islanders to refer to the undivided power of the eye of the storm.

I

INTRODUCTION

STARS OF TAGAI I

FB
Em i come, Em i break there. There's a word for that kind
of sea... Another one come. So they come. Break! Em i curl
them, Em i ... Break under our boat.

EVERYONE
Aaaaaaahah, uuuuhuh! [softly sucking in wind].
ooooohoooh!

SIS
That's why Ailanman never growl the sea or anything. Not
say anything bad about the sea when you're on it. Because
the sea we treat like a polite thing, like you say, not
criticism. Wind's like a person too. Even cyclone, that kind
of big wind, we never call the name. We just refer to it as
Em. So. We never say because it might bring it when it's
strong or when it threatens us.

EVERYONE
Bring it.

SIS
Must show respect...ah! If it's threatening us, you never call
name belong Em.

Islander Narrators

THE MYTH OF TAGAI: THEMES

The myth of Tagai belongs to all Torres Strait Islanders. Various versions are given
in different parts of the Strait. The following version of the myth was given to
a member of the Cambridge anthropological expedition in 1898 by Pasi (Passi),
the nameholder for the sub-clan at Giar Pit on the island of Dauar in eastern Torres
Strait, which is also the original owner of the myth of Tagai. Tagai is seen in the
sky as a man standing in a canoe; his left hand, the Southern Cross, holds a fishing

spear; in his right hand is *sorbi*, a red-skinned apple-like fruit (*Eugenia*). The myth tells of Tagai and his twelve-man crew, consisting of six Usiam (the Pleiades) and six Seg (Orion), who ate the food and drink prepared for a journey. So Tagai strung the Usiam together and threw them into the sea; to the Seg he did likewise and their images were set in a pattern of stars (Ray 1907, 250; see also Haddon 1912, 3–4; Landtman 1927).

The sea hero, Tagai, 'recognised alike by Eastern and Western Islanders' (Haddon 1908, 3), is a vast constellation, consisting of Scorpio, Lupus, Centaurus, Crux, Corvus, part of Hydra and one star of Ara. Tagai himself is composed of Centaurus and Lupus, who is standing in the front of the canoe, which consists of the body and tail of Scorpio, holding a pronged fishing spear, Crux, in his left hand, and the fruit *Eugenia* in his right hand, Corvus. The anchor is Sagittarius (Haddon 1912, 221, Figures 216–18, 221–22).

Among the Western Islanders, the myth of Tagai is closely associated with the Aboriginal culture hero Kwoiam: Tagai (Togai) or 'Good Eye' is Kwoiam's maternal uncle, being known as he who 'could make the best weather' (Haddon 1912, 226; 1904, 67–70). According to this version of the myth, Kwoiam sent Tagai and his brother Koang in a canoe to get turtle-shell. The crew, who had stolen the food and water for the journey, were killed, as in Pasi's version, and 'transformed into stars or constellations whose function was to usher in certain seasonal changes when they first appeared on the horizon' (1912, 226).

The myth of Tagai carries four loosely interrelated themes which signify the developing social reality and cultural identity of Torres Strait Islanders. First, it identifies a sea people who share a common way of life and manner of ordering the world. When Usiam, the Pleiades appears it is *naiger* (MM) *naigai* (KLY) or north-east season, a sign of fair weather and time for sailing. In traditional life these were known as *wauri* (MM) *waiwi* (KLY), after the cone shell (*conus millepunctatus*). It is also turtle-mating season, a time to prepare the food gardens before the first rains. Tagai thus denotes the existence of common categories of life among the people of the Islands, speakers of Kala Lagaw Ya in the western and central islands and speakers of Meriam Mir in the eastern islands.

The second theme is given in the instruction of Tagai: I cannot walk the path that is Usiam's nor can I walk the path that is Seg's (Lawrie 1970, 337), a complementary charter to that of the myth of Malo-Bomai, the culture heroes of the Meriam speakers of the Eastern Islands: stars follow their own path across the sky (Lawrie 1970, 337). The world is ordered so that everything has a place and a path to follow; in following your forebears you must keep to your own course, passing on and receiving the land you have inherited, not trying to encroach upon that which belongs to another line of people. Everything and everyone has a place within the cosmos, a conception similar to the original meaning of *moira*, destiny, the fates: among people as among the gods, each has an 'allotted portion' or province, a time and place (Cornford 1957, 16).

The third theme is Tagai as the harbinger of the new, as well as the sign of the repetition of the eternal circles of time: Tagai does not denote stasis or a closed circle of repetition — each rising is a sign of renewal.

Finally, Tagai is a mediator integrating the Kala Lagaw Ya speakers and the speakers of Meriam Mir. Among the stars of Tagai are those with special images, signifying times of significance; they are the special 'stars' of the Torres Strait and the *dramatis personae* of this book. To a greater or lesser degree, these stars are the custodians of important cultural traditions, persons with the special understanding and originality to act as mediating or bridging people in modern times.

These four themes are explored in their relation to the central motif of this book: the creation and re-creation of a Torres Strait Islander identity and its expression in self-awareness as a unique sea culture. The first, that of common categories of existence among Islanders, forms a background and an integral part of all the discussion, which will be introduced within the context of themes of intercultural encounter. This theme finds a new expression in Torres Strait Islander identity in Part IV. The second, on the notion of place set within cyclical time, is a central theme about the ordering of the world of the Meriam (Part II), culminating at the end of Part IV in a discussion of the philosophical justification of the right to land and political sovereignty. The third theme on renewal and the fourth theme on the role of mediating or bridging people form the central theoretical and methodological ambience of the whole study and are central to each of the four parts.

REPETITION AND REKINDLING: THE RENEWAL PROCESS

The Meriam word *kerkar*, meaning fresh or new time, embodies the double meaning of newness and repetition. (It complements another word, *kerker*, which means seasonal time.) *Kerkar* denotes an idiom which can incorporate new events and knowledge without losing the original: through the resolution of oppositions, a new synthesis is created which signifies the emergence of a growing identity. This occurs through a process known as gift exchange or reciprocity, the mode of exchange pervading Torres Strait Island life and distilled in custom. Reciprocity is a two-way relation between two persons or other dualities which does not involve a radical abstraction from the you and the me of human relations and their place and context of life.[1]

Kerkar carries a cyclical connotation of an eternal recurrence which is not simply endless repetition — as in Nietzsche's conception — but renewal: the new is embedded within the old, the old within the new (see Knight 1933, 111, n 1 and 106). The world, according to Heraclitus, is always coming into existence, passing away and rekindling, like Fire (Kirk and Raven 1962, 199). In this mode of being, opposites become one and 'the same' through their existence within an alternating cycle, in which their 'oppositeness' occurs at different times. Like waking and sleeping, day and night — and for the Torres Strait Islanders, the southeast dry season as against the northwest rainy season — these opposites represent 'alternating processes' (Heraclitus in Lloyd 1971, 100–01).

It is this antithetical unity which offers the possibility of a development where the creation of something new does not destroy the old. In the very experience of the 'us-ness' of social life there is the simultaneous experience of the 'otherness' of the 'other side': the non-reciprocal or the singular. The quality of having these oppositional sides or two levels pervades all reciprocal being. In a sense it is the fabric of life; concealed by a smooth surface, *Em*, the stored up energies of the 'other side', is always there ready to surface. It is towards that 'other side', which Rudolf Otto terms 'the "wholly other"', something which has no place in our scheme of reality but belongs to an absolutely different one, and which at the same time arouses an irrepressible interest in the mind', that the eyes of reciprocal humanity are turned: the realm of what 'we' call the religious imagination (1936, 29). Its quest follows the path towards what Goethe called the 'All-One' (Eliade 1965, 80), an imagination that lies at the centre of the Torres Strait Islander perspective (see Chapter 4).

Social phenomena, wrote Mauss, in explicating the nature of the gift as an integrative principle of social life and thought, are totalities containing 'all the threads of which the social fabric is composed' (1970, 1 and 76). Mauss' notion of totality, Lévi-Strauss observed twenty years later, is less important than the manner in which he conceives it: 'It is a foliated conception, one might say, composed of a multitude of distinct and yet joined planes' (1978b, 6).[2] As we shall see in the example of the Meriam people in Part II, this totality, which comes to be composed of many-layered identities, is like a flower with many petals, the rose or the lotus being an appropriate symbol of that whole.

Composed of all the threads of the social fabric, each act of reciprocal exchange creates a 'unity' which continues to carry its oppositions within it. In bringing two sides together in antagonistic unity, reciprocal exchanges create the 'differences in unity' of complementarity which has far-reaching effects. Two such effects stand out. First, reciprocal exchanges make for change: the qualities of dissimilarity of the 'other side' are bound into the new relationship. Second, the 'original' is continued, because the new 'unity' carries forward the qualities of 'this side'. The synthesis created carries within it the original, the beginning of things; it also bears the 'original' in the sense of the qualitatively new. It follows from this that what came first is not expunged or dissolved. So we have the possibility of originality in a double sense: a newness, viz something different, in union with beginnings.

The reciprocal process by which Torres Strait Islanders lived together is double-sided, moving from gift giving to pay-back. The emphasis here is on the peaceable forms of reciprocity through which Islanders integrated themselves. These forms were less subject to repression by the invader than expression of old enmities.

In past times in Torres Strait social life, oppositions expressed themselves in blood feuds, in wars which led to new and extended alliances. When the missionaries and administrators put an end to warfare, feuding and 'skull-hunting', they did not kill enmity and contradiction; they merely assisted in changing its form. Sorcery, itself driven underground by the missionaries, resumed its importance within the context of a new message which said, 'love your enemies'.

Given the powerful forces for change in the Strait from the mid-nineteenth century onwards, continuities which were expressive of the traditional idiom are characteristically manifest today in new forms. The South Sea Islanders, who began to arrive in the Torres Strait Islands from the 1850s onwards, were a critical influence in the development of intercultural reciprocities — symbolic exchange and intermarriage with the indigenous Islanders. Torres Strait Islander society is rich in social practices within the idiom of reciprocity. A highly elaborate system of adoption or fostering, which continues from pre-contact times, carries a many-faceted set of imperatives and social purposes: the strengthening of family, clan (and in the Western Islands, moiety) alliances and inheritances (Macdonald 1980, 1–70).

In reciprocal exchange the living nature of the object exchanged remains central: in the item exchanged there is the embodiment of the personalities of the giver and the receiver. In reciprocal relations, where the unique difference of the 'exchanger' remains undissolved, networks of relations are woven into a social fabric which retains all the threads which compose it (Mauss 1970, 10).

In commodity production, on the other hand, objects are equated by being exchanged: in that type of exchange relation the living character of the you–me relationship of reciprocity is removed. Things are detached from, and now substitute for, persons; exchange becomes impersonal (Marx 1949, 44–49; Sohn-Rethel 1978, 19–22).[3]

The social life of the Torres Strait Islanders exemplifies reciprocity as a universal principle, where 'symmetrically arranged groupings' exist and exchangers are equivalent (Polanyi 1965b, 250). While the sacred order of Malo-Bomai in the Eastern Islands, and the Cult of Brethren in the Western Islands, exerted powerful influence upon Islanders, corporate political structures in the form of hereditary chiefdoms were absent (Haddon 1904, 1908, 1935). As in the rest of Melanesia, highly developed reciprocal exchange systems in the Torres Strait performed the functions of the political structures which existed in Polynesia (Mauss 1970, 30).

The pattern of the universe created by ties of reciprocity is one which comes to consist of a vast web of ties within all spheres and on all planes. It is a movement with an inner rhythm. The 'world' comes to have its own impelling project, its own wants and priorities. How to break the 'binary opposition' between life and death forms the centre of life's commitment. This is the realm of the sacred, of mythical heroes, of ritual observances which recreate the Cosmos, of myths which affirm grounding truths, and of people of special wisdom who mediate the crossing points to the 'other side' of the ultimate Divide. A social life set upon that course comes to terms with the oppositions of dissimilarity in ways which differ at every point to that built upon the exchange abstraction of the commodity: time is cyclical, not linear, life is lived face to face, not impersonally.

ACROSS THE GREAT DIVIDE: SPANNING TWO WORLDS

Moving from the themes of encounter, this study traces the way reciprocal processes continued, creating new levels of integration among Islanders, in spite of the antithetical tendency of abstract relations to dissolve reciprocal exchange. The study modifies some conclusions of the Cambridge Anthropological Expedition of 1898: for example, meanings of the Malo-Bomai myth for the existence and identity of Eastern Islanders and the cultural possibilities Malo-Bomai foreshadowed. It weaves together threads of the life-world of the Islanders, making visible both the overall pattern and the separate strands of a culture often presumed to have been destroyed.

In an earlier paper, I suggested that contemporary Torres Strait Islander society had 'taken on a distinguishable form with its own integrity', which 'retained an essential continuity with the critical foundations of the Islander societies of the pre-colonial period' (1980b, 2). I designated three influences on Islanders which set going powerful processes towards the re-formation of their institutions and their consciousness: Christian universalism, a common experience of domination through the colonial process, and the social relationships of capitalism. I now add a fourth — the comparative experience of a new knowledge system. These four influences not only tended to destroy the old culture; they also created conditions for a new unity which was reflected in a shared consciousness as one people: the Torres Strait Islanders.

Islanders sought to 'get even' with the newcomers who had set themselves up as their rulers: to force them into reciprocal behaviour, or to drive them from power. The marine industry taught Islanders new skills; it also gave different meaning to the familiar — pearl shell, trochus and bêche-de-mer. Islanders were introduced to a money system different from the old stone 'money'. They became familiar with capitalist forms of labour and the selling of labour power, with the individualist-based work ethic and a linear time system. The commodity culture reduced the meaning of pearl shell to an abstract common equivalent. Money, the universal system of a global commodity economy with which Islanders became inextricably interwoven in the latter half of the nineteenth century, took on a special significance when they were denied the right to manage their earnings: it became a measure, as well as a sign, of their independence.

The impact of Christianity was two-sided. The missionaries prohibited many local religious practices. They attempted to destroy the foundations of Islanders' beliefs and customs along with their visible symbols. Yet, within Christianity, Islanders also discerned a message which completed the thought (and social practices) of their past, including recognition of the possibility of new alliances and extended networks of reciprocal exchange. It gave them, too, the moral strength to resist their rulers and to assert their cultural distinctiveness as equals. Within the new knowledge system lay the possibility of severance with the past and the taking on of new ways. Access to a new knowledge system also helped Islanders to become aware of the sources of their oppression and so find the confidence and the techniques to meet their rulers on their own ground. Through a new understanding of themselves in relation to others they set their sights on a future which contrasted with their situation of subordination. The thrust of the colonial process was towards subduing and taming the independent fighting spirit of the Islanders; yet the long period of administration of the 'Torres Strait Islanders' combined with Islanders' mass participation in the pearling industry to provide the conditions for a common experience of solidarity.

A unity created by these contradictory processes carries within it the seeds of disintegration and destruction. Today that unity is complicated, even threatened, by physical separation: by 1980 half of the Islander population was living on the mainland. This situation developed since the early 1960s when Islanders, who had been confined within the Islands for about sixty years, gained the 'right' to move about freely, an event which coincided with the collapse of their main source of livelihood — the pearling industry (see Beckett 1977, 77–104; 1987, 176–80, 201–07).

Islanders in Townsville, Cairns, Bamaga and other places, have, over a generation, formed themselves into identifiable communities with links to kinsfolk, in-laws and friends in the Strait through personal visits for burials, tombstone unveilings, weddings and recreational purposes, and through the Islander 'yam vine' — their bush telegraph system which operates actively through their churches, dance groups, sports activities, pubs, as well as kinship and Eastern or Western Islander networks. That integrative process is stimulated by moves to establish rights to land, the leading example being the *Murray Island Land* case (see *Land Bilong Islanders*, Yarra Bank Films 1990; Sharp 1990b; 1991; 1992b), and to self- government and political sovereignty over the islands and waters of the Torres Strait (Kehoe-Forutan 1988, 1–34; Cass, 1988). At the same time, the disintegrative process moves silently onwards as the Islanders of the mainland communities bury their kinsfolk away from their ancestral lands and find themselves conversing with their children in English.

In the period of invasion and occupation, Torres Strait Islanders have been incorporated into the world economic system and world market. Yet, until the 1980s, specific historical conditions prevented class formation among Islanders: a majority participated in the pearling and trochus industry on a clan basis until the mid-1930s, some as wage workers, a few as family boat-owners; some self-initiated projects outside the marine industry developed on a community basis. The reasons for this and an account of the historical experience in the era known as 'Protection' and after are explored in Chapters 5 and 6. It was only in the late 1980s that individual entrepreneurship among Torres Strait Islanders and their differentiation into social classes were being actively encouraged.

In the 1980s, the lives of Islanders in the Torres Strait area began to undergo radical changes. The 1986 'takeover' of schools on all the Islands from the Department of Aboriginal and Islanders Advancement (DAIA) by the Queensland Education Department was part of a move which began to put Islander children on an equal footing with other Queenslanders and to foster local languages and culture (Osborne 1988, 4). By the late 1980s, Islander-owned small businesses — fishing, crayfishing, trochus ventures, snack-bars and general trade stores — were beginning to burgeon, and many of these were funded by loans from the Aboriginal Development Commission (ADC) and other government agencies. These developments may be seen as part of a new integration of the Torres Strait into the world economic and financial system in which land, sea and sea-bed resources become objects for exploitation and sale as commodities. The move among Islanders for independence in the late 1980s may be seen in a double light. Many Islanders had became impatient with government refusal to recognise customary title to land and Islanders' prior rights to sea-bed resources. They had therefore come to see political independence as their one chance to retrieve what is theirs, and to stand alongside Papua New Guinea, Vanuatu, Niue and other Pacific island states as independent and equal partners. There are also outsiders to the Torres Strait with quite different interests, who see, in sovereignty, the opportunity to colonise the land and seas of Torres Strait anew.

Set within this rapidly changing milieu of the 1980s and the early 1990s, this book seeks to contribute towards a return, now in written form, of the cultural inheritance of the Islands, to the younger people of present-day Torres Strait Islander society. For the contemporary Islander, the old and the new are integral aspects of one, often contradictory, reality. Their ensemble of newer dances which have drawn spectacular, world-changing events into their creative process (see Berndt and Berndt 1987, xi), are illustrative of this union. Their forebears' assimilation of the knowledge system of Western culture provides a rare opportunity for this study in self-awareness of transition. This book is offered back to Torres Strait Islanders as a background study to the challenges of the coming period. The keynote is a cultural renewal identified by one of the central characters of the book known as Kebi Bala, as the fulfilment of the promise of ancient myths of the Torres Strait.

BEARERS OF THE STARS OF TAGAI

In 1913 Paul Radin published the life story of a Winnebago in the *Journal of American Folk-Lore*. For Radin the 'primary sources' of so-called 'primitive cultures' were oral ones which could 'be demonstrated only by actual texts from philosophically-minded aboriginal philosophers' (1957, xxx). They were not last statements about dying cultures, or responses given to him unwillingly (xxviii).

Radin believed that the anthropology of his times was going in a wrong direction. He understood, as did Lienhardt, that not 'all thought *attempts to become like our own*' (Radin 1957, xxvii, is quoting Lienhardt, *Annual Report of the Bureau of American Ethnology* 37, 1923, 394). 'The development of formal integrated philosophical systems', wrote Radin, is 'only one form which the evolution of philosophy has taken' (1957, xxv). His conclusions foreshadowed the thoughts of scholars decades later, which recognised the intrinsic worth of the mythopoeic form of knowledge (Frankfort 1946), oral tradition as a repository of wisdom, and the oral form as the text of literature on the 'other side'.[4]

In the fourth meaning of the myth of Tagai, the 'speculative philosophers', men and women of special knowledge, custodians of cultural traditions and mediators of non-destructive change, are special Stars of Tagai. Men and women of originality are not to be equated with a Torres Strait élite or 'very important families'. They are from important families, but in a very special sense: they are from important sacred stems, some of them are the nameholders of those stems. Radin makes the distinction between 'thinkers' and 'doers' in reciprocal societies where all men and women are 'doers', engaging directly in creating their own sustenance as hunters, gardeners and fisherfolk. Unlike the 'man of action' who is '... indifferent to the claims and stirrings of his inner self', the thinker is 'impelled by his whole nature to spend a considerable time in analysing his subjective states and attaches great importance both to their influence upon his actions and to the explanations he has developed' (1957, 232).

The Stars of Tagai are 'stars' in the dramatic sense that they tell much of the story of encounter, each from his or her own angle: as Torres Strait Islanders; as persons of originality in the double sense of creators of the new who are also tied to the structures and the traditions of the group. They are chosen for this twofold creativity. They are active subjects — men and women with a strong sense and explicit awareness of their identity as Islanders — and therefore able to illuminate how the 'original' was carried forward in new syntheses. Moreover, given the way in which their creative singularity is embedded within their social obligations to others within the group, they are mediators and interpreters of such change.

In the present period, a reconstitution of the social setting in which the anthropologist is formed limits and focuses his or her observation in new ways, thereby leading to a redefinition of the problems of Radin's time. The appearance of the active subject is a means whereby a new mode of social integration may assert itself. Side by side with the loss of originality which follows the consumption of other cultures about which Lévi-Strauss has written, there is a new source of concern: something like an intercultural voyeurism in which feelings of affinity with another culture are seen as a solution to the reduction in the depth and complexity of meaning of one's own culture. At a social level such a relationship may become a way of appropriating and dismembering the other culture in the service of the modern version of those system ends which parallel the old 'imperialist' study of the object.

The steps in linking two circles of understanding carry a strong component of the intuitive within a setting where one is seeking a new synthesis which seeks to bring together the 'rational' with the 'intuitive–poetic'. Steps in a transitional process of seeing and interrelating are tentative in two main ways. First, they are a preliminary stage within a larger practice which seeks to understand in order to build reciprocally rather than to appropriate and assimilate.

Second, a personal experience of searching for 'a language' is a stage in the creation of a new 'seeing' of the other, which may coalesce with the wider aim of enacting an intercultural practice which is collective as well as individual, ongoing as well as conservationist. In this aim, the double movement of the springs of originality — change in continuity/continuity in change — among Islanders offers an important message for all those of us who wish to change and conserve at the same time.

The main unwritten sources of this book are life stories based on conversational narratives with Islanders who have lived both the old and the new. The book seeks to portray a people undergoing rapid cultural change by putting together the lives of an era at two levels: recollections of events and experiences, both autobiographical and social; and a portrayal of how individuals effected a psychic integration. At both levels, the formation of the person and of several generations of men and women is seen, not as 'still life' or frozen objectified records given in speech, but as a process of a sensuous human activity, viz practice. The way in which people achieved psychic integration is also, in social terms, a story of how their culture survived: how new forms of awareness emerged which both differed from, and carried on, the themes of the old culture.

The narratives seek to gain a complete sense of individuals as real persons and so to achieve a vivid impression of Islanders as a people, to choose people from different islands with a strong sense and explicit awareness of their identity as Islanders, and to situate each life story within a socio-historical context so that the personal lives would not be 'free-floating' or dissociated from their formative social milieu.[5] The result is a highly 'peopled' work; it is historical narrative rather than the study of social form. The main narrators give a sense of the history of the era and of cultural traditions both old and new; their stories corroborate, complement and cross-check with one another, engaging also with the thematic analysis. Narratives are supplemented by self-sketches and recollections of particular social dramas: for example, the first encounters with white men, the cyclone of 1934, the 1936 strike, the Second World War and the cooperatives at Moa.

From the beginning, I thought of the narratives as whole performances with gesture and mime, each nuanced by the personality of the teller. Given a culture where life comes 'whole', I wished to retain a sense of that wholeness.

All the narratives turned out this way. Indeed, each contained drama captured as drama, often with songs and actions. 'Oral history' is the wrong word. Sound effects became a form of audience participation which, in important moments of a story told in company, became a chorus. Other narratives were given alone.[6] In an unforeseen way they were the culture revealing itself.

Primordial loyalties and sentiments relating to place and clan have going with them primordial activities: gardening is taken for granted as the ground of cultural experience, and dancing, for the Islander, is part of the cultural ground of social life. Under conditions of political imposition which denigrate or even outlaw it, it is not neutral; it may become a form of resistance. In quiet times, the cultural passes unnoticed. In times of social ferment, it may fuel and fuse with dramatic 'political' action.[7]

Islanders kept up custom unbeknown to Kole. A 'standpoint', unwritten, developed from which Islanders judged Kole. 'He's a real Kole!', a person might say. Yarning, mime, dance and drama all gave expression to perceptions and interpretations of Kole, which the latter glimpsed only occasionally.[8] In the language of Kole, something not unlike a 'reverse anthropology' developed within Islander networks (see Wagner 1975, 31).

Stories and special meanings are sometimes given as secret gifts, although this is not necessarily said in words. Where an inner strengthening has been the means of keeping the spirit alive, to take and to tell is a step towards destroying. People remain the custodians of their own secrets. The opposite holds true too. To fail to carry forward a message is to let that other person down, like Kapin's message about sovereignty, 'From east to west we want men to learn that we were given our land and never sold it. God gave it to us.'

Journeying begins from one's 'own side': the 'me' and the 'you', the 'us' and the 'they', the 'this kind' on 'this side' and 'another kind' on 'that side' are reversals of each other. It is easy to become lost. The thing is to 'read' the signs. It is the 'other' who can tell the 'me', if the 'me' can just stay quiet and listen: listen to those who carry forward their own ways, those with that originality within them. Listening to yarning, yarning, yarning. Yarning is reflecting. And yarn too and listen; not just to the words, but to quiet judgement: 'You know when you feel right'. Sometimes you are told in words as well. 'That's right, that's correct! That's the one!' (*louder*). It's like being an apprentice. But it's always done kindly. 'Listen first: our custom may be quite different to yours. Well, ours — like this!'

Through conversational narratives, one may discern the inner rhythm of the culture from which it springs, as well as its concrete social content as distilled within the life of the individual. Through social analysis, one may identify the

conflicting processes created in the encounters, which provide the life-setting of
the people from whom the narratives are drawn.

The written project has by necessity an asymmetry. It is my project
written according to the requirements and expectations of the university or my
professional colleagues. Then there is also the story of a historical epoch by people
who have lived that experience. The edited collection is seen as a return gift in
response to receiving, so completing a process of reciprocal exchange. At the same
time, the study attempts to analyse the processes
of continuity and transition.[9]

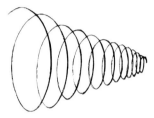

Of the ten main narrators, whose lives cover the hundred-year span from 1886
to the present, six are from families whose genealogies, on both sides, stretch back
into the 'antiquity' of the Torres Strait Islanders. They are, in order of seniority,
Kapin, Uncle, Nau Mabaig, Au Bala, Kebi Bala (Au Bala's younger brother) and
Second Meriam Man. One of them, Uncle, is a descendant of the Kaurareg, who
inhabited the off-shore islands near Cape York Peninsula and had genealogical ties
with the Aboriginal people of the Cape York mainland. First Meriam Man, on his
father's side, is linked with the many newcomers who came to the Torres Strait
region from the mid-nineteenth century onwards. Auntie, Sis and Ailan Man are
the descendants of a Pacific Islander family who arrived in the Strait in 1870. This
family, like many others from the Pacific Islands of Niue, Samoa, Lifu and Mare,
Rotuma and others, became reciprocal, integral, and influential among native-born
Islanders through marriage ties. Pacific Islanders brought with them seafaring skills,
their own custom and a familiarity with the money economy. Among them were
those who brought news of the Gospels. They brought with them, too, a pidgin
English from which there grew a creole language. This has become the *lingua
franca* of Torres Strait Islanders (Shnukal 1983b, 173–85; 1989).

Auntie's father, also a highly significant figure in the story which
follows, and in the life of the Torres Strait beyond his death in the 1950s
(Grandfather T here), is from a line of people who held sacred knowledge and
spiritual powers. They came originally from the island of Niue. His granddaughter,
Sis, describes him as '...the greatest medicine man in the Torres Strait, bar none'.
Uncle T, his son, carried on that tradition, as did Auntie, his daughter.

Importantly, the most singular personages, stars who yet remain within the sphere of reciprocity, are the bearers of the whole constellation. They are not singular in the sense of the purveyors of malevolent magic. But, in taking back the order of things into themselves, each re-creates 'the sway of that other firmament in which he sees the glitter of the visible stars' (Paracelsus 1913, 3). Paracelsus' conclusion resembles a utopian prophecy: '...man will discover that he contains "the stars within himself..., and that he is thus the bearer of the firmament with all its unfluences"' (p 3). They are like stars, leaving their impress upon the earth, until their time is finished and they are accorded their place within the firmament.

So Sis says:

Genealogy is so important because you must hand the land to the right person. The genealogy must be there because there is no written tradition. The right person carries on and that person must be trained and guided. He or she has to be firm in that right, and then that person may be an ambassador of that right. If you don't teach your children who their relatives are your sister will tell you: 'You're a really bad sister'.

I have not identified the narrators by name, even though each one is readily identifiable, a reminder that as well as being themselves, they are also selected as representatives of a certain *type* of creative person.

In following the narrators through the vicissitudes of their lives, the reader may recall that the essence of the reciprocal mode is the mediation and resolution of contradiction: their lives and their personal make-up, like the larger canvas of social life, are not harmonious but contradictory.

The lives of the narrators carry the themes of encounter in different 'mixes', and in their human manifestations. All of them are committed to the achievement of equality in difference — that is, their right to cultural dissimilarity. But they have pursued this aim in different ways, some with the accent on a personal project, others quite explicitly on behalf of their people. In each of their lives are notes of hope, of fulfilment and of tragedy. Not long before he died, a blind and lonely old man, Kapin gave me this thought together with a *wauri* or cone shell, enjoining me to let it be known to the world:

You belong to Christ. He made them like one people when they were different to one another. By and by I announce it. This sovereignty God has Himself because He won the fight belonging to Easter. God rules. He didn't make a place for thieves to come and take all our land. He'll do something to stop them. (Book of Islanders 1984, B29)

Tagai is an island man; his left hand holds the pronged spear that provided the strength to wrest a living from the sea. In the eyes of those newcomers who came from Europe that fish spear was the Southern Cross.

1 | THEMES OF ENCOUNTER IN MAGANI KES-MAGANI MALU AND TORRES' STRAIT

Well Meriam Man was different. He'd been all over the south, cut cane. A very traditional man too. He's an authority in his own right as far as tradition goes. He's there with the Zogo le. Meriam Man came into the picture as a leader in Murray Island in the thirties. It started about strike time... When he saw the Government still got power to tell him what to do he held meetings at Murray Island.
He wanted to see his culture passed on from his time from generation to generation.

Islander Narrators

BATTLES AND EXCHANGES

THE ISLANDERS MEET THE TRESPASSERS

'We are ready to exchange.' The actions of the men of Erub spoke of barter not battle, as, holding out green coconuts to the Englishmen, they brought their canoe up to the cutter of Captain Bligh's sailors. They came face to face at fifteen yards, less than a canoe's length away (Bligh in Lee 1920, 175). But the newcomers were empty-handed and the Island men would have discerned a look of fear or distrust in their eyes as they pulled for their ship, the *Assistant*. You do not want to exchange? You are not a friend: then you are *nerutonar,* those with another kind of custom, in Meriam Mir. Then we must fight you: an eye for an eye.

It was Wednesday 5 September 1792, two days after the twenty-eight gunner *Providence* with the brig *Assistant* as tender, under the command of Captain William Bligh with Lieutenant Nathaniel Portlock in charge of the brig, had entered Torres' Strait to explore a new passage from the east and to transplant the bread-fruit plant from Tahiti to the West Indies (Flinders 1814). At daylight, George Tobin, the third lieutenant, had been sent to search for a passage. Returning at one o'clock, Tobin told of an encounter with the canoes they had seen fishing in the shoals off Darnley's Island, as Bligh later renamed Erub, after the Earl of Darnley (Lee 1920, 177–78).[1] Accounts of that encounter by Bligh (Lee 1920, 174–76), by Portlock (Lee 1920, 250–51) and by Matthew Flinders (1814, 1, xxi), who was serving as midshipman on the *Providence,* agree that one canoe came close to Tobin's cutter; that the Islanders held up to him a coconut; that he rejected it continuing to row for the ship; that observing this they got their bows ready; and that Tobin fired at them, whereat they turned and made off for Darnley's Island.

Next day, the Islanders received what they were seeking: iron. Flinders records how several canoes from Darnley's Island came within handing distance of His Majesty's vessels: 'Their arms were bows, arrows, and clubs, which they bartered for every kind of iron work with eagerness; but appeared to set little value on any thing else' (1814, I, xxii–xxiii). 'A looking-glass did not surprise them', noted Bligh, 'but they cared for nothing but iron' (1920, 181). Eye to eye they met across the Great Divide. 'They took care to make good bargains, but we were honest', Bligh remarked, 'and readily gave what was agreed upon' (1920, 178).

The Islanders were strong and they sought added strength. Flinders marvelled at their skills: 'These people...appeared to be dextrous sailors and formidable warriors; and to be as much at ease in the water, as in their canoes'. Their bows of split bamboo, six or seven feet long were so strong, he observed, 'that no man in the ship could bend one of them' (1814, I, xxiii).[2] Iron extended that strength. 'Anything made of iron the Meriam called *malili*', Au Bala says: '*Malili* is hard and strong and can kill more easily than a bow; *malili* can plough the ground better than *wet*, the digging stick'. Iron toughened tools and weapons; it also strengthened the spirit and steeled men's hearts for battle.

Plate 2 The battle between the men of the *Providence* and *Assistant* with Islanders near Tutu, Warrior Island, 10 September 1792 (watercolour by George Tobin, photograph, courtesy of the Mitchell Library, State Library of New South Wales)

The daily life of Islanders moved between the asymmetry of giving the 'gifts' of arrows or of life and the re-creation of a symmetry in receiving their equivalent in return. The white sailors had hurled back the insult of war at the Darnley men by refusing the gifts of green coconuts they proffered on 5 September 1792; they returned by stringing their bows. That event over, next day they exchanged equivalences of coconuts for iron.

The processes which produced the axes the Islanders were avidly seeking also produced weapons which could be fired at a distance. In this lay the 'power' of His Majesty's men to trespass on others' ground. For Imperial Britain, iron did not mean 'getting even' through exchange of equivalences; it meant mastery. As the British vessels moved through Torres' Strait in the early days of September 1792, the question was being silently asked: Who will be master here? In less that a week it was answered by a battle near the island known as Tutu in Kala Lagaw Ya, named Warriors Island by Bligh after the battle (1920, xxiv).

THE BATTLE

On 10 September, the British vessels approached Magani Kes, the Meriam name for the Great North East Channel (Magani Malu in Kala Lagaw Ya), arriving near

Plate 3 Maino, descendant of Kebisu, Yam Island, 1911

two low islands of the central group to which Bligh gave the letters O and P. As Bligh recorded, many Islanders were on island O (Dungeness Island) and nine canoes, each with eight to twenty men, were 'paddling towards the ships' (1920, 187). Several went towards the *Assistant*, but the strongest party went towards the *Providence*, making 'signs that water and food were to be had at Island P' (1920, 187). 'They expressed great astonishment at the ship', Bligh's log continues, 'at the men at the mastheads', and would not accept the ropes offered and come alongside, 'but showed signs of distrust and design' (1920, 187). While the commandant was contemplating the meaning of this situation events took charge:

> ...I saw the *Assistant* suddenly fire at some canoes, as did our cutter, and she alarmed us by the signal she made for 'assistance'. It was now seen that the canoes had made an attack, and that those around us were intending to do the same. I knew that mischief was done to our poor little companion by these wretches, and arrows were fired at us. It was not a time to trifle. My ship might be on shore in a few minutes without being carefully handled, and it was a serious point who were to be masters of the situation. I settled it by discharging two of the quarter-deck guns with round and grape. The contents of one carried destruction and brought horrible consternation to them, and they fled from their canoes and into the sea and swam to windward like porpoises.
> Three men on the *Assistant* were wounded by their arrows. Great fires were now made on the Island P, where we saw about a hundred persons. (1920, 187–88)

Flinders' impressions evoke a dramatic impact, while still retaining the detail of the moments of armed interchange:

> ...Canoes were also coming towards the *Providence*; and when a musket was fired at the headmost, the natives set up a great shout, and paddled forward in a body; nor was musketry sufficient to make them desist. The second great gun, loaded with round and grape, was directed at the foremost of eight canoes, full of men; and the round shot, after raking the whole length, struck the high stern. The Indians leaped out, and swam towards their companions; plunging constantly, to avoid the musket balls which showered thickly about them. The squadron then made off, as fast as the people could paddle without shewing themselves; but afterwards rallied at a greater distance, until a shot, which passed over their heads, made them disperse, and give up all idea of any further attack. (1814, I, xxv)

He observes with a note of poignancy a deserted canoe with one Islander still sitting in it. '...signals were perceived to be made by the Indians, to their friends on

Dungeness Island, expressive, as was thought, of grief and consternation' (1814, I, xxv).

Kebisu, a Tutu man, was commander of the canoes that came out to meet the British ships. Here is a version of the battle as passed down through his family. As his great great...granddaughter explains, Kebisu had the discerning eye of his *augud* (KLY) or totem, the crocodile. Like the crocodile, a master of shallow waters, whenever he spoke he shut one of his eyes. Her grandfather, Maino-Kebisu told her the story.

> *Kebisu's crew went bow and arrow with them but he say, 'No! Wait till them feller come close'. They look at them snap the water like this. Well them feller look them now. Them feller speak that's what means war in the language belong to them feller. So they want to fire back at them. They wait. They're his brothers-in-law. They said: 'Soon as you're ready put your hand up'.*
>
> *They chase away them warship. You go put this one in a book. It's true he been win that battle.* (The Battle, Book of Islanders 1984, B151–53)

The Islanders, under the command of Kebisu, had brought the full power of their culture to the meeting with the strangers. The white men noted their differences to themselves and Flinders marvelled at the original qualities of their everyday activities. He discerned the distinctive way they could swim like dolphins, fight with the power of sharks and glide through the shallows with the ease of alligators.[3]

These sea people were men of power. Iron strengthened that power. Through their impelling need for iron they risked the hazards of offering friendship to the white men. They offered what they had in exchange. In that manner they had in the past made out new paths along the 'border regions' of their named world. Their 'need' for iron was itself framed within the terms of those rules: the seesaw of keeping even with those who formed part of their social ambience alternatively re-created and threatened social order. Once the multiple advantages of iron were recognised everyone had to have it. Quickly, iron began to revolutionise the technology of the Islanders. Its uneven spread foreshadowed new contradictions and the possibilities of new alliances. Moreover, at the very moment when Islanders' strength was being fortified with iron, the men who brought it began to subdue them through its alien power.

FROM MARINERS TO MASTERS: CROSSING THE SANDBEACHES

On 18 September, after identifying twenty-three islands with letters A to V, the ships passed out into the open sea. In nineteen days they had traversed the passage from the Pacific to the Indian Ocean through Torres' 'archipelago of islands without number' (Markham 1904, 463), with the bread-fruit plants 'in charming condition' (Lee 1920, 200). 'Perhaps no space of three-and-a-half degress in length', wrote Flinders, 'presents more dangers than Torres' Strait' (1814, I, xxix).

In charting a course for His Majesty, King George III, the expedition had identified new jewels for Britannia's crown. The myriad islands of the Strait, named for Spain by Luis Vaez de Torres nearly two centuries before, and the resources of the sea-beds of the region were now within Britannia's grasp. Before passing out of Torres' Strait to the Arafura Sea, Captain Bligh took possession for Britain 'of all the islands seen in the Strait', bestowing the name 'Clarence's Archipelago' upon the whole (Flinders 1814, I, xxvii). Torres' name remains attached to this area.

The newcomers shared a view that the hidden dangers of the Strait held a human quality. The men of Torres' Strait, wrote the missionary Wyatt Gill in 1876, are a fierce intractable race (200–01). The forty-two skulls of those aboard the shipwrecked *Charles Eaton* in 1831 were arrayed at Darnley Island as dramatic 'proof' of what sailors had come to believe: like all the men of the 'black islands' of Melanesia these Islanders were fierce sea warriors (Shineberg 1967, 165). The old sailing directions to mariners gave a warning of the ferocity of the Murray Islanders (Haddon 1908, 189). Yet, again and again, British mariners returned. Sailing vessels were giving way to steam ships by the 1840s and the volume of sea-traffic in the Strait was rising rapidly as bêche-de-mer and pearl shell became valued materials for burgeoning industries. Increased contact fluctuated between battles and exchanges. The battles were unequal, for the newcomers responded to the wooden arrows with the fire-power of guns.

In the three-quarters of a century following Bligh's voyage, the unfamiliar sounds of steel blades echoed along ancient trade tracks, as iron products forged in a changing 'old world' found their way across the new frontiers of contact. Always the Islanders sought iron. When the *Fly*, the *Rattlesnake* and the *Bramble* visited the area between 1842 and 1850, barter, in which the desired articles were almost always iron, mostly axes, had become a general expectation (Jukes 1847, I, 162). The keynote of equivalence remained. Even those who came in search of survivors of the *Charles Eaton* were welcomed; the Islanders were seen to barter readily once they had possession of 'what they considered an equivalent' to 'their commodities' (Wemyss 1837, 23). 'Most commonly they were ready to make friends and were eager for trade', Haddon wrote, glancing back over the century (1908, 187).

Within the first half-century the scale of exchanges widened. Exchange of turtle shell, bows and arrows, yams, coconuts with knives and axes, was supplemented by name exchange and exchange of words of friendship (Jukes 1847,

I, 196). Newcomers of fine sensibility, such as Matthew Flinders, were quick to recognise and act upon Islanders' expressions of good intent, so paving the way for others like him to be welcomed across the sandbeaches (1814, II, 107–12). Voyagers found touches of the primeval landscapes of their distant homelands in jewel-trees risen from the darkened earth. The 'huge blocks of sienite, resting fantastically one upon the other' in the darkened grove created by 'thick-leaved trees with gnarled trunks' at Yam Island put the naturalist J Beete Jukes in mind of the ancient worship of the Druids (1847, 1, 156). Men of aesthetic nature, such as the artist Oswald Brierly, responded to the fine artistry of the Islanders' craftsmanship: 'I had long admired but I had never till now seen anything that realised so much the idea of beauty', he wrote of *Kie Marina*, the canoe of Manu, a Muralag man (1848, in Moore 1979, 46). Islanders' important social customs were soon recognised by men such as Jukes and MacGillivray. They also became aware of Islanders' 'obsession' with their land, whether or not they tilled it (MacGillivray 1852, I, 28); the ambience of their lives with respect to other islands and neighbouring lands (Sweatman in Allen and Corris 1977, 36); some resemblances in local distinctions between the seasons and their own (MacGillivray 1852, I, 326–28); and a contrast between Islanders' social organisation with the hereditary chiefdoms they had observed in Polynesia (MacGillivray 1852, I, 27). The existence of 'taboo' similar to that in Polynesia was suggested by a sudden and unexpected switch from friendship to hostility among the Darnley men (Jukes 1847, I, 159–61, 250–59; Sweatman in Allen and Corris 1977, 36).

The newcomers began to realise that to the Islanders they were not humankind: they were spirits of their dead. 'She is only a spirit', Islanders of Muralag said of Barbara Thompson, the shipwrecked Englishwoman whom they believed was the departed and now returned daughter of one of themselves (Moore 1979, 9).

Many secrets of these antipodean islands remained hidden from the men of the other side: like the white pigeons Jukes observed moving northward in 'numerous small flocks'. 'In September, 1844, they were coming thickly from the northward to Endeavour Strait, and they seem to return in March. What can be the reason of this migration?' he wondered (1847, I, 157).

Of all the great British sailors who tarried awhile in Torres' Strait, perhaps it was Matthew Flinders who combined best a sensibility which could discern the original qualities of 'another' humanity, attuned to the sea in a dissimilar way to his own, with an ability to map a safe course for sailors. His pen 'threaded the needle' of the lacework of reef-strewn shallows and fathomless deeps in the navigational charts, which he drew with painstaking care and which he completed and nurtured for seven years as a prisoner of the French (Scott 1914).

Ironically, for a man so finely tuned to the qualities of the 'other', his charts and narratives made a singular contribution towards the advancement of British imperial design which came to unleash the Storm-Winds upon the Islands.

Soon trespassers seeking bêche-de-mer and pearl shell in vessels from all quarters began to force their way across the frontiers of the Islanders' sandbeaches. The riches of that old world no longer 'satisfied' the fetish which created it. The pearl shell which lined the deeps of Torres' Strait shone with a new light. The race to secure it had begun. They encroached upon island land (Haddon 1912, 146). They destroyed important food supplies and almost denuded some islands of their timbered areas; they stole Islander women and they shanghai'd young men as 'food for the fisheries' (Government Resident, Annual Report, QV&P, 1894, II, 914). The Yorke Island people complained bitterly when shellers cut down their wongai trees, which bore the prized and nutritious red plum (Pennefather, 31 October 1882). As soon as the vessels were sighted, the men of Tutu buried their women and young girls in the sand with only their noses showing (Pennefather, 10 September 1882).

On 1 July 1871, the evangelists of the London Missionary Society (LMS) brought the Light of the Christian Gospels to the people of Torres' Strait. As the two missionaries AW Murray and Samuel McFarlane saw it, the 'deed of cruelty and blood' against the survivors of the *Charles Eaton* gave new reasons for 'a softening gospel of peace' (Report, 1871, 35). They were not the first missionaries in the area. Reverend FC Jagg and William Kennett, two Anglican missionaries, had had a short-lived stay at Somerset, Cape York, from 1867 to 1868; they had dared to protect and succour the people against the destructive actions of the government officials there (The Jagg Reports, 1867–1868, in Moore 1979, 255–56; Sharp 1992a). The LMS missionaries, centred first at Darnley Island, banned warfare and the taking of skulls. They burned and destroyed the Islanders' sacred shrines and they re-educated them to bury their dead in cemeteries. Throughout the Islands the people began building churches in prominent positions near the sandbeaches (see Chalmers, Reports for 1897–99). Yet, within thirty years of the arrival of those seeking the riches of the sea-beds in the mid-nineteenth century, the populations of many islands dwindled to less than half: the population of the Murray Islands at the end of 1879, which Flinders had estimated as 700 or more in 1802 (1814, II, 111), had dropped to 374; it was reported in the same year that many of the original inhabitants of Darnley Island had died from measles some years before and that only eighty, out of an estimated 500, remained.[4] In the valley of the shadow of death the people were ready for a message of peace.

On 18 July 1879, the Governor of Queensland authorised annexation of certain islands lying between the coasts of Australia and New Guinea. In

November and December of that year, Captain C Pennefather of the QGS *Pearl*, made an official voyage from island to island to proclaim to the inhabitants their new subordinate status. On 10 November at Tutu, Warrior Island, the eighty-five inhabitants were 'mustered' and given public notification of defeat:

> I told them that in future they would be amenable to the laws of the white man as the island now formed part of the territory of Queensland. In the afternoon I fired five shells from the guns, close to the island and from a distance of 200 yards, which had the effect of showing them what could be done if necessary. (Pennefather, Report of a Cruise, 19 December 1879)

Kebisu, a descendant of the leader of the battle with Captain Bligh at Tutu in 1792, was detained overnight in irons aboard the *Pearl* as a warning to the inhabitants who, it was alleged, had tried to kill a newcomer by giving him poisoned turtle. Only at this island were the guns fired in a naval act of war, as a reminder of who had become master of the situation (Pennefather, 19 December 1879). The conquest of the Islands was over (Supplement, *Queensland Government Gazette*, 19 July 1879). The eye of the Storm-Winds was upon them.

The warriors had become silent. Six years after annexation, John Douglas, Police Magistrate and Government Resident at Thursday Island, a former Premier of Queensland reported:

> Dangerous and savage as the people of these Islands were, they are now perfectly harmless and friendly. Even at Saibai where, not more than three years ago, the most confirmed skull hunters were in office, there has been a complete change of policy. For this we are chiefly indebted to the representatives of the London Missionary Society and at this present time it is not only perfectly safe for Europeans to land on that Island, but they will be treated with kindness and hospitality. (Douglas, 1 October 1885)

A DIVERSITY OF SEA PEOPLES

For the Erub men who went out to Bligh's sailors with their land produce on 5 September 1792, it was *naiger kerker*, the northeast season, the time for slashing and burning patches of garden land in preparation for planting after the first rains; time too for the rising of the left hand of Tagai, the Southern Cross. So Erub, a most fertile island composed of lava with two small strips of volcanic ash, appeared 'scorched up' to Bligh (1920, 174).

Naiger kerker, was also the preparation time for the maritime expeditions, the *wauri* voyages, heralded by the appearance of certain stars of Tagai. Meriam voyagers went in two directions: towards Op Deudai (Papua New

Guinea) for canoes, cassowary feathers, dogs' teeth necklaces and other dance ornaments; and towards Keo Deudai (mainland Australia) for red ochre, emu feathers and emu leg bones.[5]

Unlike the people living along the coast of Op Deudai, who had single outriggers, the Islanders' seagoing canoes, sometimes fifty feet long, were equipped with double outriggers. The legend of the creation of the original double outrigger tells how the one became two. Two men were given two canoes at Mawata. To enable them to travel together they removed an outrigger from one of them, joined the canoes and put a cross-piece at each end. The Islanders then evolved the seagoing craft with a double outrigger fitted with a gunwale (Landtman 1927, 211).[6]

These seafarers lived within the arc of the southeast trade winds which blow for more than half the year. The southeast wind, *sager*, set the pattern of the outward movement of the Meriam people. They turned their faces towards the northern land they called Op Deudai, 'face land'. There they went for canoes. Haddon describes the exchanges known to the Meriam as *wauri* (KLY *waiwi*; *conus litteratis, var. millepunctatus*), by which they made friends and obtained canoes from the Kiwai people: 'a fine armlet, *wauri*, cut out of a large cone shell' is sent towards Kiwai; 'numerous presents of shell ornaments and food are added' in the course of the voyage. The *tebud le* or *wauri* partner at Kiwai in the year following the purchase of the canoe sends to the Meriam 'purchaser' a *seker lu*, usually a bamboo pole to which he affixes the gifts he wishes to send — 'feathers of the cassowary, plumes of the bird of paradise, dogs' teeth necklaces, boars' tusks, fringes and petticoats made from leaves of the sago palm, mats, bows and arrows,...'. The *seker lu* travels along the same path but in the opposite direction along the coast of Op Deudai to Saibai and then from island to island, 'each forwarder vying with the others as to the amount he adds'. Haddon notes the custom of adding 'presents' by intermediaries 'associated with the outward bound *wauri*' and the 'homeward bound *seker lu*', and their tendency 'to do a little friendly exchange' on the way (1908, 186–87).[7]

Wauri exchanges created complementary unity through the shared social code of reciprocal exchange between those who possessed what the other lacked: canoes, potential marriage partners, fishing and gardening tools, ceremonial valuables, weapons and different food produce. *Wauri* was a form of exchange of the equivalences of dissimilarity: it enhanced, enriched, and gave variety to their lives; by making *tebud le*, friends for all time, it broke through the frontiers of their face to face communities in extended networks. Among the Meriam, *wauri* voyages were made possible through the myth of Malo-Bomai.

The myth of Malo-Bomai consists of two complementary narratives, the first of which is the coming of Bomai from Tuger in West Irian just beyond the present boundary with Papua New Guinea. It is told here by Au Bala:

> Bomai transformed himself into a whale and swam down until he reached Boigu Island in the far west of Torres Strait and got stranded there. 'It's a zogo, the supernatural', the Islanders said because it whistled. So they built a fence round it and went to fetch the drums and other things for feasting and dancing, but Bomai broke the fence, dived into the deep sea and changed into a canoe, arriving at Dauan Island in the form of a huge turtle, here again being recognised as a zogo. Sailing on in the form of a canoe Bomai arrived at Mabuiag in the shape of a dugong. In turn he called at Badu, Moa, Nagir and Muralag where he met his three brothers; together they sailed eastwards passing through islands like Waraber and Paremar and Warrior. One brother's canoe drifted to Yam Island, another brother sailed to Aurid and the third stayed at Masig (Yorke Island). Finally, Bomai arrived at Mer becoming stranded at Begegiz where the people said: 'Keriba agud ged seker em', 'This is our god our protector'. Bomai moved from place to place and changing from shape to shape of different sea creatures in the deep water he arrived at Teker on the south side of Mer in the form of an octopus where he met Kabur, a woman who was line-fishing from the sandbeach, and had connection with her. Recognising it as a zogo she put it in a basket and gave the octopus to her husband Dog. They hung the basket in the house where that night they saw its two eyes shining like stars. The basket with Bomai was stolen by Dog's two brothers-in-law from Las. Then the people of Las invited Dog and they all sat and smoked zeub, the pipe of peace, so becoming friends again. And Dog and his wife said, 'All right, you keep Bomai here'. So they left the zogo there with the people of Las and the trees everywhere became painted with red ochre. The second narrative is about the coming of Malo [Malu] from Op Deudai where Bomai came from. Malo, a man with a shark's head, came with four brothers to find his uncle, Bomai, increasing his canoe-party in the central islands. Bab nade? Where is Bab [father]? Some of Malo's party speared him in the back and gave the drums they brought to the local people saying: 'These are the dances you are going to perform'. Then Malo was brought and added on to the original agud, Bomai. (Cassette 135/AB/TI/3/84)

Of critical importance, Au Bala says, is that Bomai came first. Malo, the lesser *agud* or god came after.[8]

Bomai, the secret and sacred name for the *agud* of the Meriam, combined into one the power of the manifold qualities of creatures and creations that go with the sea, from the 'other side' beyond Boigu travelling from west to east. In embodying protean metamorphoses, Bomai is the pinnacle of sacred power known as *zogo*, the ultimate power of a sea people. *Zeub*, the pipe of peace, was passed round the circle at Las in the presence of the *agud* Bomai, so prefiguring a way of living together. *Zogo* or sacred dances and chants were performed by the people at Las through the power of Bomai. They came to be known as the sacred dances of Malo because Bomai was so sacred that no ordinary mortal might call that name. So 'Malo' has always a deeper meaning. And the last and most sacred chant and dance for the eight clans of the Meriam of Mer, Dauar and Waier, was known as *seuriseuri*.

The coming of Bomai foreshadowed a way of the eight clans of the Murray Islands living together, which was embodied in Malo's Law, Malo ra Gelar; a shared custom among the Meriam prefigured exchanges with others across the seas: the networks of *wauri tebud*. The power of *zogo* also made possible the transcendence of death through rebirth in the land of the immortals or *lamar* at Boigu on the 'other side' from whence came the *agud*.

Malo made possible reversal of strangers to friends through *wauri tebud*, 'shell friends', as far away as Op Deudai and the far western island of Saibai. Far down the eastern seaboard of Keo Deudai, in the arc of the double-outrigger canoe, the sandbeach area at Lockhart River was the knotting point of the myth of Malo-Bomai with the myths of I'wai, alligator, and Pai'yamo, Rainbow Serpent.[9] Among the Meriam are those like Au Bala, whose ancestors shared a common name with a family at Saibai at the western end of the Strait who speak a different language (Book of Islanders 1984, B149). Over a time, through reciprocal ties of *tebud le* and in-laws formed in the aftermath of wars, Meriam speakers of the Eastern Islands came to see themselves as Op Ged, face islands, in contrast with Keo Ged, back islands (the Western Islands), and Eip Ged, middle islands (the Central Islands) (Kitaoji 1978). The seas which they sailed were laced with the tracks of warrior raiders, avenging expeditions and the *wauri* voyagers.

Over a time the definition of the 'other side' had undergone change; alliances were expressed in giving, receiving and returning. Through Malo close ties had begun to form between the Meriam and the Kala Lagaw Ya speakers of Tutu in the Central Islands. Kebisu, so his descendants say, exchanged messages with the *Zogo le* of the Murray Islands 'like a bush telephone'. There were other signs too: 'If he want to go to Murray, if he want to go anywhere he tell his wife: "Bring me two big coconuts". He cut that dry coconut and if that dry coconut cuts right in the middle, he says, "Come on, we go, good word". Before time they are really friendly through Malo. They make great friends.'

In describing the resource-rich ecosystems of the sandbeach people of the Lockhart River area as 'an ecological mosaic of great diversity and richness', Harris might also have been referring to the area inhabited by all the sandbeach people which supported high population densities (1975, 96–97). Throughout the Torres Strait Islands 'swidden' cultivation varied in both degree and style in different islands, ranging from regular planting in the eastern volcanic islands and the alluvial mud flats of Saibai and Boigu in the northwest, to the practice at Muralag of planting yams only when supplies of 'wild' plant and animal food were scarce (Brierly 1849, in Moore 1979, 178–79, 210; Moore 1979, 279).

The staples of the Western Islanders were yams, sweet potatoes, bananas, taro and sugar cane, but coconuts thrived no further south than Mabuiag (Haddon 1912, 132). Muralag had neither coconuts nor bananas. Exchange knotted people together in reciprocal ties necessary for life, for spice to life and for meaning. Nagir, for instance, provided coconuts for Muralag; Yam was the 'garden of Tutu' (Haddon 1890, 408; 1935, 71).

Together with their common life-ways as seafarers were vast differences in cultural practice, which probably had their origins in the variations of their ecosystems. Those variations in cultural practice meant first, that some 'needed' and others did 'not need' to garden. Second, it meant the imperative to travel for some things; for the Islanders, canoes were the basic need. In consequence, life became a many-rayed network of ties created through a wide diversity of exchanges, which were made possible by the mythical heroes who originated in Op Deudai, in Keo Deudai and in the islands of the 'other side'. The myths of Tagai and Sida, both shared by all the Islanders, and the myths of Kwoiam and I'wai are illustrative of the overlapping networks of the sandbeach people. From the far northwest of Op Deudai came the god Sida (Sido), burying cone shells in sandbanks and reefs, bringing manifold plants which he gave in varying amounts to different islands and giving the two different languages to the Islands on each side of the Strait (Haddon 1904, 28–31, 31–36; 1908, 19–22; Landtman 1917, 73–74).

In the myth of Kwoiam the might of the Aboriginal spear follows a path from the sandbeach people of Cape York into the heart of Western Torres Strait at Mabuiag (Haddon 1904, 67–83; Thomson 1934, 238): even as far south as Lockhart River the people may show you Kwoiam's footprints. In the headwaters of the upper Pascoe River lies the centre of the mythical hero I'wai, alligator. The owner of that myth tells how I'wai travels downstream eastwards to the mouth of the river, following northward along the line of the sandbeach, turning finally eastward along a path that ends at Mer.[10]

For the sea people, *malo*, the name for the sea in Kala Lagaw Ya and the languages of the Cape York sandbeach people, is negotiable. It is also awesome, contradictory, its apparent calm masking a contrasting reality beneath. The sandbeach people came to know the sea as the 'same kind' as themselves. They are born to the sea, so swimming, like walking, is 'natural'. Among Islanders a small girl or boy is taught to fish often by the grandfather and the child's first 'catch', be it even a sardine, is honoured by a personal feast: that small person has become an Islander. To be shipwrecked or *sarup* in Meriam Mir is to be rejected by the sea and hence 'another kind', an enemy. *Sarup* is a sign of danger, signifying the undivided power of the singular.

Islanders recognise the 'other side' of the sea: it is not only knowable, negotiable, predictable and tamed; it can be also wild, singular, uncontrolled and threatening. So 'Ailan man never growl the sea... Not say anything bad about the sea when you're on it.' You go with the wind and the currents. When the sea rises up in a storm-surge it threatens: 'Like an eye'; it is like danger. 'We never say because it might *bring* it...' The sea must be 'matched'. So an Islander's canoe, itself like a living thing, an extension of its owner, sails in matched union with the sea, following the patterns of its movement. Malinowski wrote of the Trobrianders' canoe 'which allows him to cross perilous seas to distant places', their long slender canoe 'skims the surface, gliding up and down the waves, now hidden by the crests, now riding on top...' and 'mounting the furrows with graceful agility' (1961, 106–07). The sandbeach people do not seek to master the sea, to harness or to exploit its 'riches': they seek to live and go along with it and that means to 'know' it. We must treat it in a proper way; where it suddenly turns to raging storm our brothers-in-law are always there to placate it. Birds sing out, too, and their cries may be the voices of our ancestors with whom, like in-laws, we mortals are reciprocal.

Here begin the frontiers of the 'why'. Why are the seas and the winds angry? The birds sing out and the noise of the wind is strange, setting 'free' the power of the wild, the singular, the unknown, unnamed. Why? Why now? Why here at this place? Why to *this* man, not *that* man? The people of *malo*, the sea-people took hold of a world alive with wilful spirits and 'enchanted crossways', a world of acts of gods, of singular events brought about by the power of *Em*: herein lies the centre of the meaning systems of the people of the sandbeaches.

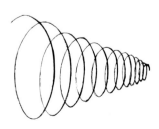

The myths had brought to the sea people diverse gifts: their similarities made possible their common life-ways and custom; their dissimilarities impelled them to seek an associative, complementary unity. Through the imperative of the necessities they lacked they created networks of peace. The Island seafarers went to Op Deudai (Daudai) above all for canoes. The myths which brought them together by turning round the danger of the wild into a named world made voyages possible across storm-prone waters. The voyagers travelled the safe tracks of the mythical heroes. Over time, the wisdom of their experience was further distilled in extension of their myths, so enabling the networks of exchange to be enlarged.

Islanders' world came to span the half-circle of the flight of the Torres Strait pigeon. These white birds thrive on mace, especially in the homelands of the Marind-Anim at Tuger, flying southward to feed on the red plums of the wongai trees (*Manilkara kauki, Mimusops kauki* and *M. Browniana*) of the islands towards the end of the southeast season, moving on to lay their eggs among the mangroves of the eastern sandbeaches of Cape York Peninsula, the place of their rebirth, and returning northwestward with their fledglings after the northwest monsoon.

The Torres Strait pigeon joins together the two continents. It is also a bird of the Islands; every Islander girl or boy knows the legend: if you eat a wongai fruit you will become like a bird and always fly back to the Islands.

COMPARISONS AND CONTRASTS

FROM SPIRITS OF THE DEAD TO MASTERS OF THE LIVING

For Islander people, the white men who arrived in *au nar*, great ships, were not part of the world of *le* with whom they customarily exchanged. 'Nothing foreign was merely human' in their scheme of things, to repeat Sahlins' reversal of Marx's famous aphorism (1976, 11). With those among the shipwrecked, who bore the discernible stamp of their ancestors, known as *lamar* in Meriam Mir, they set out to establish reciprocal relations. The rest were fraught with the power of the singular, so they killed them and kept their skulls. Since Islanders' lives oscillated between the sharp extremes of enemy raids and *wauri* exchange, the early contradictory experiences of encounters with white men may have echoed familiar contrasts. When the newcomers did not hurl back the silent insult of refusal of their gifts the Islanders did not usually string their bows; they sought to exchange equivalences.

Yet when the newcomers crossed the sandbeaches and sought to live among them, seeking to acquire the sacred symbols of their culture, the Islanders refused their requests: they were transgressing the Islanders' code (Jukes 1847). In their custom, no one crossed the sandbeaches without permission. Those who did so were either *wauri* partners, sisters-in-exchange, or brothers-in-law. The Darnley men were reluctant to receive the LMS pastors from the South Seas as residents (Murray and McFarlane, 11 September 1871). Nor would they part with their land willingly (McFarlane, Report 1875). Nothing could persuade the Meriam to part with the five *seuriseuri*, the star-headed stone-clubs of Malo (Haddon 1908, 296). It was with visible reluctance that the Meriam agreed to make cardboard models of the Malo and Bomai masks for Haddon (1908, 289).

Once the Islanders were forced or tricked into 'receiving' the trespassers on their soil, things began to fall apart. In the early stages, they had joined the new techniques and productive forces to their own ends. Only later were their old skills harnessed to new purposes. The voyages began to lose their old meanings as they were encouraged to divest themselves of their canoes and buy cutters and calico, and dive for shell to earn money. New needs were being created, new hopes kindled, new expectations partially realised. They began to press for schools where their children might come to know the white man's custom, the source of the manufactured goods he brought with him, and the key to another world.

For Islanders the non-reciprocal was always present: that was the 'other'. At times it rose up implacable as a storm-wind. Yet the coming of Kole was a contradiction of a new kind: an enforced asymmetrical relationship. Islanders soon learned that the newcomers were not spirits of the dead — but men; men who, unlike raiders known to them, did not follow Islanders' cultural principles of killing and taking skulls; of coming to terms and creating ties of brothers/sisters-in-law and of *tebud le*, through the integrative effects of the extension of their myths. Amongst Meriam speakers, *kole* meant master. In the time when white men took on the role of their rulers *kole* also came to mean white men: *kole* had become Kole. Kole did not seek to know Islanders in the positive quality of their difference. At best they taught them how to sail ships the Kole-way; at worst Islanders were denied the knowledge by which they might do so. Their oral tradition stored in myth and legend and rite was seen as part of a rapidly disappearing past.

No one was interested in their canoes as creations of use and of beauty which formed part of a living culture. The newcomers even came to forget that the Islanders made voyages to distant islands, to Op Deudai, to Keo Deudai, in their double-outrigger canoes.[11] Scholars came to see the islands as a barrier between 'horticulture' and 'hunting-gathering' (Walker 1972, 405), rather than as a vast mosaic of networks of diversities-in-unity transecting those categories.

For a brief time some Islanders shared in a new prosperity, especially in the Eastern Islands. Through schooling and an experience of a wider life which went with ownership of cutters and working in the pearl shelling industry, Islanders came to know that the '*lamar* ships' brought commodities from Kole-land, not gifts from the world of the ancestors.

Three years after the creation of a federated 'White Australia' in 1901, Islanders joined Aborigines as the faceless indigenous Aboriginal people of Queensland. They became subject to Protection. Following an all-island strike on the pearling luggers in 1936, a separate Act once again recognised Islanders' identity as a separate people. Unlike Aborigines, Islanders were not pushed off their lands; they were hemmed into them for some sixty years until the early 1960s, when a new 'right' to leave the Islands coincided with the collapse of the pearling industry. By 1980, half the Islander population was living on the mainland. Over that time, Islanders sought to break free of their containment by Kole. A double-sided imperative was created among Islanders. One was the re-creation of equivalence; the other was the need to know the 'other side', to take its measure. Together they represented the reassertion of the social code by which they lived together in face-to-face communities and came to terms with those outside their immediate world.

ORIGINALITY AS SYNTHESIS: THREE VIGNETTES

The Islander being called here 'First Meriam Man', a man of Piadram *nosik* or clan, was born in 1884 and educated first at Murray Island State School and later at the LMS seminary at Mer. Like other Eastern Islanders, he had been relatively free as a youth to move around the Islands and the Queensland mainland, so becoming familiar with the knowledge and customs of Kole society; in coming together with South Sea Islanders with customs similar to his own, like Sis' father, a contemporary born in 1888 and educated, too, at Murray Island, he came to a fuller awareness of his own changing culture. When the man known here as 'Second Meriam Man', a descendant of the *Zogo le* on his mother's side as well as his father's, was born in 1936, the older Meriam Man was fifty years old. The younger man grew up in a period when Islanders were locked into a closed situation within the Islands and largely shut out of the wider world. In his later youth, he experienced an impelling need to go in 'search of something': to discover for himself the other side of the coin of white culture that was denied him. That was a first stage.

Sis' father was a man who saw the Christian teaching as the completion of the message that came through his own family. Through comparison and contrast he was able to see the 'truth' of Malo's teaching; he developed very close associations with the Meriam, especially the descendants of the *Zogo le*.

First Meriam Man died in 1968. Some of the meaning and élan of his life is captured in memories of Ailan Man in Thursday Island, of his son and his son's age-mate in Townsville in 1980 and 1981.

First Meriam Man — Before he did anything he thought about his zogo

AILAN MAN

Well Meriam Man was different. He'd been all over the south, cut cane. He rubbed shoulders with Pacific Islanders in camps down there. He's the sort of man when he's got a go in him to do it he'll bloody do it. A very traditional man too. He's an authority in his own right as far as tradition goes. Even to the time when I came the old fellows there talk about him. They say, 'You go ask Meriam Man!' They have to confirm it with him. He's there with the Zogo le. *Meriam Man came into the picture as a leader in Murray Island in the thirties. It started about the strike time. Well during the [Second World] War he got all the Murray Island people to put money together and buy a boarding house and that's when he stands out: because Island people had never owned a boarding house. And then people talked about the Murray Island boarding house and about the Murray Island boys that came in here and cut wood and sold it in town, in TI.*

SON

Well, when he was a young fellow he and his mates used to cut timber in Daintree until he reached manhood. He went back and he got education and married a Murray Island girl. Douglas Pitt brought him up there in Daintree when he was a young fellow.

SON OF AGE-MATE

When the 'Company boats' came to Torres Strait he was a Councillor. And when he saw the government still got power to tell him what to do he held meetings at Murray Island. He liked to work by himself; he don't want the government telling him what to do.

Councillors were united on their culture and the zogo. Before he did anything he thought about his zogo and that's what made him become a great man. He believed in where he stands on his culture and on his history and on his language plus what we call the zogo. When I was getting married he said to me: 'Now we're fighting for our culture and we're still going back to where our culture is'. He wanted to see his culture to be passed on from his time from generation to generation. He talk about the land and what we're talking about now: getting our land back. He said it to me personally. '...no good to be Chairman and

*just sit on chairs; must go out and see the people'. And that flows into
the way he was doing things and make him come great in the Island.
The more Meriam Man travelled the more he got his experience from
the outside world. Go back and help his people.*

AILAN MAN

*People used to talk about Meriam Man. The Protector wouldn't have
Murray Island people in town. He said, 'They're going to come in! If
they can't come in you support their families.' I remember the time
at a meeting in 1954 old Meriam Man stood up and wanted to take
over the Island Industries Board. He asked for the balance sheet.*

*During the War there were some arguments about lands at Murray
Island, about the boundary. And after the War the old bloke he gets
very wild about this. He was the Chairman then and they went out
there. They were trying to shame him. O'Leary [the Protector] said
they got him out of office, but the people seemed to realise that he was
right.* (Book of Islanders 1984, B19–21)

Sis' father, Uncle T — They liked doing things for him because he liked doing things for them

*Grandfather was going to school in Samoa and they heard about here.
His father was an LMS priest. If you go to one of the villages in Apia,
Samoa, there's a stone there they put up in memory of all the LMS
priest-missionaries that went from Niue to Samoa and fourth from
the top is T, my great grandfather's name. He served his full time as
a missionary, seven to ten years. When they heard about Australia
he and his brother came to Sydney. He kept on coming up this way.
He came up under his own steam; and he found a lot of countrymen
when he came here. That's why today Darnley has no language; there
were too many Polynesians and Melanesians there. The same as Moa;
Moa has no language too; it had a mixture of people too, those other
people with their local wives. We all conversed in broken English.*

*My grandfather worked the Darnley Deeps; they didn't work any
shallow water. They went to Samarai and to Papua and worked there;
they'd come back to Darnley. He was the first man to go down the
deepest in Darnley and to this day that part carries his name. My
father went even deeper by accident; he fell off a 'hill'. My father was
born in 1888 and he died on the 18 May 1971. He got that date in 1935:
he knew that seventy-one had to do with his death. He started learning
medicine-man things when he was twelve. I guess he was always a
medicine man. Grandfather T took him aside when he was twelve, then
fourteen, then seventeen: then he was allowed to practise. My
grandfather was the greatest medicine man in the Torres Strait, bar
none! My grandfather became a diver because that was the only way
in those days to get good money.*

My father went to Murray Island school. In those days it was Mr Butcher's school and it was a good school, the best in Torres Strait: Butcher, Bruce and all those people. You look at the men who came from that school: they were really intelligent people. My father could do sums I can't do — and he learnt them all on Murray Island. My father was a true Polynesian: he wasn't very industrious. My father would rather sit and sing. My father's people were really kind and they are now. They could give away everything and not worry. They'd give the shirt off their back. My mother used to say that when he took a boat out all he used to do was sign on and off. Everyone did the work for him because they liked him. He'd find the right man around to do that work. They liked doing things for him because he liked doing things for them. He used to say: 'They do the work; that's because they're good boys'. All through our life we'd have people come at all hours of the night and never once did he complain. People used to call him Uncle Spear-Eye or Uncle Glass-Eye because when he was a boy a spear hit him in the eye.

The very first day that my father died we collected more than enough to pay for his burial and the taxi-driver was carrying in bags of rice and flour for the dampers. The boys went out to get the turtles. Well one family had five boys, so all the boys just went up and dug the grave for my father. He is buried here. Everything was just paid by outsiders. But then again when you come to look at my father's life he's done more than that. You know it is sort of fitting because people want to give to say 'thank you'. Then you know how the children are always the last. The children sat first because my father was very fond of children. The children came in, children for miles. That was his death — and then the grown-ups had theirs. The spirit was there.

My father was the religious one of the family. Oh, my mother believed in God and loved Him, but as my father said: 'We join other churches but we have our own belief, our own God that's different to all of these'. We have a God and we believe that we had this God long before the white man came to us. We believe that our true Church will come to us, that because He was true our God will bring our Church to us again. I didn't know my great grandfather but I believe he was a good LMS priest and I guess that's the closest they came; they had to have a form of religion. I believe that when they prayed, like my father used to, they prayed to their own God.

The way my father talked to me about Bomai-Malo was that it was a good teaching leading up to the real religion. But it wasn't the full teaching. We had this kind of religion but we didn't have the Christian message to go with it. Instead of that we had Zogo le. I'm talking about the true religion now. If we had it in its fullness we wouldn't have to come back to it again. We had something, we had some teaching, enough to recognise it when it did come, but we didn't have it in its fullness. My own family, our tribe, were the closest to the true religion than any other religion on earth. We were good LMS; we listened to the new teachings only because our religion taught all those good things anyway. The Bomai-Malo teaching was of good things too. (Book of Islanders 1984, B93–96)

Second Meriam Man — We have a coin and it has two sides

I was like a little primitive lad growing up in a tribal situation. The only thing we had was the land. I used to go to school with bare body, just a nesur. Nesur *is our term for what they call* lavalava, *a pidgin word. That was in the fifties when Robert Miles came to Murray Island as government teacher. At that time I knew nothing of English language. Then eventually I started to take an interest because Bob Miles was interested in learning Meriam. He would teach me English and I would teach him Meriam Mir.*

From then on I started to look at the whole lifestyle in the Torres Strait from a different point of view. One thought was that we have a coin and it has two sides and whilst we're looking at the side the DAIA dishes out to the Islanders we see there must be another side. It led me to think that I would have succeeded if there was an alternative education in the Strait run by my father or someone like him. And from then on the idea of a black community school came into existence. I think I was about thirteen or fourteen. It took me eighteen years to get all my ideas together and convince people it was necessary to have our own school in order that we may ensure that our future generations would remain as a proud Piadram people or whatever tribe they belong to. We wanted to be able to teach both cultures in our school.

Then I came south. In my upbringing on Murray I wasn't offered much and when I came to the mainland I saw what they knew as a thing I must have. I made an effort to admire people from colleges and universities, from societies like the arts societies, to appreciate their form of art, choral groups and all those sorts of people who have their cultural value to contribute. I continued to think that by drawing the best out of both worlds you'd come up with something totally unique. I admired very much this guy Bob Miles. He made me appreciate a lot of things that the white man had to offer: like music and art. One of the things that I did when I came south was try and see if they were around. I actually investigated white culture and discovered it for myself. Also the use of the English language. I tried to learn it the best I could and tried to follow the Oxford system.

It was only a matter of two or three years before we found ourselves sitting faced in a meeting in Townsville. It was an in-service training course for teachers in schools with predominantly Aboriginal and

Islander people. I was invited as a guest. When I started saying, 'Who
would be willing to spend some time on Aboriginal and Islander
people?', some said: 'Why would we spend time with boongs and black
bastards while we have so many of our own to worry about?'. When
I heard that of course, being a touchy issue in my way of thinking,

I got up and did my dance
[laughing softly]
Everyone stood on their feet and I walked out.

Well the thing was I really thumped the floor saying something like,
'Who the hell's going to send their kids to be taught by racist people
like these bastards?'.
    Some of them walked out with us. Yes, some were sympathetic, those
who were seeing what was going on in the state schools, walked out
with us. It took us three weeks from the time we walked out and the
school opened its doors with eight students enrolled and two teachers.
We thought it was proper that we became a school on the basis that
we're culturally different. I think I've told you before that it is my wish
that when I do return to Murray there there'll be no Department schools
at all. (Book of Islanders 1984, B134–39)

A DOUBLE MOVEMENT OF CHANGING AND CONTINUING

Unlike those who grew up at Murray Island after about 1901, in his formative years
the older Meriam Man combined the new world with his own without outright
interference from Kole. It was 'natural' for him to bring back his experience from
the outside world to help his people. The uniqueness and strength of his personal
synthesis was put to the test many years later: in 1936 as a central figure in the
strike on the luggers he came forward as a man who confronted Kole on their
own terms; as an innovator in community projects such as the first Island boarding
house and a firewood business he was also continuing the associative ties of Meriam
social life.

    The younger Meriam Man was putting the two worlds together which
Kole had kept apart. His actions spoke clearly as he thumped the floor, striking
back at Kole in a face to face confrontation with those personally stated attitudes
which expressed the ideology underlying his exclusion from the brighter side of
the coin of Kole culture. This moment was like an intense experience of his whole
life up until then, an experience which had been building up in him over eighteen
years since he had 'discovered' Robert Miles as a white man prepared to exchange
Meriam Mir with English. That had been an act which acknowledged the
equivalence of cultural difference and also a beginning of a journey to the south
in search of the 'other side' which he had glimpsed. When he set foot on the

mainland that wish became suddenly a burning need; he 'saw what they knew as a thing I must have'. Later on, after many years of coming into closer touch with that 'other side', he came to confront the underside of Kole culture. In one intense moment he got up and did his dance: he was smashing down the barrier separating the two worlds, which Kole had erected, in a cultural–political act — his dance in the genre of Meriam tradition. At that moment he re-experienced the recognition of the integrity of his own cultural difference in the eyes of the 'other', this time not just one, but a group of the white teachers present. In his project for a bi-cultural school, which then suddenly came into being, he was putting the two worlds together, not as an association which meant a melting pot of the two cultures, but in the complementarity of their dissimilarities. In 'drawing the best out of both worlds' the school would, he believed, create something 'totally unique': yet that 'something' remained explicitly within the tradition of the *Zogo le* (the *Aets*) of Malo.

As First Meriam Man's life illustrates, the originality of a new synthesis implied the cultural growth of Second Meriam Man, a growth which nevertheless remained attached to its source; a new synthesis did not mean the extinguishing of old syntheses. There is a double movement here of changing and continuing, in which 'innovation' carries with it continuity; in which continuity bears also change. This is rather like the argument crystallised by Marshall Sahlins on 'the inseparability of continuity and difference'. 'Writing of the Hawaiians' incorporation of 'breaches of tabu by the logic of tabu', he concludes, following Wagner, that new values are 'resumed within the cultural structure': 'But the structure is then transformed. Here the cultural encompassment of the event is at once conservative and innovative. It would seem that a good Heraclitean argument can be made for the inseparability of continuity and difference' (1981, 68).

The myth of Malo-Bomai had brought eight 'peoples' (clans) into one, 'strengthening' them with the qualities of a diversity of sea creatures, so giving the power to match the sea and make long journeys across *malo*, the deep seas, for canoes and for battle. That new social and cultural integration did not weaken the separate existence of the 'peoples' so brought together. In the era of the Storm-Winds that same integrative process continued. Yet, it is suggested here that the new syntheses which were created in this period hold a new component of individuation, one which, however, continues within the frame of the reciprocal based on the primordial givens of place and blood or kindred. That individuation, symbolised for instance in a 'moment of truth' for Second Meriam Man in the early 1970s — 'I did my dance...' — suggests a form of awareness and self-awareness which was foreign to the subjectivity of his grandfather or the *Zogo le* before him.

The Storm-Winds brought calamity and affliction to the Islands. With them also came the cultural traditions expressed in social processes and meaning systems through which Islanders came to reconstitute their life-form and ways of seeing. In part, the pre-existing social forms were destroyed; at the same time, both in social life and meaning, the 'new' sped up the processes of change which were already there. Perhaps one may compare the Island world in transition to that of Tangu of New Guinea of whom Burridge wrote in the 1960s: 'A pattern that was already there was coaxed into view' (1969, 458). In the Islands the pattern so coaxed came to hold a transformation of quality, the result of cultural themes from the other side of the Great Divide between cultures.

THE MERIAM AS EXAMPLE

Part II which follows, focuses on how life is constituted among the Meriam of the small trio of the Murray Islands — Mer, Dauar and Waier — in a process of change (see Map 1, inset). Islanders believe that Mer was shaped by the dugong Gelam. The myth of Gelam tells of Gelam's journey in the form of a dugong from Moa, in which Gelam transferred the rich red soil of Moa to Mer, bringing also *u*, coconut palms, and *lewer kar*, yams of many varieties, and other fruits. The everlasting daisy, it is said in the Islands, grows only at Moa peak and at the nose of Gelam, so knotting the two. Two red bean seeds which he spat out became the smaller fertile isle of Dauar and the crescent-shaped Waier, so making up the first island trio of the Meriam, a community of horticulturalists.[12] When Gelam faced towards the north the wind blew strongly, so he turned round where the wind blew from behind him (Haddon 1908, 25): that act signified the founding of a sea-culture where life followed the movement of the seas and the winds. Islanders say: 'Travel westward with *sager*, the southeast wind, leeward down to Boigu, the island at the end of the seas'.

There are three main historical reasons for taking the example of the Meriam of the Murray Islands; a fourth reason became apparent in a public setting at the end of the 1980s. First, they were an especially cohesive group in pre-contact times, a quality noted by outsiders as early as 1845. As AC Haddon asked rhetorically following his visit to Mer in 1898: what other grouping of people occupying a space of no more than one-and-a-half square miles 'can exhibit such rich variety' in their life:

> This very small island supports a relatively large population, and
> it also affords the spectacle of a people (who had an undeserved
> reputation as treacherous savages) enjoying an active economic
> life filled with a great variety of small individual and large

collective rites. The various groupings gave social and local solidarity. The spirit pantomimes emphasised the continuation of life after death. The spirits of their forbears and other spirits with whom no relationship could be claimed cooperated with the living in promoting present well-being. Finally, all the islanders were embraced within a powerful, awe-inspiring cult which gave them a new feeling of nationality and induced an increased zest to life. (1935, 183)

Second, in contrast with Darnley Island, for instance, where a dwindling native population became subsidiary to immigrant South Sea Islanders as early as the 1870s, the Murray Islands retained that integral quality. In 1885 all the South Sea Islanders resident at Mer were expelled and resettled at Darnley Island. Third, in the last twenty years of the century the Murray Islanders not only had the best schooling in the Torres Strait; the government school which existed there from 1892 until the end of 1902 was rated as equal to any other state school in Queensland.[13]

From this uniquely balanced combination of a 'feeling of nationality' among the living in union with the life-giving 'spirits of their forbears', as Haddon saw it, not only were many of the old ways replaced by new customs. *The original social processes, which gave rise to that cohesion noted by Haddon, provided the foundation for continuity: the 'conservatism' of the Malo tradition formed the basis of 'innovation'.* Those who carried a strongly meaningful message from the past were capable of receiving the new knowledge from other cultural traditions, whether these were from Europe, from the South Seas, or elsewhere. As Sis says, the two in association created the deep strength to stand up to the Administration: 'The Murray Island people were really strong and some of us used to believe it was because they spoke their language. But I think it was too that they had a better education.'

It was easy for Uncle T, Sis' father, to exchange his 'new' message with the *Zogo le*, because they had something to give in return: the teachings of Malo-Bomai through which they were able to receive a different cultural tradition. Haddon himself sensed this to some degree when he visited Mer and met the newly-won Christians there:

> I am under the impression that the most moral and pious heathen are the most likely to be attracted by a higher form of social order and religion. These are just the men that have a strong sense of reticence and of the sacredness of religious customs; in changing their beliefs and customs, their attitude of mind would remain much the same, and they would not be disposed to treat lightly that which had previously meant so much to them. (1908, xix)

When the Cambridge team visited Mer in 1898 their 'greatest difficulty was naturally with customs related to magic and religion', as Haddon reported: 'Not only had a good deal disappeared from actual practice'; the team found a reluctance to talk about certain subjects, partly because they 'were originally of a secret or sacred character', partly because they believed that white men expected that they 'ought to be ashamed of the past'. 'Even the profession of Christianity', Haddon noted perceptively, 'does not make all the difference that one might at first sight think it would' (1908, xix).[14]

Where was Malo-Bomai pointing? This was the question asked by Haddon: 'I am afraid we are never likely to find out...' (1908, 44). He saw in the sacred 'hero cult' of Malo-Bomai a way of living together; he also recognised the meaning of its funerary rite as a transcendence of death through rebirth in the place of *lamar* (1908, 45). Haddon did not discern the meaning of the power of *zogo* in beginning to overcome the profane danger of the 'other side' among the living; how the strength of Malo was with them when they went for warfare or *wauri*. Nor was he aware that in a twofold sense this 'powerful cult' was pointing to the power of life over death. It made possible an ambience beyond the face to face community, bringing Islanders together through *tebud* or partners, who were then passed down through the generations of each partner's family.

Au Bala explains the reluctance of the Meriam: 'See, they got used to keeping Bomai secret and they didn't tell the outsiders, even the anthropologists that went there'. But Au Bala's grandfather, one of the three *Zogo le* of Malo said: '...the *ged kem le*, the true one of the Island, was Bomai'. So Au Bala says today: 'Most of the time I say Malo first before Bomai... I think of the old people when I say it. Bomai was so sacred that no one was allowed to call that name' (Cassette 134/AB/TI/2/84).[15]

Keeping silent about their own world is a continuing habit among Murray Islanders. We shall find in Part III that over the past hundred years they were given ample reason for retaining and developing the habit. Given this context, it occasioned surprise among some outsiders in 1989 when one after another the Murray Islanders appeared as witnesses at hearings of a land case brought by three plaintiffs (including Second Meriam Man and Kebi Bala) against the State of Queensland and the Commonwealth of Australia (the *Murray Island Land/Mabo* case)[16] in the Supreme Court of Queensland, at Mer, at Thursday Island and in Brisbane. They refuted vigorously the claim made by PJ Killoran, for the first defendant, the State of Queensland, that intruders had effectively destroyed the way of life and custom of the Murray Islanders. Virtually to the last man and woman (including several Murray Islanders who gave evidence for the Crown), they were eager to demonstrate the continuity of their occupation of the Murray Islands, their land law (Malo's Law) and their cultural traditions to the present day. In appearing as a witness for the plaintiffs, Au Bala summed up for the court the past in the present: 'If you want to be a real Murray Islander you follow Malo's Law'. Herein lies a fourth — and highly significant reason — for taking the example of the Murray Islanders as our illustration of a rich and continuing tradition within the Islands. As we have seen, the Meriam *kerkar*, meaning 'fresh season', carries a sense of the repetition and the newness of things. Part II, a study of the *kerkar* of the Meriam of Mer, Dauar and Waier, moves back and forth between the past and the present.

.

II

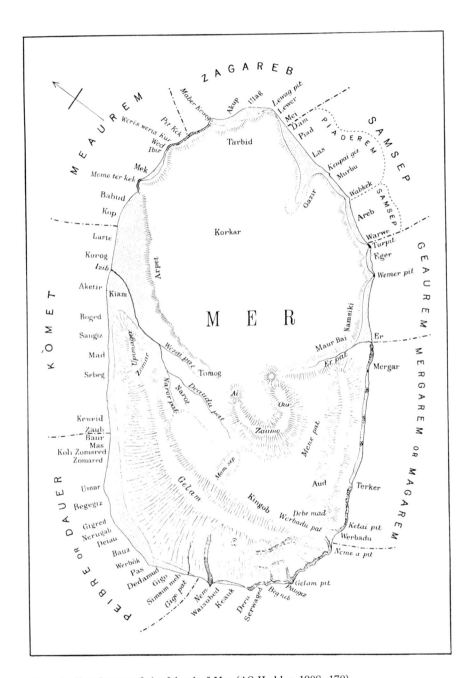

Map 2 Sketch map of the Island of Mer (AC Haddon 1908, 170)

2 | THE FLOWER OF MERIAM IDENTITIES: LINKING CIRCLES OF LIFE AMONG THE MERIAM

Yes, very important that wauri *shell. If I give you that* wauri
*you can't leave me: you're my blood family. That's why
we hold on to Torres Strait family here. These two people
are like my two relatives.*

Malo got laws like the Christian religion. When wauri
*becomes known others will see it as one part the Gospel has
left behind: 'Be kind to one another!' Because* wauri tebud
is more than one born from the same blood.

Kapin

SPRINGS OF THE MERIAM: A CENTRE OF ORIGIN

Meriam social life springs from *giz ged* at Las on the eastern side of Mer, the place
of the arrival of Bomai. *Giz* means root of a tree; it also means origin or spring.
Ged, which means home or place or homeland, is the undetachable milieu of
Meriam identity, for each individual must have a homeland. For an unborn Meriam,
ged is the mother's womb; at birth, the individual moves from this *ged* to that
ged, the land belonging to his father. *Giz ged* is the centre of the world.[1]

The village of Las lies within the *ged* of Piadram [Piaderem] clan (*nosik*)
and from here begins the first meaning of Meriam: Piadram clan, in contrast to
the neighbouring Samsep clan. From this first meaning, overlapping and widening
meanings of *ged* and of Meriam arise, which reach outward to include the island
of Mer as against Dauar and Waier, those three isles in contrast with the Eastern
Islands, coming finally to include the latter, known to the Meriam as Op Ged or
face islands, in contrast with the Central Islands, Eip Ged and the Western Islands,
Keo Ged (Kitaoji 1982, 68). Those who belong to Op Ged also share a language,
Meriam Mir.[2]

The coming of Bomai from the western reaches of Op Deudai signified
receiving the sacred power of *zogo* and with it a moral code. In the Bomai epic
the octopus with eight tentacles joined into one body symbolised the eight *nosik*
or 'peoples' of Mer, Dauar and Waier. The myth of Malo-Bomai, described by Kitaoji
as 'an epic of cultural independence of the Miriam' (1977, 212), joins the many
into the one; the one comes to express the diversity of the many. Malo, 'the name
of the less sacred individual', used 'as a cloak for that of the more sacred' Bomai
(Haddon 1908, 232), became exemplar of the sacred code known as Malo's Law,
Malo ra Gelar. In Malo ra Gelar lies the imperative of Meriam life. It provides the

rule by which people conserve the land, make it bountiful and protect the rights of those who belong to each part of it: *Malo tag mauki mauki*: Malo keeps his hands to himself; he does not touch what is not his. *Teter mauki mauki*: He does not permit his feet to carry him towards another man's property. *Wali aritarit, sem aritarit*: Malo plants everywhere — under *wali* and *sem*, the yellow-flowered hibiscus. *Eburlem, esmaolem*: Let it drop and rot on the ground. This concerns the conservation of food and may be expressed in the following way. The head of a *nosik* calls all the clan members together for the purpose of placing a *gelar* or taboo on some or all of the food resources owned by members of the clan. Signs of *gelar* are erected in a prominent place in the clan district; these may be a row of banana leaves attached to bamboo, each leaf representing the head of a lineage, who is the nameholder for a particular allotment of land. For the period of the *gelar*, Malo's Law prohibits anyone from removing any part of the trees, branches or fruit on village land, garden land or plantation land belonging to any members of that clan.[3]

The Meriam believe that it was through the coming of Bomai from Op Deudai that the fertile island of Mer became a centre of exchange of vegetable food with the sea foods from other islands. *Aritarit* means planting; it is a word in the language of the sacred chants, known as Malo language, which, like the myth, comes from the 'other (western) side' (Haddon 1908, 243; Ray 1907, 50–51). Au Bala explains how Mer became a small *deudai*, or centre of exchange to which Islanders from the Central Islands came to trade fish, turtle and dugong for garden produce.

Within the richly variegated trio of islands the Meriam developed a slash and burn horticulture (Haddon 1912, 145); law and custom (*gelar tonar*) signified the rights and obligations embedded within the Meriam land-owning system. Also, boundary markers (*nener*), known as *elikup*, cut from a variety of ironwood (*ur sekerseker*), often supplemented the ancient boundaries. The eldest son became the nameholder (*lu kem le*) for *ged*, the land inherited through the father's line (Wilkin in Haddon 1908, 163–68). Family groups within each of the eight *nosik* made gardens, *gedub* (Kitaoji 1982). For most of the yearly cycle the Meriam lived in grass-thatched 'beehive' round houses (*keubkeub meta*) along the sandbeaches, gaining ready sustenance from the sea at fringing reefs (*ter*) encircling the three islands. On the northern side of Mer the people built large stone fish-traps known as *sai*.

As gardener or as fisherman or woman, each Meriam is like a mediator between the known and the unknown, between culture and nature, transforming it by his or her knowledge, skills and relationship with it, so bringing it into the realm of the cultivated, like *gedub*, garden. In becoming reciprocal with it the person knows it and one might say, in being alive, it 'knows' the person (Frankfort 1946, 6). For the gardener there are several essentials. First is the selection of a healthy plant and this has meaning in relation to the core of the cultural, to *lewer kar* or yams, as real food. Second is knowledge of a plant in its specific interrelationship to a whole environment: the habits of the plant with respect to this soil, this season, other plants present in relation to its potential and its needs as a whole at particular stages of its development. Third are tools related to preparation for planting and its growth through to fruition. Finally, and framing everything else, is an apprehension of the cosmic world within which it is set and in Islander tradition this means *zogo mir*, the chants of garden magic. The gardener may transform wild nature, but the wild as the other side of the cultivated is always ready to break through: it is the immanent power of destruction.

Au Bala, the eldest brother, is renowned as a gardener among the Meriam; as a grower of yams, *lewer kar*, he is known beyond the Torres Strait. Through a lifelong experience of cultural contrast he is also able to perceive the unique quality of the Meriam tradition. In him many strands of knowledge are woven into one: nature has become his book.

PLACE, TIME AND IDENTITY: THE FIRST CIRCLE OF LIFE OF THE MERIAM

Mek, Signs: Au Bala, I use nature for my book

> Nature always shows signs of something that will happen in a few months. Say for instance, when there is a prolific year for the wongai it'll be for sure a prolific year for turtle egg-laying season. It's wonderful, you know, to get the knowledge straight from nature. Our ancestors didn't even know anything about the names of the months, but they knew when the cold season began to set in that so and so tree will be in bloom, like sorbi. As soon as one feels the air is cold it'll tell: nature says sorbi is in bloom.
>
> Now there was a certain thing that before an Islander went fishing early in the morning he should be making some special preparations. There were certain rules that an Islander must follow. And we understand too that a fish is a living thing and it goes from one patch to another in the right time, the proper time, to look for its feed. There are some areas which attract fish in a spring tide, while others depend wholly, solely on the neap tide and one is contrary to the other. You can't just put them together by going to the place where you should fish in a certain time of the year. If you go in the neap tide to that particular part where you can only fish in the spring tide, you're wasting your valuable time because they won't be there. That's

the knowledge we have had for so many years and it still exists. We know that it is true. So if you were to take me out fishing I first must study the tide: I must take you where the fish feed for that tide.

White society goes from books and calendars, but with our society in years gone by they used to study the stars and trees that symbolise a different thing to come. I was interested to know that there are some things like fertilisers from the outside world only newly introduced here. But we knew such a thing before. We thought that nature's own fertilisers were better than man-made fertilisers. That is why I said to E, one of my white friends: 'You can go to Australia and bring all the fertilisers you want, but you will never come close to me, because I depend wholly and entirely upon nature's own fertilisers'.

Kipa gogob is the first rain. We get heavy rain before the change in the weather from southeast to northwest. Before that time of heavy rain they knew what to do with the garden. Father used to read the clouds: 'All right now. The atmosphere: the sun start to draw water into the air.' And he was very clever. At one time he called me: 'Come here. See this cloud here. Rain is not far. This is the sign of first rain.' And I looked at him and said, 'Okay'. It's written in my brain. Indelible pencil. I was quite small then; nine or ten.

I use nature for my book and I know how to go about in my part of the world. I still am going to preserve this knowledge through the ages. I know the knowledge we have had handed down from forefathers into our time. Our knowledge is according to what nature says and we still look forward into nature which tells things much more clearly than the outside world. (A Cultural Tradition Handed Down, Book of Islanders 1984, B143, B144, B145)

THE SEASONS: GIVING LIFE'S PATTERN

Meriam life swings upon the axis of the two great seasons of the year: *sager kerker*, time of southeast wind, may last from about April to early August and *koki kerker*, the northwest rainy time, from December through to March. *Naiger kerker*, the northeast season, the dry time, and southwest season, *ziai kerker*, are almost like transitional pausing times in-between the great changes of the winds. In the movement from one season to another the Meriam experience the cycle of abundance and scarcity, of harvest and rebirth. The rhythms of the natural world are ordered but not always orderly; they are mundane and at the same time other-worldly; they are discordant, yet they are expected. They are cycles of the repetition of samenesses which also carry the new. Everything dies but all things are reborn. Yet as Mircea Eliade has written, 'nothing really dies', the world 'just rests waiting for another spring' (1974, 332). The patterns of nature are self-contradictory. Life is lived *both* as contradiction and as rhythm. Eliade discerns their inseparability: 'Any vision of the world founded upon rhythm must have certain dramatic moments; to live out in ritual the rhythms of the universe means above all to live amid manifold and contradictory tensions' (1974, 332).

The movement and pattern of the circle of nature form the fabric of social life. The imprint of surrounding nature upon the Meriam is expressed in categories drawn from it. The 'order' of its patterns holds antinomies as well as harmonies of quality: like spring tide and neap tide 'one is contrary to the other'. Yet the 'book' Au Bala reads is no fixed or frozen thing: it is the movement of a circle in which the world above, the world surrounding and the world below 'tell' or show forth signs of things that will happen later. The movement of nature — the seas, the winds, the celestial world, the land — produces the 'seasonal calendar', the rhythm of Meriam life. This is the foundation of Meriam 'time', their 'timetable' of life.

Nature's variegations of similarity and dissimilarity move upon the two intersecting axes of place and cosmic time. Among those social groupings who move from place to place with the movement of the seasons and as specified by social relations, 'time' denotes a tie to a specified place: time belonging to this place, time belonging to that place. For the Meriam as village horticulturalists there is a constancy of place, but place itself takes on a different significance according to seasonal 'time'. Meriam life goes with the tides and the winds. For most of the year the winds come from the southeast side (*sager pek*) beyond the Reef. As this breeze ends and the wind begins to turn round towards the north, the canoe voyages took place: 'Travel westward with *sager*, leeward down to Boigu, the island at the end of the seas'. Warm land breezes and calm waters blow on the lee side of Mer before the great transformation of *koki kerkar* when the voyagers to Op Deudai headed for home with the wind on their backs.

Each season has its own inner rhythm set within a larger circle of birth and growth, maturity and decline. This 'ordering' process is not a motionless equilibrium. It is a contradictory process in which each rebirth is fresh and new, both similar to the old, but also different. Thus *koki kerker* is fresh northwest: it is both not like and like *koki kerker*, northwest time.

The comings and goings and returnings of the seasons imprint all the Meriam; there is an overall similarity in the framing of their lives. From one season to the next one all the Meriam become like different people. Their diet changes. Their activities differ and with those changes go hopes and expectations and variations of mood. Like *ketai*, the perennial yam that yields all the year round yet tastes a little different at different times, the people decline and revive.[4]

THE WIND-CIRCLE OF MERIAM IDENTITIES

Like those whose camp moves in an orderly fashion from place to place with the movement of the seasons, the Meriam are both the same and different in different seasons. Their relation to their environment is also both the same and different in different places on the island. They are not similarly situated in their relation to local circumstances (Durkheim 1949, 287–89). Their life-form as Meriam possesses an overall similarity which undergoes a common seasonal transformation. Nevertheless, dissimilarities within the circle of the seasons combine with dissimilarities of *ged* to set in train a social differentiation between groups and individuals. So in a culture where all people are gardeners and fisherfolk there is also variation among them. There are especially strong gardening clans, for example Piadram; and especially strong seafaring clans, for example Komet. At Lewag, south of Ulag, where the first thunderstorms of *koki* strike Mer, one finds the rain-making *zogo*; there one finds the singers who chant the rain songs (*irmer wed*). Ulag on the northeast side of Mer is the place where the mythical hero Sida won the affections of Pekari; on the spot at which they coupled there sprang up many coconut palms laden with coconuts (Haddon 1908, 20–21). Ulag became the special place of *u zogo*, the magical power associated with the coconut. Ulag, where the northeast wind blows breezily, is good for healing; this is the centre of the *kekuruk le*, the medicine people.

Members of the Cambridge expedition showed how the Meriam classified things in the natural environment and themselves according to the same principles: through *au nei* or big name and *kebi nei* or small name, categories which correspond broadly to species and variety. The Meriam also have larger generic classes or *au au nei* (Ray 1907, 58–59). Kitaoji's work shows Meriam perceptions of themselves as a series of overlapping identities which begin with territorial/wind divisions differentiated by means of *lubabat* or totems (1980, 1–7, Figures 1 and 2).

In taking up spatial positions round the Murray Islands, the territorial groups of the Meriam simultaneously define themselves in relation to three main points of reference: first, to the land; second, to one another; and third, to seasonal time or prevailing wind. These elements or qualities are place (*ged*), clan or 'type of people' (*nosik*) and wind or season (*wag/kerker*). These three reference points give them their basic orientation to the world and its classification (see Durkheim and Mauss 1969, 48).

The interrelationship of place, clan and season (*ged*, *nosik* and *wag/kerker*) may be seen in the form of a round dial in which the eight clans of the Murray Islands are differentiated according to wind directions.

The wind-circle of Meriam identities shows that the four clans belonging to *sager* (southeast wind) are further differentiated. Piadram and

Samsep, sub-clans of the *nosik* Samsep, are associated with *mared*, the easterly division of *sager*, the former being due east, the latter east-southeast. Geauram, the due southeast clan and Magaram, are associated with the southern division of *sager* known as *gared*. Similarly, the two *naiger* (northeast) clans, Mei-Zagareb and Meauram are differentiated further into *naiger* (true northeast) and *sab* (north). Komet is the *koki* (northwest) clan. Peibre is really the west-northwest clan; its orientation is designated by a reef — Mebgorge — across which the wind arrives as the new season is heralded. *Ziai*, the southwest wind is the orientation of the two sub-clans of Dauar *nosik*, known as Giar and Teg. Within each are two further orientational subdivisions: so Giar people are differentiated by *bakei* (west wind) associated with Giar Pit; *irewed ziai* (west-southwest) is associated with two other subgroups of Giar; Teg people are associated with two divisions of south-southwest *ziai* — the Ormi Teg people with *logab ziai* and the Teg people with *ukes ziai*.

Each wind or season is imprinted upon the relevant group as a primordial quality of affinity. People await and welcome their own winds; they dance as groups — as 'southwest people', as 'southeast people, as 'northwest people' and so on. They also sing about all the winds which are always in movement round the circle of the year. In singing their songs they are living not only the seasonal

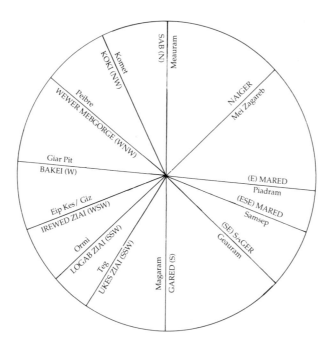

Figure 1 The wind-circle of Meriam identities

round: they are also drawing a circle round each one of the identifiable groups of people who make up the whole island grouping. Each wind imparts a character to each *nosik* and to each of its members. When the west wind (*bakei*) blows, the earth shakes, so it is said.

Within the segments created by the first three points of reference lies a further differentiation: people belonging to particular locations, clans and season/wind are differentiated from one another through *lubabat*, translated approximately as totem.[5] Reflecting their lives as a sea-people, the *lubabat* of the Meriam are almost universally salt-water creatures and seabirds. The Torres Strait pigeon (*deumer*), a seabird which arrives from New Guinea about March as the wind begins to turn southeast, and tiger shark (*beizam*), are *lubabat* of easterly southeast *le*, Piadram and Samsep. Other *lubabat* include tern (*serar*), frigate bird (*waumer*), green turtle (*nam*), mantaray (*peibre sor*), sardine (*tup*), and deep sea creatures such as whale (*galbol*), dolphin (*bid*) and mackerel (*dabor*).

Lubabat are part of a classificatory scheme in which small names form the basis of a system of generic categories. The effect is to create overlapping and many-layered identities (Haddon 1912, 229; Ray 1907, 59).[6] Giar Dauareb persons, who belong to Giar Pit (the land forming Giar's nose), are in the path of *bakei*, the west wind within the general division of *ziai*, the southwest wind. They are also *wada, dabor* and *kebi nam* (a stage of frigate bird, mackerel and green turtle) people as differentiated through the *lubabat* of that clan, in contrast with persons of the other west-southwest divisions of Giar Dauareb, whose *lubabat* are different stages in the lifecycle of the frigate bird (*sai* and *maimai*) and a different part of *ziai*, southwest wind. Both these subgroups or 'varieties' of Giar Dauareb contrast with Teg Dauareb, who belong to the south-southwest division of the southwest wind, *ziai*.

Although both the Giar and Teg *nosik* belong to *waumer* (the frigate bird), the Giar people, who belong to the big hill of Dauar, see themselves as the rightful holders of *wada*, the full grown, red-throated frigate bird, which soars to great heights and swoops on its prey. Thus the song of *wada* about occupation carries a warning to would-be trespassers:

> *Look at the top*
> *Of the big hill of Dauar*
> *They look like clouds*
> *But they blow* waumer.

The southeastern clans are differentiated and joined in multiple ways also. Thus Piadram and Samsep, who are often regarded as one people, belong to *mared*, the eastern division of *sager*, the southeast wind. Geauram and Magaram *nosik* belong to *gared*, the southern division of *sager*. The two eastern groups share *deumer* (Torres Strait pigeon), *beizam* (tiger shark) and *sap* (driftwood) as *lubabat*. Piadram *nosik* also has *galbol* (whale). The two are differentiated through their celestial alignments, Piadram with Beizam constellation (the Bear), and Samsep with *Gergerneseur*, the Morning Star, the waxing phase of Venus. The two southern groups of *sager* share *galbol* (whale) and *tabo* (snake); Geauram also has *dibadiba* (dove).

Furthermore, the Malo classifications which came into existence late in the pre-Christian era, created further layers of identity differentiation among the Meriam (which tended to obscure for outsiders the still flourishing pre-existing distinctions). The first is between the Beizam *boai*, the dancers in the Malo ceremonies and the Zagareb *le*, the song men. The territorial groups composing the former are *gedub boai*, garden groupings, as against *lar boai*, fish group, the former comprising the two easterly (to southeast) clans only, the latter being made up from the westerly clans (a division which, incidentally, retains something of the land clans versus sea clans contrast) (Kitaoji 1980, Figure 2; see also Haddon 1908, 174).

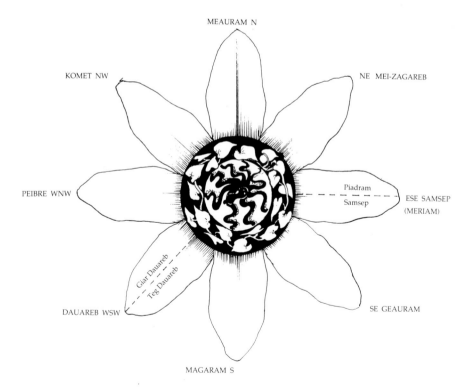

Figure 2 The flower of Meriam identities

THE CIRCLE OF LIFE OF THE MERIAM OF MER, DAUAR, WAIER
A CALENDER*

Season (Kerker)	Signs of Approach (Mek)	Characteristics	Mek for later Kerker	Activities (Tonar)	Local Foods	Approximate Calendar Months
Naiger Kerker	Adud wer, a star which appears in the south-west, is mek for Kipa gogob, the first rains. Usiam, the Pleiades, rises in the east. Usiam is part of the constellation Tagai, which includes the Southern Cross.	Very hot weather followed by Kipa gogob. Ketai, wild yams, are sprouting new shoots. Sorbi, a red-skinned, apple-like fruit; Waiwi, mango; meker, almond, are fruiting.		Garden preparation is completed, followed by arit kerker, planting time. Men move to garden houses at gedub, gardens. Planting of lewer kar, yam tubers; kaba, banana suckers, are transplanted. At peak of dry weather bunches of bananas on the tree are wrapped up to make sopsop kaba, turning the skins red and changing the flavour. Sai, stone fish-traps, are made ready for koki kerker; fish hooks are made from turtle-shell.	Turtle harvest begins. Turtle eggs are collected in nests of up to 200 on sandbeaches. Fish become plentiful. Wild yam, mango, almond, sorbi, are ready. Juice of green coconut forms the main beverage at all times. Nineteen varieties of banana and nine varieties of coconut fruit at all kerker. Varieties of banana cultivated are: aue, borom, bubuam, buruam, idzid, iweie, kud, markak, katam, mauko, moar, namepi, ornar, pas, pekai, suekakie, tereg, uop, zagraem, zeberadber. Varieties of coconut are: bebe-bebe sor, gomer, guriguri, kapkup sor, kureb, med, mes aroaro, wamerawamer, zarzar.	Mid-October to Early December
North-east Season (later half)		Turtles lay eggs upon the sand-beaches.	Wind begins to turn around to the west. Lightning and thunderstorms announce the arrival of koki kerker.	Wuuri derseri, waiwi voyage preparations, are completed. Yams, bananas, sweet potatoes (muri), are mixed with turtle fat, roasted, dried, placed in bamboo tubes and sealed. Expedition sets out. Voyagers may sail all the way to Op Deudai for canoes, bird of paradise and cassowary feathers, dogs' teeth necklaces and other valuables. From Muri and Keo Deudai the Miriam obtain red and white ochre, emu feathers and emu leg bones for digging. Gifts from Wuuri tgbud, shell friends, are taken to Las, the original place (giz ged) of Malo. Imar zogo, rain-making magic, practised by Zagareb le at villages like Lewag where the thunderstorms strike first. Rain water is collected in the valves of giant clam shells at the base of trees, from drips off rocks, from a pool near Gelam's nose and from certain places on the surface of the sand.		
Koki Kerker North-west Season	A total stillness and rainbow-like sunset is mek for arrival of koki kerker.	Maximum growth time during heavy rains.		Arit kerker continues: planting of sweet potatoes. Seeds of yams planted in preparation for following naiger kerker. Miriam take up residence in kewbkeub mari, round houses, on family lands along the sandbeaches for protection against rainy time. Fish are being caught in sai. At night men go out into sai to spear fish at low-water with 2-3 ne, coconut-leaf torches made by binding together two coconut branches about six feet long. A torch lasts about half an hour. Men go	Vegetable foods very scarce. Bananas, dry and green coconuts still available. Fishing good. Yellow tail (maiu), trevally (mekmek), long tom (paraes), black bream (menaiz), blackfish (erar), taram (geigi), garfish (sub).	December to Early March

Kerker / Season	Signs & Weather	Activities	Food & Notes	Month
Záí Kerker	Winds turn around to the south. Weather starts to become cooler.	out into *saí* in canoes carrying six *ne* to spear fish with *bazur*, spears with bamboo shafts and hardwood prongs. Islanders from the Central Islands (Eip Ged) may arrive to exchange fish, turtle, dugong, for land produce.	The frigate bird (*waumer*), tern (*sewar*), are snared.	
South-west Season		Preparation time for *sager kerker* and vegetable harvest time. Early vegetable foods begin to be harvested. *Wag zogo*, wind magic, practised by south-east *Ze* at Turpit.	Early vegetable foods may include banana, *sopsop* banana, manioc, sweet potato (three varieties), sugar cane. Fish start to become plentiful. *Tup*, sardines (three varieties), are harvested in *weres*, a conical bamboo basket.	March
Sager Kerker	Rainbow fish (*irpgar*), is sign of *sager*. The kingfisher (*birobiro*), returns to the area. *Sorbi* blooms. First vegetable foods ready.	Harvesting of *lewer*, vegetable food, begins: the three staples are yams, bananas, coconuts. Local ceremonies and rites with *wetpur*, feast offerings to reciprocal clans, begin.	Thirty varieties of yam are cultivated by the Meriam *bad lewer, borometer, buzi wauri, daibar, dob, etet, gabagaba, ged wauri, gos, irpigaba, iwaririar, kukkigaba, kepsabes, kimiar, kurkar lewer, laman lewer, madagemeo, magaram wauri, mamam wauri, mapris, musmus wauri, reg, sap, sager, sorbe kep lewer, tap, wahwel, wakman, waima-wáima, wakwar.*	Early April
South-east Season	*Kek(flawel)*, the planet Venus, is sign of *au sager*, the height of the harvest. Trade winds from the south-east make for cooler evenings.	One phase of the three-yearly cycle of the rites of Malo-Bomai are held at Las preceded by the building of *pelak*, the sacred house, at *memgiz*, the springs of common blood. Keber, spirit pantomimes and Waiet ceremonies take place.	Fish are plentiful. Shell-fish, are collected in baskets (*boz-opeli*), at low tide on the fringing reefs. Varieties include *botuar, wami, kimkim, tornpar*. The wongai or wild plum (*emeo*), is harvested late in *sager kerker*.	to
	Wongai (emeo) yield is *mek* of good or poor turtle harvest at *naiger kerker*.	House-building preparations commence. *Akur*, house-grass, collected while still half green, is used for thatch which may last up to five years. Walls are of plaited coconut leaves. *Pater*, a small variety of bamboo, is split and made into a circle about 15 feet in diameter and about the same height. Houses are ornamented with trumpet shells (*maber*). Tools are renewed and repaired from harvest of many materials, e.g. *parud*, a vine for house-joining, *sirib lager*, fish-line rope. *Apes lu*, weapons, are renewed.		(mid) October
Naiger Kerker (north-east Season (early half))	Turtle-mating time. Sardines (*tup*) spawning. Dry and becoming hot.	Grass-burning and clearing of patches of garden land in preparation for fresh gardens. *Waurí dermurí, waurí* preparation time, commences.	Fishing is poor. Vegetables are scarce. Small fruits, eg bell-fruit (*are*), are available. Bananas and coconuts become important staples.	August to (mid) October

* This calendar attempts to reconstruct the circle of life of the Meriam in past times.

In joining the *nosik* of the Meriam into one body, the octopus (Bomai) came to the village of Las, on the *eastern* side of Mer, followed by Malo wearing a shark's head. The Meriam say that they are buried there at Las, a sign of the sacred origins of the people of the clan of the rising of the sun.

Differentiations, then, are multiple and many dimensional. There are further differentiations within the 'wind-circle of Meriam identities' created by positions in geographical space and cosmic time (the winds or seasonal time). These classifications, operating on different planes, interrelate in such a way as to create many-layered social identities, so producing cultural depth; one acts as metaphor for another, so that, for instance, the naming of a season or wind readily calls up a corresponding clan and territory. Through this process Meriam identities come to resemble the face of a fully-blown Rose of the Winds[7] or lotus flower, the ancient symbol of mariners, of which the octopus is the deep-sea solar symbol (Campbell 1974, 230).

THE FIRST CIRCLE OF LIFE OF THE MERIAM: A 'CALENDAR'

Adud wer, star in the southwest, is *mek* or sign of *kipa gogob*, the first rains. At this time the constellation of Tagai begins to rise in the east. First Seg, the alignment of Orion appears in the northeast at dusk. Usiam, the Pleiades, is nearby. This is *naiger kerker* in its later half; 'Usiam time': time of planting known as *arit kerker*. The shoots of wild yams (*ketai*) break forth, signalling the arrival of *kerker*, the fresh circle of nature: this is the springtime of the Meriam. The calendar of their lives begins anew in this latter part of *naiger kerker*, as set out in the table of the seasonal year.[8] As the 're-beginning' of things, it is a time of special cultural meaning: Malo *wali aritarit, sem aritarit*; in the signs of the stars there is the message to begin planting afresh. This is the first meaning of Malo ra Gelar.

The Meriam begin to clear and burn the garden land (*gedub*) ready for the first planting: the signs of Tagai tell the right time. When the left hand of Tagai, the Southern Cross, appears that is a sign to the gardener: 'Have you planted *ketai*; have you planted *kakigaba*?' *Kakigaba* is a kind of yam that doesn't grow deep; it just goes down a little bit, spreads out 'like an octopus' and comes to the surface. It is like *ketai*, the wild yam. Before Tagai appears completely the gardener prepares his or her garden. Then *arit kerker*, the real planting, begins. 'When you plant be sure that the tide is coming up, flooding tide; and when the tide drops then you stop', as Au Bala's uncle told him: 'Use new moon to plant vegetables that bear fruit on the surface and full moon for plants that grow down; carry on with that full moon: when he rise you plant your sweet potato facing the full moon' (Cassette 135/AB/TI/3/84).

The arrival of *koki kerker*, the northwest season, may be heralded by a total stillness, and a rainbow-like sunset often appears in the northwest. Thunderstorms are followed by heavy rains and rapid growth of plants. *Arit kerker* continues; fish are caught now in *sai*, the stone fish-traps.

After the rain, the rainbow. *Ziai kerker*, when the wind turns round to the southwest and the weather becomes cooler, is a preparation time for *sager kerker*; it is a prelude to a change to the new winds.

Sager kerker is the season of new *lewer*, the vegetable harvest. *Lewer kar*, the staple food of the Meriam, are maturing. First comes *nur sager*, when the yam leaf fades. *Kek*, the planet Venus, is the sign for *au sager*, the big harvest, when the yams are ready for digging. *Sager kerker* is a time of the replenishment of many things. Preparations are made for house building. House grass (*akur*) is cut before it turns yellow. Tools are renewed and repaired. *Sirib lager*, a long-lasting rope for outriggers and houses, is made from vine; *mekek lager*, fishing-line rope, is made.

Plate 4 A performance of the Malo ceremony at Las, Mer, 1898 (AC Haddon 1908)

Sager kerker also heralds the approach of one phase of the three-yearly cycle of the Malo rites; the initiation ceremonies of *le* are also preparation times for *wauri* maritime expeditions which take place at *naiger kerker*. The first phase of the Malo ceremonies takes place at Dam lasting two days. The next year the ceremonies take place at Gazir and Las; the former ceremony of initiation and exhibition of the sacred masks of Malo and Bomai is held early in the morning of a day chosen by the *Zogo le*, followed by a public ceremony with the Malo dances in the afternoon on the sandbeach at Las. At the beginning of the following *sager*, the Bomai mask is taken from Gazir to Kiam, where it remains until the end of *naiger kerker*. When the rains come the Bomai mask is taken back to Gazir, remaining at Dam during *koki kerker*. The final ceremony, lasting one or two days, takes place at Kiam the following year. The Bomai mask is worn only at Dam, Gazir and Kiam: at each place *pelak*, the dome-shaped *zogo* house, is built in which the three sacred masks of Malo-Bomai are kept; the site of *pelak* is known as *mamgiz*, the springs of common blood.

The dances of the Malo rites are like the great waves of the first circle of the year. The movement of the Malo dances presage the great waves that will carry the *wauri* voyagers as *tebud* of Malo, Malo's friends, to other places. *Le* are readying for exchange or for battle. Kapin looks back to the times of his father and grandfathers and reflects upon the meaning of the *wauri* voyages. He does

Plate 5 The sacred dances of Malo, 1898 (AC Haddon 1908)

so in the light of the new teachings which are both the same as and different to beliefs of the past. His line of people were the ones who had the power of *zogo* and could say: 'Don't go this day it looks like trouble somewhere'; they were also the ones who 'took in' all the new stories and through the process of comparison and contrast between old and new meaning systems saw the deep message of *wauri*.

JOINING OUR SIDE WITH THE OTHER SIDE: WAURI AS LIFE-GIVER

Kapin: Wauri tebud *is more than one born from the same blood*

> *So both my parents belong to that sort of high family. They have to look after people in every move according to the season and to prepare for the trip to New Guinea for trading, for* wauri. *Yes, very important that* wauri *shell. That's the one you buy your canoe, you buy your wife and you buy everything there.*[9] *Something very important. And there's one thing. If I give you that* wauri *you can't leave me: you're my blood family. That's why we hold on to the Torres Strait family here. I sit here. These two people are like my two relatives. If I give you something, when you come to my home, my island, don't forget to call on me because I'll tell my people: 'Our friend. From that side there!'*
>
> *Malo got laws like the Christian religion. Now I find the shell for you. You want to have the* wauri? *I got it here; we talk about it today.* Wauri *is the thing that covers everything. If I belong to another tribe and I give you that one you become another one of my tribe. It covers everything; very precious.* Wauri — *it could save your life, it could give you plenty of things and make you friends for all time. You*

Figure 3 *Wauri,* cone shell

never forget your friend. You can't forget; you can't make things wrong when you have a wauri tebud *that way. Your* wauri tebud *is just like the boy or girl born from your family. Yeah! You can't be bad to her or him that way. You always respect them; you always take them to you. That's why we don't care today because we know more better than before. Before we were a bit suspicious because nobody would learn the thing. Now this is a new Gospel here and we take all these new stories in. When* wauri *becomes known others will see it as one part the Gospel has left behind: 'Be kind to one another'. Because* wauri tebud *is more than one born from the same blood.*

The blood tebud *is this way: I can have a good row with my own friend, with my own blood relation like me and G. We have a good cut up there on the hill. Yeah [excited voice]! G calls me uncle, his father's my cousin; I'm like his uncle. We growl, me and G. And all our daughters were crying in the kitchen. They see the rough way we speak. Later I stopped from talking and say: 'You give me a smoke? You got some?' He swear me, 'F... you', the word they use round the Torres Strait. They stop crying all our girls there. 'These two make us cry!' But it's true growl. 'If we'd been strangers we'd stand up and fight. I know you'd belt me!' He's a good fellow my cousin. I'll never forget him. We growl, yes! Then finish fight. No more!*

Oh you never growl your wauri tebud *because you be ashamed of yourself. You can't. People never take your part. Yeah! If you make trouble with your* wauri tebud *you get something from another man. He stop you and tell you: 'You're not Malo's friend. Be ashamed!' That's the law belong to* wauri tebud *and Malo. That's why we are together.*

These people down west they forget all these things. Those Western Island people had that law too. We were all the same Malo people until Kwoiam came from Australia. Lockhart River people and all them down there, they know something about Malo. Malo went to Lockhart for this part is known as Marilag [literally 'spiritland', KLY].
(Book of Islanders 1984, B24, B25, B26)

FROM OUR SIDE TO THE OTHER SIDE: THE CIRCLES OF WAURI

Among the Meriam the 'we' begins in the attachment to *ged*, home-place. It develops through the mediation of *naiwet*, brother-in-law. *Mam*, blood, kin, and those 'like kin' are the archetype of the 'we'. Reciprocal relations between the eight clans of the island trio, which are spread round the outside circles of the islands facing across the sandbeaches, are created through an exchange whereby two women of a particular generation marry two brothers of another clan of the same generation (Haddon 1908; Beckett 1963, 7–39). This means that a double tie binds together the two clans. Upon this relationship — one which brings the *us* of this side with the *them* of that side into a permanent alliance — an intricate network of social bonds is built up. The in-law is the cornerstone of a 'between' relation which makes life social and which, in turn, gives it a cultural code, an ensemble of meanings.

When a Meriam *le* introduces himself or herself, self-identification locates that person in *ged*, home-place, and in a line within a clan or *nosik* with its particular totem or *lubabat*. Everything else about him or her is to be judged by the other person. Together they go to the heart of what it is to be a Meriam. Yet always that expression of identity contains within it a contrast with another *nosik* at another *ged*. In Kitaoji's words, the concept of 'Meriam' is 'multi-layered', seven overlapping meanings of Meriam coming to exist over time (1982, 68). It is as though the world of the Meriam has built itself up from the first association of two neighbouring *le*: *this* side with *that* side, the east with the west, Piadram with Samsep people. And so the first meaning of the Meriam — Piadram *le* (whose centre is *giz ged* at Las) in contrast with Samsep *le* — is the beginning of successive divisions: the two northern clans in contrast with the two southern clans; the four clan *ged* facing the southeast side (*sager pek*) in contrast with the northeast side (*naiger pek*); the gently sloping southeast part of Mer in contrast with Gelam hill; the island of Mer as distinct from Au Dauareb, which includes Dauar and Waier; the trio of the Murray Islands rather than the other Eastern Islands of Erub, Ugar, and so on; Op Ged, the Eastern Islands, in contrast with both Keo Ged, the Western Islands and Eip Ged, the Central Islands (1978, 56; 1982, 67).

The contrast between this side and the other side, between themselves as Meriam speakers and Kala Lagaw Ya speakers, between themselves and those belonging to Op Deudai on the one hand and Keo Deudai on the other, follows the same pattern as the overlapping meanings of self-identification as Meriam. It is *wauri* which breaks the exclusiveness of these contrasts.

The process begins with a person who wants a canoe handing a *wauri* shell to a *tebud* (who may be *boai*, a crew man) in say Komet *nosik*. That person is not any Komet *le*; he is *this* particular *le*, not *that* one. When the canoe arrives it is the *tebud* who hands the canoe to that person, sometimes called the *giz le*. Total solemnity surrounds the preparation for the voyage, befitting the seriousness of the relationship of *wauri tebud*, one which has turned the power of death into the quintessence of 'brotherhood'. For '*wauri tebud* is more than one born from the same blood'. That is why you never 'growl your *wauri tebud*. You can't.' Framed by the spirit-power of Malo, *mam* extends through the ground of the sacred house, *pelak* at *mamgiz*, springs of the same blood, reaching out beyond the face to face community of the Meriam towards *tebud le*, like brothers for all time through *zogo*, the power of Malo. Haddon's description of diving for *wauri* carries an almost reverential note. A canoe was decorated and pushed out with the chosen man standing in it, looking intently into the clear water for cone shells: 'It was necessary for him to remain perfectly quiet and still, and he could not move even to assuage his hunger or thirst. Upon sighting a shell, he drove his spear down alongside it, then he dived and collected the prize' (1935, 183).

Wauri voyages were continuing beyond the 'octopus' a process which brought new life: the gift of *wauri* created a pact of peace. Through that solemn moment of exchange, which carried with it the sacred power of Malo, bridges were formed across dividing seas. Through Malo the singularity of difference, *nerutonar* (people with a different custom, 'another kind' of people, the hostile other), became *le* and *le* is a kinship term whose first meaning in the patrilineal society of the Meriam is brother. Haddon notes the strength and permanence of the tie created: 'These friendships once formed were never broken; they were hereditary, having come down from past ages from father to son. A man may never have seen his *tebud le*, but his name and family history were as well known to him as his own. On visiting the islands the *tebud le* would be welcomed and entertained' (1935, 183). *Tebud le* addressed one another as *le*; they had become 'like brothers'.

In the idiom of kinship, the law belonging to *wauri tebud* and Malo transforms the individual seeking *tebud*. *Ka nali wauri*, which means literally, 'I am *wauri*', is a way of saying, 'I have that feeling of friendliness towards you which can make *me* and not some other man like brothers forever'. I have called that relationship a *yumi*, from the Melanesian pidgin word meaning 'the person or persons spoken to to the exclusion of others'. It is saying that you and I will become like two blood relatives. As Kapin says, if I give you that *wauri* you can come to my place, my home. My people will not kill you now because 'I shall let them know: our friend. From that side there!' Networks of peace are formed through a multitude of *tebud*-in-Malo. Those networks bear the imprint of the 'you' and the 'me' of each *tebud* partnership. They are like pacts which do not depersonify; they are cumulations of many particular exchanges. And these particular exchanges are not transitory, for the name of Malo and the shaming of oneself is at stake. Unlike brothers, *wauri tebud* may not 'growl one another'. Such is the overarching power of Malo. Nothing is too good to heap upon *tebud*.

At their peak, *wauri* exchanges may be compared with the *kula* of the Trobrianders. The arrival of the voyagers at Saibai with shell armlets and *dibidibi* and the new gifts added upon the way was similar to the 'crowning episode' of the *kula*, climaxing a multitude of exchanges on a smaller scale (Malinowski 1961, 86; Haddon 1907, 296, 297; 1908, 186–87). By breaking through the frontiers of the immediate world *wauri* expressed cultural possibility. *Wauri* expeditions were exceptionally dangerous. Those seeking *wauri tebud* might seem like 'daring individuals' risking death to establish friendly relations.[10] Expeditions were tests of strength. For peace always held within it the seeds of war: the insult of misjudging the proper quality of giving or returning dishonoured the relationship; it demeaned and shamed the other. 'Paying back', like 'being matched', is always two-sided.

In three important ways *wauri* was a life-giver, a talisman of trust.[11] First, it made friends. In so doing it extended the world of the Meriam across new frontiers. Second, it provided the frame for life-giving things, of which the canoe was the most valued possession. Third, it reaffirmed geographical and social boundaries: 'We are a people over our side', said the Meriam: 'Don't be coming over this way without knowing that'. Like 'showing the flag', the arrival of the 'fleet' of canoes filled with as many warriors as possible announced to the others the fact of the 'we' over 'our side' (Au Bala, A Cultural Tradition Handed Down, Book of Islanders 1984, B148). The active 'presence' of the 'other' also strengthened the awarenes of oneness of the 'we': *wauri* re-created the identities of its participants.

Every canoe of the Meriam, every canoe within the networks of *wauri tebud*, arrived at Saibai to collect the new canoes from Op Deudai: without them the Meriam had no future. And as the voyagers left, at *naiger kerker* each island turned to face the way they went and to look outwards towards the horizon of their return. It was as though the whole culture brought all it had to secure its lifeline. Beginning at *giz ged*, Las, the centre of their lives, *wauri* exchange with Op Deudai brought together two circles. The first was the canoe-path which moved from east to west. The second was the track of *seker lu*, the gift-path from Saibai to Mer, travelling in the other direction from west to east. A single network has been created: two circles compose it. In Malo *wali aritarit, sem aritarit* there lies a deeper meaning than the first one, to plant. The signs of Tagai at *naiger kerker* foretell that Malo can send his warriors to the 'other side' to fight or to exchange and bring back gifts for Malo at Las.

Those in the tradition of Malo ra Gelar who have come 'before' us create footprints in which we who come 'after' may place our feet. Kebi Bala, younger brother, reveals the deep meaning of *teter mek*, following in the footsteps.

LINKING HUMAN WITH COSMIC CIRCLES

Teter Mek, *Footprints: Kebi Bala: Where my father put his foot I had to put mine*

> *For thousands of years we have owned the land and Malo who was the Meriam centre of it made sure that members of the society were*

given land. They are our laws. We have Malo ra Gelar. It says that Malo keeps to his own place, Malo does not trespass in another man's property. What belongs to others belongs to them and as you understand Nonie there are boundaries which were made. The land is so valuable that whatever dropped, whether it's a coconut leaf or whatever, if it's a rotten tree, let it rot on the ground. It simply means that we respect the land, we respect the soil: eburlem es maolem *means drop and rot on the ground and whatever it does to the ground. And so if we* Zogo le *or Murray Islanders make a garden, we don't make one big garden, we make a small patch because the soil is terribly important and we are governed by this. If we have* ketai *or yam, we don't go and in one big rush take everything out. We don't do that at all. We take what we need. We don't exploit; white men do that. We don't exploit it* [very hushed tone]. *We are very careful in our treatment with land and what is in the land.*

This law was made to govern my society. Malo keeps his hands to himself. He does not touch what is not his. That's the explanation; it's a good explanation. He does not permit his feet to carry him towards other men's property. His hands are not grasping.

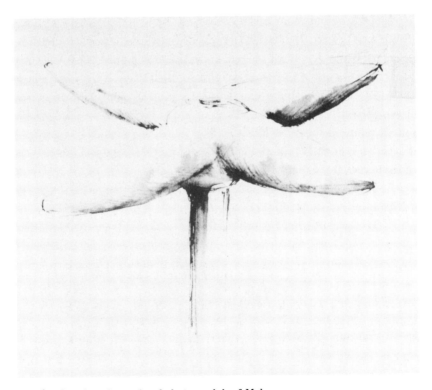

Figure 4   *Seuriseuri*, star-headed stone club of Malo

*He holds them back. He does not wander from his path. He walks on
tip-toe silent and careful leaving no signs to tell that this is the way
he took. This is very true in my father's case. He had a garden at old
Mek and there he walked on tip-toe. Where my father put his foot I
had to put mine when I was a little boy* [louder suddenly]. *Beautiful,
it is simply beautiful. I don't think you really understand it the way
I understand it. There is nothing like it as far as life is concerned.
I was brought up in it. I respect it. My heart goes for it, my whole soul
goes with it. You may not understand it, but this is true. My whole
life, there it is. Malo: Keep your hands to yourself;* teter mauki mauki,
I cannot trespass on another people's land.

*If you are a friend, if you come to my land I allow it
because you're my friend, you are my sister. When my great
grandfather died — I'll tell you something about this because it's
important — when he died they lit a fire to make smoke. They call
that smoke* tug. *They make a* tug *with the* tug *in a certain place which
indicated that the* Zogo le *had died. Mer got that message from Dauar
and after Dauar had mourned the death they took him to Mer because
he had to be buried at Mer because he was a* Zogo le. *We were told that
all Murray Island was there. That means most of the people followed
the canoes till they got to Las. And when they got to Las they took the
body to the place at Piad, the* Zogo le *place. There they put white
feathers all over his body.* (Kebi Bala, Book of Islanders 1984, B130)

Earth and heavens; sea and sky; beings of the depths and celestial beings; starfish
and stars; east and west; *sager* and *koki*; dry and wet; time of shoots and time
of yellow leaf; beginning and ending; birth and death. All the opposites are here.
Life and death and *new shoots*; wild and cultivated and *wetpur*, a ceremonial feast
for a man's brother-in-law; us and other and *naiwet*, brother-in-law; brother and
enemy and *wauri tebud*; *le*, mortals and *lamar*, immortals and *opole*, the one who
wears the sacred mask.

Naiwet and *wetpur* signify possibility in a movement of life which
swings between power (giving) and equivalence (returning). At every point the
intentional power of life engages its opposite, the power of death: the engagement
seeks to maintain a balance between these two. Relationship to *naiwet* creates
the intellectual code by which the singular is confronted: everywhere there is the
reverse side of the 'we'. It is signified by *pur*, the uncultivated, which holds within
it the double potentiality of the tamed and the unbridled singular which Islanders
refer to as *Em*. Even within the tame there lies the power of *Em*; the known always
contains the unknown. The essence of social striving among the Meriam is a quest
for equality of power, an 'equality' which also holds within it at each moment
the tendency towards its undoing. Within the continual movement between the
two sides the Meriam live together.

A quest for patterns in a universe in which the unknown, the wild, the unnamed, are always present finds answers in mythical form: Gelam, Sida, Tagai, Malo-Bomai; in social relational form: the sacred rites of Malo-Bomai, of Waiet and in *keber* or spirit ceremonies (Haddon 1908, 127–30; 277–80); and in symbolic form in 'hierophanies' which show forth ultimate truths, of which *seuriseuri*, star-headed stone club of Malo, might seem to be the expression (Haddon 1908, 296). *Seuriseuri*, the blue starfish of the coral reefs and the sacred clubs of Malo, is a sign of continuity of Malo to *ad giz*, the time of coming into being. *Giz ged* of the *seuriseuri* is said to be Begegiz, headquarters of Peibre from which spring Palai and Ganomi, the two principal warrior ancients (Haddon 1935, 161–62; 1908, 258, 315). It is also the sacred space of primordial time where spirits of the dead stop on the journey westward to Boigu, place of *lamar*, the immortals. The four-rayed, unflanged stone-headed clubs may be seen as symbols of the circles of the life-world of the Meriam. Star-shaped, reflecting the unity of sky with sea; four-rayed like the winds denoting the knot between *le* and *tebud le*; single-stemmed joining 'before' with 'after'.

Seuriseuri locates a centre, a fixed point at which all the planes of the world conjoin. It denotes the central axis of life.[12] In consequence, it represents and is *mek* for the valorisation of the world of the Meriam. It is a club, the sacred club of Malo. Unlike many other sacred objects which are formed in nature, it is the product of men's hands, men who bear the imprint of the objects they create and who in turn have placed that imprint upon *seuriseuri*. At the same time it is a sacred thing which stands for and reveals certain fundamental truths. Its existential value lies in its equivalence with the unending re-creation of the world.

At the Malo ceremonies the *Zagareb le*, the song men of Malo (*wed le*), placed the stem of the *seuriseuri* in the ground about midway on the inside of the semicircle which enclosed *au kop*, the sacred space facing the dome-shaped *pelak* and next to the *Zogo le* and *Beizam boai*, the Shark brethren, who had charge of *seuriseuri* (Haddon 1908, 308–10, 306n, 308n). In those rites through which *kesi*, the initiates, became *ume le*, those who know the truth, 'members of the fraternity', or on the death of any of the three *Zogo le*, the star-head of *seuriseuri* was adorned with two white *deumer* feathers split in two halves and bent round to form a circle (Haddon 1908, 284). Around the *Zagareb le* the *Beizam boai* danced 'counter-clockwise', left hands outstretched towards the centre (1908, 310). There were five *ikok* or sacred chants and the last one was for *seuriseuri*. When the *Beizam boai* danced, two of them carried *seuriseuri* in their left hands, which each passed to the dancer who came in behind him.

In those sacred rites, the three *Zogo le* are the embodiment of Malo, performing 'the divine order of Bomai' (Kitaoji 1977, 212) among *ume le*, who may see the masks. No one, not even *Beizam boai*, would know who are wearing the three masks. These solemn ceremonies are addressed in the language of Malo, a language whose literal meaning remains unknown to most *le*.[13] In the name of Malo there is total discipline. That is why during the dances that mark the preparation of the warriors of Malo for the *wauri* expeditions, not even a baby may cry. *Seuriseuri* is like 'frozen' foliation, foliation in crystalline form. I am not suggesting that the Meriam saw the way the planes of their world or the star-shaped circles of their lives became the star-shaped head joined with the stem, itself a 'circle' on a different plane. Patterns of consciousness and the forms in which they find expression are characteristically unanalysed by those who hold them. They are taken for granted. Like the sacred rites, like the masks, the *seuriseuri* form the centre of the ultimate order of things. They are cultural statements which are experienced as irreducible. Placed in the ground at times of crossing, passed from one dancer to another within the circle of Shark brethren, *seuriseuri* are signs for moments of metamorphosis: becoming initiates means passing into the eternal circle of sacred authority of the 'other side'.

The stem of *seuriseuri* is like the line of sacred authority of Malo: the line of the *Zogo le*. The placing of *seuriseuri* within the half circle of the most sacred ground of *giz ged* reaffirms the meaning of the centre of the Meriam. The four-rayed head is like two everlasting half-circles of time: the movement of the sun from east to west; and the movement of the spirit world, the path of the mythical heroes, of which Malo-Bomai are the high point, from west to east, from outside the beginning to life, from death to rebirth.

In the image of *seuriseuri* there is a further instruction of Malo ra Gelar: Stars travel their own path, which follows the charter of Tagai: I cannot walk the path that is Usiam's, nor can I walk the path that is Seg's. I must follow *teter mek*, the footprints made by my ancestors. The line of brothers from father to son, son, son, son, son,...from *Zogo le* to *Zogo le*, must go on: 'In passing forward the *seuriseuri* from one dancer to the next, the symbol is that the authority of Malo must continue'.

When Kebi Bala speaks about the social code of the Meriam he is speaking, too, of the authority on a second plane which valorises the first: that from 'before' to 'after' between *lamar* and *le*, immortals and mortals. 'Where my father put his foot I had to put it.' Malo ra Gelar expresses the distilled wisdom of the Meriam formed through the accretion of cultural experience. Like the Ten Commandments, it is the social morality given in religious–moral form. Kebi Bala's great grandfather as *Zogo le* stood for the whole. Like *seuriseuri* passed from one dancer to the next, as *Zogo le* he is the sign of continuity of the line of sacred authority.

When the Meriam lit *tug*, a special fire, to announce the death of a *Zogo le* they were uniting the terrestrial with the celestial. In taking his body across from Dauar to Mer and mourning him in *ged* after *ged*, arriving eventually at *giz ged*, the centre of the Meriam, they were reaffirming the many as the one; the one was being symbolised in the many. That meaning of the eight-in-the-one, made possible by the coming of Bomai in the shape of an octopus, is symbolised in the eight-rayed *seuriseuri*, which Au Bala believes may have been the most sacred and secret of all the five *seuriseuri*.

In speaking the words aloud, Kebi Bala is giving expression to the collective representation, the whole cultural experience. At the same time his words express 'the possibilities to which an individual...might aspire but not himself be able to realise' (see Burridge 1969, 415). Like the myth in which it is embedded, Malo ra Gelar is 'fecund with meaning'. It embodies a set of rules; it is a cultural statement about all the levels of the world of the Meriam. Hushed tones tip-toe with the words. Rising sounds go with the personal awareness of the contrast of this experience to the mundane. It is an evocation of the Divine: 'Beautiful. It is simply beautiful. There is nothing like it as far as life is concerned. My whole soul goes for it. My whole life', says Kebi Bala. It is true and real yet it remains ineffable; hence it is communicable only as revelation or as poetry. It is a personal philosophy within a poetic idiom, a philosophy that is lived and felt, not cognised. For the Meriam that philosophy holds within it the nascent striving to bring 'our side' together with 'the other side': all the opposites into one. Herein lies the deepest meaning of Malo *wali aritarit*, Malo sows everywhere: the promise of immortality, the harvest of Malo's sowing.

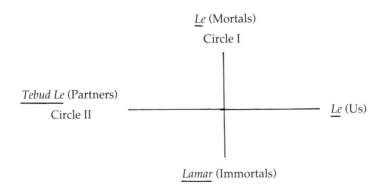

Figure 5 The axis of the circles

THE AXIS OF THE WORLD: REPETITION AND RENEWAL

Through the power of Malo two planes of life intersect at Las, *giz ged*. There rests *pelak* on the belly of the earth at its centre. Each plane of life is a circle: Circle I joins *Le* and *Lamar*, the Mortals and the Immortals; Circle II joins *Le* and *Tebud Le*, Us and our *Wauri* Partners. As planes they may be represented as shown in the diagram on page 72.

Social life moves through a circle which travels from After, the *Le*, to Before, the ancestors who have become *Lamar*. The life cycles of persons form part of this eternal circle. Among the Meriam all life moves, too, within the cosmic cycles, denoted in everyday life by the seasons, their first circle of life. The movement of that circle holds within it the promise of an endless return of *kerker*, which expresses the repetitive sameness of time for this, time for that. *Kerkar*, the fresh time, brings return: it also carries the variation which comes with renewal. In other words, each circle which follows the other, 'year' upon 'year', is both like and unlike the one which came before. There is similarity and dissimilarity.

In moving through Circle I which joins *Le* and *Lamar*, social life moves through Circle II, which takes it from *Le* to *Tebud Le* through *wauri*. That *wauri* circle is a human circle. As social 'life' the circles are not closed: they are formed by and signify both repetition and renewal. Unlike the circularity of orbital motion spinning within a closed circuit, each subsequent circle of social life remains both within the same plane and also *removed from the one before*. It is like a spring beginning to open out.

Among the Meriam, ceremonies like the harvest festival are tied directly to the first circle, which is part of cosmic cycles. Human life cycles are marked by occasions which represent the metamorphoses of rebirth. The three-yearly cycles of the sacred rites of Malo-Bomai through which *kesi* receive the spirit power of *zogo*; the rites associated with the death of mortals (*le*) and the

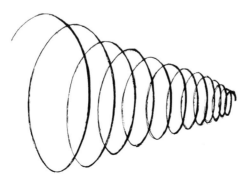

Figure 6 An uncoiling spring

birth of immortals (*lamar*), are such occasions. Both ceremonies signify moments in which the cycles of *le*, the human cycles, are brought into touch with the cosmic cycles. These are what I am calling 'foliating events', which join human with cosmic planes. That is why they are the high points of Meriam life. The time chosen for the Malo initiation rites is *sager kerker*, the height of the harvest.

In the transition from *kesi* to *ume le*, the 'death' of the boy and the 'birth' of the man, a change of quality within the human cycles is made possible through their joining with the cosmic cycles which move on the other plane. The culture is bringing all it has to bear on the re-creation: through the ceremonies at *giz ged*, in which *le*, the mortals, are brought together with *lamar*, the immortal spirits, as preparation for *wauri*, danger is changed to strong-heartedness through the power of *zogo*, turning *le* towards *tebud le*. For all the Meriam and for each *le*, these occasions are like the nexus of human and cosmic planes where all the levels correspond (Eliade 1974, 391).

The world which begins to take form within the circle of the seasons is tied diachronically in reversible time to the world of 'before' — the world of *lamar*, the ancestral spirits. The renewal and regeneration which the harvest symbolises carries with it the re-creation of the cosmos. As the 'world' passes through the zenith of its circle, offerings from 'our time', gifts from us and the places of people, are offered to 'their time' in the new circle of time.[14]

As the individual reaches the crossing point to another plane, the 'foliating event' as a rite of passage allows the person to 'pass through' to the cosmic

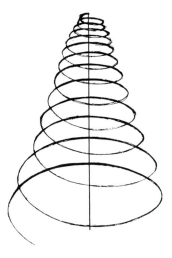

Figure 7 The spiral of life

circle. As *le*, the person's life followed the comings and goings and returnings of *kerker*, where each circle is both the same and different from the one before. As human experience there is both a repeated movement of circles and also a new experience. Human experience from 'year' to 'year' is shaped like a spring. The accretion of wisdom within the human cycle, in which life moves from beginnings to *au le*, a respected older person, a person of wisdom, moves in the form of a spiral, resembling the pattern imprinted upon the *wauri* shell. The process of the never-meeting circles which make up a person's life may be shaped like the drawing on page 74.

At the top of the spiral is the 'death' of *le*: in the process of becoming *lamar* he or she has crossed over, moving on to that other plane. It likens the shape of the spirit-power of Malo: from *kesi*, initiates, at the base, to *ume le*, who have received the power of *zogo*; to *Beizam boai*, the Shark brethren, descendants of the seven brothers of Las, who obtained possession of Bomai; to *Zogo le*, those who wear the sacred masks, when the spirit energy of *zogo* reaches its highest point in *le*.

That spiral shape, it has been proposed recently, is exactly the form in which the body of oral knowledge is stored. Writing of his people, the Binandere, in Papua New Guinea, Waiko concludes that their body of knowledge, stored within legends containing precepts and ethical rules which include plants, animals and man as interdependent parts of a whole (*kiki opipi*), takes the form of a spiral (1982, 271).

He likens the process by which tradition as text is woven into a spiral within the limits of six generations from the 'head' (*opipi*), the terminal ancestor, to the 'tail' (*mai*), who is the youngest living descendant of the clan, to the Binandere cone-shaped fish-trap (*sirawa*). The process of sorting those traditions worthy of retention within the relatively stable body of oral tradition resembles the way the fish are sorted from the debris. At the open end of the mother fish-trap, the *sirawa*, is an inner son trap, *sirawa mai*, where the sorting process begins. The mother fish trap represents the three older generations and the son trap represents the three younger generations, the oldest of which is the grandparents (*apie*). 'It is against the knowledge of the living *apie*', writes Waiko, 'that the knowledge of the succeeding generation is tested and checked for its originality and the reliability of its sources' (1982, 270). Where life is lived as a spiral of circles in which the 'bricolage' of experience is sifted and separated and then synthesised into a crystalline form, which constitutes the common wisdom and identity of a people, perception of time and sequences of events are also in spiral rather than in linear form (Waiko 1982, 271; see also Evans-Pritchard 1940, 100–08).

THE ALL-UNITY: THE MANY IN THE ONE, THE ONE IN THE MANY

In moving through the circles of *kerker* the Meriam traverse a path which moves from east to west in the *wauri* voyages to Op Deudai, a path that leads ultimately to 'another place', Boigu, at the end of the seas. The pattern of social life is formed within the movement of the seasons. It is written in the layout of the stars. Its movement is inscribed in their trek across the sky. The path of the stars becomes the language of a cultural statement. New life begins in the place of the gentle winds, like the opening of the day, with the sun's rising to its decline, like the movement of the sun beyond the west.[15] The life of *le* follows the movement from life to death to regeneration of the natural world signified by the appearance of Seg (part of the celestial alignment of Tagai): *arit kerker*, time to plant. When Seg, whom the Greeks named Orion, appears, Usiam, the Pleiades, is close by. Orion, 'he who makes water', the son of 'Mother Earth' and Poseidon, shows the way to the rainy times (see Graves 1982, 152).

The pulse of Meriam life flows from the east in helioc movement coursing westward across the sky like the path of the sun toward Boigu on the other side of Magani Kes, the isle at the end of the world, like the land of the Hesperides in the west beyond the ocean (Graves 1982, 154–55). Life rises with the sun and moves upward in the shape of an arc, descending like the rainbow to join with the 'other side', travelling down to Boigu with the wind: the 'tide' of *le*, the mortals, runs down to Boigu, the place of *lamar*, the immortals.

The movement of all life follows the very same path traversed by *le* in the *wauri* voyages to Op Deudai: travel leeward down to Boigu in the west whence come the myths upon which the world is founded and which give its meanings. It is also the arch which forms the Meriam image of cosmic space. The reverse passage being travelled by those who are becoming immortal is vouchsafed by the chant language of Malo, which came eastwards with the myth, to reach its destination on 'this side', now the side of Malo.

There is a change of form: the spirit energy, known as *mar* in Meriam, which takes a human shape as *le*, now takes a new form: *la-mar* is the undying spirit in a different form of being; *mar* is reborn in another *ged*. For the Meriam, all things can be and not be at the same time. *Lamar*, the ancestral spririts, are far away beyond the horizon at Boigu. Yet in their change of place lies the paradox of their simultaneous presence: in that moment of their rebirth in another place lies their potential to travel the gift-path of *seker lu* from west to east, to be present with *le* at times of crossing. Like the rainbow that comes and disappears, their form may change into its opposite.

The circles which meet at *giz ged* have merged. The path from *le* to *lamar* follows the path from *ged kar*, each person's real place in the given order of things, fanning outwards along the very same-shaped curve as that of the voyagers to Op Deudai. That, too, is the path taken by the stars. In moving from east to west, life below mirrors the crescent-shaped path of the stars of Tagai, from springtime, when Seg and Usiam come up to the time of their decline. They, *lamar*, are following the reverse path of the myths; they are returning from the place of their life as *le* to the edges of another world sprung from the waves of the deep sea, the 'forest regions' of the unknown; yet 'the world of the dead is close and constantly interacting with that of the living' (Waiko 1982, 281). 'Distant seas' and 'distant times' join with 'our times' and 'our places' (Sahlins 1981, 16).

In this joining of planes there is a fusion into one circle, a union symbolised by the path of *deumer. Deumer lub*, a single feather worn at the back of the head by each *kesi*, quivers in the dance like *upi*, the tail of *deumer.* The headdress of white feathers (*dari*), in the form of a half-circle worn in the men's dance, is like the arc traversed by *deumer* from Op Deudai to the islands and to Keo Deudai, the outreaches of the world of the Meriam. *Zogo le* stand for the whole world of Malo, a world marked out and signified by the flight-path of *deumer* round the circle of the year... And so they put white feathers over the body of the *Zogo le*, Kebi Bala's great grandfather (see Haddon 1908, 145).

The separate planes are illusory: 'before' and 'after', 'us' and 'other', 'this side' and the 'other side', have become joined in the 'All-One'. Just as the voyager-path from east to west has merged with the gift-path from west to east, so the movement of *le* to *lamar* is simultaneously a movement to the 'before' of beginnings and a movement to the 'here-after', a coming together in 'place' and 'time' in an immortality which unites 'before' with 'after'. The All-Ways have joined. Here begin ultimate meanings: the trajectory is towards the millennium, the 'end-point' of the Eternal Return of cyclical time which has no 'ending', only a change of form (Eliade 1959a, especially Chapter 2). So as Waiko writes of the Binandere of Papua New Guinea:

> ...these spiritual energies here act as separate but in essence they are all part of one spirit energy. Like bubbles in water they are held separate by the liquid but potentially in another medium — *viz.* air — they are all one, just as when the bubbles reach the surface they will all become, air.

Like the Binandere, this is how the Meriam 'expect their world to be — things can exist and not exist, and shapes and forms may change' (1982, 34).

3 | ORIGINALITY AND CONTINUITY

Malo-Bomai can give you something to guide you before you can learn something else. I appreciate having such rules from Malo-Bomai. Once you've learnt that you can just manage to do something that is written in the New Testament. We got the knowledge from the outside world and put it together with our own knowledge.

Au Bala

LIVING THE OLD AND THE NEW. AU BALA: MY FATHER SET ME TO GO ON A LONG JOURNEY AND I FOUND MY WAY THROUGH

Au Bala is a person of enduring spirit; until his recent death, he was the oldest living descendant of the *Zogo le* of Malo, top people among *Beizam boai*, the Shark brethren. He was born early in *naiger kerker*, or northeast time, on 29 August 1912: that is 'Usiam time' when the Pleiades begins to appear, a sign of garden preparation time. As we saw in the last chapter, Au Bala is a great gardener who uses nature for his book: gardening will never end for him 'until my time is finished'. That occasion came for Au Bala on Monday, 1 October 1990; on Friday 5 October he was buried near his home at Zomared, Mer.

As the eldest member of the family it was automatically given to him to look after his grandfather's lands. As a descendant of the *Zogo le* he has tried to set an example in his life to other Meriam: that meant producing garden food for his family, his teaching career, his responsibilities as an honorary deacon of the Anglican Church. He sees the teachings of Malo-Bomai as the foundation of Christianity among the Meriam. His life story tells of a hard life in which he managed to put the new knowledge together with his own cultural inheritance in the tradition of his family and Giar Dauareb clan. In 1898, his grandfather wrote fifty-nine pages in English on myths, custom and classificatory systems of the environment and social life for members of the Cambridge expedition, described by Sidney Ray 'as the first unassisted literary effort' by any member of a Papuan race (1907, 228). On 28 March 1980, Au Bala was called to Brisbane to be made an Officer of the Order of the British Empire (OBE). Yet for Au Bala his own *ged kar*, or real homeland at Mer is his first thought; 'in my second thought Torres Strait'; Murray Island culture, says Au Bala, is still 'three-quarters of my life'.

My father taught me gardening, that's why I love gardening

Grandfather was the first to marry into Christian marriage. He was eighty-three years old when he died. He was a youth when they first landed here and introduced the Gospel. His ancestor, Koit, was the first one who decided to leave Mer and go to Dauar and claim the lands there because he was one of the high priests of Bomai-Malo cult. Far back, many generations before grandfather was born.

My father was a real gardener and he taught me too. That's why I love gardening. It's in my veins. I give gardening my first priority. He taught me so I carry on. My mum too, she gardened. And they planted gardens; they used their own hands. We had enough; we didn't depend on store food. No! Flour and rice were foreign food for my father and mother.

I've got fresh memory, I can think right back. Because when he started to plant he would say: 'Look at this star here. Look at the atmosphere.' They used to 'read' the atmosphere, the clouds. They knew the right time to plant cassava, banana, yam, sweet potato, water melons and pumpkin. So that is why I learnt to plant as a little boy. Kipa gogob is the first rain; we get heavy rain before the change of weather from southeast to northwest. Before that time of heavy rain they knew what to do with the garden. At one time he called me, 'Come here. See this cloud here. Rain is not far. This is the sign of rain, first rain.' And I looked at him and said, 'Okay'. It's written in my brain. Indelible pencil. I was quite small then, nine or ten. My father used to do his gardening this way while I got all the smaller seeds of yam and I made my garden and practised. Since it started it'll never end until my time is finished.

It was important even for a little boy to spear a sardine

I learned a lot of things from my grandfather and my father: to take an aim with the spear. I was told how to use spear and how to use wap, *dugong spear.* Wap *is used differently from fish spear. Grandfather made me a line out of coconut fibre. In our language we say,* muti mekek: muti, *fibre;* mekek, *line. So he made* muti mekek *for me and I found it was very strong line, even when I fished for dabor, kingfish. It was very strongly made. Little boy then. My father said, 'We go out fishing'. Well, I go with my line. And grandfather [laughing softly] made me that line. It was long too. Around 200 yards. I was small but to spear first turtle, first dugong you must make a feast, for each one. It was important even for a little boy to spear a sardine; that was counted as first fish.*

When I was in school there was no such thing as 'your future'

Now you can arrange your future. Then there was no such thing as 'your future'. But my father was very strict. He wanted me to have a good schooling. And learn something in Sunday school. When I left school a few things they said: 'Thou shalt not, thou shalt not, thou shalt not...'. That is why I don't smoke. Father said to me, 'No smoke for you; no beer for you.' I learnt to drink that stuff when I was fifty-four, in Brisbane.

Mr Agnew found that I was very bright so he used to make me look after the other classes. And I left school and signed on a trochus boat. 1928. I turned sixteen. The only thing we knew was to leave school and go and sign on trochus boat. I decided to sign on a 'Company boat', Tagai. One time when we were at anchor a policeman came here and he called me up, said, 'Mr Agnew want to see you'. He said, 'There is a vacancy for a teaching staff here. What about you?' I said to myself, 'Well, after diving in salt water for so many years I think my brain is full of salt'. He said, 'Well it's good to teach. At the same time while you're teaching you're learning.' I said, 'Okay'. So early in 1931 I left diving to join the teaching staff. And I didn't think that I had a future. And later I said, 'Oh well, I take teaching for my career'. So that was that: 1931 to 1971 when I left teaching.

Father said, 'I asked God to give me a son... Now I'm giving you back to God'

The day when I was ready to leave Murray and transfer to Poid I got all of my luggage and my father said to me, 'All right, you wait here until I tell you something'. And he said to me, 'You were still in your mother's womb when I prayed to God, "Give me a son. When he grow up to be a man I will give him back to you." Now I'm giving you back to God.' But somehow he knew that my future was coming: 'You are leaving Murray to go and teach children in other lands'. Father said to me, 'Don't waste your time dancing and all that. Keep up to your work.' And from that day when I left I didn't dance any more. Songs all right but not dancing. In those days if you were seen talking to a female partner you were brought up before the court and dismissed from teaching. I looked upon teaching as my career. But if I did some slight wrong I'd be dismissed and sent back home. So I rather give up dancing. My career was first thing for me to hold on to and nothing else. In the Bible it says, 'Feed my lambs, feed my sheep'. I think that was my mission to feed the lambs of God. I didn't want to disgrace my father and mother. I looked upon them as my earthly gods.

Grandfather said, 'Look at my hands, the hands of love'

Christianity was so successful you know. It makes one wonder how it was so quick. From Malo-Bomai to Christianity: mental telepathy. I think I told you about grandfather's mental telepathy. It was so great that I wish I could have gained some of his knowledge of telepathy. It was marvellous. It was still in him [after he was converted]. *He died in 1933. I think because I left that was his downfall. I was so close being the eldest in the family. I put the family together. I was looked upon by him also as the head of the family because I was going to claim all his property. When I got there, in a month or two, he* [voice becoming softer] *passed away.*

I went to see him before I walked down the beach to catch the dinghy. 'Grandfather', I said, 'I've come to let you know that I'm leaving. So you must know before I leave I'm trying to keep up the name where you built it.' He said, 'Look at my hands, the hands of love. Go from here to any Islands from Saibai to Boigu you find friends because of these hands of love.' It's still fresh in me. Love everybody from here down to Boigu. That is why he said to me, 'hands of love'. This was more than wauri tebud *because they had been Christianised.*

Malo-Bomai can give you something to guide you

Grandfather taught me a few things then about the law of Malo-Bomai. And he and Meriam Man said to me, 'Go through the law of Malo-Bomai. If you go through them you will know how to go about in this life.' So they were right; because the rules of Malo-Bomai are very similar to those of the Ten Commandments: Thou shalt not...; don't do that; you should do this. Keep out of this! Well, Malo-Bomai was something like the Old Testament. Say for instance, Malo wali aritarit, sem aritarit. *Well that means, 'Don't stop planting; plant everywhere as long as there is soil for you to plant in'. And they said to me, 'In the New Testament it says that God sends His people to go and teach other people the message'. Malo-Bomai can give you something to guide you before you can learn something else.*

On Murray Island Christianity was accepted so quickly because of Malo-Bomai. You just imagine [raising voice a little]. *Grandfather was the high priest of Malo-Bomai. His second son became one of the first Island priests in Torres Strait whereas in other places it took hundreds of years. But here it was so quick because of Malo-Bomai. I appreciate having such rules from Malo-Bomai. Once you learnt that you can just manage to do something that is written in the New Testament.*

I felt I was a stranger at Poid then I met a few friends there. They said to me, 'Your grandfather's well-known'. So I found brothers and sisters there. I went there lonely and in two or three days people

came up and said, 'Oh, I know your grandfather'. It was a broadening
experience at Poid. I learnt how they hunt in the Western Islands. And
W taught me the use of wap, dugong spear. I learnt to meet people from
that end of Torres Strait and they taught me their language. Later I
thought I was on Murray Island.

When you're working you do it with your heart and soul

It was a bit hard for me but eventually I got through all right. But
there was something different there: the way I passed the message
through was what people call 'a success'. First there is no such thing
as 'play up' during lesson hours. No! When you're working you do
it properly. You do that with your heart and soul. I was always on
time; before school I was up there already. And school time meant
school time to me. Even during Christmas holidays I used to find my
way here and before New Year I would be back in Poid; get a boat and
race right through... Well, if you want to be My disciple you must let
go father and mother and all that.

The Superintendents in some Islands were like little tin gods

Mr Chandler was a real teacher. He understood his work thoroughly.
I first got my real foundation in teaching from Mr Chandler. Oh,
Number One! I think highly about him too because that is where my
foundations built up. Yes, the first time he taught the children there
about phonic sounds was the first time I learnt that there is such
[laughing]. By gee! He took me far enough in my teaching career. The
Superintendents in some Islands were just like little tin gods. Mrs Zahel
was teaching over the other side at Badu. The way she spoke to me
made me think that she was a little god. I think Chandler was a
different man. He came just after the Yorke Island Conference. Oh, he
might have been part of the New Law.[1]

My wife-to-be spent the night in gaol. Just think of it! She
was standing so many yards away and talking to me. Another day
I found that she was in gaol. One time I started worrying. Chandler
came up to me. He said to me, 'Do you know the song, "Look for the
silver lining"?' 'Yes, I know that song.' 'If the dark clouds appear now
in the blue today in your life, remember somewhere the sun is shining.'
Oh, I still remember him. He was great. I don't like to remember those
days again [laughing quietly]. I hate them. But I think great God was
so close.

Well to tell you the truth I felt great about my father and
the way he faced me with a future. I thank him a lot. He set me to go
on a long journey and I found my way through.

I spent four months in Brisbane in 1965. I started a special
course of teaching at the Kedron Teachers' College. That is why when

I went to Lockhart River I knew what to do. I think a message came to me saying that I was one of the pioneer teachers to go to Brisbane. Then we looked back to the life here fenced in. There it was so open in the community. We were free!

I was trying to treasure my inheritance being a descendant of a high priest

When I was elected into the Council my hopes were of treating people here fairly. I was trying to treasure my inheritance being a descendant of a high priest. Zogo le *set the example for all the others. That is why I tell the younger generation of my relations that I belong to that class of people:* wali aritarit *and* sem aritarit. *Malo never wanders to anybody's land; Malo never picks anything from anybody's land, somebody's land. Malo always keeps his hands away from other people's property. Malo can only pick from his own land, from his own property. Malo tag* aorir, Teter aorir aorir. *But when sacred people walk now they're hardly seen because they don't want anyone to see them walking in somebody's land.* Tag aorir aorir, Teter aorir aorir.

As I said, 'Gardening as a way of life was in my blood'. I worked in the garden in addition to my career as a teacher or as Chairman of the Council. I still supplied my family with vegetables from my own hard work. I think that sort of Island life must be preserved. At the moment we're trying to preserve all that belongs to the Islands.

Island culture is three-quarters of my life

Murray Island culture plus new life put together is culture today. I've plussed them: new life. Island culture, I think it's three-quarters of my life. I think of my culture wholly and solely. When I said, 'Three-quarters of my own culture' it's three-quarters of my life. That's the way I look upon Island life and custom. But then again I don't think that white men's custom is so foreign to me because I put them together: one and one are two.

We got the knowledge from the outside world and put it together with our own knowledge. I showed you that yam the other day. My yams have a full life eh! And I say to you, 'They're well fed...'.
(selected and edited extracts from Book of Islanders 1984, B54–69, B142–50)

SINGULAR AND PLURAL

All the Meriam were able to 'read' the clouds, the stars, the winds, the tides, the stages of trees. They all knew how to garden and when to prepare the land, when to plant and when to harvest. Au Bala observes: 'I don't know how the Meriam before came to understand how to burn the patch of garden land there so that when the rain falls you get coals or ash into the soil to make it rich'.

When *birobiro*, the kingfisher, returned to their area they said, 'The harvest is near'. This is part of the common store of knowledge which everyone took for granted. 'Everybody knows that. In certain ways they differ. One might be a champion banana grower. Another one a champion sweet potato grower.' The Meriam were gardeners, fisherfolk and seafarers: within their common life-form there was group and individual variation.

As we saw in the last chapter, all Meriam *le* had knowledge of the hidden connections between things in the environment. But some *le* had special knowledge of the wild, the non-reciprocal, the singular, the hidden power of *Em*, the 'other condition'. They were the *Zogo le*, men of the most sacred line from *giz ged*, the original place of the myth of Malo-Bomai. The knowledge store that went with each *le* and each *ged*, strained through the net of succeeding generations, was passed with *ged* and totem or *lubabat*, from before to after through the eldest son; continuity of the power of the full 'otherness' of *zogo* was passed through the most sacred stems. In that extra-ordinary power there existed a dissimilarity to *le*.

Zogo le shared with other Meriam the ability to garden, to recognise the signs of nature. They planted to fulfil Malo ra Gelar. They followed Malo's instruction to plant everywhere so they were always champion gardeners. In this they were exemplars for *le*. Malo showed a way for the Meriam to live and the *Zogo le*, as representatives of Malo, provided the example. Yet their daily life was also different from that of *le*. *Zogo le* did not go out on the reef to fish because they might cut their feet on the coral, which would prevent them from practising their 'sacred ways'. The younger brothers of the *Zogo le* went on *wauri* and warfaring expeditions; the eldest brothers of the sacred stems did not: each had a warrior to fight for him.

All *le* were bound by reciprocal rights and obligations and *Zogo le* were not exempted from those reciprocal relations. It was they who could 'reciprocate' with the most 'other' and through the power of *zogo* turn round the power of *Em* from danger to divine power. So they were looked upon as those most able to divine events. The *Zogo le* were the ones who would say: 'Don't go this day, it looks like trouble somewhere'. They were like ordinary *le*, but in the Malo-Bomai cult they were looked upon as divine. *Aets* were not rulers. 'That's the wrong word', says Au Bala: 'The *Zogo le* or *Aets* were sacred people. They were not such people to press others down. They were people of divine power, like we look upon the Creator as someone Divine.'

Zogo is intentional power, like spirit energy matching the coils of the whirlpool, like cosmic energy moving in a spiral. The power of *zogo* is 'knowing' that spiral process.

Other *le* had particular *zogo* associated with *kerker* and *ged*. There were divinatory *zogo*, like the shrine at Tomog facing northward towards Erub. The special powers of the *Zogo le* were more general. They had the power to communicate with others of similar power in other places; the power to foresee events; the power to communicate with *lamar*; the power to heal or to injure. *Zogo le* and *le* are both like and unlike one another.

In the affairs of everyday life they are personally similar, each bearing the qualities associated with different homeplaces. Au Bala's grandfather as *Zogo le* of Dauar, bore the stamp of people who spent about three-quarters of their time harvesting from the sea, unlike the *Zogo le* springing from Piadram clan, who spent most of their time as gardeners. On occasions of sacred rites, the *Zogo le* were most dissimilar to *le*. As *opole*, wearing the sacred masks of Malo and Bomai, at places specially set aside, they presided over the most solemn occasions: the foliating events which bring human cycles into union with cosmic cycles.

Zogo le are embedded within exactly the same network of social relations as *le*: those of giving, receiving and returning. They are therefore subject to the same ultimate restraints as *le*, both social relational and symbolic. While the singular inheres in all *le*, in *Zogo le* it is specially potent; yet unlike *maid le*, purveyors of malevolent magic, *Zogo le* are locked into and their powers are subject to the moral discourse. Their singular power is moderated by their obligations to others within the group. It is expressed through the life of *le* of which they are part. They are carriers of the consensus of the group in which they are embedded.

In contrast, *maid le* are the archetype of the anti-social: the unobliged, unbifurcated, wholly self-willed singular. While the singular inheres in everything, in *maid le* who 'go with' the wild, the singular is dominant. *Maid le* deal not in Life: they personify the power of Death.[2] As 'the antithesis of normal living', sorcerers 'go with' the untamed bush, among corpses and with the night (see Marwick 1965, 225). They are 'other', the odd ones out; they are non-reciprocal (Burridge 1969, 424). That is why they are feared. Conversely, *Zogo le*, through the heightened power of singularity of the 'other', bring the wild or non-reciprocal into the realm of the humanly meaningful: that is why they are revered.

Burridge has written that '...no moral system can abide the uninhibited singular'; yet '...a singular and non-reciprocal power cannot be wholly resolved or contained in moral terms' (1969, 459). Stability, order and stasis within community life always contain their opposite: the upsetting of that balance through the disorder of singularity. Within the logic of reciprocity lies the injunction to move from the singular to the plural: the triumph of culture over nature.

The distinction between the two types of people is integral to the differential way in which the singular is negotiated by societies on either side of the Divide. Reciprocal culture abhors the unbridled singular; yet the singularity of the 'other side' constantly re-emerges (Burridge 1969, 459). The power of *Em* must be apprehended and propitiated. The mysterious, the awesome, the death-dealing power of *Em*, is humanly impossible. As Burridge observed of Tangu of New Guinea, the singular, expressed almost always as 'bad' or evil, 'hangs broody, moody, and wild' (1969, 467). The daily life of mortals is always within striking power of *Em*. Among the Meriam, *Zogo le* carry the reciprocal power of *Em's* propitiation, a power which holds within it the qualities of the 'speculative' or meditative.[3] That is why the *Zogo le* are at the centre of the world of *le*.

Speculative thought is the mythopoeic form of thought: it is concerned with discerning relationships, not with the properties of something; it remains undetached and 'matched' with its object. Described as 'an almost visionary mode of apprehension' (Frankfort 1946, 3), its quest is the revelation of relationships, rather than the study of the object. In contrast to the mode of intellectual detachment and withdrawn appraisal, discernment engages the senses in a unity which takes in 'everything', as in 'tracking' or 'reading' the sea. Multiform signs come from a variety of sources which are held apart in the intellectual mode.[4]

Speculative thought seeks to apprehend patterns. It 'attempts to *underpin* the chaos of experience so that it may reveal the features of a structure — order, coherence, and meaning' (Frankfort 1946, 3). It involves not only the intellect but the whole being in an active interrelationship with the living 'other': 'The world appears...neither inanimate nor empty but redundant with life; and life has individuality, in man and beast and plant, and in every phenomenon which confronts man — the thunderclap, the sudden shadow...' (1946, 6).

> Any phenomenon may at any time face him, not as 'It', but as 'Thou'. In this confrontation, 'Thou' reveals its individuality, its qualities, its will. 'Thou' is not contemplated with intellectual detachment; it is experienced as life confronting life, involving every faculty of man in a reciprocal relationship. Thoughts, no less than acts and feelings, are subordinated to this experience. (1946, 6)

That reciprocal confrontation is an ongoing process of awareness, drawing upon the cumulation of handed-down wisdom, which is also integral to the categories in which social life is lived. In this mode of engagement with life

the watchwords are encounter and commitment, not detachment and analysis.[5]
As a form of reflection, the speculative quality of mythopoeic thought differs from
the scientific mode. That difference reaches a peak on occasions of sacred
significance: in the telling of a myth the individual moves through the whole range
of culture. That experience reaffirms a moral code and a way of living, for it is
a reminder and a way of reflecting upon the grounding nature of the truths it
embodies (Geertz 1966, 28). That is why the correct telling of the myth of Malo-
Bomai is of primordial importance for Au Bala (see Chapter 1).

THE CENTRE OF THE ALL-WAYS

Where life is shaped and patterned by the movement of cosmic cycles the
recognition of signs which presage a later culmination is like complex 'forecasting',
calling upon all the senses. That 'future' is not a straight line from here to there
but a continual movement of many circles. An awareness touched with the power
of 'the Other' apprehends the movement of cosmic rhythms and the signs of
approaching phases within the unending cycles of 'death' and 'rebirth'. So as Eliade
has written, a 'sign' of spring might reveal the *spring* of a new *beginning* before
'nature's spring', whose outward and visible signs have not yet appeared. That
new beginning is the spring of '...a complete renewal and recommencement of
all cosmic life' (1974, 391).

     Zogo le would hearken to the sea, voicing the tones that tell of oncoming
danger or the tunes of safe voyaging. They would foresee the approach of gentle
winds and fair weather for sailing, though they themselves did not go out upon
the sea. Their special awareness of practical possibilities was expressed in
encouragement or caution to *le*.[6] For the *Zogo le* held the spirit power of Malo,
who in mythical time voyaged from Tuger, the 'outside place', far westward at Op
Deudai, beyond the arc of the 'known' world of the Meriam, across *malo*, the deep
water, to Mer. In a profane sense, the Tugeri (Marind-Anim), living beyond even
Boigu, personify the ultimate power of danger; through the mediation of Malo,
danger is turned to 'sacred power' or *zogo*. In a metamorphosis of the strongest
order the power of the 'other' expressed in the metaphor of *beizam*, sharks of
the depths, became the power of *Beizam boai*, the Shark brethren, descendants
of the seven brothers of Las who gained Bomai. The ultimate and deadly power
of the 'forest regions' of the 'other side' has crossed over (see Sahlins 1976, 11).
It is this transcendent power — the *zogo* of Bomai — which signifies the possibility
of transformation from death to immortality (Haddon 1908, 45). Among mortals,
the *Zogo le* are the height of its expression.

In the life-world of reciprocal confrontation, 'good' and 'evil' are both expected to inhere in everything. The reality of magical chants or *zogo mir* among the Meriam is the counter to the harmful force of the *zogo mir* of another: my yams will grow at the expense of the yams of 'another kind' of person, or the other way round. Everything and everyone are two-sided. So the *Zogo le* are not only exemplars; they are also executioners, for *zogo* carries not only the power of life but also the power of death through malevolent magic. In the *Zogo le* the power of the singular is tied into the moral order so that the power of the social is in the ascendancy. So it is they who are called upon to make decisions on matters of life and death, on behalf of *le*: to perceive the right time to go on a voyage is a matter of life and death for it may mean death to 'another kind' or 'our' death; an attunement to the sea or a watery grave.

In *Zogo le* resides the 'matching' power to tame and channel that energy which hovers like a compressed spring, suddenly breaking forth and appearing, chameleon-like, in manifold shapes. Through that power conferred on them by Malo it becomes humanly negotiable. *Zogo le* are set apart, yet they are grounded in and shaped by the consensus; they are different from and the same as other persons, within a life-mode in which variation between individuals takes the form where all relationships retain the personalities of giver and receiver who are tied to place and clan. Each generation of the Meriam, and hence the common wisdom distilled over time, bear the imprint of persons of heightened powers of discernment in a social life, in which they are the principal but not exclusive bearers of an accumulating wisdom.

The form in which that wisdom is gathered together resembles the manner in which certain relationships are woven together in nature. Waiko has traced the way the body of 'oral tradition' comes to be shaped and patterned among the Binandere of Papua New Guinea: its cone-shape is suggestive of the spiral of the *zogo* (Waiko 1982, 143; see also Mackie 1985, 143 on the spiral shape of 'multilevular thinking').

At the centre of the many-rayed network of that cone is the line of *Zogo le*, stretching back to *ad giz*, the time of coming into being. Through that line whirls the spirit power of *zogo*. The *Zogo le* are not 'head' people or 'leaders'; in that sense, Meriam social life is acephalous, or headless. *Zogo le* form the centre of its all-ways: they are the linking people, of 'after' with 'before', of 'us' with 'other'. As custodians of the cultural tradition they stand for a *constancy* of identity. Their singularity signifies the possibility of a process of *change*: through the foliation or layered overlapping of reciprocal relations the quality of the 'other' is brought within a growing cultural ambience.

PERSONS OF ORIGINALITY

Differences between cultures, Lévi-Strauss has observed, 'are extremely fecund.
It is only through difference that progress has been made. In order for a culture
to be really itself and to produce something, the culture and its members must
be convinced of their originality...' The 'over-communication' of modern technology
brings with it 'the prospect of our being only consumers' of other cultures, '...but
of losing all originality' (1978a, 20).

    The originality of difference is the essence of reciprocal interrelations
between cultures, a truth which Sis apprehends deeply (see Epilogue). She is
intensely aware of the quality of originality of her culture: 'People who know their
own ways', she observes, 'can get on with other people who know theirs':

> *Well, our good manners might be quite opposite to yours. If you marry
> my brother I refer to you as 'woman'. Otherwise it's very bad manners
> to call you by the name. And you call me 'woman' back. Our in-laws
> are really important people in our lives. Their place is special too.
> They like being there because you put them there and you respect them.*
>   *When your in-laws die you have a very big part to play.
> You're the ones who look after the immediate family. That's one of the
> reasons we don't say their names any more. It's a mark of respect.
> In your way of life you say: 'Oh now my mother has gained another
> daughter by my brother marrying'. Well, it's not exactly like that with
> us. She now has a daughter-in-law with a special place in our lives.
> When that old lady dies that daughter-in-law plays a really big part.
> The in-laws are the ones that dress the body, that do everything. They
> won't sit and mourn: they will be the ones that will look after the family
> that come to mourn. They will sit and not do anything. Immediate
> family don't touch anything; that's the proper custom. A daughter-
> in-law is very important in life and death. So we look after our in-
> laws. We're very happy when somebody marries, so we don't
> understand your mother-in-law jokes.* (The Tombstone, Book of
> Islanders 1984, B159)

Islanders who possessed a strong sense of their own culture were
frontiers-people in the deepest sense. In the time of the Storm-Winds powerful
inner resources were called upon to resist the imminent danger of 'psychological
death' (the term is Riesman's: see Read 1959, 425). Their possibilities of spiritual
survival were grounded in the older wisdom and its potential to confront both
the ancient and the new 'otherness'. They responded in creative and varied ways
on terms not chosen by themselves. As Au Bala says, he 'found a way through'.
Yet it was his father who set him on that journey; so it is a journey that goes back
to 'before' as well as on to 'after'. It was the teaching of his father and his

grandfather, the old *Zogo le*, which helped him to begin. Their teachings which came from Malo gave him something to go on: 'If you go through the law of Malo-Bomai you will know how to go about in this life'. That was the deeper meaning of Malo *wali aritarit* and *sem aritarit* for Au Bala: one may find other places in which to sow the seeds of that special knowledge which comes from Malo from where to reap a harvest in the ever-enriching process of reciprocal giving and receiving. Through that wisdom he knew that he would learn something else: the new knowledge of other places.

The new soil in which to plant was found through the 'new *wauri*': the message which made it possible for Au Bala to teach in once-hostile territory at Moa Island, out westwards towards Boigu, the end of the old world, and be received as *tebud*. 'Go from here to any Islands from Saibai to Boigu and you find friends because of these hands of love.' That was the Christian message, which took in but did not extinguish the message from his grandfather, the *Zogo le*. The result of that experience is the creation of a new man: Au Bala, who is like, but also unlike his father and his grandfather. He is a man who can look into his own personal formation and say: 'Murray Island culture plus new life put together... I've plussed them... Island culture is three-quarters of my life.' Au Bala passed that same message to Meriam Man as a seventeen-year-old lad going out from Mer

Plate 6   Flo Kennedy at Thursday Island, 1989, with Torres and Joy (photograph by Yarra Bank Films)

to teach at Yorke Island: 'It's important for the benefit of this Island and your people that whatever you do outside, don't forget you bring that idea back to Murray'. Malo *wali aritarit* was finding new soil in which to plant.

Au Bala identifies with the whole Torres Strait: 'At the moment we're trying to preserve all that belongs to the Islands... what I want is for the whole Torres Strait.' Yet for him 'first things' remain first. His primordial attachment is the foundation of newer ones. New loyalties and attachments are enfolded within the old, not the other way round. Au Bala remains a Giar Dauareb and a Meriam man; he is also a Torres Strait Islander. Each one of his identities bears the imprint of himself, Au Bala. He continues to carry the inheritance of the *Zogo le*. That is so when he works in the garden, growing *lewer kar* or other vegetables. In following his career wholeheartedly, he was also honouring his inheritance; as a teacher training in Brisbane, as Chairman of the Council, in his reception of a Decoration, he was treasuring the tradition handed down to him through the sacred stem of the *Zogo le*: that was the deep meaning of 'success' and the 'disgrace' of failure.

The ten people whose life stories are given here are like Au Bala in an important sense: they are all people of strong spirit. How they managed to achieve psychic integration throws a gleam of light on how the culture grew. They are like those before and yet they are new: they know their own ways and they are aware of the originality of those ways. In differing degree and in somewhat varying form, which are tied to each person's particular historical–personal experiences, they are all persons of originality. Unlike those who were effaced by the Storm-Winds, their identity is strong. As Sis says: 'I had no trouble knowing who I am'.

Originality is a two-sided quality: it is the coming together of the new and the old; it is the synthesis created out of the mediation of the singularity of the non-reciprocal. That is the motive of the culture. The arrival of Kole gave added impetus to the process of mediating the singular. It did so in two ways. In the first place, Kole had the quality of a new singularity: among the 'enemies' of past times the outcome of warfare was not only death; it also held the promise of the permanency of marriage ties or the relationships of *tebud le*. The presence of Kole meant the continuing non-reciprocity of a master-servant relationship. That is the meaning of *Kole*. In the second place, there also arrived in the Islands a moral order borne especially by Christianity which offered new ways of accommodating the singular. In turn there followed further consequences of outstanding significance. Christianity provided Islanders with ways of 'resisting' the new destructive powers. In the process of 'coming to terms' with the logical and hence the social impossibility of a sustained asymmetrical relationship, Islanders were able to come to know and see themselves in new ways. At the level of meaning the change was expressed in new forms of awareness and self-awareness.[7]

In the changed awareness there is a differentiation of the 'I' as expressed in 'I am an ailanman, this is my custom'. This is the 'I' of faith, the individuation which is characteristic of the Judaeo-Christian tradition (Eliade 1959b, 160). It is the 'I' of detachment from the 'other' characteristic of the abstract rationality associated with the exchange abstraction of the commodity culture (Cassirer 1955, 236; Sohn-Rethel 1978, 13–29). The synthesis is created according to the same reciprocal logic as before: the social necessity of its functioning is partially changed. The 'originality' of the synthesis now holds a new component: an individuation which still remains set within the frame of the reciprocal continues to be tied to locality and wind orientation, to the group which belongs to that place, and to the *lubabat* that goes with that group, and hence to the social practice of everyday life.

Each of the people here manifests strongly and 'individually' this new form of awareness. In each there is the decisiveness of the 'I': 'I found my way through'. Yet in Au Bala, faith in the 'I' is also made possible through a new Faith: 'I think the great God was so close'. In Second Meriam Man the power of the singularity of the 'I' took on the character of a lightning metamorphosis: 'I got up and did my dance. Everyone stood on their feet and I walked out.'

The new moral order created cultural possibility. It is expressed in the 'new *wauri*' which made possible the turning round of enmity to friendship, a friendship whose social bonds are framed now by the ideology of 'brothers or *tebud-*in-Christ', which could pass beyond '*tebud*-in-Malo'. As Au Bala illustrates, those new bonds find their subjective manifestation in a developing awareness as 'Torres Strait' Islanders, a new 'us' which does not suppress or obliterate the primordial attachments to place, to kin, to clan, or to their identity as Meriam people.

The lives of the people here have a strong sense of newness. Yet that newness constantly returns to the experiences of place and kin. Recollections of childhood retain a strong sense of continuity. 'People say I have my mother's ways. My mother was a very kind woman and she always tell me to be kind and always stick up on your rights' (Uncle). Kapin recalls his mother: 'And as she sat on the *sik* [bed] I saw her watching me reading'. 'She did influence me. Amongst all the baskets and mats I could pick out my mother's ones. They were so different' (Second Meriam Man). 'I had plenty of men raising grog to my lips but I only had one mother' (Ailan Man). 'And when my father died all the children ate first at the small feast because he loved children' (Sis). They are bringing the old ways lit up by a new light — the light of comparison and contrast: so 'our good manners may be quite opposite to yours...'. In coming to be acquainted with your custom we can recognise the distinctive qualities of our own custom. We can see ourselves with eyes that are also different from before. Second Meriam Man left Murray to go in search of something: the other side of the two-faced coin of white culture. A seed had been sown in him by the white school teacher, Robert Miles: to find the originality it had to offer. In the eighteen years it took him to get the idea of a black community school together his cultural difference remained founded upon the ongoing generations of Meriam clans. Like Au Bala, like First Meriam Man, a return to the source is inseparable from the search for something else.

They are representatives of people who have been able to renew themselves and this renewal has now a quality different from past syntheses. As before, it is associated with the primordial 'givens' of place and group. Yet faith in the 'I', associated with the universalist message of Christianity, by which all humankind may come up level as brothers and sisters, represents a new individuation. This new individuation, it is being suggested here, moves within an arc which ties together personal creativity in the speculative mode with reciprocal obligation and commitment. I have chosen the term 'integrative universalism' to designate that emerging form of awareness. The word 'integrative' most nearly lights upon the nature of an awareness which brings together a multiplicity of discrete mental and sensory processes. 'Integrative' most nearly corresponds with the meaning of 'speculative thought'. Its two principal defining qualities remain: discernment of patterns of interrelationships, not the search for the properties or attributes of an 'object'; and a 'matching' of the qualities of the other which does not dissolve the 'you' or the 'me' of the *yumi* relationship. Speculative mind is more akin to the meditative than the cognitive. The whole person and all the five senses, are brought to bear in the process of discernment; some would say that a sixth, the power of the intuitive, the inspirational quality of *zogo* frames all the others. Speculative thought is a form of 'rationality' in which the intellectual is not separated from the affective, a form of reflection in the poetic mode. In the matching of the other there is something resembling a symmetry of opposites.

The following chapters explore a developing process of reciprocal integration among Islanders at the levels of social relations and consciousness within a rapidly changing context of social life. Islanders like Au Bala lived the 'old' and the 'new'. The 'old' they lived had already undergone change brought about by both the dissolutionist and the revitalising powers of the 'new'; the new in which they were permitted to participate was lamed and misshapen by the power of its own destructive forces. Over the whole period, the 'new' was itself undergoing a major transformation, a process which deepened the contradiction for Torres Strait Islanders between cultural possibility and cultural eclipse. The following discussion of the forces for change addresses some of the complexities of these processes within a social context in which cultural difference became a condition of imperial power dominance.

III

4 | THE CROSS AS SIGN

Malo came to prepare the world for a bigger truth. Jesus Christ is where Malo was pointing. You see the high priests in the Malo dance, they carry seuriseuri *[the star-headed club of Malo]. In passing forward the* seuriseuri *from one dancer to the next, the symbol is that the authority of Malo must continue. So the heritage was passed on...*

Kebi Bala

DIVINE WRATH AND UTOPIAN PROMISE: THE COMING OF THE LIGHT

THOU SHALT HAVE NO OTHER GODS BEFORE ME: THE LONDON MISSIONARY SOCIETY

'"I am the Light of the World." Thank God for the first missionaries, who, on 1st July 1871 at Darnley Island brought the light of Christ to the Torres Strait.' So the inscription reads on the memorial stone outside the Anglican cathedral at

Plate 7 Building a church at Saibai, 1920s

Thursday Island.[1] For the isles of Torres Strait, the 'bloodless crusade' of which the religious crusader Quiros had dreamed was undertaken by members of the London Missionary Society.[2] Darnley was the first island visited by AW Murray and S McFarlane in their missionary voyage from the Loyalty Islands to New Guinea. Making their way westerly they reached Dauan Island where they '...had all the natives together that they might witness an act of worship to the true God, the first act of the kind no doubt that had ever been performed on their dark shore...under the canopy of heaven, and with the great dark land of New Guinea before us close at hand we sang, "Jesus shall reign where'er the sun"' (Report, 11 September 1872).

Pastors from the Pacific islands of Mare and Lifu were placed upon the islands at the 'option of the people'. It was firmly believed that if each missionary was '...allowed to remain, he would, with the help and blessing of God, work his way among the people, and gain their confidence and affections' (LMS, 11 September 1872, 31). Within a few years Islanders were helping to build churches which soon came to occupy central positions near the beaches. Over twenty or thirty years the LMS recorded an 'enthusiastic' response to their efforts. Islanders made available land for the churches and mission houses.[3] They raised money to buy the materials to build limestone churches and they offered their labour. The missionary, Rev James Chalmers, who brought more pastors from Niue and Samoa in 1890, records the following decade of progress. At Saibai in July 1897, £110 was subscribed by the people; the young men raised the money by hiring themselves to bêche-de-mer and pearl shell fishermen and the work was all done by themselves. In Mabuiag in the same year they raised £250 for the church by selling off a great batch of copper ingots they had discovered whilst diving for pearl shell; the new church at Darnley in 1899 had enough money over for a mission house; the new church was ready at Yam Island and a new church was expected to be opened about October in the same year at Murray Island (Chalmers, 20 January 1898; LMS Report for 1899).

For the London Missionary Society evangelists, the 'living God' was a terrible power manifest in Divine Wrath.[4] The 'Light' brought to the Islanders was the light to enlighten the Gentiles. In the missionaries' view, their arrival heralded the erasing of the old ways of 'heathen darkness'. The sacred emblems of that 'darkness', the masks and divinatory skulls, the sacred places and shrines, were destroyed at the instigation of the missionaries. In 1872 the first missionaries came to Mer; they were Mataika and his wife Siau from the Loyalty Islands. The Meriam took the missionaries to *au kop*, the sacred ground of Malo at Las, and the missionaries burned *pelak*, the sacred house and they banned their sacred dances. Some objects were spared or hidden like Tomog *zogo*, a divinatory shrine at Mer, consisting of a collection of stones, on each of which was a giant helmet shell representing a dwelling place, village or district at Mer. Story has it that Siau had asked its owners to consult that *zogo* when her husband's boat was overdue; next day he arrived in a canoe from Erub as predicted by the *zogo* (Haddon 1908, 265–66). Near the end of the century, as Haddon continues, the old men still displayed 'reverent affection' for that *zogo* even though Josiah, Mataika's successor, had burned it (Haddon 1908, 265–66). The missionaries stopped 'native dancing' on all the islands at which they were stationed (Haddon 1901, 127).

The missionaries created a three-way 'peace'. First was the ending of warfare raids between Islanders and their neighbours who were also warrior peoples. Second was the protection of Islanders from marauding vessels of pearlers and pirates, a matter on which after annexation of the Islands in 1879 the government and the missionaries cooperated. Third was the making of Islanders harmless to those seeking pearl shell and possession of islands. Government and Mission applauded the success of the missionaries in 'pacifying' Islanders in similar terms to one another. Their practical results were 'indisputable', the Government Resident, John Douglas, wrote to the Minister for Lands on 1 October 1885 (affidavit of PJ Killoran, 1982, letter R). Even the most remote and least 'contacted' people in the Strait at Saibai Island had put up 'their own Church' without 'asking outside help': 'Twenty years ago', wrote Rev Chalmers in 1897, 'these people were as wild as any skull-hunting tribe, that we know of at present'; now these young men were going out in the pearl shelling boats and giving half their wages towards building their church (January 1897).

Four closely related reasons may be suggested for the quick and positive responses of Islanders to the missionaries. In the first place the message rekindled a flame that already burned within the traditional religions in all the Islands. Second, some of the coloured missionaries from the South Seas understood the same social language of reciprocity as the Islanders. Third, the context in which the evangelists arrived, one of calamity and affliction, created a climate of conversion. Fourth, in greater and lesser degree in different Islands the new message of hope was accompanied by tangible expressions of a new way of life.

'Receive that man from the east': Kapin's grandfather, the old *zogo* man of shark (*beizam*) clan, was watching from his land up on the hill, looking eastwards when the mission boat, perhaps misnamed *Surprise*, arrived at Darnley Island from the east.

> *Well I think the LMS cut Malo down to pieces in some ways. But that law was the same: Malo had talked about obeying the law, the parents. Inside them my father and mother and grandpa believed. They say, 'That's a new religion', new ways of accepting God as their defender.*

Because that's the same as that old Darnley man I've been talking about told us, 'Receive that man from the east'. When that boat arrived with supplies on July First he was there. He felt something was going to happen and he was in that story place, in our land there on that hill, and he was feeling in his heart something would happen. He was always watching from the point running down to the harbour, that's the east. The boat left Lifu on Thursday; it ran down to Papua and in the afternoon it pulled out near Keppel Point and kept sailing outside for the dark comes now. That's Thursday. Friday they were still half way yet until on Saturday the man on the lookout said, 'We soon come to an island'. Man on the mast now cried out, 'Island ahead! That's Darnley! That's the place we come for!' And they come right round that sandbank and came closer on the end. That old man was looking for something and at the same time the boat was seen coming through those trees on that point on the Island where the road is now and he saw it: 'That's the boat!' Because he saw the flag. When they anchored they don't know he's up on the hill watching them. And he call out, 'Too high!' And they look at him standing there in the bush on top that hill. They make hands [gestures] calling him to come down. They went to pick him up on the beach and the pidgin English start now. (Book of Islanders 1984, B25)

Here arrived the message they had been waiting for. That is a truth which Islanders discern: the rekindling of a flame within the Islands. Among the Meriam of Mer and Dauar it is said that only one man refused to accept the new God; he died a Malo-Bomai man.

The missionaries from the 'South Seas' brought with them many customs similar to those of the Torres Islanders which made for exchange. So as Kapin says: 'The missionary was very happy to see that we had that festival for the fruit and all that and he came to learn that story when he learnt to pray in the Island way. He prayed to the *zogo*.' They exchanged so becoming like *tebud*, brothers-in-Malo. Some of the South Sea people who became *tebud* or even in-laws, were not themselves formally missionaries, like Sis' father's father, Grandfather T, the son of an LMS priest who went from Niue to Samoa. Sis says, 'That family were the kindest, most generous people. They could give away everything and not worry' (Book of Islanders 1984, B25). The lives of those 'coloured missionaries' were governed by relations of reciprocity; they were the ones accepted as *tebud* by Islanders, and they brought the meaning of the Scriptures to them: the strengthening of Moses through his father-in-law, Jethro, was easy for Islanders to understand. And Jethro came into the wilderness where Moses was encamped at the mount of God and Moses 'did obeisance and kissed him; and they asked each other of their welfare...' (Exodus, xviii, 7). Jethro said, '...I have

been an alien in a strange land...' (xviii, 3). And Moses told Jethro how the Lord
delivered them (xvii, 8). And Jethro said: 'Hearken now unto my voice... Be thou
for the people to God-ward, that thou mayest bring the causes unto God...' (xviii,
9). And so new coloured circles began to form.

In the period in which the missionaries arrived the effects of disease
had taken their toll; in some islands the populations were down to half their pre-
invasion numbers (Beckett 1963, 65). When Captain Pennefather mustered the
inhabitants of each island late in 1879 he observed a rapidly decreasing population
at Darnley Island (Report, 19 December 1879, in QSA COL/A288). The Islanders
were suffering unfamiliar afflictions: at some islands, like Darnley, they seemed
to be dying out.

The God brought by the LMS was the God of Wrath and Redemption;
of Affliction and Hope, of Sin and Salvation: the men who came were prophets
of God to a chosen people — the Islanders — exhorting them to give up their evil
ways 'by utopian promises and punishments' (Weber 1952, 296). The missionaries
spoke the language of the Islanders' own tragic experience: the language of
mediation of singular elemental forces. After the thunder and lightning the Lord
came unto Moses in a thick cloud: 'And it came to pass on the third day in the
morning, that there were thunders and lightnings, and a thick cloud upon the
mount, and the voice of the trumpet exceeding loud; so that all the people that
was in the camp trembled' (Exodus xix, 16). And standing 'afar off...they said unto
Moses, Speak thou with us, and we will hear: but let not God speak with us, lest
we die' (xx, 18-19). The signs were those with which the people were familiar:
Moses, like the *Zogo le* of the Lord, spoke to them in the language of mortals: 'I
am the Lord thy God, which have brought thee out of the land of Egypt, out of
the house of bondage. Thou shalt have no other gods before me' (xx, 2-3). In this
way the Ten Commandments came to the people of the Torres Strait.

The abyss of their destruction also contained the beginnings of a first
wave of their hope. Especially at Murray Island the people were acquiring the
new knowledge and eagerly applying new skills in boat-building, smithing, and
other trade-skills to an old life with new qualities. The Papuan Institute, as the
Rev McFarlane named it, established about 1880 at Mer which became the regional
headquarters of the LMS, was both an industrial school and a teachers' seminary
which taught the English language to young men from all over the area.[5] Kapin's
father went there: 'They had good training and many things he could do I can't
do', Kapin observes.

Before the new century arrived Islanders had given up the observable
customs the missionaries had reviled; they were quick to learn new ways; they
had suffered one 'punishment' after another; they had quickly built churches.

The language of apocalyse is both that of an ending *and* a new beginning. Perhaps they were eager for the realisation of the utopian promises. The LMS brought to them the Old Testament prophets: Isaiah, the prophet of hope, spoke the language of the isles: of the joining of heaven and earth, of being the first and the last, of turning deserts into gardens, of comfort in desolation, of truth from falsehood, of vengeance and redemption — of life in death. Island people had given up their 'evil ways': now the Lord would deliver them from bondage.

GATHERING THE HARVEST: THE ANGLICAN CHURCH

Many Islanders had their own cutters, but before the end of the century the wave of hope which followed the missionaries' arrival had receded. They were still awaiting the fulfilment of utopian promises. Observers noted Islanders' regret at the loss of ancient customs: 'The native dance still exercises a great fascination over them...', the Rev Butcher noted in 1906 (Report for 1906, LMS Correspondence). They feel a great loss at the ending of their ancient canoe voyages, Sir William MacGregor observed keenly following his visit in 1911.[6] In 1908 the Anglican Church assumed responsibility for the spiritual care of the South Sea people now separated on 'a reserve set aside for them' at Moa Island (Report of Chief Protector for 1908, QPP, 1909, 24). Reverend John Done and Rev GA Luscombe arrived in the Strait as the first two Anglican missionaries in the Island area. John Done was a man who *did* things: he built the churches *with* the people. Some of his first impressions of Islanders' responses in those first months in the Strait are of their gifts to the Lord:

> *BADU, 20 July 1915.* The welcome given by these people and their evident appreciation of our coming was very touching and one feels the great opportunity. The people are religious in every sense.
>
> *21 July 1915.* Held service in Church and had a splendid congregation. Many young men are away in the cutters on the reefs, but about 100 present. After I was told the people wished to make me a small presentation. The whole village, men, women and children came in procession singing a native song and when they reached where I was, deposited their gift on the ground in front of me. Nearly everyone had coconuts, sweet potatoes or yam or something similar and a great heap of food soon accumulated. It does make one feel humble realizing one's limitations and feeling the absolute dependence of these people. Thank God the Church was not slow to accept this responsibility for there's a wonderful harvest only waiting and willing to be gathered. At Badu I find the people quite prepared to kneel, a posture they are not accustomed to.

MURRAY, 21 September 1915. Eight cutters and luggers anchored off the island, the crews drawn there no doubt by the prospect of a wedding feast and dance.

The double wedding: I wish I could describe the dresses, they were gorgeous. The men were gaily decorated with coconut leaves and feathers and danced up and down the village afterwards. Mabuiag and Badu men danced together and then Murray Islanders had their turn.

BOIGU, 27 October 1915. The people met me singing one of the two English hymns they know. They were gaily decorated. Most of the men wore red lava lavas and nearly everyone had red hibiscus flowers in their hair. I suggested a native church with cement floor. They are anxious to get to work soon. Boigu people are anxious for a native missionary. They 'want good man work for God'. (Diary)

From Murray Island down to Boigu, Islanders were hearkening to the Word of the 'new religion'. John Done's arrival was greeted like the coming of a prophet. He sensed some of the meaning of their gifts: 'The people are religious in every sense...there's a wonderful harvest only waiting and willing to be gathered'. The people 'went over without a murmur' into the new fold, as John Bruce, the government teacher at Mer, wrote to the Bishop of Carpentaria on 10 November 1915 on the first visit of the two clergy in April that year (White 1917). Within a few years Islander priests were being ordained. Islanders at Mer were also encouraged to revive their old Malo-Bomai dances in the early 1920s. Au Bala recalls the occasion: 'Father Done from the Anglican Church said to we Meriam: "This is your dance. You go ahead." We were so glad.' The LMS missionaries had 'told the people not to perform the sacred dance of Malo-Bomai or to sing *ikok*, the five sacred chants'. The Meriam composed new *ikok*; the words of the first *ikok*, composed by the *Zogo le*, Au Bala's grandfather, was in Kala Lagaw Ya: 'Someone is mourning, crying in the house...'.[7] Au Bala wondered at it all as a young boy:

> *I remember I was really scared at first. There were still old people there and they stood together where the singers and the drummers were and they were all in tears thinking of the time when as young men they last saw the original ceremony before the missionaries arrived. As a boy I thought: 'They're crying. Why are they in tears?' without knowing the deep meaning of it. My grandfather was there too. They must think of the time when they used to go to the original ceremony.* (Cassette 133/AB/TI/1/84)

The Malo ceremonies, last performed in 1898, had been witnessed by the Cambridge anthropological team; the masks of Malo and Bomai were made of cardboard (Haddon 1908, 306). The 'real Malo [mask]' was buried somewhere in the village of Las. 'But where was Bomai? That was the question; and they didn't tell us because everything of Malo-Bomai was in secret.' There were five *ikok* of Malo, and the fifth one for *seuriseuri* has lots of meanings: 'It is not only the emblem, but also the life that is handed down from the previous generation to the present one' (Au Bala, Cassette 133/AB/TI/1/84).

Most Islanders became members of the Anglican Church; they did not talk freely to outsiders about the beliefs and practices of their forebears concerning magic and religion. There were other churches centred at Thursday Island, but the Anglican Church was firmly established among Islanders.[8] As an institution it moved in step and in tune with the Administration. Only in the 1960s did an 'Island Ministry' as it was called, even begin to take shape. As individuals, some white priests and lay missionaries acted as go-between with the Protectors on behalf of Islanders. The Councillors' pay of 'two sticks of tobacco and uniform' is 'ridiculous', John Done told the Protectors in 1921; the teacher at Mabuiag is an 'obstructionist', he recorded (Diary). Inside the Anglican fold a 'coloured mission' soon began to grow: it consisted of a few priests, more deacons, many church wardens, mission teachers and workers. Sis' parents were foundation mission workers at Lockhart River Mission, Cape York Peninsula; Auntie followed as a teacher. The Anglican Diocese's periodical, *The Carpentarian*, contained pages and pages on the activities of the white missionaries; only an occasional sentence referred to the work of the three Islanders (see 1933). The Church contained two networks; the 'coloured circles' were almost invisible from the 'outside'. From the standpoint of Islanders that circle helped them to interpret and come to terms with the paradoxes of their experience of Christianity. In the name of God and the Gospels missionaries had come to destroy Islanders' most sacred institutions. In Kebi Bala's words, the mission-boat *Surprise* also brought 'the most precious, the most valuable gift ever to be given to the people of the Torres Strait'. The following discussion explores the meanings of that 'Gift'. It begins with the life of Kebi Bala who is from a stem of the *Zogo le*: he is Au Bala's younger brother. He is also a priest ordained in the Anglican Church. In his great grandfather's time only the eldest brother in the most sacred lines of the three *Zogo le* became *Aet* or 'priest' of Malo.

THE CROSS AS DIVINE POWER

TETER MEK, *FOOTPRINTS: KEBI BALA, JESUS CHRIST IS THE FULFILMENT OF MALO*

The zogo and the call somehow came together

> In Christianity you have to be called. I felt I was called. I was about
> twelve or thirteen years old. I had a dream of a native hut with a mat,

pillow, blanket. I slept on the mat, the door opened and I saw Jesus coming in in a long white robe; lovely golden hair, carrying the Cup, the chalice, full of wine. He was not carrying bread. He came and stood just near my head. I got up; this is the only dream that I've had in which the house looked the same. So I think it was a vision. So I knelt down and He gave me the Cup to drink. From then on I realised that I was being called to the priesthood.

But that zogo, that 'zogoness' was inbuilt in me and after the call had come, these two somehow came together and it brought about the richness which I am very thankful about. The call was a personal thing. What was inbuilt and what Malo had prepared for is being fulfilled in what I'm doing. And as I grew older I became more aware of the call. It was tested by other people who were saying that I should become a priest. I went to [Second] Meriam Man's mother and she said: 'When are you going to be a priest?' People were seeing the priesthood in me. She knew somehow. And uncle P because he was a prophet as well as a priest he knew that I would become a priest. He just left everything, sacred vessels and garments to me.

I was saying, 'Not yet Lord, not yet; give me more time'

I was working on that boat for two years and I was just thinking about it. I was saying like St Augustine, 'Not yet Lord, not yet Lord. Give me more time. When I'm ready I'll come', until one day I said, 'Well I won't go on saying "not yet" any more to the Lord. I better do it.' I went to the College at St Paul's. We began the course called ThA, Associate in Theology. It dropped during the War and after the War it started again. I didn't complete it because I was tired of six years in college. It was too much. Somehow that got through to Bishop Mathews and he came to our rescue and ordained us and so we completed the ThA. Then I went to Morpeth College to study and did part of a ThL, a licentiate in theology. Then I got a letter from Bishop Hawkey asking if I would become an acting Priest-Director whose job was to decide the direction of the Church's work in the Torres Strait. I accepted it because I felt it was a challenge.

My father said, 'The Anglican Church is the fulfilment of Malo'

You've got to be called by God to be a priest and when I became a priest I became aware of the zogo that was in me. I think it's inbuilt, yes. This awareness became more valuable and more important to me as my priestly life and understanding developed. This idea of the holiness and sacredness — the zogo — developed. I came to compare Malo more with Christianity. Also as I grew up I heard more, the tradition was passed on more to me. I understood the two more and compared them because my grandfather compared them. Not only him but other old people have said that, even my father said: 'Not LMS, but the Anglican Church, is the fulfilment of Malo'. I value this very much.

LMS did not impress the people. They learned about the
true God, yes, but when the Anglican Church took over some years
later, my grandfather, with many others, said: 'Here is something of
the complexity, the mystery that Malo expressed'. You see the high
priests in the Malo dance, they carry seuriseuri. In passing forward
the seuriseuri from one dancer to the next, the symbol is that the
authority of Malo must continue. It wasn't dropped. It has to be taken
by the next person. So the heritage was passed on all the time. It was
like the Apostolic Succession, but it was more hereditarily grounded,
you know. That was the difference. Nobody was allowed to become a
priest on his own. He was chosen by Malo through the head people,
the Zogo le.

Jesus Christ is where Malo was pointing

It's interesting because their failure shows the greatness of Malo. I'm
seeing it this way: Malo came to prepare the world for a bigger truth.
Jesus Christ is where Malo was pointing. The truth is not easy to cross
out as every Christian understands. Jesus came not to destroy but to
fulfil. The zogo of everything, the words, the actions, the zogo was
passing on to us. In our worship there are words in the form of sacred
songs; the words are important and nobody ran through them. They've
got to be sung with all reverence, sung properly to the best of man's
ability. I do not see me infusing Malo into Christianity. I see
Christianity as the fulfilment of Malo. Malo came to prepare Murray
Island for Christianity and it makes me very proud as a Zogo le to
see Malo playing that role.

You see Malo and Christianity go together. See the idea of
reverence I was talking about. It is there. The reverence must remain
there. This is the first important thing that God demands from man:
reverence. You must show it, you can't escape it. I don't see fusion.
I see comparison. The differences are that Malo was touched, but there
was that mystery about it, transcendence about it. All these things
are the sacredness about it, which is similar. If you look at what Philip
said to Jesus, 'Show me the Father'. 'If you want to know the Father,
do His will.' So it's not the saying, it's the doing. Malo is concerned
with people. Malo exists because of people. It governs people; it tells
people to work hard to support themselves. It teaches people to respect
themselves, their rights, what they possess. So it is more personal. It
exists for the sake of people.

Well, I see the value of the corporate mind. This is how Malo
expressed it and if there is an individual consciousness, the value,
the wisdom, the importance of the corporate mind still remain. You
can't escape it and if you are a priest your faith has got to be with
the whole. I see Christianity as an extension of what came before, but
it must continue to relate to this basic truth. Our leaders worked. And
so today when our people work I work with them. My priesthood means

I have to become a servant. Yes, well today I must work with my hands because of my background. It could be building, putting stalls up. I'm there too. If they work, I work. Sometimes they don't work; I work. My heart goes with it.

I talked about fulfilment. There are these rituals. Say for instance at the Solemn High Mass, when a bishop is wearing a cope there are those two tapes at the back of the mitre. When our people saw this they said, 'There is olai, the turtle'. Yes. 'There is olai [softly].' We see the two tapes as emes, one of the masks of the three Zogo le. Of course it has more meaning. I don't know whether my grandfather saw that but we did. I saw it as a young boy and many others did too.

At the worship the reverence is important. It's not that free worship that I don't like. I accept the formal reverence because I come from Zogo le. All right, there is a fulfilment now. In the High Mass the sub-deacon holds the end of the chasuble the celebrant is wearing and walks at the back: there is emes le. There's a fulfilment of the ritual — emes. Or if a priest is wearing a cope with two servers holding the end of it, this is emes.

At initiation the Zogo le, the priest, would come, stretch the legs three times over the candidates. Malo's power or blessing goes through the priest over the candidates. That's the initiation ceremony. But the ritual is there. It was not just done by the invoking of Malo. It was done as ritual and man is the intermediary. The priest is the one where the power goes through to the candidate. The idea is that in the Christian Church, Anglican Church, Jesus is the High Priest.

So I compared the values in the Light

I think it came very strongly when I made an address for July First in 1976. I'd become more proud of my culture, proud of what I'd inherited and I think that brought about values of what I had before; from Malo. So I compared them and to me Christianity came out of the Administration and all that kills; like a dinosaur: you destroy one only to build another. The only thing is the Light. We can see other things in the Light. We can interpret them in the Light of what Christ is saying:[9]

'I have chosen as our text for today, July First 1983, the day of absolutely great significance for the Torres Strait, John xii, 46 and x, 10. A hundred and twelve years ago today the ship called the Surprise *anchored at Darnley Island carrying on board the most precious, the most valuable gift ever to be given to the people of the Torres Strait. And we call it "the Light". It is in the Light of Jesus, the true Light of the world that he, the Islander, is able to see himself as he really is, his whole identity, his complete self in union with his Lord and Master, Jesus Christ. In this union with his Master and in the Light, the Light of Christ Himself, he discovers not only the completeness of his being and his identity, but he also discovers the*

true purpose of his existence and life in its abundance. He is able to distinguish between the thief that comes to steal, to kill and to destroy and the true representatives of Christ the Light of the World.'

We can have a unity yet retain diversity in that unity

My dreams are to see this, an Island Church, offering what is Island to God; not being cut off from the mainstream. It is this identity thing again. But it is being yourself, living your own life, offering what you have to God. The mainstream has been mainly European and some people talk about a sort of global village where everybody would know everything. But there's got to be some mysteries, some place to know mysteries. We can have a unity, yet retain diversity in that unity. That is the diversity which St Paul talks about: 'Now this I say, that everyone as you saith, I am of Paul; and I of Apollos; and I of Cephas; and I of Christ.' This is behind my mind all the time. It's the richness in all its diversity.

When I look to originality I look at the Gospel and my own background because Malo prepared me. And then I look at the development of what Christ meant. It's being able to appreciate 'the other'. The word 'black' in 'black theology' is an expression of the European mind. We may retain the variety of the Torres Strait Island Church, the Papua New Guinea Church, Solomon Island Church. There is variety and yet we are one. There has to be variety. With the Island Church, more and more people will see what was hidden before. People who come here from other places see it now and it is unique.

Because the Anglican Church is predominantly European to become one church often meant for we Islanders to be simply absorbed into an existing structure. Within our Island custom we retain the personality of each one of us. So unity means the yumi, *which is beautiful.* (Book of Islanders 1984, B122–29, B131)

DIVINE POWER

Islanders *lived* the paradoxes of life. They knew that '*All things are contradictory in themselves*' as 'the truth and essence of things' (Hegel, *Science of Logic*, 1929, 68, as quoted in Marcuse 1977, 147). Their lives moved within a rhythm in which the new sprouted forth from the old; they were aware that in the smooth lay the whirlpool, in the sudden calm lay the eye of the storm. From the entwined crossed-strands of resolved paradox there came life's meanings: its purpose the search for the hidden truth within the paradox. This was the realm of 'encounters of man with more than man', the powers which go beyond those rhythms which denote the orderliness of nature's cycles to the 'supernatural', the spirit, which is coeval with the 'normal'.

Zogo is like the Divine 'Wrath' of the old Testament, the Wrath of Yahweh. That was the divine Power brought by the LMS. Like a hidden force of nature, that Wrath may strike the wrongdoer who would profane God's 'otherness' by looking across the Divide. Mediating that 'otherness' is the role of the prophet: 'And the Lord said unto Moses, go down, charge the people, lest they break through unto the Lord to gaze, and many of them perish' (Exodus xix, 21). 'And let the priests also, which come near to the Lord, sanctify themselves, lest the Lord break forth upon them' (Exodus xx, 22).

The Cross was like *seuriseuri*: it joined together the circles of life. It meant also the 'answer' to the quest in a spiral of quests which led to the 'Other'. For Islander people it was the numinous arc to which their eyes were raised: the revelation of the mystery that lies upon the 'Other side'. In the 'mysterious act — the manifestation of something of a wholly different order, a reality that does not belong to our world', lies the revelation of the sacred (Eliade 1959b, 11; see also Otto 1936, 29).

In Christianity there is the message of 'before' in its fullness: in the 'holiest' moment of His Presence, *Opolera Wetpur*, the Lord's Feast, the moment of the most numinous is near. That is *Zogo* at the moment of supreme reversal. Kebi Bala speaks of the quality of mystery in the sacred rites of Malo; of total reverence in wearing the mask. His grandfather looked for that total reverence and sought to behold Him in the height of grandeur. This is the quality found in the sixth chapter of Isaiah: six wings of the seraphims covered the Lord who cried unto one another, 'Holy, holy, holy, is the Lord of hosts...' (vi, 3; see also Otto 1936, 65, 63 and 192, on the essence of the Divine in a passage from the Bhagavad Gita).

Along this same path moved the most sacred moments of *opole* of Malo. In *Opolera Wetpur*, the Eucharist, the ineffable truth of *Zogo, Zogo, Zogo*, is the moment of stillness where one draws near to revere and thence to 'know': there is reserved for this moment the 'absolute cessation of sound long enough for us to "hear the Silence" itself' (Otto 1936, 72). That 'Silence' valorises a deeper meaning of the numinous: it is like the universalisation of the *Zogo*. Through an All-Mighty God *teter mek* means we may all follow in the footprints; it also means we may *all* become 'like brothers' through His *Zogo*. Through Jesus Christ, who entered into history and was born and lived as a man the 'people-line' goes on. Through the mediation of the Son, we may all become brothers and sisters in Christ, like *tebud le*, and so the themes of 'God's People-line' and brotherhood and sisterhood are continued and placed within a universal frame. Through Malo *wauri tebud* became even closer than blood *tebud*. Those of a different origin, that is, of a different filiation, came to be as 'brothers in Malo'. The message of Christianity goes beyond this. Through God's People-line there is a common filiation which

Jesus, the Son, as Mediator makes possible. This now is universal, extending even to the four directions of cosmic space. Through Christ there is reconciliation to God through the ministry of reconciliation. But in the words of St Paul that coming together, that possibility of embracing all through Faith and Love, does not wipe out their opposites: it holds them in association to a 'higher' purpose. In the passages which follow St Paul is speaking the very same language as the Islanders: mediation through Christ does not mean the stamping out of evil and affliction. It means that truth may triumph or subordinate evil in a new synthesis: 'By the word of truth, by the power of God, by the armour of righteousness on the right hand and on the left, By honour and dishonour, by evil report and good report: as deceivers, and yet true; As unknown, and yet well known; as dying, and, behold, we live; as chastened, and not killed; As sorrowful, yet always rejoicing; as poor, yet making many rich; as having nothing, and yet possessing all things' (II Corinthians vi, 7–10). This is reciprocal language, not the language of linearity. Through the victory of Life over Death the people's heart is strengthened: 'O ye Corinthians, our mouth is open unto you, our heart is enlarged' (II Corinthians vii, 11).

Malo-Bomai was like the Old Testament: Do this, don't do that. It was a guide to learning something else; it was 'a good teaching leading up to the real religion', Sis' father explained to her. It gave people the chance to recognise the full truth when it did come: upon it rose the spire that reached up to Heaven. In Christianity Islanders saw equivalences: 'There is *olai*'. They recognised a continuity in God's 'people-line' of sacred authority. They saw fulfilment and re-creation in the universality of Divine Power. That fulfilment lay in the experience of a new transcendence; at the same time it gave the possibility of a way of living which might transcend the old boundaries: there was a new injunction to take the Message to the 'other side'. The spring of that 'new *wauri*', as I called it in the last chapter, was there already in Malo ra Gelar; Christianity turned it into a possibility and an imperative by metamorphoses of a stronger kind than had ever existed before, so creating a message of a qualitatively new type: '...all things whatsoever ye would that men should do to you, do ye even so to them...' (Matthew vii, 12; see also Luke vi, 31; x, 27, 30–36). Love everyone, even those on the 'other side'. The people on the 'other side' of the Strait signified danger to the profane. They were part of the death-dealing power of *Em*: through Christ as the Exemplar of a way to live, earth-born mortals are joined back to the heaven-born form in the Resurrection. The power of *beizam, sasrim a kelar,* the power that comes from strength, had been given to the Shark brethren of the Meriam through the journey of Bomai who came to embody the diverse qualities of whale at this place, of dugong at that place, and so on, as he travelled eastwards from the 'other side'.

In this manner Bomai brought the gift of the strongest power the people knew; through it they might begin to transcend the profane danger of the 'other side'. The *zogo* of Bomai was a power so strong that ordinary mortals did not even know the true name of Bomai; only the initiated, 'those who know', might gaze for an instant in sacred space and time at Bomai whose name remained unutterable. In God the Almighty Power, *Au Sasrimsasrim*, are all the diverse qualities. As Kebi Bala repeats the words of St Paul: '...I am of Paul; and I of Apollos; and I of Cephas; and I of Christ'. In Him are all the opposites: that is the possibility of the All-One. This is the first meaning of the Gift of 'the Light'. So Kebi Bala's grandfather revered Him in the manner of a *Zogo le*: like the angels he fell prostrate before His Presence.

REJOINING THE CIRCLES OF LIFE

MORTALS AND IMMORTALS, MATCHING HALVES: SIS, IT'S PART OF OUR CULTURE, THAT SHARING

When the people of the Torres Strait 'went over without a murmur' into the Anglican fold coming to be baptised and confirmed, they also buried the dead according to Anglican burial rites. In the days before the LMS missionaries arrived the body of a dead person was placed upon a platform known as *paier* (Eastern Islands) or *sara* (Western Islands). That was the beginning of two-stage funerary rites. The missionaries put a stop to those rites: the dead were buried in cemeteries made on each island. As the missionaries saw it, the past had ended.

In the early 1930s a custom sprang up which came to be known as 'making a tombstone', with special rites associated with its unveiling. After the person has been buried preparations are begun for the making of a tombstone and after a year or more it is unveiled. The new custom just grew unannounced: 'Who sowed the seed of that custom, who knew it first, no one knows', as Au Bala says. In explaining the two-stage process of burial and tombstone unveiling as it exists today Sis implies its deep cultural origins: 'I think that it goes back to anything they had they shared and when they came to build a tombstone they just did it the way that they felt it should be'.

> *The scene is a woman's death at Thursday Island. We have just visited the family who belong to one of the Western Islands and paid our respects.*

Time of death

> *There's the head* mariget [literally spirit-hand, KLY]. *He's the oldest of the brothers-in-law and he looks after things. When you bring your*

gifts you give them to him. That's the proper custom. You don't involve the mourners in any way. Not that the mariget *don't mourn too. But they're the ones that do the work. He'll say, 'Go to that sister. Go to that aunt.' And you go and you cry with that aunt. She receives you then. She just sits there and you go and cry there with her. There's people to receive you. They're* mariget. *They make sure there's enough mats or chairs. They look after everything and they bury the person. The brothers and sisters of the person don't handle the body at all. The* mariget *bury the person. The head* mariget *will stand up after they've buried the person and he'll say: 'The family invites everybody back for* kaikai, *for feast'. There's no music. You just sit down and eat.*

This feasting belongs to you: the tombstone

After twelve months or so, it's the mariget's *place to make the tombstone. When it's being made we let everybody know. Then they send in money. All right, then, they'll come in* [from other islands]. *The tombstone's made and paid for. Then the feasting. That's the time now the family themselves, not the* mariget, *but the whole family that sat and mourned, decorate and wrap the tombstone up. That's all their expense now. They do it with their own hands and the* mariget *don't touch it because that's a different type of thing now. They did all that mourning part. Now this is the happy part, the joyous part. The family will put all those gifts on the tombstone. Those gifts come from other relations. Gifts come from all over the place, from relations and friends and everybody. Then they give money too and they buy some more gifts to put on the tombstone. In the old days they used to pin money on to the material that covered the tombstone.*

All the gifts belong to the mariget: *they're from the family. All the gifts — those in there around and on the tombstone are to be shared by the* mariget. *The family cut the ribbon* [which is tied round the tombstone area] *and they go inside* [the area]. *Say if Ailan Man's mother died, well he is the head one now. He replaces the head* mariget. *He replaces his brother-in-law and he's the one who heads this feasting. Now there'll be somebody to talk. In the early days it was the oldest man in the village. He's the one to talk and he stands up and gives the life story of the person who died and people listen.*

Well that old man will tell how he was when he was a little boy. He can even go to the night he was born. It's a happy time. They laugh; that's better. It gives you a picture of that person when he grew up. Then all of those things there are shared: all the gifts to the mariget. *That's a thank-you for how they worked during that person's passing away. We invite them to the house now. The head of the family will thank the* mariget *publicly in front of everybody for all the good work and the comfort that they have given the family and what good brothers and people that they have married. You know, they say nice things about them because this is their day, the* mariget's. *And then he* [the head of the family] *says to them — he looks at the head* mariget *— he says to them, 'Now this feasting is yours'; and the head* mariget *is to take the head of the table. 'This feasting belongs to you. Thank you very much for your help.'*

And the head mariget *then talks. His speech is very short. He says thanks to his brother-in-law. And he says to everybody else: 'Come, we want to share this with all our family and all our friends.' So he is the one who invites the other people to sit at the table. That's the proper custom of the tombstone. It's sharing: the family sharing with the* mariget *and the* mariget *sharing with their friends. The head of family calls them together and they all sit down and eat. But it is the family who do the cooking not the* mariget *any more.* (Book of Islanders 1984, B159–61)

FROM DEATH TO RESURRECTION: THE CIRCLES REJOINED

The ghost of the newly-departed wanders 'like an errant soul' (Goody 1962, 371) without a homeplace on which to rest: it is non-reciprocal. Existing as singular it is dangerous to kinsfolk and other mortals alike. It is the shadow or 'double' of a person and his undying spirit: it is known as *mari* (KLY) and *mar* (MM). The metamorphosis of *mari* to *markai* (KLY), of *mar* to *lamar* (MM), ghost to immortal, is mediated by in-laws.[10] In the Western Islands (in former times) the body was placed on a roofed platform (*sara*) by the *mariget*, the name given to in-laws during mortuary rites, who stood guard over it: at this time the 'wild spirit' is most vindictive and dangerous (see Goody 1962, 21; Beckett 1975, 180). After a time when the mortal remains were joined with their home-place the *mari* was ready to be reborn. Funerary rites performed by the *mariget* mediated that rebirth: the *markai* in the Land of the Dead had now become reciprocal with kin (see Haddon 1904, 90; Beckett 1975, 166–67).

This process exemplifies a more or less universal custom among so-called 'primitive' peoples, in which burial and funerary rites take place in two stages. It was observed by Lafitau in 1724. Two hundred years later Hertz attempted to explain its meaning and significance. Death is linked with resurrection, so it is both the end of life and the beginning of a new existence in another world; exclusion from the terrestrial world 'is always followed by a new integration' (1960, 79). The 'double funeral', as Hertz terms it, effects this transformation. A 'provisional ceremony' rejects and disposes of the body, 'while the soul is separated from the mortal remains' (Goody 1962, 26). This is the mourning period of the bereaved, the *periode de marge*, as van Gennep termed it, the period of waiting before the 'definitive ceremony', the second half of 'the final and most dramatic rite of passage in the life cycle' in which the soul joins its forebears in the Land of the Dead (Goody 1962, 28).

The immortal is an 'ancestor', Goody writes of the Lodagaa of West Africa who 'continues to hold certain general rights in the worldly property of his descent group' (Goody 1962, 371). In the definitive rite of passage, in-laws act as *mariget*, or intercessors between the circle of mortals and the circle of immortals. In the process of crossing over to another plane of 'life' immortals become like reversals of 'us'; they are the other halves. Mortal and immortal are symmetrical and opposite. Our skins are black; theirs are the colour of white clay. We are visible; they are invisible. We to them are like day is to night, like the two halves of a single circle: we are the half that came after; they are the half that came before. We are complementary: 'your dusk is my dawn...', comes the voice of the ancestor within the spirit of a bird (Narokobi 1981, 5).

Like light and shade, like person and shadow, they go together reciprocally. As the processes which resolve the contradiction of life, that of physical death, are completed, we, the mortals, placate them, our other halves, by offering gifts. The contradiction between the singularity of the earth-born dead and the living kin is resolved in a new synthesis: the creation of a reciprocal unity between mortal and immortal. So the second phase of the definitive ceremony is 'the happy time'; people laugh and joke: in the new synthesis the two circles are strengthened through exchange of gifts.

When the missionaries forced the Islanders to bury their dead in places marked out they did not know of the cruel wounds they were inflicting. Making a tombstone as a new rite arose almost unnoticed. Au Bala's first memory of its existence is about 1933, a year or so after he went westward to teach at Poid. Who sowed its seed, who knew of it first no one knows; Islanders just did it the way they felt it should be; it was not a conscious act. It was a sign of cultural healing; in the silent spring of the victory of life it was a resurrection. In knotting together the circles of reciprocity on the two different planes it made for social cohesion and resilience. The body social of the Islands had been like a person trying to walk on only one leg. The reciprocal halves were coming together in the complementarity of dissimilarity in the 1930s, just when singular powers were approaching in their full strength.

The sharing of giving and returning *is* social life; it is taken for granted. As Sis recalls, Ailan Man struck that chord at a tombstone unveiling at Thursday Island at the end of 1980: 'It's not a day of wealth or anything, but it's part of our culture, that sharing part'. In the circles of gifts of 'calico' and 'coins', of acts of kindness given and returned, the group sees itself re-formed. In the cutting of the ribbon the soul is freed to Paradise, the Land of Immortals. The human circles and the cosmic circles have come together. The 'unveiling' is a moment of the transcendence of crossing over, a foliating event of primordial meaning: it is the triumph of the plural over the singular power of *Em*.

COSMIC RENEWAL: PATHS TO THE ALL-ONE

THE COMING OF THE MILLENNIUM: GERMAN WISLIN

At Saibai Island in the northwest of the Torres Strait 'a popular movement' heralding the millennium came into being around 1913.[11] Three leaders who were known as 'German Wislin' (Wislun, even Wesleyan), commanded all the men of the Island to be present in the cemetery on Good Friday evening, 1914, to pray and sing before the graves of two men. Failure to attend, the Islanders were told, might bring down wrath of God or the *markai*, the name of the ancestral immortals in Kala Lagaw Ya (Chinnery and Haddon 1917, 460). The German Wislin prophesied to the people that the *markai*, who would appear that night, would return very soon on a steamer named *Silūbloan*, bringing money, flour, calico, tomahawks, knives and other goods of European origin for all those who accepted the new religion. According to German Wislin, in the beginning all men were created equal and God had given all things to black and white people alike, but the latter had stolen certain goods. God was conceived as working His will through the ancestors or *markai*. Through them, God would restore to the Saibai Islanders their rightful share of His gifts (Worsley 1970, 106). They were told to cease working in preparation for the arrival of the *markai* who would embark on the steamer at 'German town' in the far west calling first at Thursday Island where they would fight and kill the white men after which the steamer would proceed to Saibai coming alongside a jetty that would mysteriously appear at the western end of the island (Haddon 1917, 461; Beckett 1975, 167). Thus the mortals and the *markai* would be reunited in a terrestrial paradise.

Similar millenarian prophecies of a Golden Age had been noted in Melanesia by outsiders as early as 1867 when a herald of the mythical hero Manseren proclaimed that the spirits of the ancestors of the Biak–Manokwari people of Dutch-ruled West New Guinea would return bringing them gifts in a new era where the old would become young and the sick would be healed (Worsley 1970, 136–41; de Bruijn 1951, 1–10).

While millennial movements had sprung up in widely dispersed Melanesian communities, Worsley has noted that German Wislin was the first such movement in which European manufactured goods constituted the 'Cargo' of gifts to be brought by the ancestral spirits, a 'notion that was to become so important and widespread in decades to come...' (1970, 104). Haddon saw a resemblance between German Wislin and a prophet cult which had arisen in the Milne Bay district of New Guinea in 1893 led by a young man named Tokerua (also Tokeriu), who had prophesied a mighty storm which would submerge the whole coast with a tremendous tidal wave. Believers, who must abandon all goods of European origin and stop tending their gardens, would be saved from the cataclysm and would be reunited with their immortal ancestors who would return aboard a ship heralding a time of fair weather and the covering of the land with yams and taro and trees laden with fruit (Chinnery and Haddon 1917, 458–60; Worsley 1970, 61–64).

The reasons for the differences in the character of the gifts with which the ancestors would return relate to differences in recent historical experiences. The Saibai Islanders were not only 'surrounded' by 'Cargo'; they had new wants and they had been imbued with new hopes, yet they had been denied the possibility of their realisation. They were very familiar with manufactured goods, yet they lacked the opportunity to know their origin. Soon after the missionaries arrived they had dived for *mai* to provide gifts for the Lord; in the 1890s they had quickly and unaided built a church to the Almighty One; they had responded to exhortation and given up their 'evil ways', but they still awaited the utopian promises; they had absorbed the Christian message that God created all people equal which corresponded with their code of reciprocal giving and receiving, yet they saw duplicity in the actions of white men.

The belief that the ancestral spirits would one day return with gifts from the land of the dead was present elsewhere in the Islands, yet only in Saibai did a millenarian cult appear. The reason for this may be sought in the uneven impact of the missionaries, the pearl shell industry, Kole rule in different parts of the Torres Strait, and variations in cultural response. The experience of the Meriam of the Murray Islands and the other Eastern Islands since the mid-nineteeth century provides a sharp contrast with Saibai. There the people had access to the new knowledge system as early as the 1870s through the teachers' training institute and industrial school of the LMS, which taught all kinds of practical skills, and through the government school begun in 1892 and staffed by John Bruce; they had been integrated into the life of a wider world through South Sea men who had come up from Sydney like Sis' grandfather; some Islanders had worked down south like Meriam Man; they were familiar with basic book-keeping; they knew the terms of the industrial society and some of them had taken its measure. The making of the 'Cargo' had long been no secret to them.[12]

The Saibai people, who had none of those opportunities, remained unaware of the character of manufacture and commerce; they had accepted the missionaries' message of an All-Father and Christ as Redeemer; and over a time they had experienced white men as their self-appointed masters. The message of German Wislin, the three 'captains' or 'generals', was that the One God was working His Will through the *markai* who would drive out the thieves, return the stolen gifts to their Islander owners, bring about a reunion of mortals and immortals so restoring cosmic unity in the joining of the All-Ways. The contradictory experiences of Saibai Islanders were brought into relationship with an original theme of ancient myth in a new synthesis of fulfilment. German Wislin was a popular movement which suddenly brought Saibai Islanders together for a time; it was also a 'religion of the oppressed'.[13]

PARADISE REGAINED: A THEOLOGY OF COSMIC RENEWAL

Elsewhere in the Islands the paths to the All-One of cosmic renewal took a different form. That Kapin's synthesis of the message of 'the Light' was theological in character is quite consistent with the social milieu of the Eastern Islands in which he grew up and with his own personal history.

He came from strong *zogo* stems on both sides and both his parents had great hopes for their one boy born in 1902 who loved school, who sat year after year reading books from the school library by the firelight inside the family's coconut-leaf hut. He was a child whom teachers call 'gifted' and in the six years between 1908 and 1914 he listened to every word of the government teachers, Mrs Smallwood and Mr Guillemot. Soon after he left school at Darnley Island he found his way to St Paul's Mission at Moa Island, accompanying Rev Done on his missionary visits to the various islands as Sunday School teacher (Diary). Kapin was one of the new fruits the Anglican Church began to harvest: 'First let me hear how the children stood round His knee...'. That's what 'He preached for all the world... He called it universal...' Kapin came to inquire into the nature of things and discern the connections hidden within them:

> *You belong to Christ. He made them like one people when they were different to one another. The two are now brothers through this religion belong to* yumi. *That's the thing He preached out for all the world: the Church we got now, He called it universal, the hope of the world here now.*
>
> *From east to west we want men to learn that we were given our land and never sold it. God gave it to us. By and by I announce it. This sovereignty God has Himself because He won the fight belonging to Easter.* Em i singaut [Jesus announced]: *'All power is given unto Me in Heaven and Earth. Go and teach all nations and tell themfeller only one God rules.' That man that been upon the Cross, He stood up: 'Today you'll be in Paradise. You come along with me.* Yumi go.' *Now*

I think that's the Paradise that Milton sat down and wrote about:
Paradise Regained. *You savvy John Milton? The Lord got up from the
grave: 'I go to prepare a place for you. I will come again and receive
you unto Myself.' That's the man who will save our souls, even if we're
blown to pieces by them bombs they're making. They don't understand
that God will protect His own. God rules! He didn't make a place for
thieves to come and take all that land. He'll do something to stop them.*

    *The land doesn't belong to anybody. It belongs to God to
help one another with. Any Christian can see well he's only looking
after the land belonging to God. He is giving it to me and you only
for a time. That law belongs to Christianity. Same as Malo. They're
good laws. God gave us this land. We got our people here and those
others come with the sword and make themselves boss. 'You can't make
yourself become boss over them fellers. You no got permission. We're
the original people!' We don't trust anybody from outside. They got
another law. You can't make* wauri tebud *with any of them. But other
Islanders and Aborigines round the coast they know us. They're all
one coloured people. Cape York people come from Marilag;* mari *means
spirit-people,* lag *is land [KLY]. So that's the land belonging to spirit-
people.* (Book of Islanders 1984, B29–30)

Islanders' interpretation of the meaning of Christian burial laid the
foundation of a new practice: the making of a tombstone. The circles of reciprocal
giving and receiving between mortals and immortals 'broken' by the missionaries
were rejoined. This is a first stage. Christianity also gave a possibility of a second
stage of completion: the path to the All-One. The vision of a new path which joined
the All-Ways was prophesied in millenarian form by German Wislin; in Kapin's
awareness it finds theological expression. In the message of Easter and the news
of a Second Coming, there is a completion of the cosmic order which promises
to bring the two planes of being together; in doing so there is a restoration of the
place of each person within the cosmos. In the valorisation of cosmic order and
therefore the circles on different planes God as Sovereign reaffirms more strongly
than ever through the fullest power of the ultimate reversal, the position of the
'landowner', the person who 'goes with' that place. For Kapin Paradise Regained
is a completion of the Eternal Return. 'I go to prepare a place for you. I will come
again and receive you...' This is neither a going nor a coming; it is both. It is the
new being and the possibility of the new becoming. The re-creation of primordial
time is not a return to the beginning of 'before'. The moment of the All-One, a
'paradise regained', is a terrestrial paradise; it is also a celestial one.

    In the cosmic scheme of things we belong to 'this' *ged* or place, just
as we belong to different *kerker,* or seasonal time. From this first attachment to
our *ged kar,* or real homeland, our place in the cosmic scheme of things is given.

We 'accompany' or 'go with' a particular *ged* thereby excluding others: they belong to another ground and have another place in the cosmic order. Malo had brought into one the *agud*, or gods, who represented different *lu kem le* or 'landowners': the many in the one so created was justification of that state of affairs. In Kapin's understanding, Jesus Christ as Son means we belong to one God who has universal sovereignty: in the universal God there is a new filiation. That God is then the valorisation of the system of 'ownership' of the land; this leads Kapin to elaborate further on the landowner and Christ as the protean seed of many generations until today. So God as the All-Father upholds the possession of the land in a way which wasn't possible before when there were many gods of 'this' people and 'that' people. In this manner a new synthesis is created. The meaning of the One God is a reaffirmation of cosmic positioning and therefore of Islanders' right to their islands. At the level of social relations this means the eviction of white men: God 'didn't make a place for thieves to come and take all that land'. God is on 'our' side; He will help 'us' because this is a cause given by Him. This is the meaning of the 'original people'. When Au Bala says firmly, 'This place is my *ged kar*, my real land', he can say it now with absolute certainty because the universal message of Christianity reaffirms that relationship to *ged kar*. The actions of trespassing and dispossession by Kole went far deeper than cutting across 'ownership' of land by Islanders. By refusing reciprocal relations, viz in refusing to 'share' their knowledge and the 'gifts' they brought with them, they were upsetting the cosmic order. By taking land they were dispossessing people of their place within the cosmos. God's 'people-line' does not refer only to the succession of sacred people: it is like a 'divine right' of original people owning the land. The head of each family 'puts the family together', as Au Bala says about himself; for the 'landowner' is the link between the *le* and the ancestors whose land he holds in trust to share among the living and those who will come after.

THE AWARENESS OF ORIGINALITY, THE ORIGINALITY OF AWARENESS

Kebi Bala's experiences of going south to Morpeth College on the mainland, of returning again to the Islands, of going 'outside' once more to become Dean of Rockhampton Cathedral, helped to create in him a way of looking 'inside' and coming to know what is 'Island' and of himself as an Islander, so coming to see 'what is Island' as 'a unique thing'. Only by seeing its relation with others could he become aware of the identity of the Islands, for without such a relation it does not have an existence (see Marcuse 1977, 124). For Kebi Bala 'compare' does not mean to look for the common properties of this and that, which is the hallmark of positivist consciousness; it means 'compare' and 'contrast', which is the dialectical imagination. It is the process in which knowing the 'other side' is the condition for beginning to know 'this side'; it is so seeing 'this side' afresh that it becomes possible to see the 'other side' more deeply and so on. The 'me' and the 'we' continue to remain bound to their opposites: 'our' Malo *wali aritarit* in contrast with 'their' custom. In the complex interrelationships of the light and shade of 'this' and 'that', patterns of relations are revealed.

In 'the Light' Kebi Bala came to distinguish between the thief who comes to steal, to kill and to destroy and 'the true representatives of Christ...'. So Kebi Bala compared the tradition of Malo and Christianity in 'the Light'. In that process of reciprocal comparison and contrast Islanders could begin to answer the question as a people and as individuals: Who am I? In this manner Kebi Bala came to recognise 'the greatness of Malo' in preparing Murray Island for Christianity; in doing so he came to identify as a '*Zogo le* of the Lord'. His 'comparison' led him to see the originality of his side: unity means the *yumi*, which retains the personality of each individual. In the 'discovery' of what was once hidden there is a distancing from the former incorporation into 'European' institutions in which Kebi Bala's existence had been partly embedded.

In seeing the uniqueness of 'what is Island' Kebi Bala was becoming aware of the dissimilarity which Islanders had to offer in reciprocal exchange; they had something to share. As Kapin says, the message of the *wauri* of Malo is not wrong as the missionaries had insisted; it's part of God's 'people-line' and one day people will recognise it as a lost part of the Gospels: 'be kind to one another' means *wauri* treasures acts of human kindness, the *yumi*, of which the 'people-line' of Malo in its widest sense, is woven from generation to generation. Malo *wali aritarit, sem aritarit* means take the message and sow it in distant lands; that is not some sort of cultural imperialism: it is what the 'me' has to exchange with the 'you'. Although 'our' dissimilarity tied to 'our' *ged* is always offered competitively it respects and seeks to become aware of the originality of the 'you'. The code of the *yumi* neither seeks to consume other cultures nor to become assimilated by them.

In offering their dissimilarity in reciprocal exchange Islanders like Kapin and Kebi Bala are also reaping the harvest of a new synthesis in which one can still see the old. 'If you want to know the Father, do His will', means to Kebi Bala an imperative for a *Zogo le* of the Lord to be an exemplar in accordance with Malo ra Gelar. So he continues to live the life of his people: he works in the garden, everywhere. For Kebi Bala the process of comparison and contrast between the teachings of Malo and the Gospels moves 'naturally' to and fro between the 'texts' and everyday life resembling the 'hermeneutic circle' of the theology of liberation in which there is a continual exchange between the text and social life (Segundo 1977, 9).

Kapin's theology is universalist in theme; at the same time it is tied to the earth. Cosmic positioning is a statement about 'land rights': He 'gave' His land to the original inhabitants who held the land for Him to look after only for a time. In sending His Son He had the power of life over death and hence gave the promise of the All-One: the miracle of the coming millennium. In the last years of his life Kapin became a blind man with a clear mind. Some say he lost his eyesight reading books; others that he lost their power searching the stars. He searched the heavens for the revelation of the answer to the overcoming of the singular power of destruction; and the heavens sent forth their earth-bound message. The universal message bears the reciprocal commitment to those born of the earth; the practical imperative of 'before' remains.

Eliade has written that the birth of Christ who lived in historical time as a man signifies the transition from cyclical to irreversible time, and from myth to history (1959b, 110-12). Through the Resurrection a new category emerged — the category of Faith — through which all those who believe in Him will inherit everlasting life. In faith there is a personal awareness of the 'I' as reflected in the Creed, 'I believe'. In Eliade's view, historically within European civilisation it was the category of *faith*, a new category of religious experience in Judaeo-Christianism, which effected transcendence of the horizon of 'archetypes and repetition'. Christianity is seen then as the religion of modern, historical man, of the man who discovered personal freedom (1959b, 160–61). Both Kapin and Kebi Bala accept the category of personal faith. In Kebi Bala the faith of the 'I' is a personal commitment: 'I felt I was called. The call was a personal thing.' The 'ordering' process has undergone change; the priesthood is no longer purely hereditary: the one who is 'called' has the chance to respond or to fail to answer, the 'free will' to say like Kebi Bala, 'Lord, not yet'. A new singularity in the *zogo* has emerged, a quality of individuated awareness which is present in certain other Meriam as well as Kebi Bala, the one who was 'called': people like the younger Meriam Man's mother, were 'seeing' the priesthood in him.

Writing of the European cultivators, whom he saw as incorporating into their new Christian faith 'the cosmic religion that they had preserved from prehistoric times', Eliade observed: 'We may speak of a primordial, ahistorical Christianity' (1959b, 164). Kapin and Kebi Bala are both expressing something different to this. The fulfilment of Malo in Christianity is not the incorporation or infusion of the old religion into the new Faith. Rather, Christianity makes possible a valorisation and a completion of the cosmic order. A new synthesis is realised in an original theology. Through the transcendence of death in the Resurrection

Christ becomes the intercessor of mortals and immortals (*le* and *lamar*), so making possible their coming together in a cosmic unity of heaven and earth. This is Kapin's interpretation of 'I go to prepare a place for you and I will come again and receive you...'. The category of Faith is accepted into the cosmic structure, the 'people-line' continues in a new, universal form. This is new theology. Radin identified the emergence of 'new theology' among the Winnebago which is different to the received doctrine of Christianity in any of its 'Western' forms: to transpose Kebi Bala's words, they were 'offering what is Winnebago to God' (1957, 279–91).

The Cross as the symbol of the Resurrection gave the possibility of a Paradise Regained; that was like the coming of the All-One from the four directions of space. The Cross was the image of Divine Power which carried on, completed and universalised the *zogo*, the spirit-power that came with Malo. It made possible cosmic renewal. By living in historical time the Son became the Redeemer of mortals and immortals. Through His mediation the circles of reciprocity between *le* and *tebud le*, between *le* and *lamar*, which were 'broken' by the missionaries, were rejoined. Through the universality of Divine Power there sprang a cosmic renewal whose path led towards the All-One, the ultimate joining of the eternal 'beginnings' and 'endings' of the cycles of cosmic time. This is the meaning of the sign of the Cross.

The coming together in a path which leads towards the All-One is not like a 'global village' of endless similarity, but a network of *yumi* where each 'you' and each 'me' is tied to cosmic 'place'. The faith of the 'I' of Christianity does not signal the ending of the cyclical: rather, it makes possible the coming together of the 'other halves' of the circles of life. This is the new heaven, new earth given as a promise by the Lord to Isaiah. To Kapin this is the moment when the circles of life resume their primordial positions within the endless creation and re-creation of 'earth' and 'heavens' so realising the word of the Lord to Isaiah: '...as the new heavens and the new earth, which I will make, shall remain before me, ...so shall your seed and your name remain'.

In the Resurrection there is the promise of the beginnings and endings of primordial time coming together in the All-One of a Paradise Regained. It is as though 'the Light' also reopened a new cosmic era; like a Star in the east of which Kapin's grandfather, a man with special powers of *zogo*, is said to have had a presentiment: 'Receive that man from the east'. And Christianity when it came was both like and (also) unlike 'those old religions' that came from the west. The 'old' cosmic circle was completed; the 'new' cosmic circle on the same plane had come into being alongside yet 'one space' removed from it.

Christ, the supreme Mediator, has the power to make dissimilar people 'like one': in the new *yumi* which came through Him we may all become *wauri tebud*, that is, 'closer than brothers'. That is Kapin's personal message. It is a distilled wisdom which synthesises the old with the new in an 'integrative universalism' carrying an originality of awareness.

To Kapin the Resurrection brought the possibility of an ultimate reversal which *wauri* had prefigured: how people of a different filiation might become the 'we'. The *seuriseuri* of Malo had handed through that message from generation to generation; the 'planting' and nurturing of Malo *wali aritarit* now yielded a larger message: that was the return Gift of 'the Light'. *Seuriseuri* is the starfish of the deeps; it is imprinted in the stars: Tagai's left hand — the Southern Cross — points to the *kerkar* of the endless springs of cosmic regeneration within which is embedded the 'exchange' of repetition and newness of the old and younger 'years' in a cosmic originality of the springs of cosmic life. *Seuriseuri* had addressed the Meriam from ancient times. These were '...the auguries that dare to plant the Cross upon your forehead sky...' (O'Dowd, Australia 1909, 9).

The new Gift had reached them; so they were offering back their *kerkar* — the enlarging circles of 'sharing'. Within the centre of these circles were those who were at the joining points of the circles: persons of originality.

5 *KOLE*

Next morning Em *come. Southeast. Come now. It go!*
[blowing] *Keep keep up. Go listen* Em. *Brrrrr. Two down.*
Join me below. Go go go go...go...go. Half noon. All them
bloodwood; all them tree under that Cape, that's where we
anchor. Em *been smash all them stem, all them been smash,*
all them been killlllll, snnnapp.

Nine days. We look. Small black in the head
been come, like a small black eye. Wind, seas, noise been
urururururururururrh... rrrrrrrrh Come from sea now,
on the east, north-east. And now we broadside. It come and
hit us.

Cyclone 1934, First St Paul's Man

We been work for JW Bleakley. He come out all the Islands,
he said, 'Oh I'm your big mamus, *here are two sticks*
tobacco, here are two blankets'. Oh, so we bend the knee and
bow down to him because he's the big mamus. *I get one stick*
tobacco; that's my pay for Chief Councillor. Well we used
to go down to the office and you know those little Pass
Books? They stop me if I want to draw money today,
Monday. 'It's not for today. You have to wait for next week.'

Uncle, Chairman Kubin Council

THE DOUBLE EDGE OF PROTECTION

BECOMING INMATES

On 30 January 1903, the Department of Public Instruction, Queensland, announced immediate removal of the school at Murray Island from its lists. 'The school at Murray island is now wholly under the Home Dept: we neither pay the teacher nor inspect the school', the report ran (QSA EDU/Z1993). Queensland School Number 774, the Murray Island School between 1 September 1896 and 29 January 1903, became Stannary Hills from 1904 to 1930 and Woorabinda from 1956 to 1967. Two days later, on 2 February, the Under Secretary, Home Secretary's Department, was advised by the Secretary of Public instruction that 'the school for the children of Aboriginals at Murray Island' was now wholly under the control of that Department. The name of the school was to be deleted from the books of the Department of Public Instruction and the list of schools to be inspected.

The 'disappearance' of the Murray Island School Number 774 was a quiet announcement that the Islanders were becoming subject to 'Protection'. They were now Aboriginals for the purposes of the Aboriginals Protection and Restriction of the Sale of Opium Acts, 1897–1901, coming within the jurisdiction of the first Chief Protector of Aboriginals, Walter E Roth in 1904.[1] The meaning of that change was a move towards a closely watched segregation; in 1918 the Aboriginals Department was placed alongside the other sub-departments of Home Affairs:

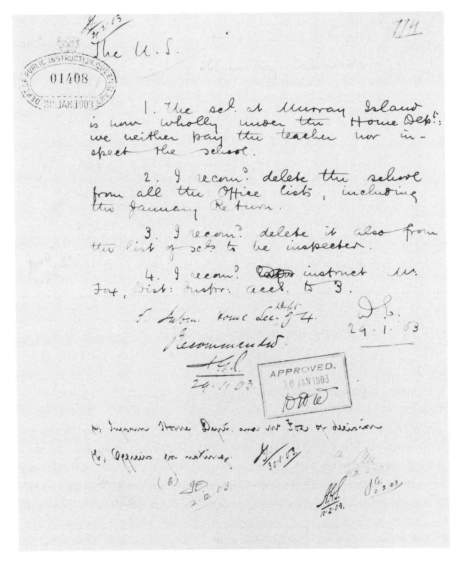

Plate 8 Announcement of removal of Murray Island school from the Department of Public Instruction, 30 January 1903 (photograph from Queensland State Archives, courtesy of Department of the Premier, Economic and Trade Development, Queensland)

prisons, benevolent asylum, chronic diseases, inebriate institutions and institution for the blind. They were all inmates.[2] Islander children were to be taught 'the elements of the three Rs; where possible the boys would be given instruction in agriculture and handicrafts; the girls in cooking, laundry, sewing, and domestic duties' (QPP, 1908).

Murray Island had had a long history of formal government schooling; on 7 September 1886, Hugh Milman, the Acting Government Resident had promised a school on condition that the Islanders found the materials for the school and teacher's house (QV&P, 1887, 5). J Chalmers of the LMS had remarked in 1897 that progress in the Murray Island school had been astonishing:

> I am told that the Murray Island school, would class as high, if not higher, than any other school of the same standing in the colony [of Queensland] — I think it would too. English only is taught and attendance is compulsory. Reading, writing, arithmetic, geography and grammar are taught. (Reported in Butcher, 4 January 1907, LMS)

On 22 December 1896 ninety-four children were enrolled; in the same year the government school teacher, John Bruce, reported to John Douglas that 'the fourth class are working compound sums in money, weights and measures, and Bills of Parcels' (Department of Public Instruction, 6 February 1897, QSA EDU/Z1993). Long before, in 1879, the LMS had begun the Papuan Institute, a teachers' training school at Murray Island.[3] By the time the Cambridge anthropological team arrived at Murray Island in 1898 the younger generation was bilingual: some of the Murray Island children's writing and composition was classed by the linguist, Ray, as 'quite equal' to those of children of the same age in English schools (1907, 166, including footnotes). 'My father could do sums I can't do', says Sis, 'and he learnt them all on Murray Island'.

How could Kole limit the wish to know when the new knowledge was already there? In some islands of course the people had little acquaintance with the three Rs of the English language. Efforts to restrict Islanders' schooling to the third-grade level were often successful. Yet many of the government teachers in the Islands who were employed by the Protector's Department met the demands of the Islanders to 'know'; and in imparting the knowledge of the 'new' they fed into the process begun long before schools were established whereby Islanders 'plussed' the new with the old and made their own syntheses. Many white teachers did much more than that, for example, McIntosh Murray who taught Kapin and Auntie at Darnley Island: 'Everything good came from McIntosh Murray', Auntie believed. 'Don't go where another man takes you', Kuki, another Darnley man recalls his message: 'Stand up and fight, don't just go with the tide'.

Nevertheless the 'removal' of School Number 774 from Murray Island represented the safeguard against Islanders ever gaining formal access to those educational institutions through which they might come on to an equal footing with Kole. It signalled a long-term restructuring of Islanders' lives so as to prevent them ever gaining access to the higher educational institutions: only a decade ago did those opportunities open up for them and even in 1984 there were still only five Islander graduates with the necessary qualifications of 'government teacher' (Noel Loos, personal communication).

THE SUPERVISION OF EXCLUSION

Kole rule in the Torres Strait was inaugurated in July 1879; the inhabitants of each island were mustered later that year by Captain C Pennefather and told that they were now 'amenable to the laws of the white man' (QSA COL/A288). The relationship of dependence established then underwent important changes which arose out of the changing needs of the colonising power. Elsewhere I have distinguished three distinct yet overlapping phases of that rule (Sharp 1980b, 56–90). The first phase covering the two decades leading up to federation in 1901 was characterised by a form of supervision known in British colonial practice as *indirect rule*: in 1886 a code was drawn up delegating powers to a *mamus*, or head-man who chose assistants or 'police'. The *mamus*, who had magisterial powers, was directly responsible to the Government Resident at Thursday Island.[4] The second phase, that of *paternalist exclusion*, which began soon after 1901, found expression in policies and practices which combined racialist segregation with paternalist rule. In its paternalism, phase two provided the frame of Islanders' lives for most of the period until the mid–1980s. That was the mentality which would not let them have inboards on their dinghies because they might burn themselves; which would not let them 'see the face of the money' (the 1930s); which limited the Island freezers to a twelve-volt system; and which restricted the number of village lights in the outer islands to five because they might electrocute themselves (the 1970s). Formally speaking, this phase was replaced by a third phase of *controlled integration* which combined the labour needs of post–Second World War capitalist expansion with a continuing paternalist segregation.

The character of the second phase was shaped above all by the emergence of the Australian capitalist nation in 1901 as a white monoculture, or what van den Berghe has called a 'Herrenvolk democracy' in which egalitarian ideals are limited to 'the people', that is to the whites (1967, 16). By the time of federation the 'ascendancy of the British race' had been established in the pearling industry. That industry had brought many nationalities and races into the Torres Strait area. The Honourable John Douglas, Government Resident at Thursday Island, expressed a common sentiment of white Australia in 1900: 'Nearly every nationality is represented... The Europeans, I am happy to say, still head the list in spite of everything and the Japanese come next' (1900, 32). Apart from the Japanese pearlers and divers there were Malays, Filipinos, Pacific Islanders, Torres Strait Islanders and Aborigines.

In the years of the second phase interrelated moves were made to effect a more and more complete colour segregation and so protect white Australia (QPP, 1920). The first was a more comprehensive and closer supervision of those protected as Aborigines and Islanders. The second was an extension of the categories of people supervised by Protection in order to widen the 'colour gap'.

In relation to the first move, the supervision of exclusion, three measures were taken. The first, announced in 1911, substituted the power formerly delegated to the *mamus* and Council for that of the government teacher on each island who was appointed by and subject to the Aboriginals (Protector's) Department: 'The School Teacher represents the Government upon the Island and must be consulted upon all matters by the Council and any directive or decision given by him must be carried out by the Council.' With these words the Home Secretary, George Appel, announced the changeover during his visit to Murray Island on 22 May 1911 (Murray Island Native Court Records, No 55). Kapin, who was a nine-year-old schoolboy at the time, recalls the changeover at Darnley Island:

> *The Government came then and George Appel came in his small boat Otter. He was one of the government officers there I think; he's got his name down there somewhere in the archives of Queensland. We were looking through the window, the young people there. No one caught us; we were looking in this court-house. Well, I was listening to this government officer who was right in the middle and he was pointing to himself: 'Me bigfeller government', introducing himself to the people in the court-house and 'this man, Mr Guillemot' [government teacher], on his right, 'him smallfeller government'. And no notice was taken of* mamus.

A second step soon taken was to force every able-bodied man to do 'a fair day's work' (QPP, 1912). An 'Island Fund' was established through which deductions from Islanders' boat earnings contributed towards the upkeep of the Islands (see Chapter 6). A third measure, the reduction of all aspects of personal autonomy with associated punitive powers, concerned earnings, crewing of boats, restrictions on movement of boats, on personal movement (a curfew), and on being seen walking or talking with a member of the opposite sex, especially a white person. In 1918 and in the early 1930s men from Darnley and Murray Islands were convicted under 'the morality laws' and deported to Palm Island off the coast of Townsville (see Thaiday 1981). In each sphere of their being the 'protected' Islanders were constantly reminded: they were less than equals. The *mamus* had been supplanted by the government teacher; the 'Chief Councillor' as he was now called, received a 'jumper' as 'pay', the word 'Councillor' sewn into it in large yellow letters. Islanders came to see the writing not as a badge of honourable recognition, but of dishonour and belittlement. The first interisland Councillors' Conference held at Yorke Island from 23–25 August 1937 successfully called for its removal (minutes, in 37/9577 in QSA A/3941).

A PATTERNING OF RACIAL SEGREGATION

Those who came under the provisions of the Protection Acts after 1901 — Aborigines and Islanders — were excluded from Thursday Island society, and, where possible, from the Island itself, the business and administrative centre of the area of the Torres Strait and the northern part of Cape York Peninsula (QPP, 1920). As boat crews their movements were restricted to the area of the boat houses.

The policies of total segregation signalled by the so-called 'Betterment Schemes' announced in 1918 had foreshadowed closer surveillance of the 'protected'; they also prefigured important changes in the pattern of race relations based on Thursday Island. In the early 1920s the Thursday Island school was 'de-integrated': behind that move to widen 'the gulf' between the black and white races lay the perceived fear of 'the half-caste evil', as the Protector's Report for 1923 makes clear.[5] In the context of a multi-racial community at Thursday Island, the sudden awareness of government officials that the indigenous peoples of Queensland were 'not dying out fast' produced new fears.[6] Where the ideology of racism had become rampant their continued existence posed a new threat; in this mental attitude the colour bar was paramount; there were also 'grades' of colour. An Islander recalls the distinctive multicultural patterning in Thursday Island society in the 1920s and 1930s on the other side of the colour bar as it presented itself to an Islander of South Sea Island origin who did not come under the Act:

> We had those indentured labourers before, but some half-caste people
> here in TI forgot that they were children of indentured labourers. They
> were people without anything. They couldn't own anything. They were
> owned by people. Some silly Islanders looked at it this way: Manilaman
> always wore a lot of jewellery and dressed up, you know, so he must
> have had money. But other Islanders looked down on the whole lot of

*them. You should have heard our mothers in the early days. They'd
say to us: 'If you don't learn to work' [and work is plant your garden
and do all that kind of thing], 'you'll finish up marrying a waster
and sit at the gamble table all day long and have him come back to
you drunk'. Now they looked down on us too because they wore shoes;
we didn't. They wore better clothes. I know a lot of them were pretty
poor living in town here, whereas the better Islanders of those days
always had plenty to eat; the ones that had yams from one season to
another. One time they'd harvest the yams, build little houses and keep
their food like that. You'd go and just get them off these trays inside
these houses where they harvest them and put them there.*

*Of all the Japanese who were here only four ever married
our girls; they're the half-caste ones here now and all those four still
lived like Japanese. One even sent his daughter to Japan to learn
something more. From their own point of view, they were too good to
marry any of us. They were above even the white people. But they lived
their own culture. You couldn't fault them. When they came they still
lived like Japanese. They even brought their own women with them.
On that side of the street that runs up to the school was called 'Jap
town'; 'Yokohama', they used to call it. Now everything was there. You
never went past there. They had their own little streets. Whereas some
of the half-castes were kind of drifters because they didn't want to be
Islanders and they weren't proper Malays and we looked down on them
and they themselves looked down on the Islanders. Looking at it from
the half-caste point of view, people who were part Aboriginal were half-
caste, but they were lower still in our Islander point of view. The worst
thing that could happen to you was to marry one of them. Have I ever
told you about a boy who came here from Brisbane? Some white people
grew him up and when he came here everybody thought he was white.
And he had a trade: he was a mechanic. I mean we'd never seen
anybody with a trade before. People ran boats and things, but then
trades were not for coloured people... And he was a very handsome
boy. I guess most mothers would think, 'He's nice'. White mothers too,
I think. He couldn't speak broken English, only English; brought up
by white people and he's just like white... He must have been quarter-
caste; more white than black, might have had one black grandmother.
Still that was Aboriginal. That cancelled out any white blood and made
him Aboriginal.* (Cassette 093/TB/TI/1/81)

The 1934 amendments to the Protection Acts extended powers of
control to those previously exempted; the issue of certificates of exemption was
temporarily suspended; finer separations were made among 'grades' of non-
Europeans. Paradoxically, the 'finer grading' and closer supervision ushered in
the new phase: the intention was to supervise this transition. A 'half-caste colony'
was envisaged in which those with the right ambition would be selected for

apprenticeship to suitable trades in European communities subject to the 'moral protective powers': this was the phase of *controlled integration*.[7]

THE OTHER SIDE OF THE COLOUR BAR

Auntie, Uncle and Nau Mabaig lived their lives on the 'other side' of the colour bar. Within their overall similar situation there were some important differences in their life-chances. Auntie was a 'native-born' Islander, but having no Torres Strait lineage she was not a 'native'. Her own origins were from Pacific islands known locally as 'South Seas', mainly Niue, and therefore she was exempted from the Protection Act. Uncle and Nau Mabaig were wholly indigenous and 'natives' under the Act. The life-story of each of these two is typical of people of the western side of the Strait who were subject to Protection.

AUNTIE: THERE ARE PEOPLE ALIVE AND WALKING AROUND NOW WHOSE LIVES SHE SAVED

Auntie was born at Darnley Island in 1903; she died at Thursday Island in 1981. Her immunity from the provisions of 'the Act' gave Auntie the possibility of moving about within, but not outside the Islands and the Cape York Aboriginal communities in the 1930s and 1940s in the teaching service of the Anglican Church.

Auntie was a woman of intellect, fortitude and patience, with special power to heal those who were suffering in body or in spirit: when the Storm-Winds came strongly she faced the full blast so to shield others from their powers of affliction. For sixteen years in the thirties and forties she worked in a harsh social environment at Lockhart River Mission, an Aboriginal community on Cape York Peninsula. She was obliged to create the compliance of an unwilling, oppressed and often hostile people, who came to love and respect her.

Scenes from Auntie's life as told by herself and others begin at Sis' place, Thursday Island, continue at Waiben hospital, TI, where Auntie spent her last years, and continue at Lockhart River.

SIS (at Sis' place, Thursday Island)

> *Her figure was perfect when she was young. She had beautiful slender ankles, nicely shaped legs, nice narrow feet, very small waist. She was a good-looking girl. Very straight the way she carried herself. She was reared by the old man K on Darnley Island. That old man had no children of his own. He took all these children, five of them and Auntie and they were all reared like brothers and sisters. It's just the custom to foster children. She knew who her parents were but she loved the old man.*

Plate 9 Kitty Savage (later Ware) c1920s

SIS (at Waiben hospital with Auntie)

> *K's wife was half-caste and she taught the girls to sew. Auntie was quite
> a good dressmaker. She could do fancy work, crochet. She learnt all
> those things that a girl should know. At the same time she knew all
> about making gardens and all about fishing and everything to do with
> how you get food. So she was quite independent when she was at
> Lockhart.*
>
> *Grandfather T, her real father, was a Polynesian medicine
> man. He was the greatest in the Torres Strait, bar none! From that
> day till today. And Grandfather T taught Auntie. Really only boys get
> taught. Before she went back again to be at Lockhart on her own, her
> father said to her: 'I never grew you up. You cost me nothing and I
> gave you nothing.' So he said, 'I'll teach you these things. You'll be
> on your own.' And he taught her lots and lots of things. It wasn't only
> good for herself, but for a lot of lives not only at Lockhart but in the
> Torres Strait as well. There are people alive and walking around now
> whose lives she saved. You ought to have seen her mother! Strong-
> hearted, brave. She was afraid of nothing. Then Auntie's mother was
> educated. All her schooling was in Brisbane. So you can imagine how
> a brave little girl like Auntie came up from both sides.*

AUNTIE

> *I did that job in school every morning, then lunch time came. Then
> at the end, we stayed over, cleaned that part. They used to play; we
> had to watch them all the time. They never forget what I taught them.*

SIS

> *And the worst one — he's the Chairman now — came one time to TI
> and gave Auntie some money; years back: 'Here's a present for you'.
> She believed that if you say you're going to do something you must
> keep your word always. In the year I spent with her the thing she liked
> was her tea in bed. So that was the only luxury she had. By this time
> there'd be one person, at least one, waiting outside to see her about
> a problem. It could be any problem,* anything, *even to a dream that
> might have had him worried.*

YOUNG LOCKHART MAN (in the canteen at Lockhart River)

> *Before I went to be a member of the traditional* bora *she realised what's
> behind all this very very sacred thing. We were initiated here and
> Auntie understands it all. That* bora *song you are listening to now,
> she know what's behind this. She understood that one they're singing
> now. She respected it. She wanted the kids to keep that culture.*

SIS (at Thursday Island)

> *Auntie would tell any of those Kole off and yet all the laws had to be
> kept. If she found she couldn't live her life the right way because the*

laws stopped her she would always go up and have a row with them.
With her there was no monkey business to this DAIA. You see Auntie
learnt my grandfather's medicine. Once you start practising that kind
of medicine you have to live your life to suit your God because you
can't serve two masters. (Book of Islanders 1984, B31–42)

UNCLE: MY MOTHER ALWAYS TELL ME TO BE KIND AND ALWAYS STICK UP ON YOUR RIGHTS

Uncle sprang from the Kaurareg of the islands off-shore from Cape York Peninsula just north of Endeavour Strait, a people who between the 1860s and the 1880s were almost wiped out. They were Islanders who had great double outrigger canoes, sometimes more than fifty feet long. Their close ties with clans at Adai, the Cape York mainland, are reflected in their physical characteristics like their scarcely 'frizzed' but curly hair. The invasion of their lands and the treatment of their people was a story of tragedy and destruction more like that of Aboriginal Australia than of the Torres Strait Islands (Sharp 1992a). The Kaurareg had begged the missionary-teacher William Kennett for a school in 1867 (Kennett in Moore 1979, 241). In 1913, as W Lee Bryce, Resident and Protector at Thursday Island, observed, their survivors, now at Hammond Island, had no school and no medical care (QPP 1914, 13). Attention to their situation, which had been described by the Anglican Missioner, Rev J Done as 'the worst in the Torres Strait', helped to bring them back on to the map of the living (Diary). Uncle's people were moved from one place to another: they became successively the POW (Prince of Wales/Muralag) people, the Hammond people, the Poid (Moa) people and finally the people of Kubin Village, Moa Island.

The Kaurareg 'paid back' and defended themselves from oncoming death according to custom. Uncle tells the story handed down to him of the death of Tamate (Rev) James Chalmers, the LMS missionary, who was killed at Goaribari on the New Guinea coast in 1901:

At Muralag there is a special place of water where people go when they
are sick. The Zogo *[Uncle chose the Meriam word] man used to climb*
up that hill there and on top they did special things. That hill belonging
to them fellers is sacred. We say: 'You have to close your eyes before
you can find that place'. Only those sacred men can find that place.
When the missionary Chalmers went up to New Guinea people
belonging to Muralag were warned before. One small boy of Muralag
remembered that the Zogo *man there had said that if Chalmers went*
to New Guinea and took all their sacred things and told them to
worship another God, more people would come here to Muralag too
and take away everything belonging to us, so we must do something.

He said, 'So we kill em'. *So the Zogo man went on top to that place at Muralag and he cast a spell on that feller Chalmers from on top that sacred hill. All the Muralag people understood that old man Chalmers had been killed that way.*

Uncle was born in 1908, a time when 'the old-time dispersals' were being replaced by 'protection' (QPP 1905, 23). He became a respected and beloved leader of his people for more than forty years; he was 'Uncle' to many people beyond his own community. In a world set to stifle all initiative and to remove people's feelings of self-confidence he was able to find channels for positive and practical expressions of hope. Uncle's life was not a life of heroic deeds; it was a life of steadfast purpose. He carried a strong spirit with him and he imbued his people with that spirit.

UNCLE

That Aboriginal boy was handed over to the Muralag people

They came from Adai along the beach behind Prince of Wales (POW), Muralag. My mother's father's father, he said, 'Don't kill this boy, he's mine'. And that baby was handed over. He was the child of the mamus *that Adai boy, an Aboriginal boy, and Muralag people gave him their name and when he grew up he married a Muralag woman. That is where my grandfather on my mother's side came from and his name was Kaubarees. They named him Kakakuk, which means something like a coconut that floats on water, because he floated like that. He must have come from someone important to be in that fighting canoe, and so that piccaninny must be from first-class man, because they give good men in them canoes. Some of our people used to travel as far as Moa Island because some of our women had married to Moa men. In that time Moa people didn't make canoes, but POW people did and they gave them to Moa to be friends. They too had 'swaps' like* wauri.

The police said, 'You jump in the dinghy you cheeky boy', and put a revolver to my chest

I was born at Hammond Island. My mother married a Horn Island man. They live there and POW people live at Yata, Port Lihou. When Jardine shoot all these people he forget about [ignored] *those he didn't shoot. (There were people left at Muralag, at Nurupai and at Adolphus.) So he said, 'You'd better go to Hammond Island'. I grew up at Hammond Island until 1914 war. When I came to age about eighteen here comes an order from the Chief Protector Mr Bleakley. He sent a man out to Hammond Island and tell all these people to get away from Hammond to Moa Island. Oh, terrible! I saw my uncle that brave, just go and push all those white police who come out with revolvers. He was*

Plate 10 Wees Nawia, Chairman, Kubin Community Council, Moa Island, 1980

*something like a giant, a strong-hearted man. I was frightened they
might shoot my uncle. So the police said, 'You jump in the dinghy you
cheeky boy', and put a revolver to my chest and pushed me into the
dinghy. The mothers and sisters all cry and go and take all their things
and Badu and Moa people made grass houses at Poid, Moa. It was oh,
big cry that night. Moa people come and the Hammond people cry and
the Moa people they didn't like us to have to leave Hammond. I don't
know why they moved us.* (Book of Islanders, B46)

SIS (at Thursday Island)

*Everybody was against the Hammond children going to the school at
TI. The white mothers were not going to let their children mix with
them. So they separated them and sent all the coloured children to the
other school.*

MOAN WOMAN (in Townsville at the home of Uncle's granddaughter)

*Yes, we cry with them. The boat that bring them come here called
Goodwill. I'm eighteen then; I born 1904. We have to go and cut the
grass for the houses and help these people. Five boats go to pick all
them things, them mats they sleep on. They're weeping all the time.
The Government wouldn't let them go back and visit [afterwards].*
(Cassette 087/MW/TN/1/81)

BADU MAN (at Badu Island)

*Uncle was six or seven years older than me. I went there with 'Old
M'. Elderly Moan people come and met them and talk very nicely to
them. They can feel the friendship from Badu and Moans. All the
houses Badu people made for them. When Hammond people settle, they
and Adam people, the Moans, start to fall in love with each other.*
(Cassette 076/BM/B/1/81)

UNCLE

*It was called Adam, but when we got there we changed the name to
Poid. We stayed there from 1921 to 1940. When we leave Hammond
in 1921 we live in those houses which had little mangrove floors. The
Moa and Badu people built them for we and we lived there and in 1932
I married Aunty [not the same person as Auntie]. I became a Councillor
and went to the Yorke Island Councillors' Conference in 1937. So I was
Chief Councillor from 1934 onwards. I stayed at Kubin as Chief
Councillor during the War.*

My mother always tell me to be kind and always stick up on your rights

*Always in my mind I live in Hammond Island, but when I got married
to Aunty I tried to forget Hammond Island. I love the place where I
was born; better I live on the place I was born. But I can't leave Moa
just because my mother's buried there. Me and my brother-in-law make
a garden more than anyone in that Moa Island, all over the place. Even*

the place where their grandfather was buried at Dabu, we grew a
garden around there too. It's a long way but we walk there. I got small
wages, £3 a month. I got to do all my gardening to keep all my family.

My father used to be a good fisherman. I used to go out with
him when I was a boy and I see him track all these dugong one night
and next night my old man said, 'Dugong come tonight here'. He knew
the grass, what tide they been come on, if they feed on this tide or that
tide. He could tell by the grass. And Aunty can tell you, nobody, no
Badu people good as me today in telling that dugong come tonight here
or dugong not come. Dugong may come tonight on the low tide or the
high tide. He leaves a mark on the sand and me and my sons leave
a stick here at that place. We make a platform we call nat.

When I think of my mother, well this old lady she teach
me all perfect things: not to be selfish, which is the big [respected]
person, which is the low person. My mother was a very decent polite
person. That's why I think I'm a different boy from all my family,
because I take all that advice from my mother. She might come up from
fishing. She won't pass us. She come up here with the fish and she say,
'Take what you like'. That's why people say I got my mother's way.
Yes, I say my mother was a very kind woman. She's a big woman.

She never interfered; a very good-hearted woman and she
always tell me to be kind [louder] and always stick up on your rights.
My father died when I was ten or eleven years of age.

JW Bleakley said, 'Here are two sticks tobacco, two blankets', so we bend the knee and bow down to him

This Act belonged to the time of me and Tanu Nona. We been work
for JW Bleakley. He come out all the Islands, he said, 'Oh I'm your
big mamus, here are two sticks tobacco, here are two blankets'. Oh,
so we bend the knee and bow down to him because he's the big mamus.
I get one stick tobacco; that's my pay for Chief Councillor. Well we used
to go down to the office and you know those little passbooks? They stop
me if I want to draw money today, Monday. 'It's not for today. You
have to wait for next week.' That's why I talked about the Act. Tanu
Nona is finished now. This Act has to go. In those days we always do
things like gardening. The Church in those days was not much, but
we were very Christian people those days. Calm sea-people, not
disturbing the village, very honest. (Book of Islanders 1984, B46–48;
see also Sharp 1992a, 125–32)

NAU MABAIG: COLOURED TEACHERS MAKE US MORE UNDERSTAND; THEY'RE OUR PEOPLE

Nau Mabaig's name means songman. He was born at a time when total segregation
was being effected. When Badu became 'top island' for pearling, 'clan' structures

and custom became subject to concerted attack and 'native' Islanders fared badly.
A strong working boy like Nau Mabaig, who went to the boats at fourteen years
of age to escape one evil only to be engulfed in another, returned to his Island
twenty years later a non-working man with the disabling effects of beri-beri, his
eyesight almost gone.

His father, a Councillor of Argan clan, was 'the strongest man to fight
for the freedom of the people'. Nau Mabaig carried on that tradition, often in a
secret way with his songs, and as 'bush lawyer' along networks invisible to the
'other side'.

Our fathers mostly grow up we on bush tucker

> Right. Now we'll start to tell my story. I'm Nau Mabaig. I was born
> here at Badu in 1919. I was baptised Anglican. When I came to have
> sense, I found I'm living under State Government. I lived here. I found
> my father was a Councillor of Badu Island and of the Argan tribe.
> So we are living here happily and our population is 700 altogether
> at Badu. Our mission is on St Paul's. A priest used to come from there:
> come round to Moa Island, then to Badu. Goes on and on. I grow up.
> We live mostly on bush tucker because our money-line is very little.
> Three pound a month when our boys used to sign on the 'Master boats'.
> And for the pearl shell fishing, we used to have cutters here. The Argan
> tribe cutter is called Argan. Wakaid tribe cutter is called Wakaid and
> the Badu tribe cutter is called Badu. Well our fathers mostly grow up
> we on bush tucker: banana, yam, taro and sweet potato. We were grown
> up in that way. When I came to be fourteen years of age, I'm a big-
> headed [smart] boy in the school class. My teacher is Mrs Zahel.

She was the Government's right-hand man

> Mrs Zahel she was very strict with us. She don't even trust us to buy
> an inboard engine dinghy. She reckons we might burn ourselves in
> the sea and drown. She hadn't got faith in us and she make a law.
> We wanted to come up and get something but she'd stop us. She didn't
> even want us to go to TI and stay in there like a month or three weeks.
> She wanted we to go out and come back with her permission. She noted
> us. One person went out from here to visit the woman who loves him
> at St Paul's Mission, but he forgot to get a permit. And when the police
> caught him, they stood him before the court and fine certain money
> from him for going without a permit. We don't like her but Government
> still wants her to stay. She was their right-hand man. All the good
> things we needed we were too frightened of her to ask about. And we
> haven't got that knowledge like we have today. Now we see many good
> things and we've got the knowledge. We can fight and work too.

I made up my mind to come out from the school

Before the War when our people fall in love, younger people fall in love and police find them — if they meet together, kiss or walk about together — they must come to stand before the court. The law punished them by making their hair cut into two parts, shaved on one side. I was a boy then. I worked beside it. Looked at them people with shaved heads personally. In the time of McLean.

When I come to fourteen years of age I was a schoolboy. Mrs Zahel called me up one time to her table and she said: 'One old fellow wants you to go up to the store and get him a bag of flour and bring it to him'. Store is at Dogai. I go up there get a bag of flour. When I come back a woman is standing up there, white woman. She's pretty, young woman, wife of the clerk at the store, white clerk. Yes, nice woman. She called out to me: 'Wait me up there.' I stood up there waiting her. We walked along. Come out on the beach and come on towards her place. Well I found we got [did] wrong. We had a law about walking with white ladies. I told her about that. Well I'm going that way inside. That means keep away from Mrs Zahel. I come from the beach on a kangaroo road, a small road, meet that big road, main road. I wanted that teacher not look me come with this white woman. That's why I'm scared of her. That's why I made up my mind to go this way inside. When this pretty white woman said this to me I did this; I had an eye for a girl too. On the other hand I fright from her [frightened of being with her], scared. But what I was scared of next afternoon was the policeman coming to me. They caught me just because I come side road. Someone seen me.

Mrs Zahel blew the whistle. But anyway it comes out what I do. They put me in gaol. I'm fourteen years of age. I schoolboy, I'm tall boy, I'm pretty boy. That's why that young lady wanted to come with me. But that one's wrong for the law. I can't say anything because I'm kind to her. So when she asked me, I said, 'Yes, I come with you'. So anyway I stand before the Native Court and they punish me. I have to work for three months in the gaol. Work on the street. Hard labour. Not go to school. Work along the road. When it's finished, I made up my mind to run away from the school. All my age know it. I told them, 'If the school break on December month I'll come out from this door. I will lose [disappear] from here.'

We used to leave school everywhere in Torres Strait at sixteen years of age, but I'm strong-headed. I ran away from school at only fourteen years of age. Went down on the trochus lugger. I signed on the lugger Wakaid *and my skipper is Tanu Nona. He was a great and good skipper in all the Torres Strait, so I signed with him, but I'm not a real age to sign on the boat and went down south with* Wakaid

to work trochus outside Cooktown, Cairns, Townsville, Bowen, Mackay
and Grafton right up to Swain Reef.

The glow was so strong in the heart

You might have heard the love song, 'Linda'. That's the time when we
sang that song [composed by Nau Mabaig]. It really means darling:

> We are sailing away to work in the sea,
> We can see the light shining through the coconut trees,
> I don't know where you are over in the island;
> In your dreams I hope you see us sitting together.

The girls were waving white sheets. We can see them between the
coconut trees and some are shining pieces of glass. That's because we
are going for so many months to work outside in the sea. But they
are doing this in a secret way; keeping it from their parents because
the glow was so strong from the heart. If a parent or somebody find
out they do that they must report it to the police and the police would
make them stand before the Native Court. It was the law in those days.
In my young days.

He said, 'I want him, he's a good working boy'

Then I came back. In December month we come back. We are successful.
Well in Wakaid we always throw twenty-seven tons when we get inside
the port. Then after that we are going out for work on the diving boat
again. That's the next year. We work here outside behind Badu on the
western side. It's called our 'old ground'. When we work behind Badu
it's only eleven fathoms, thirteen fathoms when it comes to high water.
When you go down over Booby Island and come to the south side near
Red Island, Weipa Point and Weipa, it's more than twenty-five fathoms.
Yeah, I worked on the diving boat and come back home end of season.
        Next year I sign on again because my diver wants me back
again. He said to me, said to the Council: 'I want him, he's a good
working boy. I don't want another Island boy, I want him.' So Council
told me I had to sign on back again. We go out that year, work behind.
When Easter comes we all went to Thursday Island, that was tucker
time. We unload shell and prepare the boat, loading and cutting
firewood and then went to Port Darwin. We stay there; then I became
sick. It's a sickness called beri-beri. That's from the wet. Well my boat
diver took me back to my home, Thursday Island. We were two
Islanders on that boat, but one was dead; half-way back when we sail
back he died and I'm very ill when I get to Thursday Island harbour.
I was very ill. I stay inside the hospital for nine months. When I come
better the doctors make me swim outside in the water where I could
move my legs and very slowly start to walk.

Coloured teachers make us more understand; they're our people

When I was young my teacher was Mrs Zahel, then black teacher comes
to us. Murray Island man and then Darnley man. I left school before
1935, two years before the strike. We learn a lot from coloured teachers.
They help us in school and when they go back we have knowledge
ourselves to fight against, fight against... When they teach us, they're
our people. Sometimes they talk to us in broken English, make us more
understand. Taught us any way [all ways], half in broken English and
half in good English. That's why we come to knowledge. Island teachers
school up that way, Darnley and Murray Islands. Three of them come
with the dinghy and say, 'Kapin looking for you'. [Kapin was then at
St Paul's Anglican Mission, Moa Island.] McIntosh Murray he taught
them; they more good educated than our Islanders here. Better
government teachers there.

Tanu Nona got a hard life for us

When I was coming out of the school I go to Tanu Nona and work under
him. I find him a good teacher but he got a lot of hard life for us. Treat
we so bad. Well we still work. When end of the season comes we're
discharged. When next year comes, again we sign on the boat. The
police blow the bu whistle in the street. We go to meeting and Tanu
Nona told us: 'First sign only for the Island boats'. But those Island
boats belong to him. First to sign go only for Island boats and what's
left, them go for 'Masters boats' to Thursday Island. Every year come
round he made that law. But we've been trained by him. One time
when I sit down I think we could work just like Tanu Nona because
we've been long enough with him. Then I ask one of my brothers,
'Another day I'd like to become skipper on a boat'. He said, 'Yes, I'm
getting tired of working for Tanu Nona and all you brothers too'. 'What
about I search for the boat up there at Thursday Island and if I get
it I'll come back'. If you give me time I'll get a boat.'

The crews want men to come up level

Right, I go up to TI. I stay there for a month. Going down to all those
'Masters' asking for a boat. Well three sons of 'Old M' they work
Duffield's boat, and we're like brothers because we grow one place, 'Old
M's' place. When I come there they ask: 'Where you go brother?'. Me
and my brothers getting sick and tired of working for em. 'We'll get
a boat for you if you stay with us a bit', they told me. So I talked myself
to those boys and they helped me. They supported me to get that boat
of Duffield's. So one time when recruiting time came, Duffield told
me: 'Tell your brother I'll give you a boat'. He gave us one boat. When
we work we stand like [are equal to] Tanu and he gets jealous of us.
Oh he gets cross. So bad.

But we still work and stand. Goes on and on. And afterwards now my two brothers they tell all the crews of the boat: 'Say, water is not the home of a man. It's the land of the fish. We're now all going to the shore and looking for a job.' So. They all go work at Duffield's station. 'Old M's' sons too. All the crews been coming out too. They don't want to work under someone. They want men to come up level. Everyone come up [equal].

People want me to say something for them

Goes on. We brothers support ourself now. But my father when he teach me to say something for the people, the people find me a little bit good man. They wanted to put me in the Council, but I refused. There's a man in our time who was enemy for us. That's why we don't want the Council. But at any time if bad things come for us, we stand firm and fight for it. So from that time people wanted me to say something for them. People wanted me to fight. If they were in trouble, they'd put me like a lawyer bloke [whispering] *in the court case for them. That's after the War now. They make me like a 'Badu lawyer'. I finish off from the cargo boat as skipper. I make myself come to crew of a lugger under him to work here at the Island. Maybe one year I work at that boat. Then the next year come, I refused. I only stay at the Island now. My eyesight is no good. I go under the doctor and he made me a pensioner. In 1951 I was inside the hospital. They check me up 1951, 1952, 1953, 1955; they gave me a pension and I'm all the time here.*
(Book of Islanders 1984, B73–83)

THE VIOLENCE OF ASYMMETRY

INMATESHIP AS SOFT VIOLENCE

Mateship is for equals. Rulers and ruled are non-mates. By their existence those who are 'outside', beyond the social boundary, define what lies inside. They are the inmates of 'benevolent' institutions for the 'disabled', the 'handicapped', the 'mentally retarded', the 'insane', the 'criminals': they all share a status as captives of institutions from which they cannot pass in and out of freely. Inmates are usually confined further within a space demarcated for them beyond the physical boundaries of 'normal' life: those spaces are asylums with a double meaning. Inmates are all poised on a path that leads to nowhere; souls on ice.

Inmateship is the obverse side of mateship. It represents the other side of how a 'mate' in white Australia can also behave as a self-defined supremacist in relating to 'inmates' (see Nelson 1972, 223). If you scorn or deride a mate that person becomes something else: the definition has changed because your derision has altered the relationship. You cannot be mates with those you suppose to be your inferiors because mateship is the everyday face of egalitarianism. 'Inmateship' can become an institution of soft violence: that is a paternalist system.

Van den Berghe has described 'a *paternalistic* system' as one in which a dominant 'group rationalises its rule in an ideology of benevolent despotism', regarding members of the subordinate group as inferior but lovable — childish, immature, exuberant, good-humoured — 'as long as they stay in "their place"'. At least in official policies, race prejudice takes the form of genteel benevolence and *noblesse oblige*, rather that virulent hatred. 'The relative stability of these regimes is partly a product of coercion, but, at least as importantly, of close, intimate, albeit highly unequal symbiosis' (1967, 27, 29). As the second phase of Kole built up to total segregation the 'soft violence' of inmateship was institutionalised for Islanders. They were offered not bags of poisoned flour: they were offered a specially close relationship as a 'chosen people'. The price of that relationship was the weaving of their lives into a seamless cloth on which was imprinted on its indivisible sides the double motto of the 'legend' of Queensland: the social inferiority of the ruled and the fatherly enlightenment of the rulers. Over a time the situation was so regulated as to 'prove' the legend in a circularity of self-fulfilment. It was a 'benevolent despotism' that made people *feel* dependent. Islanders were cut off from learning and having the 'new'; they were then ridiculed for their ignorance ('bush-ways'), their calicos (*lavalava*) and their bare feet.

Islanders' situation was one of 'being-for-other' in the language of dialectics (Marcuse 1977, 135); in Islanders' language it was being 'monkey-men'; the same as monkeys in the zoo performing tricks for the purposes and amusement of others. Such a relationship means a loss of self, an incompleteness in which external conditions contradict what a human is. Before the Storm-Winds there was no category of a person-for-other; anyone who tried to create person-for-other was soon struck dead.

The dependence of being-for-other creates feelings of worthlessness, of self-depreciation, denial of self. In the end one wants to be other than what one is; like somebody else: 'I wish I were a white man instead of a coon, coon, coon...' sang the African slaves in the 'New World'. Self-depreciation, wanting to be not oneself, is also expressed in identification with the father-figure. Being noticed by him becomes terribly important: 'He knows me' expresses the cruel truth of not really knowing who you are. There comes a line of looked-for favours: being one of his favourites, being chosen to 'chair' (carry) him from his dinghy across the shallows to the shore, to carry his bags, to cook for him according to his custom, to be near him, to touch him, to hear him call your name, to be 'almost' one of his family, to be allowed to mind his children, to draw very close to him. Intimacy is the key note. From the other side, symbiosis means *these* ones are nice: not so coarse or rough as others; a better kind of 'native', not like those *others*. And among those chosen the ones 'we' like are trying to improve themselves. Symbiosis for the one leeched on is like a spreading poison through diffusion. There is no way of stopping it except by attacking it at its roots. It is endless, for it is the touch of death of the spirit. Psychic immiseration breeds compliant slaves. It makes people frightened to rule themselves. That is its intention; it is self-fulfilling like a closed circuit. Where it has taken its toll that is true; that is its success. It is very effective and very cruel. In the clash between being-for-other and what a person properly is there comes a sense of incompleteness which makes a person restive.

SHAMING AS SOCIAL CONTROL

The worst thing that can happen to an Islander is to be 'be-littled': to be made less than a person. Shame is the reverse side of prestige. To hurl an insult, to give a mean gift, is to belittle, to humiliate. In Island social language it means war. Where social life is regulated by the process of creating and re-creating structural equivalence, fear of ridicule takes on a special meaning. The oscillation between prestige and 'getting even' is experienced subjectively as a fear of shame. Among the Meriam to fail to follow the example of Malo was to feel the shame of derision. Only stupid people do not plant or waste the fruit of the gardens: 'Look at him — plucking green bananas and fruit before they are ready!' (Lawrie 1970, 337–38). A shamedness in Malo's name! Malo ra Gelar is invisibly woven into personal make-up. Where social behaviour is regulated by a state and state apparatus, respect for the rights of persons may be inscribed in the law of libel: hatred, ridicule or contempt are punishable by law. Among Islanders to deny that right not to be belittled is a denial of self: it is to put their humanity in question. Kole did just that to Islanders: ' "I'm your big *mamus*; here are two sticks tobacco, here are two blankets". So we bend the knee and bow down to him...' For people whose lives were founded upon the bedrock of equivalence the very presence of Kole was a matter of shame. That asymmetry began in 1879. For the first generation of Islanders (in phase one) power had been muted; the Islander *mamus*-system 'mediated' that relationship. The post-1901 era of phase two became an encompassing era of a shame unspeakable or spoken about only softly.

Radin has written about just how far a Winnebago person would go to avoid public ridicule. Among the Winnebago fear of ridicule is 'the preserver of the established order of things', a force 'more potent and tyrannous than the most restrictive and coercive of positive injunctions possibly could be' (1957, 51). Fear of ridicule can be seen as the obverse side of 'prestige hunting'; at rock bottom the latter is but a defensive mechanism against ridicule. 'If you travel in the road of good people', say the Winnebago, 'it will be good and others will not consider your life a source of amusement' (1957, 50). Radin relates the story of the man who dared to say he disbelieved in the powers of the holiest and most terrifying of the Winnebago deities, expressing contempt for him in public. Shortly after the deity in question appeared and pointed a finger at the sceptic, an action intended to cause immediate death. 'The man stood his ground and did not budge and the deity...begged the man to die lest people make fun of him!' (1957, 51). Islanders may be likened to the African Ceŵa among whom 'Shame is said to make grown men weep and to drive impetuous transgressors to suicide' (Marwick 1965, 224).

For the individual person ridicule disturbs psychic unity: it produces horror and fear because the person's feelings of human worth and personal dignity are outraged. That is true for all people: a child who is persistently ridiculed makes a defensive, 'prickly' adult. But personal make-up and archetypal social reactions have their structural underlay. Gut reactions of outrage, the unspeakable horror of personally pointed fun-making have their origins in exchange relations which lie at the heart of reciprocity: the reasons lie in the social grammar of life regulated solely by reciprocal mediations. It begins in the simple fact that you demean a person by not giving him or her the appropriate due — a proper 'gift'. You are insulting and devaluing his or her worth as a person.

Rite affirms the value of symbolic patterning of the universe; each level of patterning is validated and enriched by association with the rest. Jokes have the opposite effect: they do not affirm accepted values: they 'denigrate and devalue' (Douglas 1978, 102). Joking is like stretching social boundaries by the process in which the 'other side' is glimpsed: by devaluing it is boundary testing. Where joke or frivolity takes too much liberty with a central cultural support the joker is likely to be reprimanded or admonished by the silence of a joke 'falling flat'. Where it devalues another person it is likely to be met by angry action. In either case fear of going beyond the boundary is a strong preserver of established order. So while joking is anti-rite, fear of being made fun of is a protector of established norms. Kole possessed the power to shame to the point of utter destruction by contradicting the very essence of being human for Islander people. Ridicule became a form of social violence: as a personal experience it was psychic violation. Where it is combined with built-in means to frustrate all initiative its 'success' is denoted by total dependence: being part of another which may lead to psychic emptiness...to the bottle — or the rope. Kuki, a Darnley Islander, sought to follow the advice to stand up against the tide; for a time he was swept along by its self-willed power of destruction: 'Inside me it's cold now; I feel wreck now. Something cold inside me now; something wrong. When I came round all of a sudden my two leg now cold come up and I can't move no more now... I could feel myself dying. I finish now: "Lord, give me one more time, one more chance. I want to look you now"' (Cassette 053/KK/TI/1/80).

For an Islander the essence of being human is the reciprocal being of the 'me' and the 'you'. To lose the 'me' is to be without anything to give in exchange: to cease to be human. That is social death. Benevolent despotism is a form of psychic violence: it violates a person's sense of self; it defiles by poking fun, by belittling, by finding amusement in different custom, by finding fault, by inducing feelings of worthlessness. Even the way your natural presence comes across, for example strong (frizzy) hair, is used to belittle you. It is like sustained brainwashing, which, as Gellner has written, not merely induces maximum confusion. It strips the person of all those facets of the self which hold the norms in place: 'The key ideas...are made as loose and shaky as possible. In the end, nothing can any longer be interpreted with confidence...' (1974, 13).

COLOURED NETWORKS

Kole had a double-edged impact. In throwing all coloured people into the same house of bondage they provided the condition for them to find common cause: they were all unfree. Yet by their differential treatment of the 'grades' they had created Kole put one against another. Within this contradictory situation Islanders began to weave new networks. What they did quietly and secretly on their side of the colour bar was not necessarily known or bothered about by Kole so long as they looked like 'calm sea people'. On those occasions when 'the peace' was disturbed Kole hardly believed they were the same people; it appeared to them as one big mistake.

Badu people and the Moans built houses for the Hammond people: together they cried for those who were moved and for the mothers and fathers buried at Hammond Island who were now alone. Uncle's people could 'feel the friendship' of the Moans and the Baduans who in former times had been the enemies of both. Over a time the 'Hammond people' and the Moans intermarried, eventually becoming one community. With the arrival of the Eastern Island teachers the new knowledge was passed to Islanders at the western end of Torres Strait by people like themselves in a manner and a language they could understand: the pidgin language coming to be known as 'Broken', 'Blaikman', and more recently, Torres Strait Creole, had become the language of cross-island coloured networks (Shnukal 1983b, 173–85). Through their experiences of the 'new', Islanders could distance themselves from their current situation and see themselves afresh. In beginning to satisfy their need to come to 'know', that is, to come to terms with the singular, they could overcome the 'disnomy' of their experience with Kole.[8] By beginning to restore psychic unity they could begin to resist the tide which led down to destruction. When Au Bala came to teach at Poid in 1932, the charter given him by Malo *wali aritarit, sem aritarit* (Malo plants everywhere...) gave him something to go on through which he could learn something else. He offered the children in the school and the parents what he had to exchange; men of the Western Islands offered *their* custom and *their* language; how to use the dugong spear and dugong platform, and in so doing became like an uncle, like a father, like a brother to Au Bala. In those exchanges they became as *yumi*, a solidary experience of dissimilarities in-unity.

In all the Islands the circles widened and multiplied in a similar way as the Island teachers (and priests) went out first from the Eastern Islands and later from everywhere to teach and preach. As Nau Mabaig says: 'We learn a lot from coloured teachers... When they teach us, they're our people. Make us more understand.' And so at Badu and Poid they were given the knowledge of the three Rs, the custom of the 'other side' — and inspiration, confidence that they themselves could stand up and fight against... The new networks were the antithesis of 'being-for-other'. The accretion and strengthening of custom within these widening circles were a renewal and strengthening of the 'me': that meant the possibility of survival. Auntie, Uncle, Nau Mabaig, each reflect the identity of the 'me': each had something of great importance to give.

In the coloured networks which were forming, marriage exchanges and exchange of knowledge and things and symbolic meanings did not make the 'two sides' of each exchange all-the-same: the varied threads of their associations were visible within the (overall) patterned network which constituted the whole. The dissimilarities of each side were not extinguished by the exchanges. People were 'coming up level' which meant 'equivalent to' *and* 'dissimilar from': such a combination gave the possibility of reciprocal exchange.

Kole were the personification of the power of death: all that destroys and kills. They coalesced with and strengthened the power of the unequivocal singular that was already there: the power of hostile magic (*maid* and *puripuri*). In a social life where the power of death is woven into every aspect of everyday life there had to be the power of curing. Auntie had that power. She grew up in the Eastern Islands and spent most of her post-Lockhart years in the Western Islands. In all these places she was an exemplar; she could do anything: teach the new in the white man's schools or in the Mothers' Union; teach the old by her example and her words. In either world she knew and respected other custom;

most of all 'She realised what's behind all this very very sacred thing [the bora at Lockhart River]'. Above all else she was life itself because she had the power of healing: 'Any coloured person who knew her knew about that; every single person in the Strait and every single one at Lockhart'. The truth of her life for the Islands is intimated in Ailan Man's words about her: 'Others are aunties of the Eastern Islands, but Auntie belongs to the whole Torres Strait — from Murray Island to Saibai'. She served only one Master. The message of her life was as Saint Paul's to the Corinthians: overcoming the power of evil and keeping it at bay.

In the 1920s and the first half of the 1930s Islanders did not make any visible attempt to drive out Kole; no movement like the short-lived German Wislin at Saibai arose. In that period new reciprocal ties had strengthened the circles of life. In the first place the new marriage links which crossed old boundaries in turn brought those in-laws within the circle of mortals and immortals. 'The tombstone' unveiled widening circles of giving, receiving and returning. The one God gave promise of the All-One: the 'seeing' of Islanders had begun to extend far beyond the old *wauri* networks in a new circle of 'partners'. In the strengthening of those two circles of life lay the possibility of deliverance through those chosen by God. Among the Islanders were those who began to reveal those possibilities in hymns of praise — and deliverance.

Christmas, the birth of a Saviour, of resurrection and the freedom from the chain of the Devil, the opening of the heavenly gates to all people, became the central themes. The crossing of the Red Sea by a people who saw themselves as God's people led by the prophet Moses, out of the land of bondage was the theme of one of countless hymns composed by Sis' father, Uncle T. Islanders began to sing this hymn in Meriam Mir:

> *We praise your name above all gods*
> *All earthly lords bow down to you.*
>
> Chorus
>
> *God, you sent Moses your servant,*
> *He delivered all your children, the people of Israel.*
> *He stood up and struck the Red Sea*
> *And by Your blessing the sea divided.*
>
> *Pharoah rose up with his army*
> *The sea was their grave forever.*[9]

The power of the singular was being returned like the healing of affliction. The moment of death had become the moment of rebirth. In the words of the prophet Isaiah: 'Keep silence before me, O islands; and let the people renew their strength' (xli, 1). The time of a resurrection was drawing near.

An occasional ripple disturbed the smooth surface of a 'calm sea people': the Poid men refused to crew their 'Company boat', the lugger *Manu*, until the Protector agreed to replace his chosen skipper from Badu with Uncle from Poid. Nau Mabaig recalls: 'When it's come time to recruit here at Badu all the Poid people stood up and they walked out. "We refuse to sign. If you want you could take that boat for the Gov'ment." They go down the beach, policeman try to stop them. They went down on the dinghy and paddle across to Poid. Government put Uncle skipper on that boat and all the Poid men agree with him' (Cassette 076/NM/B/1/81).

Killing softly does not light the flame of physical rebellion — unless the iron hand which inhabits the soft glove hits out. It is then that the bonded sometimes strike back.

6 FROM MAI TO PEARL SHELL

> *Before the War men and women go out and pick up*
> *wolfram. Then we say we'll come together to form some*
> *cooperative; so we formed this Moa Island Investment Co-*
> *operative. Everyone went to the wolfram. They just walked.*
> *Each family sold its own bags of wolfram to TI. All of Kubin*
> *and St Paul's, even some people from Mabuiag come out,*
> *Boigu, Saibai; everyone come out and camp round there,*
> *some from Murray Island. That's why people still talk*
> *about that wolfram mining today.*

> *Uncle, Chairman of Kubin Council*

> *We started the cooperative movement in 1958. Then in 1964*
> *I went down to school again for the bakery course in East*
> *Sydney Technical College. Kubin people all for it, Badu,*
> *Saibai, all the Torres Strait Islands and the Co-operative*
> *Society was coming good from all the people. But most they*
> *want their freedom. They thought this society would give*
> *them a freedom so they joined.*

> *Second St Paul's Man*

ENDOWING MAI WITH A NEW LIFE

THE ALLURE OF PEARL

They came from all quarters in search of bêche-de-mer and trochus and most of all golden-lip mother-of-pearl to meet the changing needs of the Old World: human labour-power of divers was indispensable to that purpose. Some of the intruders drawn to *magani* seas were brigands and pirates who looted the sea-floor and ransacked the islands for food and water and firewood and most of all slaves, especially women.[1] Many of these intruders did all that and left; the lives of others ended among the coral; fewer still were buried side by side with the indigenous people in the island cemeteries which the missionaries insisted they make. The activities of the pearlers joined a new thread into the enlarging networks of nineteenth century capitalist expansion though the sea-kings often came into conflict with the structures of law and order of capitalist powers. In the period following annexation of the Torres Strait Islands in 1879 they came into conflict with the resident sprigs of Imperial Britain (see Pennefather, 10 September 1882, ML).

Bêche-de-mer fishing began in the 1840s and pearl shelling had begun in earnest by the 1860s (MacGillivray 1852, 308). A shelling industry based on the Strait rose to world peaks by the end of the century. For the people of the area the establishment of that industry meant the tragedy of violence and violation.[2] In the Torres Strait Islands most distant from Cape York the destruction of the inhabitants came to a halt in the decade following the arrival of the London Missionary Society (LMS) and the annexation by Queensland, a situation contrasting sharply with the surging tide of destruction in the Cape York area which followed the withdrawal of the two Anglican missionaries from Somerset in 1868.[3] The Government Resident at Thursday Island, John Douglas, and some of the LMS missionaries, saw a potential for a trading centre in the Strait for pearl shell and copra in which Islanders would be integrated as petty producers on their own account. Although the passing of the Imperial Pacific Islanders Protection Act in 1872 (the Kidnappers Act as it was called) had begun to reduce unrestrained 'shanghai-ing', in the 1880s the activities of the pearlers were subjected to further regulation. In 1880 the schooner *Pearl*, flying the blue ensign of the British Navy, was commissioned by the Queensland government to supervise the outlying pearling stations (see T Hoghton, QV&P 1880, 6).

Among those so supervised was the Jamaican Douglas Pitt, who fondly and enigmatically called the honourable John Douglas, 'Black Douglas'. Douglas Pitt, a strong man in physical stature and personal make-up, had come to the Strait in 1870, a year before the missionaries. He began a 'floating station' off Murray Island, occupied land there without a licence, and was summarily expelled from Murray Island on 20 September 1882 by Henry Chester, at that time Commissioner for Lands.[4] He was fined one pound and three-and-sixpence costs and together with his Lifuan wife, Chopa, he was removed to Halfway Island against his will.[5] The life of Douglas Pitt is not uncharacteristic of men of that era who sought to divide up the oceans between themselves at a time when the imperial powers were jostling one another for lands on which to hoist their flags. Not for nothing did the notorious king of piracy, Bully Hayes, call Pitt 'the black pirate'. Life was raw and dangerous for those who ruled with the revolver: in a world where no man could be trusted those who went down to remove the wonders of the deeps had their wives hold their life-lines. Yet whatever his misuse of those who worked within his power (and Chester impugns his character in his report to the Minister for Lands), Pitt's influence in the area he adopted as his home was permanent and many-sided. It was with Pitt and his sons that early generations of colonised Islanders cut their teeth in the watery deeps and on the canefields of Queensland. First Meriam Man went south with the younger Pitts, cut cane around Daintree and rubbed shoulders with white workers. Top Islander divers and lugger captains among the Eastern Islanders readily acknowledge their debt to the Pitts. Sis, his great granddaughter, an Islander born in 1924, tells his story.

He used to wear a flowing beard; he used to wear two revolvers and he was said to be a good shot. He was six-foot-four, might be six-foot-six. He died in 1933 when he was living with us here at TI. He lived most of the time on Halfway Island. You ever hear Paul Robeson? My great grandfather had that kind of voice. He sang a lot more when he got blind. The reason he left Jamaica was he shot his sister's fiance. I mean she wanted to marry that boy and the parents didn't like him. Then he had to leave Jamaica. He settled in New Caledonia. He married Chopa who was a daughter of Chief Kalimo from Lifu.

Old Douglas Pitt followed Bully Hayes; he got back those two old ladies Bully Hayes stole. He followed them in his two-masted schooner; he ran it alongside Bully Hayes' boat, stepped on to it and said: 'Name your weapon!' And Bully Hayes said to him: 'I own half the Pacific; you join me and we'll take the other half.' But he used to tell stories about Bully Hayes: he was a dishonest man, a wicked man. But takes a thief to find a thief. It was Bully Hayes who called old Douglas Pitt 'the black pirate'. Douglas Pitt tells his story about how he was coming to Australia in 1870. He had to leave New Caledonia because he fought a duel. It was in order. They had seconds and everything and he killed the man. He had a business there, but my mother said it was probably a front for smugglers. It wouldn't be below him to make money that way — smuggling.

In those days they didn't have all the companies here on TI. A lot of them had floating stations as they called them. A lot of them had islands and my great grandfather's island was Halfway Island. He got right away. There he took his workers and he bred his own workers. He got wives for his men — as bad as Bully Hayes — but he had to. He only married strong women to his men and there was no fooling around with another's wives on his island because he ruled them with a revolver.

Well, old Douglas Pitt had Maryann; he brought his daughter Maryann with him. He had other children too: Chopa, his wife, just kept on having children. Then he sent Maryann to school in Brisbane from when she was seven years old to when she turned fourteen. When she left school she came back from Brisbane and her father had a West Indian man, twenty-two years old, to marry her. She didn't want to marry him; she didn't want to marry anybody. Must have been terrible in those days: to come back after going to school and living with white people treating you like a little girl. Well she was just a little schoolgirl. Her father had this twenty-two year old West Indian, his countryman. I bet he looked him over. He, Douglas Pitt was terr-ible. I mean he was a real boss; he ran everything, his

*whole family. One day he told her that she was going to be married:
'Well Maryann, today you make up your mind. It'll either be your
marriage or your funeral', he said; 'but we're going now, as soon as
you're ready'. And while he was talking he put a revolver away in
his coat pocket. Yeah, he even threatened his child. Maryann got
married but being his daughter she got back at him... Later, after her
husband died she married Grandfather T who was the son of an LMS
priest-missionary from the island of Niue.* (Summarised and edited
from Book of Islanders 1984, B90–93)

Maryann's strength of character stood her in good stead in the days of colour
segregation to come. In the mid-thirties when the terms of Protection were being
extended she refused to let C O'Leary, the Protector, come beyond high-water mark
at Rennel Island (Mauar) until he promised to give her family a paper of exemption
from 'the Act'. Auntie is one of her children: the qualities of strength and self-
willedness went down the line as courage and endurance.

CULTURAL DISSIMILARITY, A SEEDBED OF CONFLICT

PHASE ONE: THE 'COMPANY BOATS'

Islanders' participation in the marine economy took place under conditions chosen
by others. In the first years indigenous inhabitants came to own and work pearling

Plate 11 Sorting bêche-de-mer at Warrior Island (Saville-Kent 1893)

and trochus boats as clan owners, or as employees of 'master' pearlers. Many South Sea Islanders worked their own family boats. As I have mentioned (see Preface, xiv), given the long era of Protection which was extended even into the early 1980s through provisions of the Torres Strait Islanders Act, a class of Torres Strait Islander independent producer-owners only began to emerge in any sphere of the economy in the mid–1980s. The three phases of colonisation discussed in Chapter 5 provided the framework in which Islanders took part in the money economy.

From the earliest days after annexation Islanders began to take part in the economy of pearl shell on their own account. In less than a decade after 1879 Islanders were paying off newly acquired cutters (QV&P 1888, 6). They were given official encouragement to participate: through 'contact with the white man' and his 'constant supervision' Islanders might be taught to give up 'their idle useless life' and work for themselves, as the acting Government Resident at Thursday Island, Hugh Milman, wrote in 1886 (QV&P 1887, 6). By 1890 the prospects of a trading community in which Islanders participated in the area between Cape York and the coast of New Guinea were seen as promising (QV&P 1891, 3).

Islanders' wants increased rapidly: money to buy calico and groceries and hymn books soon became a 'necessity'. In response to his suggestions Islanders approached Rev FW Walker, who had been a member of the LMS Mission since 1888, requesting his assistance in buying their own money-earning boats (Bleakley

Plate 12 Grading pearl shell at Badu, 1920s

1961, 265). In 1904 Walker established Papuan Industries Limited (PIL), a Christian trading station with headquarters at Badu Island, whose purpose was to encourage Islander participation in the pearling industry to increase their self-reliance (Austin 1972, 38–62).

The response was rapid and enthusiastic. In the first year two boats were purchased at Mabuiag and three at Murray Island. The latter three which had an earning capacity of £300 per year were fully paid for that year; they had been completely overhauled, and the people were taking 'great pride in their possession', it was officially noted (QPP 1905, 21). The Meriam were already conversant with basic accounting and soon became competent at handling the sale of the catch and the distribution of the proceeds from the activities of the 'Company boats' as they came to be known, which were owned on a clan (or community) basis. In 1904, the Chief Protector of Aboriginals described the procedure:

> The cash is made up into a sealed package and is taken to the Island, where the seal is broken at a public meeting of the tribe, and the cash distributed among its members, male and female, the actual swimmers receiving more than the others. A copy of the balance-sheet is always sent out with the natives for production at their public meeting; the younger individuals are

Plate 13 Papuan Industries Limited, Badu, 1920s

quite competent to make the same intelligible and there is always
the school teacher on the island to refer to. (QPP 1905, 21)

Soon Islanders from all over the Strait were buying cutters and luggers
through PIL. By 1907 there were eighteen boats; half of them had been fully paid
for with the interest by the Islander owners. The catch for the year 1906 when
they were working off their debts was sold for £2,756. By 1912 the PIL vessels
sold catch worth £3,895 reducing the debts to £450 (Bleakley 1961, 266). A fleet
of vessels recognisable as the 'Company boats' by the 'common badge' of black
and white striped railings often carrying Island or clan names like *Argan* and
Wakaid of Badu Island; *Tagai, Meriam, Erub* and *Ugar* of the Eastern Islands,
were operating alongside the pearling luggers of the 'Master' pearlers, as the private
employers were known. In the 1880s, Islanders, along with Aborigines and Asian
indentured labourers, had participated as boat crews: now as boat owners Islanders
had 'come up level' with the employers, most of whom were European.[6] As it was
passed down to Ailan Man who grew up in a later period: 'In those days we were
free; we took our shell to Thursday Island; we sold it to the firms we chose'.

PHASE TWO: CONTROL OF THE 'COMPANY BOATS'

Soon after 1901 the priorities of a White Australia began to have widespread
repercussions in the pearling industry. The context of Islanders' activities was a
labour shortage in the industry which had three main causes: the exclusion of
any more Melanesians entering Queensland from the Pacific Islands after the end
of 1890; the unattractiveness of the industry to white workers; and the decision
of the Royal Commission of 1908 not to lift restrictions on the introduction of Asian
workers from abroad.[7] Unlike the Queensland sugar industry mechanisation was
not an option: 'neither mechanical harvesting nor controlled cultivation of shell'
had become established (Bach 1961, 203). The industry remained labour intensive
with Japanese as the main 'dress divers' up to the outbreak of the Second World
War, and Pacific Islanders, Asians, Torres Strait Islanders and Aborigines as crew.[8]
The 'Master' pearlers perceived the Islander-owned 'Company boats' as a source
of competition.[9] For the Administration, Islanders' ownership of their own fishing
vessels was a source of independence which threatened its power over them.

Four changes were made over a time to the functioning of PIL which
effectively meant the passing of control of the 'Company boats' from their Islander
owners to the Administration. First, the ultimate control of recruiting boat crews
passed into the Protector's hands. Second, there was a change from sale of shell
by tender or auction to automatic sale to the Aboriginal Industries Board (AIB),
the renamed PIL, which was sold to the Administration in 1930 (QPP 1931, 9).

Third, control over earnings became total; part went to an Island Fund (established in 1912) and part went as credit to the Islander producer in the AIB stores.[10] Fourth and finally, where boats were not worked 'satisfactorily' in the eyes of the Protector, he confiscated them.

In 1912 the PIL produced its second prospectus, stating as its main objective the promotion of the 'material, moral and spiritual welfare of Islanders by encouraging them to make efforts for their own improvement, through the cultivation of marketable products' (Methodist Church Overseas Mission Papers, 167, paraphrased by Austin 1972, 52). Yet already its position had come under attack. In LMS circles the argument was advanced that Christian missions should not compete with traders like Burns Philp (Austin 1972, 49). In 1916 the Administration prevented some Islanders from selling their produce directly to dealers rather than to the Protector (QPP 1917).[11] In 1920 a number of boats were confiscated for not being worked 'satisfactorily' (QPP 1921).

In the first days of the 'Company boats' officials had supposed that Islanders were developing as a race of independent petty producers in the marine industry; in fact their participation was substantially on a clan basis. Despite the destructive effects of the invasion the material social base of Island communities remained: customary land tenure and inheritance patterns continued as did kinship relations (Haddon 1904, 284–92; 1908, 163–68). Island culture continued to grow within those spaces which indirect rule had left free: Islanders had their own priorities concerning the ways they used their cutters and luggers.

Cultural dissimilarity was soon noted: since the climate and soil favour 'spontaneous growth', it appeared to Hugh Milman, the Government Resident at Thursday Island, that no trouble is taken by Islanders 'to improve the natural state of things in any way...' (QV&P 1887, 1026). The people are so '...wanting in vigour and in the incentives to industry...that they are scarcely likely to rise very rapidly in the scale of civilisation', John Douglas reported on a visit to Murray Island in 1885 (QV&P 1886, 2).

Although it was hidden by the enthusiasm and application with which Islanders first greeted the new experiences, two or three decades of the events which went with foreign rule were to deepen and intensify cultural difference. That Islanders would come to mirror the social make-up of their overseers was the first expectation. Several decades later, their failure to become replicas of those who appointed themselves to remould them was to baffle their rulers (QPP 1912, 21). Look, they leave coconuts to drop and rot on the ground, Milman declaimed in a tone of exasperation in 1887 (QV&P 1888). The Mabuiag Islanders gave away thousands of 'surplus' coconuts despite a big demand for copra, the government teacher reported in 1910:

...the natives annoy me over the coconuts...'In September they gave Papuan Industries Company 3,000 nuts for carriage of cement from Thursday Island for their new church in course of erection, and in October another 4,000 as a present for their native friends in Badu. During the Christmas holidays their Moa friends, over 80 in number, came for a fortnight's visit and took back with them over 7,000 nuts. (Minnis in QPP 1911, 20; see also report on Yam Island 1911, 23)

Islanders preferred to share their new produce with their friends rather than to sell it (see QPP 1910, 20; QPP 1912, 21; QPP 1913, 26 and throughout).

To the Administrators of the first decade of White Australia, Islanders appeared as people for whom 'time is no object' (QPP 1910, 20). They were seen to work their cutters in 'fitful spurts', and in a casual way. For men with fixed ideas about the superiority of the capitalist work ethic Islanders were like quicksilver. The cutters and luggers were becoming 'free of debt'; Komet clan at Murray had bought a new lugger, and the boat crews were active, it was reported officially for the year 1911; yet there was a failure to 'work the boats regularly' or 'to keep them in good order'. The same Report identifies the qualities which the Administration was not prepared to tolerate: Islanders take a 'keen interest' in the subject of the boats and how they are governed and 'do not readily assent to anything which appears to curtail their liberties or tends to spur them on to

Plate 14 At Mabuiag Island (photograph by Frank Hurley 1924)

improve their methods of living or working' (QPP 1913, 22).[12] Moves were being made to make Islanders 'responsible': 'stringent regulations somewhat on the lines of those now in force for the regulation of Papuan villages' are needed, the Government Resident at Thursday Island wrote in 1911 (QPP 1912, 15). That was the purpose of the Island Fund which was instituted in 1912: the owners of the 'Company boats' supervised by the Administration were to be forced to contribute to the upkeep of the Islands. A new system which resembled indenturing in Papua emerged whereby Islanders were to be forced to work their own boats. Its disciplinary character was made explicit in the Chief Protector's Report for 1914: 'I am convinced that persuasive methods have failed to produce the desired results, and the only alternative is legislative authority to insist upon every able-bodied man doing a fair day's work. In some quarters this procedure would be termed "slavery"...' (QPP 1915, 12). As the fortunes of the pearling industry fluctuated over the next two decades the assessments of Islanders by the Chief Protector oscillated between two extremes: criticism of their 'thriftlessness' (QPP 1923) and praise of their ability to 'work well' and achieve results (QPP 1925). Following the appointment of JD McLean as local Protector in the early years of the Great Depression, measures were introduced which effected the final transition from the limited delegation of powers to cast-iron rule.

PHASE THREE: BREAKING CUSTOM, THE 'FREEING' OF LABOUR POWER

In 1929 the Minister for Home Affairs, the Department responsible for 'Protection', offered the prize of a silver cup to the 'best' boat. Tanu Nona, skipper of the lugger *Wakaid*, whose father was a Samoan and mother a Saibai Islander, was born at Saibai in 1900. Nona, who had become a 'Badu man', related to Jeremy Beckett how the prize was won:

> The government set me to race with Douglas Pitt [Junior] from Darnley Island. In six weeks I got ten ton of trochus; Douglas Pitt only got five. That's how Badu got the *Wakaid*, the biggest lugger in Torres Strait. For six years we kept the cup until the competition was cancelled... Some skippers work only half day, six in the morning till dinner time, then sail onto the next reef. That way they lose half a day. But I keep them there till six in the evening. We cook the shell and sail on to the next reef night-time. Making the crew work is the main thing. (Beckett 1977, 89–90)[13]

This event foreshadowed a changing of the rules by which the boats would be worked: they were to be clan boats only in name. In the name of Badu the *Wakaid* now claimed the 'best' divers. A new custom and a new 'nationalism' were being instituted: 'this' side would compete with 'that' side. Nau Mabaig recalls the change: 'Our custom been pulled down. Tanu Nona tell all the tribes and the people of Badu: "I think the better way we finish with these tribes. I want to get even the youngest teenagers to sign on *Wakaid* and we'll fight for the Silver Cup." They break our custom.'

New land laws introduced by the Badu Council under Tanu Nona forced men onto the boats; Council by-laws required that all able-bodied men must work and deserters were expelled from the Island (Beckett 1963, 253–63). On the other side of the Strait the 'Silver Cup' was lost. As Ailan Man explains: 'The Darnley blokes got lots of small shells, but Tanu was a friend of the Government, so they let him pass all his small shell, but they treated the Darnley boys' small shell as rejects...'. The 'Company boats' were finished: a 'Nona-fleet' emerged over a time with hand-picked skippers (Beckett 1963, 247; 1977, 93).

Islanders began to search for alternatives to fighting for the Silver Cup and being obliged to eat their midday piece of damper on the reef by attempting to get their own boats once again or to move outside pearling altogether. Like Nau Mabaig and his brothers, wherever they could, Islanders turned away from diving on these terms towards something else. The aim was always the same: to come up level. First Meriam Man initiated cooperative ventures with Murray Islanders: a firewood business, a boarding house, a welfare society at Murray Island.

The first of the three groups of narratives which follow gives a picture of the 'work' of diving; the second is a story of the making of a Torres Strait Islander; and the third group consists of brief illustrative accounts of three social alternatives to pearling initiated by Islanders.

REVERSING THE COIN

WORK

In the context of pearling Islanders' special competence as seafarers, swimmers and divers took on a new meaning. They began to fit old skills to the changed purposes. They had their own ways of knowing where to find pearl shell: 'When there is a swell and no surf you just take a coconut and split it. Bite the nut. Throw the nut in the water. The grease goes, the smoothness from the surface of the water. So you go out. Jump down. Black-lip [mother-of-pearl] down there. All the boys look down there. Just throw down the nut. Thick!' (Cassette 049/FB/TI/1/80).

First St Paul's Man from Moa Island, recalls diving as a way of life:

> You go out. Time to come out now. It's low water. Go out. Four in one
> dinghy. Off we go. Just flour; we no food I tell you. You ought to see

hard work. Ooh...too hard. So we work all year round. 'You fellers go
out now.' And we carry damper belong we. Damper. Damper enough
for four. Four slice: One, two, three, four. That's all that's for dinner.
Go down catchem shell bringem come. Go, go, go, go. Right down... We
pick up shell and we shout to our mate, 'Come, shell, plenty shell.' Shark
go come. Watch them cross one, hammerhead! That's the one. Oh dear,
careful this one. Come home, that's our best time. From December,
January, February go start again... Money belong we three pound a
month. That money last one year because mummy work too in garden.
(Cassette 049/FB/TI/1/80)

And a Badu Islander recounts what it meant fighting for the Silver Cup:

Competition on under Tanu Nona and we Western ones won the
competition, but it was very bad. Before sun-up you have your one
piece damper. That's all you get. You can't get no more than any other
crew. And God knows when you're going to have a second bite. Terrible
those days were. We eat raw clamshell meat to keep ourself alive; or
floating coconut. It doesn't matter whether it stink or not. Who gonna
complain 'gainst Tanu? You just have to cop it. Anyway, we were the
people which obey the orders given to us whether it's right or whether
it's wrong. We just have to do it. (Cassette 076/BM/B/1/81)[14]

CALICO AND COINS: I'VE GOT THAT FEELING OF PRIDE IN ME OF BEING AN ISLANDER, AILAN MAN

Ailan Man was born at Darnley Island in 1926. His childhood ambition was to
'match' Tanu Nona as a sea-captain: in the process of following that early ambition
he came up 'level' with him in an alternative life to pearling. In the process of
coming to 'walk abreast' with Tanu Nona he became a Torres Strait Islander who
could set an example for others.

I thought I'd work my way up and match this bloke

I think I might have started at a very early age to become something.
I don't know whether I told you the other day about a time I was helping
my mother and father doing the chores. After I said to myself, 'There
they go again talking about this Tanu'. I could be ten or nine. I said,
'Well if Tanu can be all they say he is, I'd like to find out his beginnings
too. How does he get up there?' Even at that time I thought I'd work
my way up to be a sea-captain and match this bloke and stand beside
him. Well it didn't turn out that way, but I did come up to be a group
representative of the Eastern Islands at an early age and I walk abreast
with Tanu Nona.

> *My mother read whatever fell into her lap and she would*
> *tell the yarns to the village people. She never talked to the lady next*
> *door about her son. It was years after that she started to relive the*
> *old times and talked to somebody: 'That Mr Chandler told me my boy*
> *is going to be going a long way'. And that's the first time I ever heard*
> *it. In school the teacher used to get me to come up to do mental*
> *arithmetic with the bigger grade.*

'...I want to know like a white man'

> *You see my mind opened to the world the first time I heard about*
> *university when a signalman during the War said he's going back*
> *to the uni. It's a new language the blokes spoke during the War. They'd*
> *often come to me and talk about things. So I thought to myself: Well,*
> *if I join up it's not going to be the bloody Torres Strait Light Infantry*
> *for me. I'm going to join a white unit because I won't learn nothing*
> *in the Torres Strait Light. But I'll be able to learn more by serving*
> *next door to a white bloke and be able to ask him things, because I*
> *want to know like a white man.*
>
> > *When Tom Chandler came [to Darnley] he taught us the*
> *English grammar and how to use words. Before he came there was*
> *very little about 'has' and 'have' and all that sort of thing. Then I found*
> *that the old Island teachers changed their voice to make them say things*
> *like white men, but their grammar is all wrong. And I said, 'I'd rather*
> *keep my voice like my own voice and my grammar right'. I thought*
> *then, One good thing that I'm able to find out for myself and judge*
> *is what the other bloke did: he's not talking right in this language.*
> *I like to find mistakes by white men in their own language and I laugh*
> *when they spell wrongly. Then I wanted to join the fortress signals,*
> *to learn about the radio and talk to someone to improve my English.*
> *I think it's just that I always wanted to find out more about things*
> *and inquire about them. At the end of the War I wanted to become*
> *a leader of Torres Strait. Well, as I said before, my goal was to stand*
> *alongside Tanu Nona.*

With the five bob I bought my first double calico...and the other two bob I gave to my mother

> *When I started to work for the Island Industries Board, they don't give*
> *you wages, they just give you a bonus. My first bonus was fifty cents*
> *— five bob. Well I started off that year, 1940 I think. My mother said,*
> *'You're not going to wear that double calico, that* lavalava'. *We wear*
> *single piccaninny suit, just one cloth when you're still a little boy.*
> *'Oh', she said, 'when you can earn money yourself, then you can buy*
> *yourself a double calico'. So that fifty cents was like five hundred*
> *dollars. I bought myself a double calico. I looked like a man. Even boys*
> *much younger than myself had access to their fathers'* lavalava. *But*

me, I didn't. I wasn't allowed. My mother: talk about strong! I know
you're going to ask me how with five bob could I buy that: Well it was
ninepence a yard, nice pink cloth, heavy rose pink, seersucker sort
of material; three bob and the other two bob I gave to my mother.

When I came to TI, I used to walk round and round the
shops looking in that bloody window and see those toys in there. I'd
wish they were mine. After the War I bought every toy that came into
the shop; to satisfy myself. I worked in TI now. I used to stand outside
with no money and can't buy the bloody thing even. I'd buy the thing,
take it home to the camp where I stayed and after it'd been sitting on
my table for a couple of nights I gave it to one of the kids.

I've got that feeling of pride in me of being an Islander

When my old man asked me to come ashore, I went and bought myself
a pair of shorts. 'This is town', I thought. 'I can't go ashore with my
little bit of cloth'. You can't wear calico in TI. It's like you're belittling
yourself. It's a feeling of shame to walk around in lavalava. And I
thought of adopting the opposite attitude to that. I said, 'I put lavalava
on whether you bloody like it or not'. You know, I've got that feeling
of pride in me of being an Islander. Well, that's the feeling in me. I
wore lavalava when I met the Queen. They took me and measured me
for that bloody penguin suit, dinner suit and that bow tie. When he
took me around to look at the coats I bought a white tie and shirt that'll
go with my blue lavalava. And that night when we all come out to get
into the government car to go to Parliament House in Canberra, they
saw me walk out with my blue lavalava. They didn't say anything.
I'd like people to accept me as I am and not what they might want
me to be. I'm a Torres Strait Islander and that's all. One of these days
I'll wear a lavalava from this wharf and hop on the plane and get off
in Townsville. I'm a Torres Strait Islander and that's my dress. You've
seen me knocking around Darnley. I just go around with that piece
of calico. The Islanders used to carry them across the shallows to the
shore before: with the bishop and the government people too. I said,
'No more! Finish, finish!' I called out to the man who had the job of
carrying him ashore, 'You Ailanmn, you stop here, you nothing lesser
than him'. I said, 'You might as well go put a bloody saddle on your
back and go ride em ashore'.

I planted a flag and I was going to work towards it

I decided at the end of the War, that the opening is there by working
through Meriam Man in order to get to Tanu. All the other boys were
looking for grog here. I went looking around where Meriam Man
stopped. After I get into Council and went to meetings I felt that I could
match Tanu and even go further than Tanu; and the access to it is
via Meriam Man. I still had my childhood thing to look to. I planted

a flag, my ambition, and I was going to work towards it. Lots of things now I could do, even outsmart Tanu, because I could feel what I've got in me, what I was equipped with. I've got to pass through a lot of ranks, a lot of people with pips to get there. I built up an animosity towards the other leaders, especially those who were pro-Protector.

This Meriam Man was standing up to them in an unbelievable way. That's when I saw now, 'I can see myself going to be the Meriam Man type of leader...and [more quietly] the Tanu type of leader'. I've always believed that whatever happens you have to support the feeling of the masses, which way people want things. You must try to do it their way. Well let's say, 'That's just politics'.

The older blokes talked about freedom and getting out of bondage

When I came in there in 1943 or '44 for civil construction I was a young fellow. All the older blokes belonged to the movement and talked about freedom and getting out of bondage. When Meriam Man went round the Islands to conduct the elections in the late '40s and '50s I asked to accompany him and do his clerical work. I got close to him in '46. All this group representatives thing was born out of the work of one South Sea man. He came and talked a lot about citizen rights and freedom in the Torres Strait and Murray and Darnley Island Councils wanted to meet with the Director [of the DNA] with him as their spokesman to get out of the house of bondage. (Book of Islanders 1984, B111–19)

PEOPLE'S BUSINESS: WE'VE GOT OUR OWN CUSTOM, SECOND ST PAUL'S MAN

The wolfram mine at Kubin, the bakery at St Paul's, the housing cooperative, MAW, linking Moa, Thursday Island and Cape York, were all cooperative, self-managed projects. They arose as alternatives to endless diving from sun-up to sunset, the humiliation of begging for one's earnings from the government's 'right-hand man' and dependence on the mercy of the Protector/DNA to provide houses and stores.

THE WOLFRAM MINE

UNCLE

Come, dig! People still talk about that wolfram mining today

Before the War men and women go out and pick up wolfram little by little and sell it to Island Industries Board [IIB] in TI. Then we say we'll come together to form some cooperative; so we formed this Moa Island Investment Co-operative. So this began with wolfram mining. Everyone went to the wolfram. They just walked. Each family sold its own bags of wolfram to TI. One man used to be there to buy it and IIB took it across by dinghy. It was hard; we got no outboards in those

days, only sailing dinghy. So we used picks and shovels. Oh dear me,
hard work! Some families went out there and camped. All of Kubin
and St Paul's, even some people from Mabuiag come out, Boigu, Saibai;
everyone come out and camp round there, some from Murray Island.
Several hundred people were there. That's why people still talk about
that wolfram mining today.

The Department did their part when they found one of these
old miners and sent him out here to teach people how to mine for
wolfram, how to make a shaft like they used to do it in the old days.
He was a very smart old fellow and when the crowbar was blunt he
showed we how to sharpen it. He was like a blacksmith. He was a very
old white man, oh lovely old fellow; showed we how to make a hut,
split wood right down the middle, take all the stuff out and make
corrugated iron and build a stove, make bread. Something new, we
never thought like that. We been try to do the mining and it's big rain
and there was water at the mine. We grow good gardens: banana,
pawpaw, yam, pineapple. No stores there; you had to live on bush
tucker. Long way to get them; you had to carry them. Tanu himself
came here and mined wolfram. People all came here.

THE BAKERY

UNCLE

Co-op means to pull together, so we try to come together

It was started by Rev Father Clint. He came over here to St Paul's and
called for Kubin people to go over there and he explained what a co-
op is. Co-op means to pull together, so we try to come together and form
this Christian Co-op at Moa. We been talking things over and Father
Clint said, 'What about starting off with something we eat every day?'
Well we said, 'What about we start a bakery?' So everybody agreed
that the bakery start off in small way and they make some small huts
first to make the bread in. The village people just built them. We baked
the bread in wood stoves at the beginning. So we said, 'We want a man
go down to Tranby College and learn how to make bread and learn
how to make a stove for bread'. And P, one St Paul's man agreed to
go down and he learnt about this bakery business down there. He
bought some of these things where you can bake bread and he get some
material and cement for making blocks, and when he came back all
this stuff was coming too. So P and one or two other men from St Paul's
made this house, this bakery, and they built up this big brick-work
at St Paul's. When it's finished we call for a priest to bless that house.
It took over a month to make this bakery. They did good work. it was
a village project; everyone helped to do that work. (B48–49)

SECOND ST PAUL'S MAN

The Waterside Workers gave us the bakery

We started the cooperative movement in 1958. Then in 1964 I went down to school again for the bakery course in East Sydney Technical College. So when I'm down there I went round making appeal for help for our bakery. Then I went to the Waterside Workers' Federation Conference and they asked me to speak. I told them all about our bakery, all the materials and then after they gave us money to start the bakery. It might be around £1,300 or £1,400.

The Melbidir, *DNA boat, took all that machinery over and put it on the Island at St Paul's, Moa. We do that building, we put that motor in the machine, we put that lighting plant down: build everything. Kubin people all for it, Badu, Saibai, all the Torres Strait Islands and the Co-operative Society was coming good from all the people. But most they want their freedom.*

They thought this society would give them a freedom so they joined. But it's not going to: it's people's business. So anyhow we worked. Lots and lots of people outside Moa joined because they thought this was the answer.

It belongs to the people; it's people's business

Well, when we start our bakery we sell the bread to Islanders, but all our goods we get through the DNA, from their store. They take them over on their boat. They take flour over first from TI to St Paul's. Next trip they take yeast over to the bakery. They don't take everything one time; they leave it in half there. When yeast's supposed to come over to the bakery they say there's no yeast on the boat. That's the DNA! On purpose. I tell you straight, on purpose! Then after they change over the manager [of DNA] new man say: 'That's a business principle that you'll have to pay cash'. In business they give you thirty days. Well, that was on purpose too and we got no boat to take our flour any time.

I know there's plenty of people who come before you and say, 'I am a Christian'; but when I myself go to see them they're too far yet to go near God. Even if you read your Bible all day but you haven't got occasion to love God it profit you nothing. There was a Mission boat, but if I take my flour on that boat it might dirty the boat, yet that bakery stands on a mission field. But it's not mine; it belongs to the people. It's people's business. That Father Peter Hand help us. But some old other ones, no! They're brother to DNA. Well everybody looks at the Cross, but everybody got same price, a penny a day. You might not get the same here on this earth but 'up there' it'll be a different story: everyone at a penny a day whether you be bishop or just workers.

We go round in a dinghy and deliver the bread

> The time when Father Brown came up the Co-op taught us how to run
> cooperative business methods of accounting. Well the first thing they
> told us about is bookkeeping: 'It doesn't matter whatsoever you do you
> must know how to sell it: that's part of bookkeeping.'
>
> At St Paul's, Kubin, Badu, we got to go round with a
> dinghy. If it was blowing really hard I can't make it, I put the bread
> in a carton, I cover it with plastic. We started in 1965 and in 1970–71
> things were going down: flour one trip and then yeast another trip.
> In the early part the DNA do that, so we have to buy the flour and
> yeast from the IIB store on the Island at St Paul's. That's their store;
> it belongs to DNA. It cost more and we paid cash. When we sell the
> bread we bank all the money in our number two account to pay for
> the next lot. Yes, you have to look after the rainy day; before you could
> just fish or garden. But the bakery's all right. We've only got our own
> custom: working together, live happy, share things together. (B162–65)

THE HOUSING COOPERATIVE

UNCLE

Moa-Adai-Waiben is a housing cooperative

> MAW is a housing cooperative. M stands for Moa, A stands for Adai,
> that's Northern Peninsula Area [NPA], and W stands for Waiben, that's
> TI. Mr Killoran, Director of DAIA he said that we couldn't build any
> more houses at Kubin or St Paul's, although we can go on building
> at TI and Horn Island, not 'Reserves' under the Act.
>
> MAW build these houses at Kubin. When a house is
> complete it no more belongs to the MAW, it belongs to Moa Island
> Investment Company. Same with Adai ones. We in the community
> choose this person to be in that house and that same person pays his
> rent, $15 every week to Moa Island clerk here who looks after his books.
> When Mr Killoran stopped this MAW from building these houses at
> Kubin and St Paul's he meant it and he said he will never change his
> mind about this unless the Co-operative gives the money to the
> Councils. The same thing applies to NPA. (B50)

REFLECTING UPON CULTURAL SHELL

ENSEMBLES OF MEANING

Mai, as the nacre or the shell of the pearl oyster in the languages of both sides
of the Strait, had always been subtly woven into the lives of Islanders. From this
centre meaning upon meaning had been built up. Among Western Islanders *mai*

means grief or mourning; it also means to take or to hold. Like *mar, mari*, associated with shadows and reflections and with the spirit world, *mai* too is the prime stem of a host of other words, many of them common to most languages of the sandbeach people of the region, even though they have slightly different meanings (Ray 1907). In Meriam Mir *zogo-mai* is a sacred ornament shaped like a crescent moon; and *kemerkemer mai*, a beautifully worked circular fretted pearl shell (Moore 1984, 402–07; Mer 1898, 79 and Plate 47).

Whether in 'natural' or in a worked-up form, wherever *mai* circulated there was no substitution of the qualities of *mai* in itself for those of the person who was giving it to another individual. In other words, *mai* had no 'value' of its 'own' apart from its placating of, or creating further bonds with, another person: 'The shell itself, even a part of it is *mai*', Au Bala explains; 'one side of the shell, is still *mai*. When it is cut into crescent, new-moon shape, it's still *mai*. Must have been a very valuable thing, because even the part of it is still *mai*.' Nowhere did the word *mai*, alone, as a stem of a word-symbol for something, or as a component of a compound verb, denote an impersonal relationship. Nowhere did it serve to represent a relationship among strangers, nor be emptied of the human message of an exchange. *Mai* lay everywhere beneath the sea. Islanders took what they needed for their use and exchanges of dissimilarities, and to create sacred ornaments that went with moments of passage. Shells of different kinds were 'valuable' to Islanders in the context of mutual personal relations. Tools and the items they fashioned with them retained what Marx called 'the particular and natural form of labour' (1949, 49), namely, the labour of *this* man, not *that* man: they did not want *mai* in order to 'go into production'. Their labour was concrete and personalised. The 'values' they produced were use-values and the exchange relations, which began with gifts to brothers-in-law and went further afield through *wauri* creating networks of *tebud* in other lands, remained personal human relations. External 'barter' had not been 'a disintegrating influence' upon the interiors of their communities (Marx 1970, 50). The networks of reciprocity strengthened and extended over time. 'Alliances' made through *wauri* and intermarriage were like 'post-war' pacts that came to group islands together. 'Shell' was 'valuable' in creating *tebud*; it had not 'stepped forth' as a commodity.[15]

Underlying and framing all these relations were the constitutive meanings of the society: in the traditional life of the Meriam the *zogo* which came through Malo framed all social life. *Zogo* joined mortals into the cosmic circles: in exchanging 'valuables' they were exchanging the complete ensemble of their life-meanings. At the pinnacle of this cultural frame were the *Zogo le*: the intercessors of the forces of 'more than man'. The fine finish of tools and sacred things was a result of careful handcrafting, intense and long-lasting labour by a sequence of individuals who were 'gifted' at fine crafting. The finished object was 'valuable' in the sense that a part of this person or chain of persons was embedded in it (see Malinowski 1961). Au Bala explains the way the 'labour process' was enveloped by culture:

> What I was told by a few old men was that when these old men made tools they used some sort of magic words which we call zogo mir. I've seen one seuriseuri with eight points; those eight points stand for eight tribes of Murray. Right, and how it was made you'd hardly believe. It was polished, well polished. Which tool they used to shape it I don't know, but some old people say that they grind it with some sort of hard piece of rock or stone. It must have taken days and months to shape one because to grind it with another stone now is impossible in our day. But in days gone by I think they used those magic words. (Book of Islanders 1984, B147)

Convivial tools and human-scale modes of gardening or fishing were set by Island custom, which did not resemble those 'habits of industry' which government officials themselves valued and which they hoped to instil in Islanders. Theirs was a dissimilar code: eburlem esmaolem means drop and rot on the ground, which, as Kebi Bala explains, means that 'we respect the soil... We don't exploit it.' The same is true of fishing; they took what they needed. They didn't exploit the sea or the sea-bed and go out and 'in one big rush' grab all the mai. For the mai of the sea-ground is not 'inert matter'; it is part of a living cosmos to which a person's relationship is not uni-directional but 'matched'. (See Chapters 2 and 3 above.) As two-way processes reciprocal relations are antithetical to physical exploitation, just as abstracting the properties of the environment are inimical to the 'speculative' mind. Commodity relations stamped mai as a valuable thing irrespective of the yumi of a living relationship. Mai as pearl shell has taken on a singular quality: it has a meaning in itself becoming interchangeable with money, a new thing one step removed from the reciprocal relations of life both natural and social. Mai is a metaphor for exchange gifts carrying within it the ensemble of meanings of existence; pearl shell carries the 'thingness' of commodity exchange.

NEW THREADS FOR BROKEN NETS

In reciprocal relations the existence of similarity pulled apart from dissimilarity is logically impossible. The logic of commodity relations is to make that separation; its thrust is to homogenise, to create 'all-the-same'. That logic came to impinge on Islanders from the earliest days of 'contact'. The tendency of capitalist social relations based on commodity exchange was to dissolve the reciprocal relations of Islander communities. Yet given the priorities of colour segregation the tendency of White Australia was to keep the pre-existing social relations together.[16] Even the attempts to integrate Islanders into the commodity economy as 'free' labourers dispossessed of their own means of production had going with it a continuing control of their lives by 'Protection'.

An important consequence was that Islanders did not live the exchange abstraction. They continued to belong to place, to home ground, to the myths of *this* place, not *that* place. As people undetached from the reciprocal relations which tied them to place and to primary social group 'things' were not separated from their producers and exchangers. They had not been drawn within that web in which *solus ipse*, I alone, to the exclusion of others, own this thing, whether that thing be land or coconuts or *mai*, or whether it be money, the universal equivalent of them all (Sohn-Rethel 1978, 41–43). Commodity relations impinged on them personally; as divers, crew, skippers they took part in the production relations of capitalism. They sold their labour power to the 'Master' pearlers which created surplus value, but they were not wage slaves stripped of their means of production, although from the mid–1930s onwards, especially at Badu, there was the attempt to make them so. Islanders desired money for goods which characteristically they shared with their kinsfolk or contributed toward affinal obligations on occasions of 'gift-giving'. Calico and coins became equivalents for items of exchange of *wauri*-time: the new things were fitted within their social relations and symbolic systems. In this sense their involvement was peripheral (see Read 1959, 429).

Certainly Islanders used money when they could get it: indeed they had been 'measured' by it, or (at least) their labour had. The '*mai*' they dived for, brought to the surface, weighed, scraped and transported, had within it now their congealed labour: it had become a commodity. It was that labour which determined its *value*. In consequence, they were being measured one against another anew: the best man was he whose labour produced the latter's greatest formal equivalent — money. They were being sought after: as a boat crew the summation of their equivalences meant success or failure as 'winners' or 'losers' and the prize of a silver cup was 'shared' by men as atoms, not by men tied together in humanly meaningful ways, viz, in clan groups.

Islanders were aware of the use and 'value' of money long before they were denied control of amounts of it due to them. Yet the denial of their right to it helped to crystallise its necessity for them. They perceived it as offering them the freedom to live on the same terms as Kole as well as the chance to buy those things which had become indispensable to their social life. Money had also become integrated into their own exchange relations; it often became the new form of secret gifts. So money came to play a double role for Islanders. In the first place it was a way of measuring themselves against Kole so that denial of it diminished

Islanders in their own eyes. That presented itself as the humiliation of 'tobacco and blanket and ten [store] items': so they sought to control their earnings and their passbooks as free men and women. In the second place, money was a means of extending their social relations; it had become an 'equivalent' for gifts in a context where Islanders' 'needs' had expanded to include many other things from 'Kole-land': first, iron tools, then calico and groceries and so on.

At this level 'things' and 'money' were now part of the processes of giving and receiving which had themselves gone beyond the old social networks. New ways of 'seeing' other Islanders had come into being. So the Mabuiag Islanders in 1910 gave away thousands of 'surplus' coconuts (which in days gone by had not been plentiful at all) to the Moans nearby, who only a generation or two before had been their enemies (Haddon 1912, 132). The circles of giving went beyond the old boundaries. The boats were being used to enlarge those circles despite the logic of commodity relations which was to prize them open and throw life tangentially on to the straight-line of the one dimension: *selling* commodities as an act of 'I alone'.

Wolfram mining meant money. 'Come dig!' came the call from Kubin a generation later, to which hundreds of Islanders responded: from the nearby islands of Badu and Mabuiag, from Saibai and Boigu and even from the Murray Islands in the far east they joined with the communities of Moa pitching tents and erecting bush houses on the wolfram hill. 'Uncle never knocked anyone back', Nau Mabaig recalls; 'he gave us so many acres to work on. I was working there at Kubin.' Those who came together were different to before: people from this side and the other side had joined hands.

Built into the 'people's business' of the wolfram mine, the bakery and the housing cooperative, was the knowledge of the 'other side' of the coin of white culture. The 'very old white fellow' who taught them to make a mine shaft; Father Clint of Tranby College in Sydney, who taught them how to build and run the bakery and the methods of accounting that go with 'business'; the white fellows of the Waterside Workers' Federation and so on, were not 'the brothers to the DNA', their tormentors, with whom Islanders were so bitterly, painfully and intimately familiar. They were the sort of people whom the younger Meriam Man went in search of in the 1950s and eventually discovered when he was founding the Black Community School.

It was in searching for answers to his inquiries about the customs and meanings of the 'new' that Ailan Man tried to get close to the 'white units' and learn 'to know like a white man'. He was no longer looking through the closed window of Kole-land. He had passed through to its outer reaches. Money was the ticket of permission. It also gave the promise of moving towards the big goal of matching Tanu Nona. In that process he was moving into a third stage; towards a separate identity as Ailan Man. He came close to Meriam Man and the War veterans, to hopes for 'citizen rights' and 'getting out of bondage'; he confronted the contradiction between becoming the Tanu type of leader and the Meriam Man type of leader. Through this experience and especially through the exemplary behaviour of Meriam Man in standing up for his rights and his culture, he too came to turn round 'the coin' Kole had given Islanders: 'I put *lavalava* on whether you bloody like it or not'. *Lavalava* were a source of humiliation; a way of belittling Islanders was to scorn their 'calicos' as outlandish. You couldn't wear them in TI. They were a way of putting Islanders down and keeping them 'outside'. The reversed coin of 'calico' revealed an independent identity: Ailan Man. That was a breakthrough for everyone. He achieved his young man's ambition to stand level with Tanu Nona; he also became a man who is able to understand and practise Island custom.

In their self-sprung projects Islanders were achieving their first goal; 'coming up level' with Kole. Having reached that place the cooperative form was a means of pursuing Islanders' own cultural purposes. They were 'people's business' projects where everyone took their share. They were also more than this in many people's eyes; they heralded 'citizen rights' and 'freedom'; they were the way out of 'the house of bondage'.[17]

Those who came and took part in the wolfram mine at Kubin on the western side of the Strait were circles of Islanders from right round: wider circles than before were coming together in their dissimilarity and finding common cause. Meriam speakers from the eastern side as well as Kala Lagaw Ya speakers were taking part. The meaning of 'Islanders' was changing: 'Be kind to one another!' had new possibilities. That's why 'Torres Strait is full of all our people, right 'round', as Kapin says. A 'new *wauri*' was in process.

In Islanders' eyes the size of the earnings they battled for in the 1920s and 1930s was secondary to the issue of their right to control them and their own affairs. As the events of 1936 and 1937 were to show dramatically, in order to regain that right the Eastern Islanders were prepared to give up their boats rather than work on the Protectors' terms. That occasion on which they refused to work their boats is a fleeting moment when they came to see themselves in a process of re-formation; in these moments they could catch a glimpse of themselves mirrored within the reflection of the 'other side'. Four further events stand out as special times of 'taking stock' of themselves in relation to others. They are the experience of the Second World War, in particular, that of the men of all the Islands who were placed together in the Torres Strait Light Infantry Battalion between 1942 and 1946; the experience in the 1970s of the so-called 'border issue', which followed a proposal to divide the Torres Strait into two; and in the 1980s, the right to political sovereignty and the issue of land ownership, which extended into the 1990s. As these moments were to show, a new identity was forming which carried the 'old' within a larger ambience.

IV

STRIKING
BACK

God, you sent Moses your servant,
He Delivered all your children,
The people of Israel.
He stood up and struck the Red Sea
And by Your Blessing the sea divided.
Pharoah rose up with his army
The sea was their grave forever.

Uncle T

When it was explained to them that it was impossible for
any aboriginal to be free of the Aboriginal Protection Act
in its entirety (which is what these men were asking) they
said 'We are in a closed box and wait for the lid to be taken
off'.

Deputy Chief Protector, 1936

BREAKING OUT: PUBLIC IMAGES

It was January 1936. The Islander pearling fleet of cutters and luggers bearing the black and white striped railings of the 'Company boats' lay at anchor off each island. January was pick-up time for the 400 'Company boat' men when the local Protector, JD McLean was to go from island to island to sign up the men on the vessels owned by Islanders and controlled by the Protectors (QPP 1937, 12).

On Tuesday 14 January the *Brisbane Courier-Mail*, the *Brisbane Telegraph* and the *Cairns Post* announced that, with two exceptions, all the men of the 'Company boats' were on strike: 'Natives on Strike, Decline to Work Island Luggers', 'Islanders on Strike, Official Inquiry Ordered, Payment for Fishing', 'On Strike, Torres Strait Boys, Dissatisfied with Pay'. The day after their refusal to sign on, JD McLean set sail again for the outer islands now accompanied by two of Thursday Island's four police. As the *Cairns Post* noted on 16 January 'a grave view of the situation developing among the Torres Strait Islanders was being taken'. C O'Leary, the Deputy Chief Protector, was instructed to leave the settlement at Palm Island near Townsville and proceed immediately to the Torres Strait Islands (*Brisbane Telegraph* 14 January 1936).

The Islanders' refusal to work had caught the Administration by surprise. The local Protector at Thursday Island had noted a 'revulsion' among Islanders towards working the 'Company boats' in 1935 (QPP 1936, 15). Yet, later that year, the Inspector of Pearl-Shell and Bêche-de-Mer Fisheries reported 'a very successful period' for twenty-seven 'Company boats'. When the time came for recruiting in January 1936, his report continues, '...it was discovered that a strike amongst all the islands of Torres Strait had been organised'. C O'Leary soon joined the local Protector 'in his efforts to break the strike and get the men back to work', the Inspector concluded (Report 30 July 1936, QPP 1936, 13).

The day after the strike began, EM Hanlon, the Minister for Health and Home Affairs in the Forgan-Smith Labor Government, stated its cause simply: Islanders 'had the impression that they should be allowed to spend their money as they earned it' (*Brisbane Telegraph*, 14 January 1936). For the Minister '...some misunderstanding was quite evident, because the earnings of natives of the boats owned by the Aboriginal Industries Board were much larger than on those of the privately owned boats' on which they were still prepared to work (' "Lugger Boys" Strike at Thursday Island, Official Inquiry', *Cairns Post* 15 January 1936). Islanders were pressing for 'the actual payment' rather than credit in the government-sponsored stores of the Aboriginal Industries Board, a position of 'slavery in all but the name', the Communist Party newspaper, the *Workers Weekly*, claimed on 21 January under the title, 'Terrorism against Aborigines'.

On 12 February, following the arrival of three constables and three officers of the Aboriginal Department from Brisbane on 9 February, it was reported in the *Brisbane Telegraph* that thirty men had been gaoled at Badu Island 'evidently because of their refusal to obey orders and join the boats on which the Aboriginal Department directed that they should work. '...There is reason to believe', the news report continued, 'that the department will give a concession in the way of some cash payment for their working periodically, instead of credit only at the aboriginal stores'.¹ The Islanders had 'made their complaints over some time past and have not been heard' and 'no sympathetic effort' was being made to remedy their complaints, the same issue of the *Telegraph* explained: '...so great has become the resentful feeling of the natives that — though naturally as between island and island they are not sympathetically disposed towards each other — they have "solidified" on the matter of their treatment by the Protection Department'. On 21 February the *Workers Weekly* reported the gaoling at Badu: 'Torres Straits Strike, Natives gaoled by Queensland Government'.

Following a silence of four months, on 6 July the *Brisbane Courier-Mail* announced Islanders' reaction to the sudden removal of the local Protector, JD McLean: 'As the result of the transfer of officials, the Torres Straits natives are jubilant at what they consider a victory in their recent strike against the Aboriginal Department' (Trade Disrupted by Natives, Old Thursday Island Firm Closes). Two days later, the Minister, Mr Hanlon, announced that McLean's transfer from Thursday Island was not a victory for the Islanders; it was merely part of routine Public Service procedure.[2] The public debate continued on 15 July when Fred C Hodel, the former owner of a Thursday Island trading firm which had sold Islanders' produce in the twenty years prior to the 1930s, stated in the *Brisbane Courier-Mail* (Torres Strait Strike, Protectors and Island Trade) that despite the efforts of the 'discreet' Mr O'Leary since January, in spite of the presence of four policemen on the Protectors' visits to each island, and even with the assistance of GA Cameron, a Public Service Inspector (and a popular former Protector) sent to investigate the Thursday Island Administration, the great majority of the 'Company boats' remained idle (see *Cairns Post*, 8 July 1936). When the Protector 'threatened to take away their boats', Hodel challenged, the Islanders replied: '"You take 'em. We live before boats come here"' (*Cairns Post* 15 July 1936; see also Fred Hodel, *Brisbane Courier-Mail* 27 July 1936).

The Protectors were being belittled in the Brisbane press. From Murray Island across to Boigu the inmates had broken out. On whose terms would they work and live, was the question being silently asked. Two contrasting historical experiences were forming in answer to that question, one by the Islanders, one by the Protectors, which are presented here as two narratives. The first is drawn from the recollections of Uncle, who volunteered the story of the strike in 1978, and Nau Mabaig of Badu.

Nau Mabaig, who told his story for the first time, completed his narrative with the words: 'What I've got in there [the recorder] is the truth... Even if I spoke in front of the public I would tell them what I'm telling you. So the youngsters will know this one and it will grow in them.' The second narrative, drawn mainly from the internal correspondence within the Aboriginal Department which found its way into public archives, gives the 'inside' story of attempts by the Protectors to manage the situation and restore their control over Islanders in the years 1936 and 1937.

The narratives are prefaced by an account of the build-up of hostility towards Protection and a spirit of protest among Islanders.

BUILD-UP: THE TIGHTENING OF PROTECTION, 1930–36

> In Queensland there was too much, 'In the opinion of the Minister' about aboriginal administration... A man could be dealt with by the Protector without any opportunity to answer a charge, or to defend himself. At Thursday Island, the Protector was the Police Magistrate, and in the dual capacity he had given a man six months and sent him off to Palm Island.

These words of the Right Rev Dr Stephen Davies, Bishop of Carpentaria, at the Synod of the Anglican Church in September 1935, were published in the *North*

Queensland Register of 14 September 1935. He was referring to a situation of intense disciplinary control in which waves of protest among Islanders arose like a sea storm in the early months of 1936.

The 1930s had opened with the banishment of several Islanders from the Torres Strait and their deportation to Palm Island. They had been charged, tried and convicted by the local Protector who possessed the dual powers of local Protector and Police Magistrate. In moving a resolution at the Synod of the Anglican Diocese of Carpentaria that the responsibility for indigenous inhabitants should pass from state governments to the Commonwealth, the Bishop was pinpointing a state of affairs in which all aspects of Islanders' lives were being subjected to tight ministerial control.

Following the appointment of JD McLean as local Protector in 1932, a series of disciplinary measures were taken: police were appointed to islands other than their own; a night curfew known as the 'Bu' whistle was enforced; and boats not worked to McLean's satisfaction were confiscated and transferred to other islands. The Protector controlled the recruitment of crews and skippers of the 'Company boats'; the books of the Island Fund and the personal earnings of the men were managed by the government teachers. Islanders objected to McLean's dictatorial style as well as to the restrictions upon their freedom.

Papuan Industries Limited (PIL), sold to the government in 1930 and renamed Aboriginal Industries Board (AIB), set up branch stores at Murray, Darnley and Yorke Islands in 1932 and at Saibai Island in 1933. Each store was placed under the control of the government teacher on each island who was empowered by the Protector to control the bank passbooks of Islanders and to make available to them not money but credit in the AIB stores. The practices which heightened and intensified supervision following McLean's appointment completed the process registered publicly in 1911 when George Appel, the Home Secretary, described himself to Islanders as the 'big feller government' and the government teacher the 'small feller government', that is, his representative upon each island.

The appointment of McLean was itself integral with the extension and tightening of the powers of Protection in the early 1930s. He had served as a *kiap* or patrol officer in Papua where direct rule and rigid and zealously enforced segregation had become entrenched tradition. In Papua, where 'the "mailed fist" is a predominant feature of native control', O'Leary wrote in May 1936, the 'native constabulary are armed and native police are drilled as a machine for the protection of the Patrol Officers'.[3] The recently introduced combination of the offices of Protector and Police Magistrate was bound to lead to trouble.

Not only did increasing restrictions bring relations between the Administration and Islanders to flashpoint — three other groupings within the

Thursday Island community became embroiled as opponents of the Aboriginal Department's actions. These were the Anglican Church and the Bishop in particular, whose sense of justice was affronted; the descendants of South Sea Islanders in the Torres Strait, who until 1934 had been exempt from Protection; and the Thursday Island shopkeepers and traders whose livelihoods were seriously affected by the new moves of the Aboriginal Department. These three groups provided the moral support the Islanders needed. They had been isolated and confined, now their beleaguered situation as inmates underwent a change. The Administration had overstepped itself.

Between the years 1933 and 1935, the Anglican Bishop of Carpentaria had become increasingly critical of the Administration's dictatorial methods. In this context, in September 1935, he pressed the idea at Synod that control of all indigenous inhabitants should pass from state governments to the Commonwealth. This idea was transmitted verbally to other Islanders by Islander priests who had participated in the Synod. Copies of the publication, the *North Queensland Register* of 14 September 1935, with details of the Bishop's statements, also found their way to the outer islands. His proposal diffused rapidly through the Island 'bush telegraph' system which operated through the men on the luggers and the crews of government boats. As will be seen, this was the message they had been awaiting, their cue to begin a general strike.

The Islanders were also aided by developments among the descendants of South Sea Islanders in the Torres Strait, who, until 1934, were not defined as 'natives' for the purposes of the Protection Acts. Following the Aboriginal Protection Amendment Act of 1934 which widened definitions of 'natives' subject to Protection, Torres Strait residents of South Sea Island origin and others known locally as 'Thursday Island half-castes', formed an association known as the Thursday Island Coloured Peoples Workers Association, which sought repeal of the amendments. A Darwin solicitor, Mr Fitzgerald, engaged by the Association, visited the Islands at its request to discuss the situation and prepare an opinion about the constitutional legality of the amendments. Under threat themselves and given the position taken by the Bishop, they became allies of the 'native' Islanders. Their lives were already tied together by common customs, by obligations to in-laws and by a creolised language, which had developed from Pacific Pidgin English, and was now the language of communication between speakers of Meriam Mir in the Eastern Islands and Kala Lagaw Ya speakers of the Western and Central Islands.

Important allies for the Islanders were also to be found among the Thursday Island townspeople: traders and others who, for a variety of reasons had become antagonistic to the Administration. The opening of government stores on the outer islands took credit away from Thursday Island shopkeepers; control of the passbooks and the issuing of goods rather than the free use of money secured a monopoly position over Island commerce for the Protector's Department and the effective exclusion of entrepreneurial trading. For this reason alone the townspeople became the Islanders' allies in their fight against restrictions. The 'Master' pearl shellers too, had for long had a 'hip-pocket' grudge against the 'Company boat' system: they were in competition with the Protector's Department for the labour power of the Islander.

The Islanders were not without allies in 1936; they were also not without material resources. In consequence, they were by no means totally beholden to the Aboriginal Department. They continued to hunt and fish in Torres Strait waters, to cultivate gardens on the more fertile islands, and they owned their own cutters and luggers, some of these being family boats, but the majority being known as 'Company boats' owned by whole clans. They also had long experience with the knowledge system and customs of the newcomers, an experience that developed in them both the spiritual resources and the understanding to confront the Administration as an organised force on its own ground.

ENCOUNTERS: NARRATIVES OF THE ISLANDERS

REFUSING TO CRAWL ON HANDS AND KNEES

Islanders recall today a rendezvous of a number of 'Company boats' at an appointed reef late in 1935 where the general strike was organised. 'The strike was made "outside"', that is, at sea, the Protector was eventually told (McLean Report 24 January 1936, 2, QSA 36/5997). They also recall messages to one another written on large stones on the reefs: *Binabin* was here; gone to Yam Island.

Meriam Man was a central figure of the strike at Murray Island. Born in 1886, the year when his father's and mother's generation had pressed successfully for a government school, he was fifty in the year of the strike and Islanders today still talk of his unfailing strength and ability to meet Kole on their own terms: 'He was a man before his time', as Ailan Man says. Meriam Man was schooled well in English, maths, geography and many other subjects at School Number 774 at Murray Island and at the Papuan Institute of the LMS; he learned of the white man's culture first-hand through his working experience as a timber cutter 'down south' on the Queensland mainland. As one Meriam of his son's generation said of him, '...before he did anything he thought about his *zogo* and that's what made him become a great man'. As a Councillor he thought about his

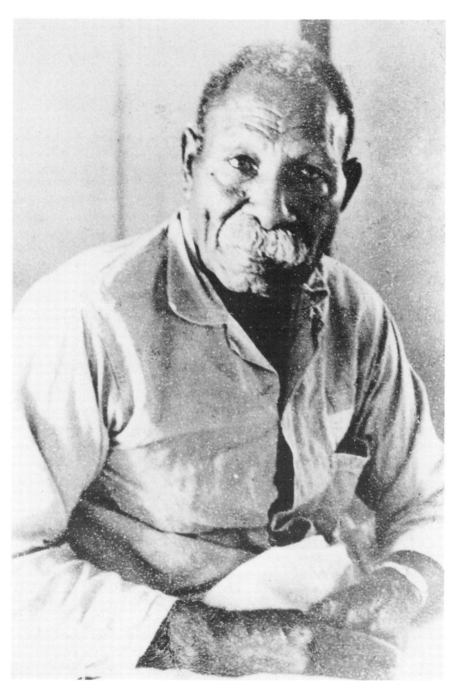

Plate 15 Marou Mimi, Chief Councillor of Mer, and leader of the maritime strike, 1936

people and, strengthened by the 'old' and the 'new', he called meetings at Murray Island when the power of Kole was rising towards a peak in the early 1930s.

The government had the power to make them crawl on their knees; that was what the strike was about, as Uncle explains:

> *For a long time the money was controlled by them. The money we earned had to be entered into a passbook and when you walked into the place they would say, 'Oh, you have drawn money on Monday, you can't have any more this week'. So that was what the strike was about. Yet the money was ours; we battled to get it. We used to crawl on our knees and say, 'Please, please, I would like more...'. If she said 'no' that was it. If we spent the money the wrong way, well that was up to the people themselves. We wanted to take care of it ourselves. For a long time we had one lady, Mrs Zahel. She was a very hard lady. She was a good teacher but she was the boss over the whole Island. So it started from there. You could hardly see a piece of money.* (Book of Islanders 1984, B48)

NAU MABAIG, RECEIVING THE MESSAGE, THE BADU STORY

We will never sign back

> *In that time there was a cargo boat used to sail. It was a boat called* Darton [renamed Mulgrave] *and the skipper was called 'Old M'* [a Badu man]. *When he goes to Murray Island the things they decided there they sent as a message with him to bring up here. That strike's been coming to us by 'Old M', skipper of that cargo boat. When he sails through Torres Strait, whichever Island he comes to he yarn* [talk] *there with them. Cargo boat of Aboriginal Industries Board carrying cargo and taking message* [laughter]. *Carrying cargo and loading messages! When he calls at some of the islands like Central Islands, then come down to Badu, he let us hear the message on the island of Badu. Then when he takes cargo to Saibai, Dauan and Boigu he takes the message and tells them.*
>
> *So that strike was going one week. So when Mr McLean goes round all the Islands this time, he goes to Murray Island first. They do it there: they jump through the windows. Then when he comes here the strike was happening here too; we give Mr McLean a surprise.*
>
> *When Mr McLean comes here he puts up the board and writes down the names of the boats:* Wakaid, Ngainga, Yasa, Argan, Badu. *Then he sits down and asks for the men: 'Now come along and put your name on the board what boat you choose'. But nobody stood up. There's only one man stood up and read a statement. It says: 'You can take the boats and sail to TI. We refuse. Tow them with the* Melbidir *to TI or sell them at TI. Wakaid and the four cutters.' The two Councillors are sitting down quiet. Then a second man and another*

stood up, they in rough screaming [loudly] *and told Mr McLean: 'You can anchor up the boats and sail back to TI. We refuse* [voice getting louder]*, we can stay on the land doing gardens.' They stand up and they walk close to Mr McLean.*

Then Mr McLean asks them: 'Why is that? Why do you refuse to go on boats?' I stood up in the middle of the public. I'm only about sixteen years of age and I told all the public: 'Come on, all of us, jump through the windows'. And all of us jump through the windows with red lavalava *and bare skin and singlets on our shoulders and others continue, all jumping through the windows and two doors* [voice getting higher]. *Mr McLean, Mrs Zahel and the other native Councillors sitting beside him. They were sitting watching us, never say nothing because we jumping out all wild. Nobody was left in the room; everybody coming out. We all come rush to the village way and everybody's whistling and calling out: 'We will never sign back'.*

'We going to take that bell from our church'

So when everyone was coming to the strike, well, as I told you Mr McLean coming back here and going back to TI and coming back here a third time. He came back with six police. He come back with Mr O'Leary. When they get here, that's number three time, all the people have been here making that meeting come strong. They said: 'We going to take that bell from our church; otherwise that bell will ring for the school children. We no work today, our children starve, so we stop them from school.' Those big [senior] *men made yarn and said: 'I think we take out that bell'. That bell was standing something like seven feet from the ground, so I stood up and took out the bell. Bell might have weighed something like thirty pound. I hid it behind the church in the thick grass.*

My cousin says, 'I'll join them for the gaol'

Mr McLean gives me a surprise. He called out my name. I stood up and he said, 'Come along'. I never thought they found me taking out the bell. Then, he said 'Anybody stand up and come and join him? Did you all make this arrangement to take out the bell?' 'Yes.' We all agree on that. 'Well everyone who been on that meeting that stop children from school, come up here.' Everybody walk up, walk up, to go inside gaol. 'Yeah, come on, come on, come on...; you fellows going to be inside the gaol for twenty-four hours.' Everyone, even my father too because he stop them from school. Well, my cousin stood up and come to us and says, 'I'll join them for the gaol'. Others refuse to stand up, they're frightened. So Mr McLean and Mr O'Leary go away on Melbidir *and leave us with two policemen. So when that thing been come for find out this message been carried by 'Old M', them put em inside the gaol at TI.*

That used to be a bad life: that's why that strike's been coming

> The strike's been coming up and going ahead because some of our friends told us, 'You work for little', but some other things too. If I'm one of the crew of the boat the police here on the village kick me out soon as it's nine o'clock at night. Whistle used to blow here through the village. That used to be a bad life; that's why that strike's been coming. You must ask teacher if she will agree you go to another Island. If you come back late you have to stand before the Native Court or they kick you out of the place. That's why that strike's been going on.
>
> After that when Mr O'Leary been get around people mention to him about Mr McLean doing things only by himself. When people go to him and say, 'I'm in trouble', he kicks them out from the DNA office. That's why everybody make up their minds to chase him away from here. All round the Islands they mention to Mr O'Leary: 'We don't want McLean to be in that seat'. So when the strike's been finish Mr McLean get out. Those boats handed over to Tanu Nona, made DNA boats. We give up from those boats. We sign on the 'Master boats'.
> (Book of Islanders 1984, B79–81)

'Old Lady W' is from one of the original Moan families now living at Kubin in the same community as Uncle. She remembers how 'Old M' transmitted the message through the Islander 'bush telegraph', or, more accurately, the 'blue-water telegraph' system. The incident she mentions at Murray Island is not confirmed by other Islanders, but it expresses the feeling of the time.

> You know what they do. They want freedom. So one man, skipper of the Mulgrave — 'Old M' — takes cargo from TI to every island. Soon as he lands there he tells them: 'Don't take the boats out any more'. That's their plan: 'All strike'. Anchor their boat. Strike this time now. He go round everywhere in that cargo boat.
>
> At Murray Island Mr McLean leave his big boat right up on the shore and gets out. Then all of them rush out and sink his dinghy and wet him.
>
> So we've got our own story round Torres Strait. Not white people [laughing loudly]. (Cassette 087/MW/TN/1/81)

ENCOUNTERS: NARRATIVES OF THE PROTECTORS

CLOAKING THE REAL REASONS FOR STRIKING: McLEAN'S STORY

When Mr McLean visited the Islands between 7 and 23 January 1936 to recruit the crews of the 'Company boats' he was surprised to find that a general strike had been organised. At each Island the procedure adopted by the striking Islanders had been much the same: the assembled men stated their refusal to work the 'Company boats' and when he asked the reasons they left the room without answering. They were on separate islands but they were acting in unison.

On 24 January Protector McLean reported to the Chief Protector on his patrols of all the Islands except Murray (by which hangs a tale I shall tell shortly) from 7–12 and 15–23 January 'for the purpose of recruiting natives for the forthcoming year':

> At all Islands visited, with the exception of Dauan Island, I found the men insubordinate and uncontrollable. The procedure at each place visited was the same. After addressing the meeting the men would stand up at a signal from their spokesman and say 'We do not agree to work on Island boats'. When I requested their reasons they would walk out of the room without answering.

He became aware that they had laid down their plans with care and in unison:

> As I went from Island to Island it was remarkable how similar the procedure was at each place, showing that there had been careful organisation. By the time I got to Boigu Island I tested the natives saying to them, 'I know what you are going to say "We do not agree to work on Island boats"'. The natives immediately stood up and said in loud voices 'We do not agree to work on boats' and then walked out. (Report 24 January 1936, 1)

A 'general strike', as McLean described it later, hung in a delicate balance between silent civil disobedience and open rebellion. 'At Saibai the natives were especially hostile.' After walking out they 'paraded up and down past the Government teacher's residence catcalling and yelling,...' (Report, 1). They had special reasons for their indignation with Mr Bryant, the government teacher, whom the Saibai Islanders, it was revealed to O'Leary later, sought to have dismissed in 1935 (Report 11 May 1936, 16).

Their fury was then aroused further by the action of the two Councillors, assisted by the Island policeman, in conducting a ballot for the 'Company boats' in their absence and then dispatching notification of its result. Seventy or eighty men rushed to Bryant's house and having located him in the AIB store ordered him out and asked: 'Why you sign us on "Company boats"?' When he stated that he had been carrying out the law and the orders of the Protector who would be back that night from Boigu, one strike leader said: 'The boys will not work the "Company boats" this year and they never will, they want to work where they like, when they like and do just as they want to' (Report, 2).

On McLean's return a 'hostile crowd collected' behind him as he passed along the main street. On 18 January he took punitive action gaoling three of the 'boys', as the Protector called the Islanders, for one month seeking, with Mr Bryant, 'to make an example of these boys who were the most violent'. His continued account to the Chief Protector reveals the latter's assessment of the dangerous situation which existed for the Administration: 'In view of your advice that it would be injudicious at the present stage to prosecute natives refusing to engage on "Company boats" no other persons were dealt with' (Report, 2).

At Badu and Mabuiag he was given such 'trivial reasons' for the strike as: the Protector broke his promise of two months' holiday; Mr May had cut off wages (promised by McLean) in slopchest (earmarked for work clothes for seamen) in the Badu store. McLean saw the issue of small wages given by the Badu and Mabuiag men as the cause of the strike for what it was: a substitute for the *real* reason behind it. Given 'the fact that the wages paid last year were better than any paid since the year 1929', their statement that the reason for the strike is inadequate wages 'is undoubtedly merely a pretext', McLean concluded. He believed 'that the real reason behind the strike is to force the Government's hand in transferring the natives of Torres Strait to the Commonwealth', a conclusion borne out by the statements made by the Islanders to Sergeant Peters, who accompanied him round the Islands (Report, 4).

After dealing 'conclusively' with all their trivial objections so 'obviously framed to cloak their real reason for striking', McLean and Sergeant Peters, who accompanied him from Thursday Island, were met by a wall of silence in the Native Court at Saibai Island. Rightly, he recognised the signs of labour solidarity, observing that the defendant in the court was more frightened of the consequences of breaking ranks than of the strong arm of Protection and white law. 'I think that some of the more advanced boys have been reading the papers and are trying to emulate the Seamen's Strike now being carried on in Australia', he reported (Report, 4).

As the unfolding events were beginning to show, Islanders believed that if they adamantly refused to work the 'Company boats' over a substantial period of months, their goal of detachment from control by Queensland and their transfer to a Commonwealth administration would be achieved.

On 4 March McLean submitted his report to the Chief Protector rebutting the complaints against him submitted in statements of grievances 'alleged to have occasioned the recent strike', the principal complaint being that he paid smaller wages to 'Company boat' crews than his predecessors. Quoting figures refuting this claim (1928–35) he continues:

It is unfortunate for the cause of the strikers that they should have made this plea their main reason for justification of their strike as the allegation is so easily refuted. The statements clearly disclose that there was indeed a general strike actuated by a common purpose as the alleged reason given on my initial visit to the Islands after the declaration of the strike was 'We do not agree to work the "Company boats"'. Up to this point the organisation of the strikers was perfect. When they were pressed for their reason as to why they would not work the 'Company boats', the strikers were, however, placed on their own resources and temporarily evaded the question by getting up in a body and walking out. (Report 4 March 1936, 1, 36/861 in QSA 36/5997)

As events were soon to show, refusing to confide in the Protector was part of the 'careful organisation' noted by McLean. McLean could not admit to the Chief Protector (or perhaps even to himself) the reasons why they wanted to be transferred to Commonwealth control. A Saibai Island strike leader had already indicated the reasons when he had said the men wanted to work where and when they liked 'and do just as they want to': to be free citizens, this was the aim.

It must be recalled that the context of JD McLean's account and interpretation of the events of 1935 and early 1936 was one in which he had been personally responsible for many of the complaints for which Islanders now sought redress. It is also likely that in imposing and administering an increasingly restrictive set of rules relating to Protection, he was unaware of the effects he was having. He was not a man to mix with his 'subordinates'. As Islanders said later to C O'Leary, when they brought a problem to him, he did not listen and 'just kicked them out of his office'. He made only infrequent and brief 'patrols' to the outer Islands. Not surprisingly then McLean sought to refute 'the allegation that the strike was due to acts of commission or omission by my staff and myself' (Report, 16).

When the men both refused to work the 'Company boats' and to talk to him, they were, as he rightly observed, acting in interisland concert. Similarly, he recognised that the reasons they gave him were not the real reasons for the strike, but a cloak for the latter. It is also evident that in those early weeks before O'Leary's arrival, few of them gave any information, an exception being an Island policeman.

The purposes of McLean's efforts were twofold: to justify his own actions in the period leading up to the strike in the eyes of his superior, C O'Leary; and related to this, to bring representatives of the strikers to the conference table with O'Leary. With respect to the former, he wrote to the Chief Protector on 24 January 1936: Mr O'Leary 'will be of great assistance in instilling into the natives a proper sense of gratitude for the excellent work that has been done by the [Aboriginal] Department on their behalf for many years' (Report, 5). On the latter, he reported on the same day that 'All Islands except Badu have appointed representatives to confer with Mr O'Leary at Yorke Island on 7 February 1936 (Report, 4), a statement only partially true, since he had not even visited Murray Island. Only three islands were represented by the strikers at this conference at Yorke Island — Mabuiag, Stephen and Yorke (Report 12 February 1936).

After he made his two visits, Mr McLean was aware that the strike would continue beyond January. Mrs Zahel, the government teacher at Badu (and a pillar of the Aboriginal Department establishment) had advised him that 'she had consulted the Bishop' who had 'said that the strike would continue until the grievances had been rectified' (Report 4 March 1936, 15).

LIFTING THE LID OF THE 'CLOSED BOX' OF PROTECTION

DISCOVERING THE CAUSES AND ORIGINS

Several weeks after C O'Leary arrived in the Strait to investigate the causes of the strike, he promised the Chief Protector 'to accurately analyse every phase of the dispute' (Report 2 February 1936, 5). In issuing his full report of forty-three pages on 11 May, he was carrying out that promise.

In the three months from his first cabled report to his superior on 12 February, to his main report on 11 May, his perception of the causes of the strike altered substantially: of the five causes he lists in the former written in February, four concerned the activity of outsiders, while only one related to Islander discontent; *all* the eleven causes listed in his final report concerned discontent with the Administration, seven directly involving Islanders, four concerning members of other groups within the Thursday Island community.

In his preliminary report of 12 February, following his visit to five Islands — Badu, Murray, Coconut, Yorke and Darnley, with others yet to be visited, the one reason given to O'Leary on 'native discontent' concerned limiting advances on wages and this, as he rightly concluded, was 'not sufficiently serious...to warrant the general strike which has been proclaimed' (Report, 1). He was as yet unaware of the surging discontent among Islanders concerning virtually every aspect of Protection. At this point the role of outside 'troublemakers' was seen as paramount. The fourth cause pinpoints 'The undue influence by Church Authorities over the Islands and harmful propaganda by native Priests' (Report, 1).

After visiting Mabuiag, Saibai, Boigu, Dauan and Yam Islands to continue his investigations of the origins and causes of the strike, O'Leary submitted a 'further progressive report' to the Chief Protector on 22 February, 'with a record of my endeavour to induce the men to again enter employment' (Report, 1). The new terms of employment on the 'Company boats' proposed by the Minister for Health and Home Affairs, which concerned a guaranteed wage equivalent to that on the 'Master boats', O'Leary reported, were 'never even considered by the men', being 'summarily rejected without discussion'. They continued to show a 'unanimous determination not to work the boats under any circumstances' (Report, 5). Not surprisingly, O'Leary believed at this stage that the conditions of work on the boats were secondary causes of the strike being used by the Islanders 'as an excuse to cover over the more important causes...' (Report 12 February, 1).

O'Leary sought to find out the causes of the strike by requiring written statements of each Islander at as many Islands as possible, and this was done with the aid of one of the Brisbane policemen who took down what each man said. Many of these recorded statements on the causes, the initiatives, the leaders, are based upon hearsay; yet many of them are corroborated by Islanders today, or by circumstantial evidence. Mr Fitzgerald, the Darwin solicitor who visited the Islands soon after Christmas 1935, is said to have told the men at Murray Island that if they 'refused to work the "Company boats" they would be taken over by the Commonwealth Government within six months', a statement corroborated by others made to Protector O'Leary, and a belief with wide currency in the Islands (Report 22 February, 5). For example, Mr Frith, senior teacher at Mabuiag, reported the Island priests as saying that the Islanders would be better under the Commonwealth.[4]

After O'Leary had visited all the Islands, he still did not know where the instructions for the strike originated. This information he sought to obtain by 'discreet questioning' by the civilians employed by the Aboriginal Department and the police stationed on the Islands.

Like McLean, he continued to be given trivial reasons for the strike during his visit to the second group of Islands in February. At Mabuiag for example, he was told that wages were inadequate, that the Protector had not honoured the price of five pence per pound for shell, and that the boats had to leave early in January. These reasons, wrote O'Leary on 22 February, were 'shown to be fictitious and without foundation' (Report, 1).

By the time he wrote the full report of his investigations '...on the origin and cause of discontent among Torres Strait Islanders' on 11 May 1936, he had become aware of 'a serious state of mismanagement that warrants urgent rectification', which he proceeded to document in forty-three pages. Discontent even among the fifteen of the twenty-seven 'Company boats' which had begun working is such, O'Leary wrote, that 'Unless immediate action is taken to institute the measures recommended in this report, it is definite that the trouble will recur next year, and then probably with greater intensity than marked the 1936 outbreak' (Report, 24).

Predicting a slow process of regaining the confidence of the Islanders, his report cautions the Chief Protector to look to January 1938 as the earliest time when the knowledge of improvements in the Administration could serve to undermine 'the deep-seated antagonism' against it by the sailors of Murray, Saibai and Boigu.

The report elaborates in detail eleven causes of the strike. Seven concern grounds for discontent directly among Islanders themselves, all of which relate to acts of 'omission and commission' by JD McLean. The first gives five aspects of his maladministration: his 'unsatisfactory manner' of handling the 'Company boat' men; his failure to gain their confidence; his inability 'to reveal any interest in the individual'; his lack of understanding of 'the psychology of the Island Race'; and 'the general deepseated dislike of him by all the Islanders'. The other six causes concerning Islanders directly are the system of allowing too little advance against wages; failure to pay sufficient of the wages due for additional Christmas comforts; failure to advise the men of details of the catch and apportionment of the proceeds; the system of compelling 'Company boats' to pay in the first year the capital costs of gear whose life is several years; enforcement of highly restrictive clauses in the Island regulations which had been ignored for many years (the curfew is an important example); and the practice of dismissing elected Councillors and replacing them with his own nominees (Report, 4).

The remaining four causes concern other members of the Island community. They are given as causes six to nine:

6. The common desire of the Anglican Authorities, Pearl shellers and business people of Thursday Island to discredit the Aboriginal Department's policy of protection of the Islanders and the failure of the Administration to counter such propaganda by:
    (a) Recognising that some of the criticism may be warranted and justifying action for remedy.
    (b) The adoption of such methods as will allay any suspicion in the native mind of unfair treatment and the creation of greater confidence in the Protector.

7. Propaganda by all sections of the Thursday Island community for the transfer of the control of aboriginals to the Commonwealth Government.

8. The failure of the Bishop of Carpentaria to prevent erroneous and harmful propaganda by his Native Priests and the fear of the powers of such priests by the people.

9. The possible application of the provisions of the Aboriginal
    Protection Amendment Act of 1934, particularly those
    Sections covering quadroons and halfcastes. (Report, 4)

O'Leary had been made aware of these deep-seated causes through
the continuing refusal of many Islander men to accept any solution short of release
from Protection. He had also put together the statements made by individuals.
Events at Boigu, Saibai and Murray Islands were instructive to the Deputy Chief
Protector.

At Boigu three of the four reasons given for the strike by the men which
concerned money were accurate, but had nothing to do with wages. They were
that insufficient information was available to Islanders about how their wages were
deducted; that they were unable to draw money through the Saibai Island store;
and that they did not receive interest on savings bank accounts. Significantly, the
fourth reason concerned 'The provisions of the Aboriginal Protection Act', and
this reason lies close to the central aim of the strike: to be free of the strictures
of Protection. O'Leary himself gives this interpretation:

> When it was explained to them that it was impossible for any
> aboriginal to be free of the Aboriginal Protection Act in its
> entirety (*which is what these men were asking*) they said 'We
> are in a closed box and wait for the lid to be taken off'. (emphasis
> added, Report 22 February 1936, 3)

They wanted the freedom of other Australians to handle their own
money themselves, as Uncle explains, and to seek employment in other parts of
Queensland whenever they wished. Nothing O'Leary offered them altered their
resolve, including work on the 'Master boats' or the 'Master boat' rate of £3.5.0
per month, which they rejected 'without consideration'. The build-up of resentment
and hostility had been distilled into common resolve. 'Ultimately', reported O'Leary,
'they stated: "Until we get new Government we will stay on shore"' (Report, 3).
Their rebellious spirit perplexed the Deputy Chief Protector: 'There is a spirit
prevailing amongst the Boigu Island men that is difficult to understand but it is
evident that on the slightest provocation they would break out into open rebellion'
(Report, 3).

It was Saibai, according to O'Leary, which 'held the key position of
the strike in the Western Islands...' (Report, 4). Like the neighbouring Boigu
Islanders, the Saibai men responded with one voice when they were asked by
O'Leary if they would agree to work the 'Company boats' on the old terms, or
at £3.5.0 per month. Their leader then gave expression to '"the voice of the Saibai
people"...' — a refusal to work any boats until they got another government and

were not 'under the Aboriginal Act' (Report, 4). The outlook and aims of the strikers were becoming apparent to O'Leary.

Trouble at Saibai goes back at least to 1935 when two Councillors were dismissed for writing to the Protector asking for the removal of the government teacher, Mr Bryant, a 'request submitted in the name of the Saibai people', and a justified action in O'Leary's eyes. On a visit to Saibai in February 1936, O'Leary had felt it necessary to leave arms with the police sergeant and a revolver with the constable, being careful to inform the Chief Protector that 'there are shotguns and ammunition on the Island' (Report 22 February 1936, 4). The Saibai people, it would seem, had no firearms; as in 1792 and 1879, power was unequal. On 23 March the Chief Protector reported to the Under Secretary: '...Saibai and Murray now only dangerous islands' (36/861 in 36/5997).

Following an incident at Murray Island in December 1935 when JD McLean had struck Marou, the Chief Councillor, and then dismissed him, the Murray Islanders had refused to elect Councillors until the authority of the Protector to dismiss Councillors was revoked. It will be recalled that in January 1936 Murray Island was the only island not visited by McLean. In February, O'Leary reported one informant as saying that a Murray Islander had told him that 'following the Marou incident the Murray Islanders had determined on the next visit of Mr McLean to kill him and bury him in the Murray Island cemetery' (Report 22 February 1936, 3). Whatever the truth of this accusation, the possibility was treated seriously by McLean, by O'Leary and by the Chief Protector; the latter drew the Minister's attention to such 'an alleged plot' and of plans to remove those involved in it (5 March 1936, in QSA 36/5997).

It was not until GA Cameron, a Public Service Inspector from Brisbane who had been instructed by Cabinet to proceed to the Torres Strait, began negotiations with Murray Islanders that they agreed to go ahead with Council elections towards the middle of 1936 (which were held before 28 May that year).

On 18 May 1936 O'Leary reported to the Chief Protector that Mr Cameron was investigating the incident between Marou and McLean, that he, O'Leary was 'still convinced that the threat against Mr McLean's life was genuine and serious and [that] it will be unsafe for him to patrol alone to Murray Island' (36/1232 in QSA 36/5997). Drawing attention to comparable features of an incident between himself and Murray Islanders in 1929 when Councillors had refused to do village work, and 'certain phases of the existing discontent', he concludes that provided the services of Mr McLean as Protector are terminated (the alternative being 'a ridiculous position...when a Protector required an escort on his patrol'), that no further action be taken for the removal of the five Murray Islanders from the Strait. The time lapse and the election of one of the five as Councillor, O'Leary concludes, 'indicates the futility of proceeding further with the removal of any or all of the men'.

THE PROGRESS OF THE STRIKE

Badu had become 'top island' for the pearl shelling industry; since 1904 it had been the headquarters of Papuan Industries Limited (PIL). Through the achievements of the lugger *Wakaid* under Tanu Nona, which had not only won the Minister's Silver Cup for its output, but had 'consistently beaten the record of all other boats in the marine industry', Badu Island took the limelight of competitive entrepreneurship (QPP 1936, 18). It was the Protector's showcase and the two Councillors there neither took part in nor gave support to the strike. A month after the strike began O'Leary singled out those Badu Islanders who were prepared to be counted for their defiance leaving thirty 'troublemakers' guarded by armed police. The inside story at Badu recalled by Nau Mabaig after forty years, appears briefly in correspondence with the Chief Protector (McLean Report 4 March 1936, 16).

By 26 February, six weeks after the strike began, O'Leary reported that the strike was finished at Badu: 'Returned from Badu Tuesday leaving for Murray Islands today Strike at Badu off four boats manned', his cryptic message ran (Report, nd, 36/469 enclosed with 36/1761 in QSA A/3826). The course of the strike in the other Western Islands was different. On 20 February, after returning from a patrol of the Western Islands, he had cabled:

> Boigu Saibai and Yam refuse man Company Boats any circumstances and rejected the Minister's suggestion payment three pounds five monthly Saibai stated will await change Government good or bad and pending such they and Boigu have determined stay ashore full stop Saibai Boigu also refuse sign Master boats Yam and Mabuiag men while refusing Company boats are willing sign Master boats. (with 36/1761)

The 'change of Government good or bad' referred to the reported 'desire to transfer from State control', which was carried by an Island priest who, according to government sources, had 'insisted continuation of Strike until Commonwealth Government took over' (O'Leary Report, with 36/1761). On 2 March, the Chief Protector relayed O'Leary's message to his superior:

> Strike finished Eastern Islands except Murray. Stephen men signing Master boats. Murray still refuses elect Councillors and decline provide crew. Sent unwanted vessels Thursday Island. Jensen and Constable remaining there. Constable withdrawn from Badu. Anticipate withdrawing civilians by end of March and probably Police exception Murray. (with 36/1761)

On 6 April, O'Leary had been joined by GA Cameron, a former Protector and now a Public Service Inspector. Accompanied by four police they visited Saibai and Boigu. The decision to send GA Cameron to the Islands 'to investigate and report upon the administration of the Protector of Aboriginals at Thursday Island and that of the Aboriginal Industries Board', was made at Cabinet level. The Under Home Secretary's letter begins: 'With reference to the Strike amongst the natives of Torres Strait, I have the honour, by direction, to inform you that Cabinet considers the position in Torres Strait to be unsatisfactory...' (13 March 1936, with 36/1761).

On 17 April, O'Leary reported an unchanged position, 'indicating that the natives of these Islands still refused to man either Company or Master boats' (with 36/1761). Following that visit, police and 'special civilian officers' were retained at Saibai and Boigu.

At the end of May, O'Leary left the Islands for Brisbane returning in mid-September as local Protector. McLean had been removed as a result of the strike. In September O'Leary took up duties in the Thursday Island office of the Protector of Aboriginals and on 9 October outlined to the Chief Protector his schemes to meet 'the still existing discontent amongst the crews of the "Company" boats'. He drew Mr Bleakley's attention to the 'altered outlook' of the crews despite his abolition of the 'Bu' or curfew whistle, the provision of copies of boat returns to each 'Company boat' captain and crew, and the holding of meetings to test Islanders' opinions on a proposed reorganisation which would transfer many of the powers of the government teachers to the Councils (36/6292 in QSA A/3874). Schemes for reorganisation had resulted from investigations by both GA Cameron as well as C O'Leary. Bleakley quotes Cameron as saying: 'In his desire to enforce discipline Mr McLean introduced methods, some of which the natives resented... The appointment of a native of one Island to act as policeman on another Island was not a happy innovation' (17 August 1936, 36/7838 in QSA A/3860). O'Leary notes the enthusiasm with which all the men received 'the amended system' when 'Company boats' from Badu, Mabuiag, Saibai, Boigu, Yorke and Coconut Islands landed produce in Thursday Island. They 'were particularly pleased when the whole transactions were given them openly and the Captains received copy of the boat Returns' (9 October 1936, 36/6292 in A/3874). He follows with a cautionary note on the lasting imprint of the encounter on Islanders:

> I am not sufficiently optimistic to imagine that the existing discontent has been swept away during the last three (3) weeks. My knowledge of the mentality and altered outlook of these people compels me to recognise that it will be many months before the incidents of January and February this year are forgotten.

> I am adopting the attitude of not appealing to any man to join a 'Company' boat. The results of the reorganisation will be my argument for the remanning of the boats next year and I feel that already there is an inclination amongst some of the malcontents, who are employed on 'Master' boats, to angle for work on the 'Company' boats next year. These men will have to ask to join the 'Company' boats. If I appeal to them, in their present suspicious mind, they will imagine that there is some catch in the appeal. I am basing my hope for success on the results which I can show with the men employed at present and at the moment I have no fear of failure... (Report, 2)

In his letter of 9 October, O'Leary also reported on discussions with the Pearlshellers' Association, the Anglican Bishop of Carpentaria and the 'Town people' (whose attitude to the Department remained 'antagonistic to a degree') on the proposed reorganisation. His comments on the reactions of the local Administration officers are as follow:

> I feel that there might be some discontent amongst the Government teachers when greater authority is given to the elected Councillors. The general tone of correspondence from the Manager, the Aboriginal Industries Board and Government Teachers indicates that they have not learned the lessons which the recent trouble should have forcibly taught them. Naturally people in a groove, as these officers are, are inclined to ignore the important features arising out of the progress of a race such as the Torres Strait Islanders. I shall suitably deal with these officers as the opportunity offers for patrol. (Report, 2)

Announcing to the Chief Protector his plan 'to visit all the Islands before Christmas', O'Leary ends on a reassuring note: '...in the meantime you can save yourself any worry regarding the future of this district' (Report, 2).

The Chief Protector responded supportively to O'Leary's achievements and proposals for a changed organisation, but his memorandum of 27 October held a note of caution: 'I...learn with pleasure of the good progress made in restoring the confidence of the Island people and the crews of the Company boats', but abolition of the curfew whistle and the permit system on interisland travel 'seem to go further than either Cameron or your own report originally intended' (36/10166 in QSA A/3874).

Commenting further in the same single-page memorandum on O'Leary's statement on reactions of local government officers, Bleakley expresses concern that O'Leary might have gone too far:

> The question seems to arise as to whether in their opinion the reforms proposed may be in the direction of granting the natives

too much liberty... However I shall be glad to hear further from you as to your own views as to how far such additional relaxation of restrictions can be given without detriment to the authority of the teacher in charge.

The hours worked by O'Leary and his staff at Thursday Island over Christmas and New Year 1936–37 'were practically unlimited'; 'the big problem to be faced now', he reported to Bleakley on 4 February 1937, '...is the retention of the hold which the administration has over these crews' (37/1580 in QSA A/3941). The elected Councillors, not the Protector, were to recruit the crews of the 'Company boats' and O'Leary sought the compliance of the Councillors in his selective policy of 'obtaining the best crews voluntarily' while rejecting 'the trouble-makers', as he went on to explain to the Chief Protector in the same letter.

O'Leary's awareness that the Islanders were turning the tables on the Protectors came to imprint itself upon his mind. Islanders recall his retirement speech at the historic Bellevue Hotel, Brisbane, thirty years later: in his years of office the outstanding occasion for him in the Islands was the meeting at Murray Island in 1936; when he raised the question of the 'Company boats', all the men refused to discuss them and jumped through the windows. Today out at Murray Island the older men will incline their heads towards the village where the schoolhouse once stood as they tell you: 'When Mr O'Leary came we refused to talk with him; we all jumped through the windows'. In Island folklore, engaging in that style of saying 'no' has come to be known as giving someone the 'O'Leary treatment'.

CONFLICTING MOTIVES AND PERSONAL STYLES

There is reason to believe that the hostility towards the Administration manifest in each Island was most long-lasting and well-organised at Saibai and Murray Islands. These were islands with large populations; they were also traditionally gardening islands, where people could readily 'live off the land', an option not open at such coral islands as Yorke and Coconut. Given this fact and the strength of continuing custom on these Islands, it was at Murray and Saibai islands that the strike lasted longest, a situation anticipated by the wily O'Leary. 'It is safe to anticipate', wrote O'Leary in his preliminary report on 12 February, 'that the strike will continue at Murray Island for another four to six months and on the other Islands for a shorter period as the supply of European foodstuffs runs out and the Savings Bank balances become depleted' (Report, 5).[5]

The Islanders knew also that without financial independence they could not be free of the Protectors, whether in the longer term, or in their efforts to carry on the strike. As we shall see, it was only at Murray Island that people combined the knowledge and skills with their independent means of subsistence to allow them to continue to stand up to the Aboriginal Department and the Minister for Health and Home Affairs.

For a time they had shown a common resolve, standing firm on their refusal to work or to give the real reasons for their action. They were in basic respects following the principles of industrial unionism. McLean reports how the Darnley Islanders had agreed to 'give a hiding' to anyone who revealed their plans to the government representative. In the labour tradition they were more scared of scabbing on their mates than they were of the Protector (Report 24 January 1936, 4).

Nevertheless, once the state as an institution stepped in with its Cabinet-appointed investigators, such as GA Cameron, Deputy Chief Protector O'Leary, various other Brisbane appointees (WS Munro, for example), and several armed police, the Islanders were to a greater or lesser degree, beleaguered once more. Island by island, man by man, they were dealt with, individuals being summoned for questioning and recording by O'Leary, whose power was protected and legitimised by the armed men taking it all down. Each Island community became more isolated from the others, from the Church and other allies at Thursday Island, and in the main, from the rest of the world. They were not just engaging in concerted industrial action: in practice they were confronting the state and the state was deploying its forces to crush them.

In rejecting the Minister's proposal for increased wages all down the line, Islanders were ruling out one important possible reason for the strike: whatever they had said, inadequate wages were not its primary cause. From island to island in January 1936 they acted in unison in their unwillingness to confide in the Protector as well as in their refusal to work the boats. At some islands at least they had made a pact among themselves adhering to labour solidarity. They were acting on the belief that if they refused to cooperate *in any way*, they would be rid of Protection.

A difference between McLean and O'Leary was that the latter treated them 'as individuals of ordinary intelligence', capable of engaging in 'candid discussion' (Report 11 May 1936, 11). This attitude was fundamental to O'Leary's attempt to resolve the dispute. He saw Islanders as people with some knowledge of unionist principles, rejecting the belief that 'these people are possessed of a child mind to be moulded in accordance with the whim of the government...': the 'suggestion that the Islander is a child subject to dictation of his father, the Government, is wrong and any policy for his protection based on this assumption must be fatal to its sponsors' (Report, 19).

Nevertheless 'appreciating their intelligences' did not preclude inducement and manipulation into accepting their lot as non-citizens in a continuing paternalist relationship: '...it should be the policy by sympathetic treatment of the aboriginals to induce them to recognise the benefit which they can obtain from the measures designed for their protection and assistance' (Report, 28).

It was this that the Saibai Islanders, for example, had specifically rejected when they demanded the freedom to move about in Queensland and to sell their labour power as they wished. Only at Murray Island were the conditions conducive to a continuing fight, which, in 1937 was engaged with the highest level of executive power in Queensland — directly involving the Minister for Health and Home Affairs.

In a variety of ways, the idea of freedom was central to the demand for transfer to the Commonwealth: free choice of work, freedom to travel, freedom to spend their money as they pleased, and the right to run Island affairs and control their own Island funds. Among Uncle's people at Poid, who had been forcibly moved to Moa, it had a special meaning. As HN Armstrong, government teacher at Poid reported to the local Protector: 'The Hammond Islanders are jubilant at the idea that they are shortly to be allowed to return to Hammond Island — their idea of the Millennium' (27 May 1936, 36/5997 in QSA). He continues:

> Lately some of the men have been working around Thursday Island with dinghies and the *Karabai*. They returned on Saturday and brought news that an aeroplane had arrived at Thursday Island with Commonwealth Government officials who had visited the Court House, had a look at various books there, were dissatisfied with them and ordered them to be burnt and replaced with new ones. The books were burnt in the backyard of the Court House.

There were Islander people alive who recalled the time they were placed under the Protection Act in 1904; and long after the mid-thirties many Islanders continued to believe that in this earlier period their forebears had been subject to the 'Commonwealth alone and not to Queensland'.

DIVINE INSPIRATION AND COMMUNITY ORGANISATION

A SIGN

'...I am convinced that the natives regarded the general strike as a holy crusade and prosecuted it with religious fervour.' These are the words of JD McLean in a confidential report to the Chief Protector on 4 March 1936. Although it seems likely that he had little understanding of the springs of their motivations and actions, he was, I believe, noting an important truth.

Through the early years of the 1930s when the cloak of Protection had been wrapped more and more tightly round them, Islanders had strengthened themselves through the development of custom — the tombstone rites being a key example; from among themselves composers had emerged who created hymns of spiritual resistance. By the middle thirties there were visible signs that their church — the Anglican church — in their locality was giving them a sign. The leadership, the moral support they were awaiting from the Bishop and ordained Islander priests were forthcoming in their time of pressing need.

According to O'Leary's main report on the causes of the strike, two preliminary reports and four months' investigations, the first person to call for a strike on the 'Company boats' was the Murray Island priest, Rev Poi Passi. He is reported as having advised the Saibai Islanders on 31 January 1934, to 'leave the Company boats like Murray Island did, the Bishop will see you afterwards, do not be frightened' (Advice of Protector to Bishop of Carpentaria, in O'Leary Report, 11 May 1936, 11).

In October 1935, several weeks after the Bishop of Carpentaria placed his proposal before the meeting of Synod in Townsville, Islanders in the outer Islands anxiously awaited his message. In that month the captain of the Aboriginal Industries Board boat *Mulgrave* conveyed the Bishop's published speech 'to the various native priests' in the outer Islands (O'Leary Report 11 May 1936, 11).

According to both McLean and O'Leary Islanders were aware of the Bishop's intention at Synod: 'The report of the Provincial Synod at Townsville created great interest among the natives, who were aware that the Bishop would speak on the aboriginal question', McLean wrote on 4 March 1936 (Report, 15).[6] 'You have already been advised of the anxiety by certain Islanders to ascertain from Mairu, Captain of the *Mulgrave*, what the Bishop had said in his Synod speeches', O'Leary reported to the Chief Protector on 12 February.[7]

The Island priests had attended the Synod at Thursday Island and heard the Bishop report on the speech. As we have noted, Rev Passi had already raised at Saibai the issue of transfer to Commonwealth control as long before as 1934. In February 1936, the Saibai and Boigu Islanders had indicated that one of the priests had encouraged them to continue the strike until the Commonwealth Government replaced Queensland as administrator.

In the Protectors' eyes, the Island priests took the Bishop's address to Synod to mean that if the men refused to work the 'Company boats', they would be transferred to the Commonwealth and would 'be free' (McLean Report 4 March 1936, 13).[8] The Island priests, O'Leary wrote on 11 May, 'were the instruments for the propaganda which subsequently spread throughout Torres Strait' (Report, 11). Neither Protector suggested that 'the gospel' preached by the priests necessarily represented the actual *intention* of the Bishop (Report, 13). McLean wrote in March: 'Whether the Bishop intended such a conclusion to be the outcome of his address is immaterial. All that I am concerned with is the reaction to it by the natives' (Report, 13). Irrespective of his intention, the Deputy Chief Protector concluded, the Bishop 'succeeded in implanting in the native mind a fanatical desire for transfer to the Commonwealth Government' (Report, 11).

Those conclusions are based partially on circumstantial evidence relating to the keenness with which Islanders appeared to await the arrival of the Bishop's 'message' in the *North Queensland Register*. They are also based on statements which began to reach the Protectors' ears especially after C O'Leary, an official with highly developed persuasive skills and visible authoritative power, arrived from Brisbane with several police. On 12 February he reported how two informants at Badu (the island where the strike was broken early) 'definitely state that following the Synod meeting in Thursday Island', one of the Island priests 'had told them when the Commonwealth Government took over the Torres Strait Islands everything would be alright' (Report, 3). On 4 March McLean reported that the same priest had told Islanders 'to keep up the strike' (Report, 13).

It is clear that some Island priests became the spark which lit the fire of organised disobedience in the Torres Strait. Seen by Islanders as intercessors of the Bishop — the *Zogo le* of the Lord — they had enormous influence. Not only were they bearers of Divine love; Islanders saw them too as the carriers of a two-sided magical power. So they were not only revered; they were also feared.

Two of them were considered 'dangerous' enough by the Protectors to be in 'need' of transfer, and on the matter of their future the Deputy Chief Protector attempted to extend Departmental control into the domain of the Anglican Church. Recommendation Ten of O'Leary's major investigative report proposed that 'The Bishop of Carpentaria be informed that Sailor Gabey and Poey Passi are regarded as a menace to good administration and their appointment as Native Priests in Torres Strait should be cancelled' (11 May 1936, 25).[9]

Their role had special force through the institutional support and encouragement of the Anglican Church to which virtually all Torres Strait Islanders belonged. This powerful support is also intimated by a statement attributed to 'Old M', captain of the *Mulgrave*, by an Island policeman, that he had told the people at Dauan in 1935 that the return of the Bishop from the South was the signal for the men to leave the 'Company boats' for good (McLean 4 March 1936, 15). And as we have seen, this is exactly what the men did throughout the Islands. That Islanders had reason to feel a strength which came from the Bishop's blessing is underlined by the fact that the Darwin solicitor, Mr Fitzgerald, who had been engaged by the South Sea Islander-based Thursday Island Coloured Peoples Workers Association, 'toured the islands...under the wing of the Church' (Munro Report, 36/1761 enclosed with 36/4901 in QSA 36/5997), with the Bishop and on the Anglican boat *Herald II*. As the school teacher, Mr WS Munro, reported on 20 April 1936, Fitzgerald is said to have reinforced the view that if they persistently refused to work the 'Company boats' they would be freed from Protection and would be brought under Commonwealth control:[10] '...having regard to the company in which he travelled, such statements would carry weight with the natives' (Munro report, 4).

As McLean commented in his report in March, the Islanders conducted the strike 'with religious fervour'; the Murray and Saibai Islanders would not have dared to challenge the Protector at Murray Island in December 1935 or 'attack' the store at Saibai when the men struck in January 1936, 'unless they believed they had the backing of the Church' (4 March 1936, 13). Of this there is little doubt. It will have been noted that the Church was only part of the Spark of the events of 1935 and 1936. In taking a copy of the *North Queensland Register* containing the Bishop's address first to the priest at Darnley Island, Rev Francis Bowie, and

Plate 16   Sam Savage and Maryann Savage (nee Pitt) at the 'Coming of the Light' stone, Darnley Island, 1 July c1930s. Maryann Savage had just completed her 1 July speech

then to Rev Joseph Lui at Murray Island, Mairu ('Old M'), captain of the *Mulgrave*, did not leave it with one of them: he finally left it with Mr Sam Savage at Rennel Island, the head of a South Sea Islander family whom the Protector had unsuccessfully tried to bring under the Protection Act following the 1934 amendments, and who was a paid-up member of the Thursday Island Coloured Peoples Workers Association.

Sam Savage, a professed Christian, was also known among Islanders as the most efficacious 'medicine man' in the Torres Strait — Grandfather T in this book. The strike had the blessing of the Bishop. His gift had travelled from island to island; it came to rest in the safekeeping of a man recognised by the Islanders as having the strongest spiritual power in the Islands. A Sign was visible in the Torres Strait Islands in 1935; the 'new *wauri*' was acting with potency.

ISLAND COMMUNITY ORGANISATION

If the hand of God was working through the *Zogo le* of the Islands, the 'Company boat' men, some of the Island Councils were engaging in secular organising activity to secure their rear through the building up of food store supplies, and by seeking to gain control over their earnings and their bank passbooks. Without stores of food and money for general necessities being available as 'strike relief' they could not withstand a long period of economic inactivity. They conducted much of the food stockpiling activity in total secrecy; in the same way they quietly found allies among the South Sea Islanders and supporters among the townspeople of Thursday Island, especially the traders whose livelihoods were threatened by the enforced transfer of Islanders on to a 'rations-only' regimen. The Islanders may have been gripped by a religious fervour in forging a path to freedom; the signs of a 'holy crusade' were imprinted upon their actions, which in many ways took on the character of a millenarian movement. But unlike the latter where the day of reckoning and freedom in an earthly paradise was heralded typically by the destruction of food supplies, this movement for freedom was characterised by the highly rational activity of securing food supplies in anticipation of the lean days of strike-bound islands. The only news of an impending strike to reach the ears of Mr McLean was from Mrs Zahel, the government teacher at Badu who got it from the Bishop soon after Christmas 1935.

They knew the principles of labour organisation and solidarity. The best crews could read and news of the International Seamen's Strike had reached them, as McLean had noted early in 1936. They had made a 'labour' pact among themselves to stand together; they had intimated that anyone who betrayed this trust would be taught the lesson of scabs everywhere. Islanders also had weapons at their disposal unavailable to the white seamen or other workers. A Divine Spark set them off and provided their guiding Star. Certain people in the Islands possessed mysterious priestly powers of blessing *and* cursing: the former strengthened their resolve and steeled them for battle; any boats that broke the pledge of the strikers and ventured out to sea felt a special fear.

In January 1935 the crew of the lugger *Erub* at Darnley Island refused to work after the Protector, JD McLean, had foisted a captain of his choice upon the crew. After a meeting the men decided 'that they would never work a Company boat again' (O'Leary Report 11 May 1936, 5).[11] This meeting, it appears, was held after the Darnley Islanders returned from Thursday Island. (There is no record of the date which appears to be well into 1935, some time after the *Erub* was transferred to Murray Island but before December when an incident occurred at Murray Island between the Protector and Marou and other Councillors.)

According to McLean, the meeting agreed that the men write to other Islands asking them not to work the 'Company boats' so that the Commonwealth would take over the Islands. The government teacher at Darnley heard about the meeting and told them they needed his permission and his presence at any further meeting. McLean reports that the teacher's 'action had resulted in turning these men from hostility to the administration to compliance with orders during the holidays'. He 'had the natives well in hand' (Report 24 January 1936, 3). However, in the same report, McLean stated that a letter approaching men from other Islands to refuse to work the boats went from Murray Island to Badu. He also stated that the captain of one boat 'came from Thursday Island about 20 December and said that it was arranged at all Islands to give up the "Company" boats...' (Report, 3).[12] Certainly too the conditions for a strike existed in all the Islands and the 'Company boats' were the focus because they were Islander-owned and Administration-controlled. Discontent was so strong everywhere that in 1935 an Island consensus had emerged: the Islanders were 'bubbling over' with the feeling that their situation was intolerable. In this situation, they were ready for the Spark that lit the fire of rebellion.

The Spark that they awaited came as a message from the Bishop, carried and explained by a Western Islander, 'Old M' of Badu, to the Island priests in the Eastern Islands, Darnley and then Murray; and then vouchsafed for safekeeping with Grandfather T at Rennel Island. The decision to strike was made at sea by a consensus at boat meetings and Islanders today mention both Darnley and Murray as starting places of the strike. Importantly, it was Divine Blessing vested in a number of mediating people which brought that consensus about. Their prefigured dramatic action at each island took on a mass character like crackers going off simultaneously.

The message which Nau Mabaig says was carried round the Islands by 'Old M' is the same 'message' carried by the Captain of the *Mulgrave* in October 1935: the Message Islanders had all been waiting for. They had their plans in readiness; their own priests had given them the word that the Bishop believed they should be transferred to the Commonwealth. Freedom was on the way; they were organising and preparing for its arrival. In this they understandably underestimated the character, the tenacity and the strength of those who held power over them.

OUTCOMES: THE NEW SHAPE OF POWER

In 1935 Islanders had outwitted and out-organised the Protectors: moving along Island networks invisible to officials the message had been carried to each Island in turn by 'Old M', the Badu skipper of the *Mulgrave*, the cargo boat of the Aboriginal Industries Board itself. 'Carrying cargo and loading messages!', Nau Mabaig recalls humorously. 'Take the boats, tow them to TI!' Islanders were turning the tables; by their action they were now ridiculing Kole.

Yet the singular power of Kole continued to prevail. Even before the sound of the Badu men's defiant actions ceased as they disappeared from the government schoolhouse to the safe home ground of the village refusing ever to sign back, the government's specially chosen representative, C O'Leary was on his way to the Islands to secure their compliance. He began work quietly and persuasively with armed police at his side. Badu Island was the key link in the chain of pearl shell, and the two Councillors were the Protectors' men. As in all the Islands there were many many strong people, old and young, like the sixteen-year-old Nau Mabaig, an experienced working boy toughened by two years of hard life on the *Wakaid*. Yet the Protector, with the power of the state behind him, had the resources to bring into effect well-planned backstage manoeuvres of which Islanders were unaware. O'Leary was just the man to judge how much rope to let out; he was flexible, cool and calculatingly divisive.

THE NEW LAW AND THE FIRST INTERISLAND COUNCILLORS' CONFERENCE

By the end of 1936 a set of amended rules or 'New Law', as it became known among Islanders, which transferred many of the powers of the government teachers, the Aboriginal Industries Board (AIB) and the Protectors to the Island Councils, came into effect. In some Islands, a new type of government teacher was appointed: 'I think Chandler was a different man', Au Bala concludes about the teacher appointed to Darnley 'just after the Yorke Island Conference...he might have been part of the New Law'. In December the AIB published the first edition of *The*

Islander, a quarterly in English for free distribution among Islanders which sought to explain the new organisational measures to them in preparation for an interisland Councillors' Conference planned for August 1937 (QPP 1937, 15; edition 4, 15 September 1937, enclosed with 37/9577 in QSA A/3941). Communication reached a high point in June 1937 when the Minister for Health and Home Affairs, accompanied by the Under Home Secretary, the Chief Protector, the Minister's Private Secretary and two Brisbane newspapermen visited the Islands ('Results of Ministerial Visit', No 4, 1). When the time for the Torres Strait Islanders Councillors' Conference arrived the situation had been stabilised.

From 23–25 August 1937, thirty-four elected Councillors from fourteen Torres Strait Islander communities met together at Yorke Island in the presence of Mr CD O'Leary. There the authority of the Councillors was underlined at the outset by the election of an Islander to the position of Chairman of the Conference, the vote being taken by a secret ballot at the request of the Councillors. It was a historic occasion in a minor key, the atmosphere one of conciliation.

Prior to the Conference the Councillors of each Island had endorsed the 'New Law' as it had become known among Islanders. It remained only to make decisions upon straightforward matters. The controversial issues, which had been the focus of a sometimes bitter struggle since the strike against the restrictive and disciplinary powers of Protection began in January 1936, had been largely resolved through the 'New Law'. Now the eddies still active below the surface were hidden by the long-awaited calms, like grease upon the sea.

Only six days before the Conference the Murray Islanders' demand for home rule and full citizenship rights had been registered at Ministerial level. As the Chief Protector reported to the Minister on 16 August, at Murray Island the 'general request was for the right to full control of all village affairs', including the administration of the Council, the Court and the Island Fund. The conciliatory overtones of the Conference contrasted sharply with events of the previous eighteen months. Just over a year before, Islanders had achieved a significant victory: the local Protector JD McLean had been sacked as a result of their actions.

Since January 1936, when Deputy Protector O'Leary had suddenly been sent to the Torres Strait to investigate the cause of the strike there, the Torres Strait area had been a focus of Ministerial and Cabinet attention. In June–July 1937, the Islanders were paid a special visit by Mr EM Hanlon, Minister for Health and Home Affairs. Travelling along the west coast of Cape York the government party began their Torres Strait visit at Badu on 22 June, calling at Mabuiag the next day and going from there to eight other Island communities. In preparing the way for a conference of reconciliation, the Minister promised to consider sympathetically all the requests made to him by Councillors.

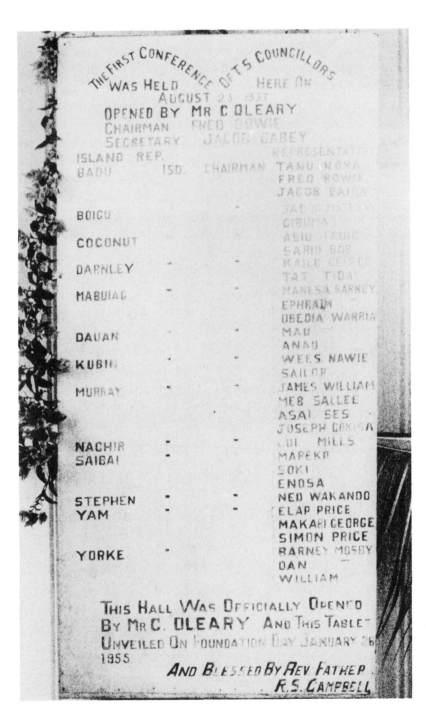

Plate 17 Plaque at Yorke Island commemorating the first interisland Councillors' Conference, 1937

This visit was the culmination of sixteen months' hard work by CD O'Leary and his officers who had given the Department's Torres Strait Administration a complete overhaul. The reorganisation curtailed the powers of the local Protector and the government teachers and, in giving greater authority to elected Councillors, it also relaxed restrictions on personal rights and movement. The Island Councillors 'took good care', reported *The Islander* (the post-strike publication created by the Department expressly for Islanders), 'to bring forward those important questions which only the Ministerial head of a Department can decide', leaving the 'small matters' for themselves at the coming Conference (No 4, 1). The establishment of a secondary school, the need for better hospitals in the Islands, and greater control over Island affairs, were matters raised with the Minister.

Given their new role in choosing crews and captains of the 'Company boats' the Conference concentrated on the practical details of the 'New Law' essentially put into operation at the end of 1936. In approving these details in the presence of Mr O'Leary the Councillors were acknowledging that substantial agreement had finally been reached with the Administration. On O'Leary's side the Conference allowed the Councillors 'to feel that the Department is placing a trust in them that they are in duty bound to uphold', as he reported to the Chief Protector on 7 September (enclosed with 35/9577).

The Conference resolved matters concerning the sale of pearls, the registration of fishing grounds, Councillors' wages, and voted unanimously for distinctive Councillors' badges instead of the existing compulsory uniforms inscribed with the word 'Councillor' in large letters. The Councillors expressed support for the newly established stores on the outer islands, and called for their extension. They recommended higher wages on the boats of the 'Master' pearlers; they varied the colours of the 'Company boats', and they also discussed the Scout Jamboree and the cup and flag competition for the best catch in the 'Company boat' fleet.

Several resolutions which sought to alter their position as a race apart foreshadowed by many years the demands for equality and 'citizen rights' put by the Torres Strait Islander ex-servicemen after the Second World War. The unanimous resolution asking that the Commonwealth Government pay maternity allowances sought to put Islanders on the same footing as other Australians. The Conference proposed that Islanders be trained as pump or dress divers like the Japanese divers, Islanders having been until then exclusively 'swim' or skin divers. Islanders had for a long time been taking part in the money culture: they were seeking their rightful share in its rewards.

At the same time the Conference reaffirmed fundamental traditional rights in land according to Island custom as an integral part of the 'New Law'. It was moved by the Chief Councillor of Murray Island and seconded by a Mabuiag Councillor 'that all land be used as our forefathers [used it] because it was boundaried up by them'.

Councillors affirmed the new rules by which they would appoint men to the 'Company boats'; resolutions expressing 'confidence' in the office of Protector at Thursday Island and thanking O'Leary for arranging the Conference were passed.[13] As O'Leary wrote to the Chief Protector, 'confidence had been restored': the Conference 'had created in the minds of the Councillors a greater confidence in the administration than existed previously' (7 September 1937, enclosed with 37/9577).

FROM TOTAL RESTRICTION TO LIMITED AUTONOMY: THE TORRES STRAIT ISLANDERS ACT 1939

Two years later, on 12 October 1939, the Torres Strait Islanders Act 1939 formalised the provisions of 'indirect rule' in the 'New Law' for Islanders as a separate people. An Act of the Queensland Parliament passed earlier in 1939 had instituted a new system covering both Aborigines and Islanders: the Aboriginals Preservation and Protection Act 1939 substituted a Director of Native Affairs for the Chief Protector and the Aboriginal Department was renamed the Department of Native Affairs (DNA). In both Acts local Protectors supervised 'natives' living on 'Reserves'. A difference between the two Acts is significant: local government provisions in the Torres Strait Islanders Act delegated to Island Councils 'the functions of local government of the reserve...in accordance with island customs and practices' (3 Geo VI No 7, 1939, Part III s 18(1)). In the Act relating to Aborigines local government was absent; a 'Superintendent' managed each reserve (3 Geo VI No 6). As a political institution 'Protection' was virtually abandoned in relation to Islanders.

The short-term outcomes of the strike were contradictory. For Islanders, the removal of McLean as local Protector in the middle of 1936, the transfer of powers from the government teachers to the Island Councils (which took place between 1936 and the Councillors' Conference in August 1937), and the recognition of Islanders as a separate people in the Torres Strait Islanders Act 1939, represented a victory for their immediate demands. As a former government teacher who had been at Darnley Island in 1935 and 1936 summed up the strike and its results in a conversation at Thursday Island forty-three years later: 'Partly they wanted to get rid of JD McLean and partly they wanted their independence. Prior to the

strike they had a curfew on all the islands... That strike led up to a partial freedom'
(Cassette 010/CT/TI/1/79).

The Aboriginal Department had lost some of its directive powers; the
Island Councils had once again become '*mamus*' of each Island; but the power
of the 'big *mamus*' in Brisbane, as Uncle called the Chief Protector, remained,
only he was now the Director of Native Affairs (DNA). The new Torres Strait
Islanders Act conferred a circumscribed power on Island Councils: first, the local
Protector retained the power '...to suspend any resolution or order of the island
council or prohibit the expenditure of any moneys from the Island Fund' (Part
II s 8(1)); second, Island police were to be appointed by the Councils 'subject to
the approval of the protector' (Part III s 19(1)).

Islanders were seeking the full freedom of home rule, a purpose
sustained only at Murray Island where within a week of the 1937 Councillors'
Conference the elected Council was continuing to press for control of the
Commonwealth Savings Bank passbooks. Following his visit to ten islands, the Chief
Protector had reported to the Under Home Secretary on 16 August that at Murray
Island the 'general request was for the right to full control of all village affairs',
including the administration of the Council, the Court and the Island Fund. The
Murray Islanders saw control over Commonwealth Savings Bank passbooks '...as
giving them the right to draw the money direct...and spend it as they thought
fit' (37/9577 in A/3941). The following day, Bleakley cabled the Minister's reply
to the question raised by the Murray Island Councillors with O'Leary: 'Murray
request operate savings bank account direct impracticable under Audit Act which
directs that all collections through government department can only be controlled
by qualified government official authorised act as public accountant...' (enclosed
with 39/9577). Each of the two parties recognised the power inherent in control
over Island finances. The state 'won' this contest which was to continue in various
forms for the next half century.

At least in the world outside the Islands the Protectors controlled how
the strike was remembered, what it was about and its outcomes. Uncle was right
when he recalled to me at the end of 1978 that the purpose of the 1937 Councillors'
Conference was 'to make everyone forget about the strike'. His view is borne out
by the official public statement of the Department on the strike which trivialised
its significance:

> Early in the year a feeling of unrest was manifested among the
> Torres Strait Islanders resulting in a partial stoppage of work on
> the boats controlled by the Department for the benefit of the
> natives. The many stated causes of discontent were immediately
> investigated, and necessary action taken to safeguard the

property of the Department. Fortunately, the prompt measures adopted by the investigating officers resulted in an early resumption of work by the discontented natives. (QPP 1937, 11)

In like manner the Chief Protector represented the cause of the strike as Islanders' dissatisfaction with 'the Department's control of their business affairs stirred up by bad advice from Thursday Island shopkeepers who resented the loss of trade from Islanders'.

Scholars fell in with this trivialisation. Beckett emphasises the meagreness of the pay among the various 'grievances': 'The grievances seem to have been various. The Chief Protector of the time supposed that the men wanted to handle their own money. Veterans of the strike cite the wretched pay, and the seeming lack of correspondence between effort and reward' (1977, 88).[14] Importantly, the build-up of events which climaxed in the 1936 confrontation were buried, so simplifying the meanings of its outcomes. Even Peel, who explicitly declared himself a champion of the Islanders' cause for freedom from the DNA, saw the strike simply as a 'defeat' for Islanders (1947, 111).

Inside the Department it was not forgotten just how hard it had been to get the men back to work, the consternation it had caused in the highest places, the long-lasting intransigence of the Murray Islanders, and the way Islanders had become a changed people. New lock-ups were built at Saibai, at Badu and at Murray Island in the years immediately following the strike (QPP 1937, 13; QPP 1938, 16). Meanwhile, they gaoled 'Old M', the Badu man who carried the message on their boat.

RESHAPING POWER IN THE ISLANDS

The singular power remained in the Islands: it had been forced to find a new shape. Over a time, the O'Leary style of picking out 'the troublemakers' and working through the Councils, of finding 'yes-men' ('monkey men' in the local idiom) and extending favours, giving houses to some and not to others, became the new style of management. At some islands, for example Badu, the iron fist was ready to push Islanders back to their knees, to thump or starve into submission those who dared to disagree.

The Islanders had experienced the jubilation of being-for-themselves, a time of transient hope; it changed them. Over forty-five years the new Act was amended and supplemented by regulations; the local Protector was replaced by a Manager; the DNA was twice renamed as the Department of Aboriginal and Island Affairs and the Department of Aboriginal and Islanders Advancement (DAIA); however, ultimate control remained in the Department's hands: Island Councils were not self-managing bodies.[15] Uncle expressed a general feeling when he said in 1980: '...this Act has got to go'.

The strike ushered in a new form of 'Ministerial' management which came to be known locally as the 'O'Leary style'. In his efforts to break the strike and 'restore confidence' in the Administration, over the years 1936 and 1937, CD (Con) O'Leary, who had been rushed to the Islands on the instructions of the Minister, foreshadowed the style of supervision which became established practice in the Islands from 1937 until the 1980s. In those two years one can discern the main shape of the 'O'Leary style': one which continued the two-way relationship of close paternalist interdependence in combination with manipulative methods which sought to influence the choices of individual Islanders in electing Island Councils. The following incident reported by O'Leary to JW Bleakley, the Chief Protector, on 4 February 1937, exemplifies the style nicely. The setting was 'the big problem' of retaining the hold of the Administration over the crews of the 'Company boats'. O'Leary had used his influence to persuade the Councillors to support his selective policy of 'obtaining the best crews voluntarily' while rejecting 'the troublemakers', an action he saw as 'unique and important' and a result of his own 'official propaganda' (O'Leary to Chief Protector, 37/1580 in A/3941).

The 'O'Leary style', passed on to the next director of the Department of Native Affairs (DNA), PJ (Pat) Killoran, was perfected over half a century. Curfew whistles were no longer blown after 1936. But in 1937 a two-way wireless system linked the outer Island communities to Thursday Island — the signal of a new form of power. Islanders were no longer isolated: they could obtain medical and other advice and send messages, so making closer contact with one another — *and* with 'the Department'. The Administration could keep in touch with everything Islanders were saying, reaping too the reward of Islanders' gratitude at their release from isolation.

Through direct personal contact in which knowledge of each Islander family became the norm a constant visibility was achieved. Surveillance under the guise of informality became the key to a new disciplinary control. Through a pastoral style in which the face of each Islander featured upon the mental map of the local DNA manager and the director (O'Leary and Killoran each rose from the former to the latter position), combined with the self-appointed function of professional adviser and friend, Islanders were being disciplined into a state of docility, conformity and passive obedience. The pastoral style, part of oppressive structures, came to be in subtle 'league with its victims' (Nandy 1985, xiv). Thus homespun versions of what Michel Foucault calls 'bio-power' and 'pastoral power' came to be honed up with a highly visible system of unequal rewards.[16] Personal attention was the watchword: 'We know them; you can't tell us anything about the Islanders', as the Queensland Premier at the time, Sir Joh Bjelke-Petersen, would say. 'He knows me', a phrase common among Islanders undergoing a loss of self and developing a psychic reliance upon the 'protector'.

In some Islands, from the 1930s through to the late 1970s, the DNA succeeded in finding Councillors who thought their way, or managed to school them to their way of thinking. At one Island, when the elected radical Council called for 'citizen rights' in the early 1950s, it was dismissed (Beckett 1963, 248–49; on control of local government and the pearling luggers, see 253–63).

Ministerial supervision features prominently in the formal provisions of the community services and land holding legislation of 1984 and 1985, which created Deeds of Grant in Trust (DOGIT) on lands formerly reserved under the Torres Strait Islanders Act repealed in 1984. The two Acts — the Community Services Act 1984 and the Land Holding Act 1985 — are complementary. The two key areas of finance and police are the direct responsibility of the Minister. Island police are chosen by the Island Council but with the approval of the Minister (Community Services Act 1984 s 39). All Council expenditure must be made under a budget approved by the Minister with a financial statement of receipts and expenditures every three months for each fund operated by the Council as well as an annual financial statement (s 33). Accounts of Councils are audited 'as if the Council were a department of government of Queensland' (s 32(2)).

In relation to Ministerial supervision of finance and police these clauses echo the provisions of the Torres Strait Islanders Act passed in 1939: the 1984–85 legislation substitutes the word 'Minister' for 'Protector' in relation to Island police; prohibition on 'the expenditure of the Island Fund' is now replaced by provisions of a less circumscribed nature.

It is this kind of 'self-management — a partnership of non-equals with the right of veto by the self-appointed senior partner — that the Minister and the Department of Community Services (the renamed DAIA) seek to foster in their supervision of the members of communities in 'trust areas'. And as Bob Katter Jnr, the relevant Minister, indicated in a radio statement on 22 July 1987, agents of the Ministers are the sort of men whom Islanders can talk to. A self-assured cultural arrogance.

STARS OF
TAGAI
II

Malo tag mauki mauki, Teter mauki mauki.
Malo says, Keep your hands and feet off
other people's land.

Four events were to strengthen and give further definition to Torres Strait Islander identity: the Second World War, the 'border issue' of the 1970s, a move for sovereign status and a case for customary rights to land.

As we shall see, over a fifty-year period, Islanders' activities reveal a set of developing themes which had come to the surface in the events of 1936–37: 'getting out of bondage', 'citizen rights' and equality with other Australians; autonomy; and the right to control over land and resources, were translated into a call for self-determination by an identifiable people: the Torres Strait Islanders. The idiom of their identity continued to be that of diversities in unity.

REKINDLING THE FIRE OF FREEDOM MOVEMENT: THE SECOND WORLD WAR

In 1942 the threat of a Japanese invasion of Australia provided the context for raising units manned substantially by Aborigines and Islanders who had previously been excluded from the military forces (Hall 1980, 30). The Torres Strait Defence Force established at this time was composed of 1,355 Torres Strait Islanders, Aborigines and Thursday Island people mainly of Malay origin. It consisted of a Light Infantry Battalion, Coast Artillery and Water Transport, and was staffed below the rank of sergeant largely by Islanders (Hall 1980; QPP 1948, 2). The unit was racially segregated and the monthly pay of Islander and Aboriginal privates was £3.10.0 in the first year compared with £8.0.0 for privates in integrated units (Hall 1980, 31; and see Beckett 1987, 62–65). Some 700 Islanders arranged in four companies (A, B, C and D) came suddenly face to face in the context of a new enemy (the Japanese) and a new relationship to some white men which contrasted sharply with the master–servant relation to the Aboriginal Department, renamed the DNA in 1939. The following brief narratives give a picture of the many-sided comparisons and contrasts suddenly available to Islanders, particularly those in the military forces.

NAU MABAIG, JAPANESE NOW ENEMY TO US

The Second World War came to Islanders quietly and suddenly. Immediately before the War the Torres Strait Islands had the greatest concentration of Japanese in

Australia; 96 per cent of divers on the boats of the Master pearlers were Japanese. Action preceded explanation as Army patrols swooped upon Japanese divers and skippers and placed them in barbed-wire encampments at Thursday Island with guns on three sides. Nau Mabaig recalls the first moments of the Pacific War:

> *When we get into Thursday Island we find there are many Army men there. They grab all the Japanese and they drag the diving boat from behind Badu. Anchored the boat and took all the Japanese ashore and put them in the prisoners' camp. Maybe 300 or 400 Japanese men: many, many, many... because there were lots of boats at that time and each boat harbours six Japanese men, two Island men crew. It gave us a surprise. Only leave us in the boat. The patrol boat called* Reliant *with an MP on it, water transport soldiers, comes alongside the boat. They only grab the Japanese and left the Island men to look after the boat. I heard the news when we get into the harbour. I was crew on the cargo boat then, so the Protector told me the War declared: 'Japanese enemy to us'. We heard the War is on the other side of Papua New Guinea.* (Cassette 020/NM/B/1/80)

Soon Islander men were themselves brought together in the Army. A white soldier who joined the Army as a Private, rose to the rank of Lieutenant and was part of a detachment which organised A, B, C and D companies, recalls the Islanders and the Islands nearly forty years after the War:

DIGGER, I HAD NOTHING BUT THE GREATEST RESPECT FOR THEM

> I could just hear the thump, thump, thump of feet in the night. I felt sorry for them because half of them didn't know where the hell they were; just marched into camp dead of night, marched in under white men, in the army; didn't know whether they were going to be slaughtered or not.
>
> In the four years I had with the Torres Strait Light Infantry Battalion from 1942 to 1946, I had nothing but the greatest respect for them; I still think they're the equal (given the right weapons and further advanced training) of any soldier in the world. At that time we didn't have the full training; we trained them as far as we could without weaponry. I loved them. I like to think that that was thrown back at me, that they loved me. I know they respected me.
>
> We went to Murray Island. Here I was finally sailing to Mer, and we come ashore there; I had about twenty-five to thirty boys on leave; come to the shore there and all the women are dancing and singing along the beach; and they got the first fire lit along the beach among the coconut trees. Old Meriam Man had them build a special little thatched hut for me, and when we left and sailed away they'd made up a song that used to be our marching song:

> *Goodbye boys we're leaving,*
> *We are sailing away to the west...*
> *We couldn't see the foam*
> *But only the rising sun afalling on Gelam hill.*

They're musical born eh? (Cassette 138/CM/TN/1/84)

The white soldiers had shown Islanders how to work machines, to fix motors and radios and electrical gear, a knowledge they had been denied in the past. 'The Army got some boys to come into TI from Darnley, Yorke, Badu, to learn about engines', Ailan Man explained: 'That's the first time that Islanders were allowed to touch the knobs on the radio. The Department [DNA] people didn't trust our fellows to do these things.' The Murray Islanders returned the white Diggers' reciprocity with an Island welcome and a song which was to become the unit's marching song. Not only the men in the defence force, but whole Island communities were to experience for the first time relationships of equality with white people, which white veterans who had been stationed in the Islands also verified with me. Islander women, children and men not eligible for army service experienced the War differently to those in the fighting forces. Organised in small detachments away from the villages by the Army — Malay Town, Wild India, Hollywood and Arizona — they experienced both privation and a new solidarity within each Island community. 'And when the War was finished we praised God and were so happy that the tears rolled down our faces', a very old lady at Badu recalled to me (Cassette 039/BL/B/1/80).

In June 1947, the Director of Native Affairs described the Torres Strait Light Infantry Battalion as having 'performed an excellent war service for the nation' (QPP 1948, 2).

Islander men found themselves together and they spoke the pidgin language of the Islands with those from the other side of the Strait. Kuki, a Darnley Islander, recounts his memories of the sudden reversals of enemies to friends which arose out of the special context of Islanders' wartime experiences:

> *The War start. We anchored at Badu now and man came to recruit from army now. We stay in the army and we go shift from place to place, go training Goody Island, go — everywhere and after we come all right into a battalion. We got three groups — Eastern, Central and Western. Couple of boys from Yorke, couple of boys from Yam Island, but mostly from Darnley and Murray; one battalion the same time now, and we finish training now and we ready now. We can stay and do much good job in that kind of spirit now, the spirit was very tough in us. We all in our own battalion. We've got no feeling of hate towards the Western and Central, no growl now. From Western to Central, they come out from one. When it come time for us now, the priest come round and go tell the churchwarden it's time to go for prayers, and*

the church warden from us he take the service in A company. And
when it's time for Western or Central Islands, or when it's Eastern,
well, I'm an Eastern Island boy, when my time to take the service I
do it. A, B, C, D companies they never forget about God. (Cassette
053/KK/TI/1/80)

REKINDLING THE FIRE OF FREEDOM: IDENTITY AND CITIZEN RIGHTS

Many of the white soldiers, especially the older men who went to the Islands in
the Volunteer Defence Corps (the VDC) to take over the fortress signals when the
younger men were sent to the centres of action in the Pacific, supported the
Islanders in their wish to be free of the DNA, and in the immediate situation, in
their attempt to get the same pay as the white soldiers. A, B and C companies
went on strike for equal pay and the same rights as white soldiers, and in 1944
their pay was raised to two-thirds of the 'white rate'. As Hall notes, to award them
more would have created problems when the War ended (1980, 31).

Only eight years before, Islanders had struck for freedom from
Protection and for citizen rights, and in the case of Murray Island home rule had
become an explicit demand. First Meriam Man and other leaders of the 1936 strike
were people of longstanding experience in the principles of trade unionism and
direct action. As Ailan Man explains, for Islanders like First Meriam Man especially,
who had associated with unionists, with the white left, and with communists, there
was a continuity between Islanders' conceptions of 'sharing' and the ideals of
communism. Ailan Man says of him:

> *I think he was with the communists before. He had a lot of contact with*
> *old-time buddies like one South Sea man in Cairns. He'd been feeding*
> *him that stuff from the watersiders in Cairns. Tell you why, I think*
> *what must have sparked him off was that Volunteer Defence Corps —*
> *the VDC unit. The older men were rejects from the fighting forces. They*
> *formed a unit and they kept the forces going. They were sent up here*
> *to relieve the fighting soldiers when they got moved up north and they*
> *took over the radio from the signal men there. They were out in the*
> *Islands and that's when they rekindled that fire of freedom movement.*
> *And they said, 'You Island people should be this way'. It's those old,*
> *mature people that came up; they were old union men. The way they*
> *talked is the way Island people talk: it's easy to the Island people.* (Book
> of Islanders 1984, B19)

According to Digger, even on the matter of Army pay the Islanders saw
their main adversary as the DNA:

Plate 18 Kittyhawks and bombers dance, Badu Island, 1987 (courtesy of Bob Scott)

I remember talking it over with my officers that they took the
same oath; they could be ordered to go anywhere same as me
or the others and they were only getting a pittance in pay. I
always have thought it was unfair. As the months went on they
got wiser; they knew and they asked, 'Why do we get small
money [*compared to white soldiers*]?'; but it was not against the
Army personnel, it was against the DNA, because of allotment
money. It happened at Thursday Island at the DNA office; it never
happened on Army grounds. I heard that the main blue was at
the DNA. Little grapevine bits coming back by word of mouth
found out that the women were getting nothing on the [*outer*]
islands, they were starving practically. There was no money, no
food, nothing for them and they couldn't get it unless they had
the necessary papers sent over by the DNA. That's what they
always resented. Everything had to go before the DNA and the
DNA was god; he was god sitting up on the throne. He said yea
or nay and that was it. (Cassette 138/CM/TN/1/84)

Given this background, the VDC men and some regular soldiers became
the spark that lit the fire of freedom movement; the harbingers of fresh times.
Islanders travelled too beyond the old boundaries; and the water-transport men
who sailed down westwards towards the US base at Merauke sang freely of new
places:

> *Goodbye my love, farewell to thee*
> *Soon I'll be sailing for the Arafura Sea.*
> *While I'm away I'll think of you*
> *Memories come by dear, love-dreams come true.*
>
> *While I'm away forget not me*
> *Till I come back to you from the Arafura Sea.*

Islanders returned to their homes with a new sense of purpose, talking
openly of 'freedom' and 'citizen rights' for the Islands. Given the renewed powers
of Island Councils under the New Law and the 1939 Act, their wartime experiences
led them to hopes of a new deal. As Beckett observes: 'Their experience of what
they called "army time" had left them with a distinctive consciousness of their
worth and the means to construct an alternative to their present situation' (1987,
65). Post-war organisations, emanating from Australia, strengthened their
confidence by championing their cause as men and women equal to other
Australians. The Legion of Ex-service Men and Women was seen by Islanders as
their organisation, extending the mateship of wartime. When the State Secretary
of the Legion came to address them in TI in the early 1950s on the subject of

deferred pay, it seemed to him that the Islanders gathered together, perhaps two hundred, were seeking a voice. Thirty years later, the attentiveness of the adults and the silence of the children still continued to remind him that they had seemed to be waiting for something: 'they seemed to expect a great deal of the Legion', he recalled, 'and at question time it was very evident that they saw the Legion as able to do for them much more than the Legion would ever be able to do':

> The meeting was held in the main hall. Whites showed a great interest peeping in at the door to see this hall full of Islanders being addressed by a white person. It seemed to me that they were seeking a voice and the Legion had taken up their cause. It was as if at last they had an organisation that could gain some of the things they were wanting. There were thirty or forty kiddies with a couple of Island women and they played among themselves quite happily all night. I have never seen a group of kiddies so well behaved. It was quite unusual; it really impressed me. (Cassette 121/ST/BN/1/82)

The War bred new Islander organisations which were expressive of a hope it engendered. Welfare societies, which arose in different Islands often came to be fused with Christian cooperative associations which preached a gospel of equality. The Assemblies of God, which proclaimed racial equality and preached a gospel of freedom (Beckett 1963, 131) became like a 'religion of the oppressed' (see Lanternari 1963).

In 1954 the Communist Party published a comprehensive program for the Torres Strait Islands, *Let the Sun Shine!*, in Kala Lagaw Ya, in Meriam Mir and in English (1954, 1-22). Its proposals were for self-rule based upon indigenous structures within Island communities, with an elected council of chiefs who then elected a 'paramount chief'. A book by Gerald Peel, a leading communist of the time, *Isles of the Torres Straits*, was published as early as 1947 and the Communist Party newspaper, *Tribune* commented on the program (6 and 10 March 1948; Beckett 1963, 118).

The militant mood and rising hopes were soon dashed, especially at Badu Island. The Badu branch of the Legion of Ex-service Men and Women was banned. The Badu Council, now composed of elected ex-servicemen who were strongly anti-Administration in outlook and champions of 'citizen rights' and 'freedom', was dismissed; Tanu Nona was elected chairman for life. Badu was still top island for pearling: between 1946 and 1958 a 'Nona-fleet' emerged which took more than 50 per cent of the earnings of the whole 'DNA fleet' (Beckett 1963, 248–50).

At one level Islanders in the defence force became the lost legion of a lost people, a culture of outsiders. At another level the War and its aftermath foreshadowed the emergence of Torres Strait Islanders as one people with an awareness of a territory in common. In Kuki's words, 'They come out from one': they are 'like brothers'.

SPEAKING WITH ONE VOICE: THE BORDER ISSUE OF THE 1970s

In 1973 a proposal to divide the Torres Strait at the ten degree parallel, the half-way line between the Australian mainland and Papua New Guinea, began to take shape (The Torres Strait Boundary, 1976; Griffin (ed) 1976; Seminar on Torres Strait Border Dispute, 1977). This move for boundary changes, which came to be known as the 'border issue', concerned rights to sea-bed oil and other marine resources (Griffin 1977, 219). Since the late 1960s the Strait's energy resources had begun to beckon foreigners to the area with an intensity even greater than that which had propelled pearlers there a century before. By 1970 two oil permits covering a major part of the Strait had been issued.[1] In 1967 oil search permits for the Torres Strait region were issued in Port Moresby, and competition for oil began to define the so-called border issue. To the Premier, Mr Joh Bjelke-Petersen, the Strait and the Islands were part of Queensland. On 14 September 1975, on the eve of Papua New Guinea's independence, Ebia Olewale, Papua New Guinea's Foreign Minister and member for the Western Province which adjoins the Torres Strait, stated that ethnically and historically the people of Torres Strait were part of Papua New Guinea (PNG). In February 1977 the PNG parliament passed an Act empowering itself to make a unilateral declaration on its boundaries. (At this time, Esso Australia was drilling for oil eight kilometres off the Fly River delta.)

Given the new and heightened significance of the sea-bed resources of the Strait, in the early 1970s, the Australian Government began to make a reassessment of the political–strategic implications. The islands of Saibai, Boigu and Dauan, which had been seen as sites for command of the southern shores of New Guinea in 1879, had become stepping stones on a walk 'into and through Queensland', in Prime Minister Gough Whitlam's dramatic words in the *PNG Post-Courier* on 26 September 1972. Given this new context, a proposal to divide the Strait at the ten degree parallel, the midway position between Australia and Papua New Guinea, gained support in Canberra with the assistance of a policy survey conducted by a group of researchers.

In 1974 a survey conducted by a research team concluded that Islanders living in Townsville and Cairns identified not with their home islands but solely as Torres Strait Islanders. Furthermore, unaware of the 'bush telegraph' system between Islands and mainland, it suggested that Islanders maintained little contact with the Islands (Fisk et al III, 1974, 44, 42; VI, 92). Events of the late 1970s and the 1980s proved both these conclusions erroneous (see Sharp 1980b, 18–32).

The proposed change in boundaries meant that nine of the seventeen islands inhabited by Islanders would become part of the newly independent state of Papua New Guinea. In response to this proposal Islanders saw themselves as indivisible; they spoke almost with one voice through a Border Action Committee, as a sea people, inseparable from the total milieu of the Torres Strait: 'Even winds, tides, currents, the air, the cays and reefs are part of our culture', one Islander leader said on their behalf (Lui in Griffin (ed) 1976).

Those Islanders who had migrated to towns in north Queensland following the collapse of the pearl shelling industry in the 1960s also left no doubt as to their opposition to the border change (Fisk VI, 1976, 79). Islanders were 'now one community' and despite their geographical dispersal they spoke together. That inseparability included a refusal to be parted from their ancestors, many of whom were buried in the northern islands. As Sis explains: 'That's one of the main things that made us fight for the border too; our people were buried in islands there and if we were to come down this way [south of the ten degree "line"] then our mothers and fathers would be left there. You see how we think of our dead; for us they're still alive and nobody would be looking after them...'

On 18 December 1978 a Treaty between Australia and Papua New Guinea on Maritime Boundaries signed in Sydney left the border unchanged. It marked out a 'Protected Zone' in Torres Strait and placed a ten-year prohibition on mining or drilling of the sea-bed in that zone.

In the 1970s the Strait had become a centre for conflicting political–strategic and economic interests. A battle for land and resources had begun. Islanders as a people had stood up for themselves in public for the first time: We are the Torres Strait Islanders, they had said, with homelands in common. They had won a significant victory; they had also strengthened their will, just what they needed in the 1980s.

A SELF-DETERMINING FUTURE? THE MOVE FOR SOVEREIGNTY

On 20 January 1988, a meeting of 400 Islanders at Thursday Island made a public call for secession from Australia. This move followed developments within Islander communities both in the Torres Strait and in Townsville during 1987 on the theme of 'sovereign independence', the term used by the Island Coordinating Council (ICC), a statutory body set up under the Community Services Act 1984–86 (Qld) (see Scott in Babbage 1990, 406), in July 1987 for the main theme of a set of demands relating to autonomy put by the ICC to the Minister for Aboriginal Affairs.

An Islander organisation based in Townsville, known as Magani Malu Kes, also emerged at this time spearheading efforts for recognition of the separate identity of Torres Strait Islanders.

The idea of a separate Islander state had been foreshadowed explicitly by the Townsville-based Torres United Party (TUP) in 1977 and 1978. The TUP, founded in Townsville in 1976 by two expatriate Torres Strait Islanders, James Akee from a Murray Island family and Carlemo Wacando, a Darnley Islander, made a public call for Torres Strait independence under the banner of 'the sacred Island nation' (TUP to the United Nations Special Committee of Twenty-four on Decolonisation, 8 August 1979).

On 12 December 1978, six days before the Treaty on maritime boundaries between Papua New Guinea and Australia was signed in Sydney, Wacando brought an action in the High Court challenging the 1879 annexation of the Islands.[2] This claim, rejected by the High Court in 1981, was integral to a request to the United Nations to make 'independent inquiries' into the case for sovereign status as a separate nation (TUP Submission to the United Nations Special Committee on Decolonisation, November 1978, 1–31).

These moves clearly reflected and promoted the separate identity of the Torres Strait Islanders. The first sought to test the 'legality' of annexation. Had it been successful, Islanders outside the sixty-mile limit would have become 'detached' from Australian control. The second raised the issue of Islander sovereignty over the Islands, aiming to secure a place for an independent Islander state in the world community of nations. Together they raised the right of Islanders to run their own affairs as sovereign people (see Sharp 1979; ABC Radio April 1980, 1 October 1980).

For the first time the Torres United Party put forward a program for the development of an independent and economically viable Torres Strait nation (Scott 1987, 11). 'Power Hope from Strait', ran a headline in the *Townsville Daily Bulletin*. Hydro-power, fishing, tourism and, significantly — oil and gas — were to form the basis of a viable economy. The tidal generation of marine hydro-power would create 'enough electricity to power the entire east coast needs of Australia, plus the needs of [the southern coast of] New Guinea and West Irian as well as the Islands' (Akee and Wacando, Cassette 016/JA–CW/TN/1/79). The waters of the Strait, the spokesmen for the Party claimed, represent 'the leading, viable, energy-from-the-sea potential in the world' (TUP, 8 August 1979). Associated with the party's formation and taking on the role of adviser to and public relations officer for the Torres United Party was Roland Cantley, a European with many years' association with the Torres Strait. A journalist with a flair for flamboyant promotion, Cantley made significant links between the TUP and interested investment and exploration companies such as Essington Investments Pty Ltd, which became the Party's main financier (TUP, 9 April 1980). The latter approached the TUP seeking a full-scale impact study on resources of the Torres Strait. A link was made too with Oil Company of Australia NL, formed in New South Wales on 27 October 1978. Through one of its directors, Neville C Green, the company expressed interest to Mr Wacando 'in pursuing a relationship with you upon sovereignty being obtained', and in particular, 'in taking up [oil search] areas in and around the Torres Strait Islands'.[3] The TUP responded in its public program by offering Islanders a 'package deal' whereby, through an 'oil auction' in the Torres Strait, Islanders might become the 'Arabs of the Indo-Pacific'.

In 1987, after a seven-year silence, the TUP moved the centre of its operations to the Torres Strait, Akee and Wacando remaining its leaders. Two important consequences followed. First was the espousal of independence for the Torres Strait Islands by the Chairman of the Island Coordinating Council (ICC), George Mye, in mid-1987, Roland Cantley becoming about that time the unofficial information officer or adviser to the ICC (Kehoe-Forutan 1988, 18; see also 16–25; Scott in Babbage 1990, 383). This move set a course towards the public call for independence at the January 1988 meeting at Thursday Island; for the establishment of an Independence Working Party Committee in 1988; and, of historic importance, for the public recognition of identity of the Torres Strait Islanders as a separate people.[4] A second consequence was the creation of some public awareness of the TUP's links with big developers. In 1988 a newly-established Torres United Party Prince of Wales (TUPOW) consortium proposed the creation of a 'Torres Strait Island city' on Muralag (Prince of Wales Island), an island unprotected by the Great Barrier Reef Marine Park Authority, by a land claim on behalf of customary Kaurareg owners or even by Deeds of Grant in Trust. The projected city, it was proproposed, would coexist in integral combination with international tourist resorts on various sites across the island. According to Turi Condon (*Australian Financial Review*, 14 September 1988), whose information was understood to have been supplied by Roland Cantley, 16,000 freehold low-priced blocks for Islanders on a twenty square kilometre area on the eastern side of the island together with development of the new city would be subsidised by tenderers for the resort half. Mr Akee's press release of the following day states that 'similar subdivisions on other parts of the island would be sold to white development'.

In opposing the proposal, the Muralag Tribal Committee, representing the Kaurareg customary owners, reacted with expressions of outrage. The local and the southern press made explicit why Muralag was chosen as the proposed resort site: it had a permanent water supply (*Age*, 26 November 1988, 60). That water source lay at Rabau Nguki, the sacred home of the Kaurareg culture hero, Waubin (see Sharp 1992, 105–08; Wees Nawia in Lawrie 1970, 6–7). The Kaurareg protest centred upon the move to construct a dam at Rabau Nguki.

Speaking for the consortium, Akee claimed that 'The granting of freehold status to the Prince of Wales Island...may result in the case for sovereignty becoming unnecessary' (*Australian Financial Review*, 14 September 1988). Was he inadvertently expressing the opinions of the financial interests with 'their own agenda' for the Torres Strait? (Beckett 1987, 205). Certainly very major development interests had become involved. In 1988, they were focussed on tourism (Sharp 1992a, 141–46); clearly the companies with close connections with the TUP at the time of its formation, had interests in oil and gas. In 1988, Essington Limited, which had become the joint vehicle of Kerry Packer and Malcolm Edwards, was the major interest behind the proposal to develop tourism on Muralag. Essington, now a large company, was about to establish new links. In the middle of that year, 48 per cent of the capital of Essington Developments was sold to Axis, the Japanese EIE group vehicle. In August 1988 Essington acquired the share capital of the Cape York Space Agency, which until December 1990, was the main company involved in plans for a spaceport at Temple Bay, Chatungun (Sharp 1990a, 32–40).[5]

By the end of the 1980s, the Torres Strait region was beginning to undergo a transformation. Its land, sea and sea-bed resources had become subject to competition. Who was to control and develop these resources and for what purposes, was the question being raised: customary owners or developers? It had become clear that behind the calls for sovereignty and self-determination lay cross-currents of interest (see Cass 1988, 59–60).

A SENSE OF PLACE: THE CASE OF THE MURRAY ISLANDERS

1992, A LANDMARK YEAR

'If you wish to be a real Murray Islander you follow Malo's Law.' Au Bala's words sum up the best of Meriam tradition given during a drawn-out hearing of a case for recognition of Meriam customary land ownership by Australian courts, brought by five Murray Islanders in May 1982 and known here as the *Murray Island Land* case (*Mabo and Others v State of Queensland and Commonwealth of Australia*).[6]

In reaffirming their continuing right to the Murray Islands according to ongoing traditional law and custom, in their pleadings and as court witnesses, Murray Islanders demonstrated the unity and identity of Murray Island people today; they also spoke the sentiments of other Torres Strait Islanders and communities. We are one people and we are culturally different to you, the coloniser, they argued in response to a claim by the first defendant, the State of Queensland, that the activities of pearlers, missionaries and officials had destroyed the former culture of the Murray Islanders.

The *Murray Island Land* case was precipitated by a major threat to Islander communities, clans and families. In 1980 Islanders became aware that rights to land which most Islanders had taken for granted were under threat: the Queensland Government was foreshadowing the repeal of the Torres Strait Islanders Act 1971–79 and the degazetting of the Island reserves which had existed in Queensland law since 1912 and in government practice since about 1885. In their place, fifty-year leases were to be offered to Islanders. In response to this proposal, representatives of the Torres Strait Advisory Council visited each island to find out the kind of land tenure Islanders wanted: 'inalienable freehold', most Islanders replied. Uncle summed up the shared sentiment of several generations when he said in July 1980: 'Torres Strait is ours and we want our lands returned to us. My great grandfathers and great grandmothers, my grandfathers and grandmothers and my father and mother before me were here in these Islands before white people came. It is my wish and the wish of all the people of the whole Torres Strait for us to own all these Island ourselves' (Cassette 027/ABC/K/ 1/80; ABC Broadband, 1 October 1980).

That hope was given concrete expression in May 1982 when a writ was issued in the High Court of Australia by five Murray Islanders claiming distinct rights to traditional lands which form part of lands continuously occupied by the Meriam people from time immemorial until today. The central events of a ten-year history of that case may be summarised briefly.

Three years later, the Queensland Government took the offensive. On Easter Eve 1985, a Bill, which was to determine the direction taken by the case for the next three years, was passed by the Queensland parliament. Known as the Queensland Coast Islands Declaratory Act 1985, it sought to extinguish retrospectively any rights to land at the Murray Islands which may have survived annexation in 1879, so leaving the plaintiffs with no arguments to put to a court and thus ending the case.

In response, on 19 June 1985, the plaintiffs challenged the validity of this legislation in a legal action known as a demurrer. The plaintiffs claimed that the Queensland parliament lacked the power to extinguish their proprietary rights to land retrospectively. Before hearing arguments on the substance of the demurrer, the High Court referred the case to a remitter court, the Supreme Court of Queensland, where Judge Moynihan was asked to hear evidence and make a determination on the facts raised by the plaintiffs and responded to by the defendants.

In October 1986, Judge Moynihan began hearing evidence in Brisbane. A fourteen-day hearing produced 630 pages of transcript and the (first) defendant, the State of Queensland, raised 289 objections to the reception of oral testimony, given principally by the first plaintiff, known here as Meriam Man. Within the common law system, oral testimony may be classified as hearsay (that is recounting somebody else's impressions), and therefore inadmissible in evidence. The defendant employed the 'hearsay' rule in an attempt to leave the plaintiffs without admissible evidence to support their case. The question arose as to whether repetition of statements made to witnesses by deceased persons was hearsay or, as the plaintiffs claimed, traditional evidence based upon a set of principles different from those of British law. Counsel for the plaintiffs argued for the authenticity of an 'Oral Register of Title' among Murray Islanders, and for oral testimony as an expression of a different system of law (Supreme Court of Queensland, transcript, T148). At this point the judge deferred rulings on questions of admissibility; an opening was appearing for a hearing of legal issues raised in the plaintiffs' demurrer to Queensland's 1985 legislation by the High Court.

On 8 December 1988, the High Court, by a majority of four to three, ruled that the Queensland Coast Islands Declaratory Act 1985 was inconsistent with section 10(1) of the Commonwealth Racial Discrimination Act 1975, which upholds rights to equality before the law (*Mabo v Queensland*, before Mason CJ, Wilson, Brennan, Deane, Dawson, Toohey and Gaudron JJ, Canberra, reported at (1988) 166 *Commonwealth Law Reports* 186). The court was asked to set aside issues concerning traditional legal rights to land and their survival at the Murray Islands: for the purposes of the hearing these rights were assumed to exist. The majority view expressed an entirely new position, which recognises the right to own and inherit in ways qualitatively different from those recognised in Australia so far. Recognition was given to expressions of sovereignty clothed in a form unknown to English law (*Calder v Attorney-General of British Columbia* [1973]), a position taken by Judge Hall in *Calder's* case in Canada.

When the hearing of evidence resumed before Judge Moynihan in the Supreme Court of Queensland in mid-1989, the defendant's technical objections to oral testimony appeared 'to recede from centre stage'. The plaintiffs' counsel had argued for a course in which a good deal of evidence from the heads of many families and community leaders would create a picture of the structure and fabric of Murray Island culture, revealing a system in which a 'system of succession' and 'oral recording of title and ownership' are complementary (T193). After the first plaintiff's evidence had been interrupted by some 300 objections, the judge foreshadowed a difficulty for the court — twenty-seven more Murray Islander witnesses were waiting 'to say more of the same' as the first plaintiff (T62).

To persist with this line of challenge would have meant suffering the consequences of impeding completely the work of the court. An abrupt change of tactic was made by the defendant. The central argument now shifted from questions of admissibility to those of continuity and discontinuity in Murray Islander traditional law and custom.

In August 1982, the first defendant contended that 'the former modes of life of the Murray Islanders' had been fundamentally and irrevocably modified by outsiders (affidavit of PJ Killoran, 16 August 1982, Eighth Street, 14(e)).

When the Supreme Court of Queensland met to hear Islander witnesses at Mer in 1989, the issue of continuity and discontinuity moved to centre stage. Murray Islander witnesses argued for an essential continuity between the present and the past: they saw themselves as customary landowners socialised in Murray Island law and custom, and at the same time well acquainted with Western ways.

After hearing evidence from Murray Islanders, expert and other witnesses over a period of sixty-six days, Judge Moynihan accepted the plaintiffs' claim that the system of land tenure 'is a continuing and enduring one':[7] there are undoubted changes of circumstances, 'but the underlying basis has not

Plate 19 The Supreme Court of Queensland sits at Mer (courtesy of Yarra Bank Films)

Plate 20 The late Mr Sam Passi and Mrs Passi in the foreground at the Supreme
Court hearing (courtesy of Yarra Bank Films)

Plate 21 The late Eddie Koiki Mabo and Eddie Mabo Jnr with legal counsel,
Greg McIntyre, at Mer, 1989 (courtesy of Yarra Bank Films)

changed' (D11). After listening to many Islander witnesses repeat and explain parts of Malo's Law in court — 'Tag mauki mauki, Teter mauki mauki', 'Keep your hands and feet off other people's land' — he concluded that Malo's Law 'is a manifestation of social attitudes deeply imbued in the culture of Murray Islanders' (D137).

Judge Moynihan concluded: 'I have little difficulty in accepting that the people of the Murray Islands perceive themselves as having an enduring relationship with land on the [Murray] Islands and the seas and reefs surrounding them' (D137). Referring to 'deeply ingrained social and cultural attitudes' of respect for others' land and for land boundaries among Murray Islanders, he noted that these attitudes were part of the personal make-up of Murray Islanders. They are like our good manners, he remarked perceptively. He saw how 'a strong sense of the observation of propriety in respect of land' and 'of the appropriateness of being in your place or locality' rather than in somebody else's was reflected in such words as 'shame and trespass' (D157).

The judge found further, that each of the three plaintiffs had claims to some lands in accordance with Murray Island law, that Murray Islanders continue to make and cultivate gardens, hand down land through their families in accordance with custom, and recognise the rights of other landowners at the Murray Islands. He also noted that the Queensland Government had given recognition to customary land ownership by purchasing land from traditional owners after the Islands were annexed to Queensland in 1879.

On 3 June 1992, the Full Bench of the High Court recognised Meriam rights to the Murray Islands: '...the Meriam people are entitled as against the whole world to possession, occupation, use and enjoyment of the lands of the Murray Islands' (*Eddie Mabo and Others v State of Queensland*, High Court of Australia, Order).

This judgement is a major victory for the Meriam people: it secures for them legal recognition of their customary law. The judgement has also profound and long-lasting implications for other Torres Strait Islanders and for Aboriginal people. In recognising Meriam rights, the High Court reversed the legal position upon which *terra australis* as a political entity is founded. The voting was six to one. The court's recognition of 'common law native title' sweeps away forever the force of past judgements which upheld the legal invention known as *terra nullius* — that is that Australia was unoccupied at the time of white settlement.

Terra nullius took for granted that the Meriam were primitive and uncivilised, without recognisable land laws or social organisation and hence lower in the scale of humanity than the newcomers. This judgement shatters the whole structure upon which their subordinate status has rested. The Murray Islanders,

Judges Deane and Gaudron concluded, undoubtedly possess 'a local native system under which established familial or individual rights of occupation and use were of a kind which far exceed the minimum requirements necessary to find a presumptive common law native title'. Moreover, after annexation of the islands in 1879 Meriam title was 'recognized and protected by the law of Queensland' (reasons for decision, 107).

A radically new assumption underlies the 1992 judgement: equality before the law now means the obligation of Australian law to respect the Meriam law even though it is a form of title radically different ('unknown') to British law. As we have seen, this is known to the Meriam as *Malo ra Gelar*, Malo's Law. Precedents had been created for this position (see *Adeyinka Oyekan v Musendiku Adele* [1957] and *Calder's* case [1973]). In placing Meriam law on some sort of par with the British common law, the judiciary is providing the condition for reciprocal relations of mutual respect and exchange possible only among equals. This recognition of a system of land ownership and inheritance at the Murray Islands as a local legal system coexisting with the common law clears the way for recognition of more than one system of law within Australia — often referred to as 'legal pluralism'.

In the past twenty-five years, changes in the law foreshadowing the present judgement have been embodied in federal legislation of 1967, which gave indigenous peoples formal equality as citizens, and in the Racial Discrimination Act 1975 (Cth), which inscribed equality before the law into legal statute. These changes would appear to have framed the thinking of the court. Thus Judge Brennan concludes: '...it is imperative in today's world that the common law should neither be nor be seen to be frozen in an age of racial discrimination' (29).

Despite such Commonwealth legislation, until 3 June 1992 Australian courts have rejected claims by previous plaintiffs that proprietary rights to land of any indigenous people are capable of recognition in Australian law after Britain acquired sovereignty over those lands. The only case which had considered this question was *Milirrpum v Nabalco Pty Ltd and Commonwealth of Australia* (1971) 17 *Federal Law Reports* 141 (*Milirrpum*) heard by Justice Blackburn in the Supreme Court of the Northern Territory, which left standing the British government's assumption of Australia as *terra nullius*, a land belonging to no-one when it came under British sovereignty (see Hocking (ed) 1988, *passim*; see also *Coe v Commonwealth of Australia* (1979) 53 *Australian Law Journal Reports* 403, as discussed by Schaffer in Hocking (ed) 1988, 19–28, 36–38).[8]

The position taken by Judge Blackburn contrasts sharply with that taken by courts in New Zealand, Canada and the United States in the 1970s and 1980s. Before 1992, Australia remained the only former British colony which did not recognise the prior rights to land of its indigenous peoples, and which had concluded no treaty with them.

A reversal of such proportions as that signified by the 1992 judgement may occasion deep emotions. Within the 218-page document containing the judgements of different members of the Bench, one finds words which denote indignation, at times anguish, statements which contradict the pretence that the law is outside the realm of the passionate. Judges Deane and Gaudron make explicit reference to their use of language 'unusually emotive for a judgment in this court'. Their use of 'unrestrained language' in commenting upon dispossession of Aborigines is not intended as an intrusion into the area of 'attribution of moral guilt': an understanding of the facts of dispossession is of critical importance in assessing the legitimacy of the twin legal propositions that the lands of Australia were unoccupied and that ownership of these vested in the Crown (111). Judge Brennan likewise takes issue with the proposition that British sovereignty led to absolute and exclusive ownership. In a forthright and eloquent manner he condemns the way the common law 'made the indigenous inhabitants intruders in their own homes and mendicants for a place to live' (15–16).

The Meriam and their counsel have reason to be proud of their role in assisting members of the judiciary into these new ways of seeing. They have also the rich reward of inflicting defeat upon the Queensland defendant in matters of deep significance to themselves. They are a forgiving people. Yet not far from the surface of their collective psyche are the unhealed scars of past wrongs which they associate with authority figures behind whom stands the power of the state.

During the decade of the case the Meriam have been completing a process of rediscovery and reaffirmation of their identity as a people. They have 'offered' their difference to the court, and in an unprecedented way their giving has been reciprocated: 'The strength of Malo's Law brought a light into the eyes of justice', Father Dave Passi, known as Kebi Bala here, reflected upon the judgement. The Meriam greeted the decision in their own way. Their response, as they whistled loudly in exaltation, reached back into the strength which Malo's Law could bring: 'We have won! This is something big we have done.' In keeping with Kole legal tradition, the case bears the name of the first plaintiff, Eddie Koiki Mabo; sadly he did not live to celebrate and enjoy the victory. He would empathise with the name used here — the *Murray Island Land* case. As Meriam Man in this book he was a Meriam *le* who hearkened to the advice of Au Bala: whatever seeds you sow abroad in Malo's name always remember to bring the harvest back to the Murray Islands...

This is only a beginning. If the judgement is received simply as an ending of an old era without the effort to understand the past on the part of Kole,

Plate 22 Ron Day, Chairman Mer Community Council, addressing a community meeting, September 1992

Plate 23 Murray Islanders consider future plans, September 1992

then the ideas of *terra nullius* — 'the rights and interests of indigenous inhabitants being treated as non-existent' (Judge Brennan, 29–30) — remain alive.

STRENGTH FROM THE PAST

While Judge Moynihan saw the Murray Islands as 'the home of a dynamic society' (D13), he found difficulty in grasping the ideas of Kebi Bala and others of Christianity as the fulfilment of the ancient promise of Malo. In suggesting a tendency of two of the plaintiffs (Kebi Bala and Second Meriam Man) to ignore some of the darker aspects of the (Malo) cult (D132), he found it hard to understand a cultural continuity which arose out of a process of comparison and contrast. As we saw in Chapter 4, through comparisons with his own culture and that of Kole, Kebi Bala had been able to crystallise his own and Murray Islander identity as something to offer to others. Appreciating the two-sidedness of *both* cultures (one takes heads and practises sorcery, the other kills with bombs and missiles), he differentiated between those who came and stole his land and the Christian message which came out of the thieves' culture.

Kebi Bala was not ignoring the continuation of a two-sidedness in the Murray Island tradition; but in the positive side he sees a future. Through his

Plate 24   The Magani Malu Kes committee members discuss the land judgement, Townsville, September 1992

selection of the most powerful theme of his tradition — diversities in unity brought about through reciprocal exchange — he was fortified against oncoming difficulties. He was able to overcome practical problems to attend a conference in Townsville in 1981 where the move for a land case originated and so become a plaintiff with a message emerging from the Malo tradition. Like others, he is aware that we are living in times when conscious choice about what we will conserve lies at the forefront of social awareness. Under conditions of acute environmental crisis, it is 'natural' for him to draw heavily upon that part of Malo's Law which says plant, make things grow, look after the land and conserve its produce.[9]

Directly and indirectly the main characters of this book have played a key role in the steps towards recognition of customary land law. Au Bala, Kebi Bala and Second Meriam Man were three of the original five plaintiffs; a fourth was Meriam Man's aunt; the fifth plaintiff — James Rice — is a Dauareb man deeply versed in the law of Malo, in the heritage and ways of his own clan and *lubabat* (totem), and a firm Christian. Meriam Man, along with Kebi Bala and Sis, was one of the main initiators of the case, which began to take an organised form at a land conference in Townsville in August 1981. The lives of Uncle, a son of the Kaurareg, who died about that time, of Kapin ('He [God] will do something to stop them [taking our land]'), and of First Meriam Man (who wrote Malo's Law in his diary in the 1930s), pre-shadow the basic ideas put by the Murray Islanders to the court.

The case has offered a focus and an example for other Islanders. Its significance has been grasped far outside the Torres Strait. Firmly rejecting the idea that Murray Island culture and custom had faded long ago, Murray Islanders brought to the public realm living proof of the existence of the past in the present. In doing so their evidence illustrates in a major way the central theme — and the unresolved problems — of this book. In rejecting the (first) defendant's proposition that they had made a complete break with their traditional culture and were now assimilated into the coloniser's culture, the plaintiffs and other witnesses argued for an essential continuity. In their eyes, only a Kole could see continuity and change as mutually exclusive: at no time had their system existed in a fixed, crystalline state; nor had it now been destroyed or abandoned.

Practically speaking, the existence of a continuity in change among Murray Islanders involves a selectivity which conserves and develops a *form* of interchange — reciprocity. In doing this it is consciously drawing upon *some* but not all of the content of that mode of interchange (see Sharp 1989, 5–17): in Kebi Bala's words, an eye for an eye and 'all that kills', may now be subordinated through a process which reverses enmities and creates diversities in unity. That reversal has been made possible through an all-powerful Mediator personified in God the Son. Evil is no longer met with evil, death with death; evil is turned round. At a theoretical level, the problem is how one might find a way of putting together the more abstract forms of interchange characteristic of modern society on the one hand, with the forms of face to face (inter)relations of reciprocity on the other, in such a way that the impetus for cooperative relations subordinates the impulse of thingified relations to create instrumental, competitive social relations which the current social forces coming to prominence in the Torres Strait Islanders are so ready to encourage.

The land case not only developed a reflective process among Murray Islanders, which has led to the reaffirmation of the cultural integrity of Murray Islanders. Its ramifications encompass the Torres Strait Islanders as a people, providing a focus for the aspirations of others. Thus for example, the Kaurareg or Muralag tribal people, the most heavily assaulted of any Islander group by colonial expropriation, had indicated their intention to put a land claim before the High Court pending the outcome of the *Murray Island Land* case (Wasaga, *Torres News*, 8–14 February 1991). Moreover, in the light of his own heightened awareness, Meriam Man was able to identify with others. When Kaurareg people were threatened by a move encouraging Islanders living in Townsville to buy up blocks of land on the island of Muralag, the mother island of the Kaurareg, Meriam Man quickly reminded the Murray Islanders of the Kaurareg people's right to customary land, and, it seems, no blocks were requested. When the Wuthathi people were threatened with a 'second invasion', through a proposed spaceport on their land at Chatungun (Temple Bay), Sis, Kebi Bala and Meriam Man readily supported the Wuthathi landowners. Meriam Man's support for them was quite explicitly derived from his recognition of the parallel between his own situation and theirs: '...we Meriam people respect the rights of the Wuthathi tribe... Because of our law [Malo's Law] we have a high respect for the rights of the Wuthathi people' (see Sharp 1990a, 38–39).

TESTING TIMES IN A SEARCH FOR AUTONOMY

Dramatic events may throw into relief underlying themes which, in the ordinary course of life are simply taken for granted or presumed to be absent. They are testing times which may feed into a reflective process, whereby the participants live and relive the event; under certain circumstances that process may fuel a new solidarity. Despite efforts to school Islanders to forget about the strike, it was not forgotten. Nau Mabaig's recollections of the drama enacted at Badu forty-three years before are clear as a bell. They found expression under conditions in which the political violence of shame was being transcended. They have the power to light up for an instant a picture in shadow.

Given the stranglehold of the Protectors and the government teachers around Islanders, the organisation of an all-island strike was an extraordinary feat; given Islanders' belief in the singularity of the 'other side' of the Strait, their common action was a sign of a new awareness. In the face of a singular power which threatened them all alike, ancient enmities were reversed: they had come together.[10] The message was passed like a secret 'gift' from island to island, bringing their dissimilarities into reciprocal unity. That reciprocity was a gauge of the strength and extent of Islanders' networks: they had 'come up level' in the diversity of their differences. Kole had created the conditions of that testing.

At that time the 'other side' of the Strait continued to hold the profane danger of the power of *Em*. As Ailan Man recalls, *puripuri* talk remained rife in the thirties and people on the eastern side would say: 'Oh, that Badu man he can change to alligator; he can fly like an eagle'. Through the build-up of the singular powers of Kole across the Islands, another level of meaning was attached to *Em*, producing new priorities in 'striking back'. The message of the 'new *wauri*', as we called it in Chapter 3, had begun to find adherents when the Islander priests and teachers like Kapin, Au Bala and Auntie moved along the coloured networks invisible to Kole. The message from Mer in 1936 was a message for everyone in the Strait: Malo *wali aritarit, sem aritarit* was received with thanksgiving. It was the moment of a new integration of the Islanders of the Torres Strait.

The three themes inherent in the strike — equality, land and autonomy — were to reach a fuller expression in later events. They constituted the essential preconditions of Torres Strait Islander identity. Without them, the multi-layered identities which characterise Torres Strait Islanders' overall identity could not find its full expression. 'Getting out of bondage' and 'citizen rights', which implied equality with other Australians, was an explicit theme of the strike, its frequent expression being the right to sail about freely and the determination to move from State to Commonwealth control. The rights of customary landowners were completely taken for granted at that time: they were not demanding land or sea rights, they assumed their existence. (On customary marine tenure, see Johannes and MacFarlane 1991, Chapter 4.) The third theme — autonomy and self-determination — which was to become the focus of the sovereignty call of the

1980s, became quite explicit in the Murray Islanders' demand for home rule and control over the Island Fund in 1936 and 1937.

The experience of reciprocity with some white men during the Second World War helped to reinstate Islanders' sense of identity as equals; in contrast with the past, they were not shamed by their war experience into a loss of self. On the contrary, their sense of self had the chance to flower. From it came their post-war demand for 'citizen rights'.

The experience of the border issue gave Islanders the understanding that their lands had been formally annexed, so feeding directly into the demand for land.

An important aspect of Islanders' support for political sovereignty in 1987-88 was a growing awareness of their basic vulnerability under the Deeds of Grant in Trust (DOGIT), accepted in 1986 by all Island Councils except that of Murray Island: DOGIT meant continuing Ministerial supervision and Departmental control of finances; their long-run consequence will be the extinction of customary title (Sharp 1987). The long wait for the decisive judgement of the *Murray Island Land* case created frustration and a loss of confidence in the possibility of gaining land rights through the Australian judicial system. The article, Land Rights Claim leads to Torres Autonomy Call (*Australian* 8 February 1988), pinpoints Islanders' frustration.

Torres Strait Islanders as a people of 'unique identity' with an 'ultimate goal of independence' was raised during the border controversy (see Mabo in Griffin (ed) 1976, 35). In a new form, the sovereignty issue taps that yearning for autonomy. Beckett notes the recurrence of an old theme within a modern idiom: 'The bid for sovereignty translated the longstanding desire for local autonomy into the language of decolonisation...' (1987, 209). It also brought that desire from the closed world of the Islands of the pre-1980s into the public arena (including the southern press, see *Age*, Melbourne, 19-21 January, 13 February 1988; see Kehoe-Forutan 1988, 1-34; Cass 1988, 1-68).

The processes of coming together in the strike and the battalion brought about new ways of seeing men from other communities. Ancient enmities were reversed: A, B, C and D companies 'are together' because they 'never forget about God'. Kuki sees how an awareness which transcends old boundaries and ways of seeing has taken possession of the men: the new 'we' have all come from one, a common Father. That shared filiation made possible a readiness in different Islands to come to Kubin to dig wolfram. Without that new awareness of oneness each Island might have voted for the narrow needs of its own face to face community of villages when put to the test on the definition of Island homelands in the 1970s.

On the first occasion they had struck back together as Islanders interlinked in what Kebi Bala calls diversities in unity. On the second occasion — the War years — they had experienced themselves thrown together against old and new singular forces. The contrast provided by the new white men with whom they had 'come up level' in relations of reciprocity and the first-hand experience of their custom underlined their common bondage as 'Islanders'. The third was a test of the toughness and resilience of the circles which tied them together: the Islanders with each other, the living with the ancestors.

ISLANDS IN TRANSITION

Torres Strait Islanders have moved into the 1990s with a strengthening identity as a sea culture with a common way of life. A Torres Strait Islanders' flag unveiled in 1992 symbolised that identity: green for the islands, blue for the sea, and a white headdress (*dari*) for the people. Carried within that shared custom is a sense of place which implies a diversity.

Through the long haul of the generations, a consolidation of the modern Torres Strait Islanders as one people carried a strength born of the strength of its diverse communities or subgroups. Torres Strait Islander identity, which we have seen as embodying the new within the old, is characterised by many overlapping and layered identities within an overarching 'generic' identity.

Each island community retains 'a clear sense of identity and distinctiveness' Beckett wrote in 1963. Larger networks of complementarities have grown, yet older networks of separatenesses-in-unity remain; the eight clans of the Meriam of the Murray Islands joined by the octopus retain their strength within a larger one, as do the other overlapping 'identities' of Meriam and of Kala Lagaw Ya speakers. Justice Deane of the High Court of Australia recognised these multiple identities when he said in 1988: '...the Torres Strait Islanders as a group constitute persons of a distinctive "national or ethnic origin" ...So also do the Meriam people as a sub group' (*Murray Island Land* case, High Court of Australia, transcript, 8 December 1988, 50).

Islanders enact Island custom by themselves and for themselves; as Beckett has observed, this gives them the confidence to 'negotiate their minority status' (1987, 235). Their successful public deferred pay claim for Second World War veterans in the mid-1980s illustrates this confidence.

As demonstrated so vividly and so forcefully by Murray Islander witnesses in the *Murray Island Land* case, such negotiation draws upon a generally silent strength: 'Hands off' my land says plaintiff James Rice in all his ancestors' names, in the name of Malo. 'Your feet must not take you to steal what is other people's', say Kebi Bala, second plaintiff (Land Bilong Islanders 1990; Sharp 1990a). Nobody can take away our ownership of the Murray Islands — Ron Day, Chairman of Murray Island Council, speaks on behalf of all the Meriam of the Murray Islands (Land Bilong Islanders 1990; Sharp 1990b, 28–29).

In Islanders' eyes Judge Moynihan's report on the evidence was a milestone in the fight for recognition of customary ownership. The judge's chair was still warm when they were reaffirming the past in the present as a guide to the future. 'What kind of people will the Murray Islanders be in the future?', they were asking themselves (see Sharp 1991, 90–93).

Direct control over land and resources means a recognition of the legal right of Islanders to determine and regulate who comes into the Torres Strait to fish, to mine, or to develop tourism. This view, expressed by Getano Lui, Chairman of the Island Coordinating Council (an advisory body set up under the Community Services Act 1984 with a mandate for increasing autonomy in the outer islands), crystallises a sentiment common to modern Torres Strait Islanders (interview with Trevor Graham, 23 August 1988). It also touches the central nerve of Torres Strait life before the late 1980s, a time when such matters were determined exclusively by Kole.

In the second half of the 1980s, the situation of Torres Strait Islanders began to open up, especially in relation to equality of opportunities in education and loans for small and cooperative businesses. Men and women of varied ages took the opportunity to study at higher levels;[11] indigenisation of the public service in Thursday Island followed. This followed the move into Islander affairs by the Commonwealth Government which began with the establishment of a DAA area office on Thursday Island in 1973; Islanders' demands for 'free communication' were met at the end of 1980 with public telephones on each island, an ABC radio relay and a plane service inside the Torres Strait. Funding agencies, such as the Aboriginal Development Commission, became active in the 1980s. The departure of PJ Killoran as Director of the DAIA in 1987 marked the end of an era in which he is reputed to have administered 'the Torres Strait Islands personally from Brisbane by telephone' (interview with J Burgess, DCS, Brisbane, by Kehoe-Forutan; see 1988, 10).

In 1967 Islanders were finally recognised as citizens, being 'given' the right to vote. Today they are coming to share a full political equality with other Australians. They will also share the social and economic right to become entrepreneurs of capitalist enterprise, or to be exploited with the majority. Given the exclusion of Islanders and Aborigines from participation in business on their own account under the old regime of 'the Department', the opportunities opening up first under the DOGIT legislation and more recently under the Aboriginal and Torres Strait Islander Commission Act 1989, are seen as very positive by many Islanders.[12] Yet the spirit that sprang the wolfram mine at Moa, the Murray Island guest house, or the MAW cooperative, has so far found no significant expression in contemporary social and economic life.

Understandably, Torres Strait Islanders and others see the chance to participate in business enterprise on their own account as a lost right for which they are now being compensated. Islanders see themselves as 'coming up level' with the rest of Australia, and securing loans from the Aboriginal and Torres Strait Islander Commission (ATSIC) is part of this process. Today some Islanders are at last running their own snack bars, stores and fishing projects; but, without the guiding principles of the give and take of cooperative sharing so 'natural' to Torres Strait Islanders, a type of society may emerge that will disappoint many Islanders: a sprouting capitalism will weaken relations of reciprocity. The Department of Community Services (DCS), successor to the Department of Aboriginal and Islanders Advancement (DAIA), for example, is actively encouraging Islander entrepreneurship (Reports for 1988–90). So far, crimes against property remain few and nobody is hungry; but as some of us witnessed in post-colonial Papua New Guinea, given the free operation of the commodity market, a society of 'haves' and 'have nots' may quickly displace the old system.

The issue of who will control the resources of Torres Strait and for what purpose arises more starkly than ever. 'We are fighting for our lands and they [the developers] are fighting for our lands', Sis' quip at a meeting on land in the mid-eighties, carries a message of real danger in the 1990s. The clash of interests which came to the forefront in 1988 between the projected Torres United Party Prince of Wales resort developers and the Muralag tribal people is a sign of new dangers.

A changing mode of integration of Islanders into Australian society and into the market system is set within the wider context of the changing economic, political and strategic significance of the Torres Strait area. Plans are underway for a military airfield and possibly a spaceport on Cape York Peninsula, which may result ultimately in the transformation of a quiet, peaceful place to an area of high strategic significance and intense activity (Sharp 1990a, 32–40; Sharp 1990c, 29–33). Moreover, Torres Strait Islanders live in the shadow of a threat to their basic wellbeing through chemical pollutants from the OK Tedi copper mine entering Torres Strait waters from the Fly River.

AN ONGOING IDENTITY, A NEW CHALLENGE

In moving into the 1990s with an orientation that identifies more and more as one people, Islanders' awareness has also been drawn into the mainstream of modern consciousness. The challenge facing Islanders is how to maintain a balance between their own customs of reciprocity and respect for others' property on the one hand, and participation in money enterprises in a manner that does not place those traditions in jeopardy on the other.

Two particular conditions exist which may qualify Torres Strait Islander unity. The first concerns the cultural and social implications of physical separation between the 'two halves' of the Islander community. Today more than half the Islander population no longer live on their ancestral lands; they live at Thursday Island, northern Cape York Peninsula and in places such as Townsville on the north Queensland mainland. As we have seen, some of the major initiatives which consolidated and defended Islander unity came from expatriate Islanders. Yet a sense of place in its original sense becomes eroded as new generations are born away from home. In June 1984 there were less than seventy Islander graves in Townsville cemetery. However, with the passage of time, many Islanders will feel unable to return to the Islands and leave their parents and grandparents alone in southern graves.[13]

Wherever they reside today, and this is the second qualification, Islanders face the full onslaught of the powerful forces of the commodity market which must lead towards the dissolution of their culture. They do so under conditions of 'new wave' assimilation which denies any special distinction between them as indigenous people and other 'outback Australians'.

The force for Islander unity made itself felt publicly during 1991 and 1992 when a move was made by the Torres Strait Islanders Corporation based in Brisbane to establish a National Forum. The first Torres Strait Islanders National Conference titled Road to Recovery, held in Brisbane from 22–25 July 1991, was attended by 200 Torres Strait Islanders drawn from home islands and from the mainland. This new expression of unity held a strong note of independence: criticising the way in which those responsible for drawing up land legislation had failed to consult Torres Strait Islander people, the conference foreshadowed a follow-up seminar in 1992. This second conference, held in Rockhampton in April 1992, passed a resolution opposing the Torres Strait Islander Land Act 1991, awaiting the High Court's decision in the *Murray Island Land* case, and announcing that 'if we don't like the decision we will take the matter to the World Court' (these are Sis's words).

In contemporary life the assumptions of primitiveness inherent in the coloniser's ideology have been firmly rebuffed by the Murray Islanders. The inclusion of their islands as part of *terra nullius* took the form of legislation reaffirming them as 'waste lands of the Crown'. In resisting the definitions of them as landless people or trespassers on their own lands, the Murray Islanders have dealt a firm blow to contemporary manifestations of assumptions of assimilation.[14] They did so by drawing upon unseen layers of culture. Like a coiled spring suddenly released with unswerving force Murray Islanders drew upon their 'cultural arsenal'. Plaintiff James Rice, for example, spoke about the sources of his strength at places named after 'sacred ancestors' handed down to him. In telling me how the strength of his *lubabat* or totem was with him in court, he recounted the sources of many of his nineteen names which begin with that of his great grandfather, include names (and places) from his grandmother's side, and end with his father's name.

Once again Islanders' identity was being reborn in a new struggle against cultural annihilation. This is a struggle with vast implications for all Islanders and for Australia, which Murray Islanders were especially well equipped by history to shoulder. It will be recalled that Murray Islanders successfully insisted in 1885 that they keep Murray Island for themselves; that they led a strike for self-determination in 1936 and in the following year held out alone for full home rule.

A century ago, a member of the ethnographic team from Cambridge was struck by 'the lack of the impulse of rivalry' among Islander adults and children (McDougall 1912, 115 note x), an observation seconded by administrators a generation later. Since then the competitive spirit of capitalism — I alone shall win the Silver Cup — has taken firm root in the Islands. Yet, as the lives and thoughts of the main characters of this book have illustrated, the impulse for cooperation remains alive.

At their best, Islanders' actions have turned round the contradictory and the dangerous into a means of their self-realisation. Those stars of Tagai who are the custodians and defenders of important cultural traditions have been called upon by history to play a mediating role. We have seen the varied ways in which they have come forward. A conclusion to *Stars of Tagai* reflects upon their experience.

EPILOGUE

REFLECTIONS UPON THE STARS

To my father Bomai-Malo was a good teaching but not the teaching. It was teaching like John the Baptist: his job was only to bring them to Jesus.

The Eastern Islanders had their Bomai-Malo teaching of respecting other people's property and sharing with them. Well, those teachings were the golden rule, the Christian rule, I guess. If each people lived their own teaching they got on all right.

If you do your share you don't worry about the other side.

Sis

STRIVING TO REJOIN THE HALVES: A MERIAM EXAMPLE

When the second wave of missionaries arrived in the Torres Strait Islands in 1915 they told the lambkins of their new Anglican fold out at Mer that they might perform the Malo dances which had been halted by the LMS two generations before in 1872. So in the early 1920s the sacred dances and chants were performed again. Au Bala was about ten years old: 'Those dances I first saw when I was a boy are like replacements of the old ones before my grandfather's time'. The fifth chant, says Au Bala, goes with the dance for *seuriseuri* which 'signifies the life that is handed down from the previous generation to the present one. The first dancer goes with the *seuriseuri*; the second dancer comes in behind him ready to take the *seuriseuri* from him. That means that tradition must be left to someone who comes behind him.' The new chant for *seuriseuri*, it is said, came to Sis' father, Uncle T, in a dream.

> *O brothers knotted into one,*
>
> *Let the trumpet sound!*
>
> *O brothers knotted into one,*
> *Let the sound of the blue fly tell*
> *That* lamar *[ancestors] are approaching.*

Au Bala recalls how the older people said, 'It's just suitable for *seuriseuri*'. Sis' father, a man of almost visionary apprehension, could see the truths in the teachings and practice of Malo-Bomai. The new chant brings together the two planes of *seuriseuri*: of the living joined in one community and the living with *lamar*. At the same time the composition is in a different genre to the mythical mode of Malo *wali aritarit*. It is evocative of the revelatory experience of death and its transcendence unique to Christian teaching: 'In a moment, in the twinkling of an eye, at the last trump: for the trumpet shall sound, and the dead shall be raised incorruptible, and we shall be changed' (1 Corinthians xv, 52).

The older Meriam, who had not been allowed to perform the dances since they were young men, wept with sadness and joy. Those who had been born into Christianity saw the dances for the first time in the context of a second wave of 'prophets', the Anglicans, in whose teachings and rituals they could see the fulfilment of their old religion. Given the contradictory behaviour of those who held the 'right' to ban and to say 'now go ahead', Islanders' ways of 'seeing' necessarily took many forms. This was a moment of hope at a time when the sinister power standing behind the paternalist word 'Protection' was constantly present to nip in the bud any murmur which held a note threatening 'originality'. Certainly in the 1920s and 1930s Islanders came to be supervised closely even in their leisure hours. Stripped of the practices associated with warfare and death which went with the Malo dances, they now looked harmless enough to outsiders. From time to time people like the Anglican priest, Rev Done glimpsed the existential cruelty associated with the forcible exclusion of the visionary, transcendent experiences which had framed and sustained the meanings of their lives (Diaries). Like the Winnebago, the Islanders, who were people of 'essentially religious natures', found the wretched, drab existence they were compelled to lead especially difficult (Radin 1957, 397). For the children of Au Bala's generation the 1920s and 1930s were years of timid and frightening pleasures. Islanders recall the moments of release from the life of daily drill and the three Rs when they scrambled for bright boiled lollies tossed to them by the visiting Protector confused in their experience by the unsmiling watchfulness of their fathers whom they had stared at chairing the 'big *mamus*' across the shallows now standing silently in their double calicos.

In this circumscribed and supervised world Uncle T's inspiration was timely. He played an especially important mediating role among Islanders: he was able to see the distinctive qualities their custom had to offer. He could discern good teachings in Malo- Bomai, and through a process of contrast and comparison with the message of his own inheritance, help them to see their own teachings in relation to the teaching of Christianity. When Uncle T composed the new chant for *seuriseuri*, the dance was not performed in secrecy, nor were all the proper symbols of Malo present; the young men were not initiated as before, and the strict rules of succession had disappeared. Importantly though, the new *ikok* brought together the human with the cosmic circles — *le*, the living with *lamar*, the immortals — their matched halves on a different plane. That is why old men like Au Bala's grandfather sensed it was 'just right' for *seuriseuri*. It answered people's needs for a spiritual strengthening.

A STAR OF TAGAI: SIS, I HAD NO TROUBLE IN KNOWING WHO I AM

In Sis' life one glimpses the inspiration of her father (Uncle T) and her mother. Her father's father (Grandfather T), a man with special powers of healing, taught her father well before he was twenty; his powers were well-known by every Torres Strait Islander and every 'coloured person' at Lockhart River Mission, Cape York, where he worked in the 1920s. Sis, a person aware of her own identity, has herself made important syntheses which make her a creative person who can offer a guide to her contemporaries and to a new generation of Torres Strait Islanders about how to meet the new challenges.

Our identity was quite safe

> *I was born in Moa. About the same year we went to Lockhart and I grew up there; the first language we spoke was Lockhart River language. The troopers used to bring the natives chained together to the Mission. All my father knew about was just 'love other people'; black or white man there was no difference. He just loved everybody. Life was lovely amongst the Aboriginals, they were lovely to us. We just felt a whole lot of love from there and we got lots of it. We knew we belonged to Torres Strait. Our family used to live on Rennel Island (Mauar). Every school holiday we went back there and we learnt our custom. I think we always knew about being different, but we liked being like the other children at Lockhart.*

I didn't tell the girl at the Adult Education I only had a Grade Three schooling

> *I was eight when I left Lockhart first, then I went back there with Auntie. I taught school as a pupil-teacher when I was twelve years old. I only spent a year with her there in 1936–37. I was only earning five shillings a week as a pupil-teacher and my sisters were earning twelve-and-sixpence a week. So I came into town, to TI to work as a housemaid. My mother got me a job working for Alice Vidgen and asked her to teach me everything, teach me how to cook. I had two years and two weeks of hell working for her, but my mother loved her. She was a wonderful woman and she could do anything: she was smarter*

*than my mother. She could steer a boat, start the engine or just rig
the sails...*

*When we were living in Cairns I went along to Adult
Education. Oh, I was older then, early forties, and I thought, 'Now's
the chance; this Adult Education teaches schooling too!' The girl said,
'They start from sub-junior'. I said to the girl: 'I'm not even educated
to sub-junior'. Oh, she looked at me kindly. I didn't tell her I only had
a third grade education...*

To my father Bomai-Malo was a good teaching

*What a lot of them didn't understand then was that the Gospel was
eternal; it was before Adam. It was given to Adam, it was given to
everybody else and the people scattered round the earth took bits of
that teaching: that's why everybody knew a little about God.*

*My father said: 'When Bomai came to Murray Island, it
was picked up in a basket by these two people that were out fishing.
He wasn't an octopus; he just came like an octopus. They took him
home and they felt it was something good. When they kept it in the
house a kind of glow emanated from it. They found out that was like
a living thing that taught them good things. And people began to notice
how really happy the two people were. But they never told their secret
to anybody else. Yet it was a thing that they should have taught other
people. Then because they were selfish, keeping it to themselves, it was
taken from them. These other people stole it from them. When they
learnt the things from Bomai they taught them to other people, and
as they taught it to others they became happier and other people became
happy. That's what it was meant to do and so it remained there. And
when they had these teachings they became very clever people too.'*

*To my father Bomai-Malo was a good teaching but not the
teaching. It was teaching like John the Baptist: his job was only to
bring them to Jesus. Malo was good enough for the people of those days.
You don't teach people more than they can understand; so that teaching
was right for them. They can all understand that and they can all live
it. It's just as though you understand the Gospel more than I do but
if I live it and you live yours too 100 per cent we'll go to the same place.
The Eastern Islanders had their Bomai-Malo teaching of respecting
other people's property and sharing with them. Well those teachings
were the golden rule, the Christian rule. If each people lived their own
teaching they got on all right.*

*Well, we've been reared so we know everything about our
own custom. Our good manners might be quite opposite to yours. When
we meet other people that know their own custom, we get on very well
with them. I've been amongst white men who don't know their own
custom. We don't get on with them very well because they can't
understand why we are like we are. But we get on well with the white*

people that have learnt their custom properly, the ones that have been
well brought up to be thoughtful, considerate. We really are brothers
and sisters in the eyes of God. Perhaps we really did have one
beginning. (Book of Islanders 1984, B87–89, B96–97, B101, B104–05;
see Kennedy 1991)

NEW CONTRASTS AND COMPARISONS

In the version of the culminating part of the myth of Malo-Bomai given to Sis by
her father the genre has undergone a change. Through the *zogo* of Bomai the
selfishness and secretiveness of those who found him were overcome. Those who
gained Bomai at Las were people who wished to share their new wisdom, they
were people who were happy in that, and in so being, they became imbued with
greater wisdom. Surely this has become an allegory which speaks the message
and transmits the élan of the New Testament while simultaneously remaining
meshed with the original myth. The power of *zogo* bound together people in a
new wisdom and a new social practice overarching, but not extinguishing, the
competitive processes of giving and returning 'equivalences' through which the
clans lived together.

In the original version of the myth (given by Au Bala in Chapter 1),
the people made peace by passing *zeub*, the pipe of peace, round the circle: the
victory over the singular power of death is given in the sacred dance of the
seuriseuri which brought the eight clans into one. In Uncle T's version, the people
at Las are exemplars of the *agud*, Bomai, as before; but they are explicitly imbued
with Christian virtues: they wish to share their inheritance and, so sharing it, they
become both happier and wiser. The Christian qualities of the Good of generosity
overcomes selfishness, which is a new message resonant with the words of St Paul:
'Oh ye Corinthians, our mouth is open unto you, our heart is enlarged' (II
Corinthians vi, 11).

The new genre of the myth is suggestive of a transformation of
subjectivity which is visible in each of the life-stories here: one may discern a
new faculty of contrast and comparison, which is expressed on the one hand in
the emergence of the 'I', and in reversals of 'another kind' to people 'like ourselves'
on the other hand. One may discern the qualities of good and evil which, in the
history of Western civilisation came with Judaism where the numinous came to
be charged with ethical import (Otto 1936, 19). With the moral values of the Good,
of a 'loving Father' through whom comes recognition of the supreme virtue of
sharing beyond the family to one's neighbour, came new practices: 'When I'm dead
give that special recipe away to everybody that wants it... Always teach somebody

something else.' This, the message of Sis' mother, is expressive of a moral code different to before, one which is carried into a practice of universalism by her daughter: 'I feed *everybody* who comes by', is the creed by which Sis lives.

In that universalist practice there is the 'free choice' to act for Good or Evil; this is the new power of the 'I' of faith and the 'I' of 'rational choice'. In that transformation comes also a redefinition of the death-dealing power of *Em* as the Devil who may take the shape of the old forces of death, in the *maid* and *puripuri* of sorcery and the new *Em* epitomised by the Storm-Winds. So for the sorcerers the new instruction is: 'Cut off communication with God and do everything the Gospels tell you not to do'.

Sis' father was an exemplar and a creator of ways of accommodating the Death-gods in all their varied external appearances. His hymn about the Israelites resonated with the theme of German Wislin which prefigured the striking down of the white Pharoahs and the deliverance of the people into the Promised Land: in that teaching was Exodus as myth. The countless hymns composed by Uncle T and some others are like new narratives in the mythical mode; through a metaphor they make statements of hope.

Universalist discernment or integrative universalism, the expression I suggested in Chapter 3, is characteristic of the way people like Sis' father, Kapin, Au Bala, Kebi Bala and Sis looked at Malo-Bomai in the universalist light of Christianity: they were seeking to find *relationships* of difference and similarity rather than the common and exclusive properties *of* something. And so through this process Sis' family came to believe 'that if each people believed their own teaching they got on all right'. This is the process that led Kebi Bala to distinguish between the thief that comes to destroy and kill and the true representatives of Christ who follow his message in practice.

Under conditions of enforced culture change, signs of the plural may take shapes which appear quite contradictory to the visually minded. So, for instance, the time when Au Bala's grandfather was seeing in Anglican rites something of the mystery of Malo was also the time when Sis' father, an 'adopted' Islander, gave the 'Zogo le' and hence the Meriam the fifth *ikok* for *seuriseuri* in which they also discerned the *kerkar* or renewal of Malo. In giving me the new words of that *ikok* Au Bala acknowledged their aesthetic-religious meaning; yet again, in the same conversation, he went on to chant the *ikok* of Malo *wali aritarit*, the one that continued to hold the deepest meaning and significance for him. For Islanders the potentialities of the hidden connection within the antitheses of opposites, the contradiction hidden by the appearance of unity, are easy to comprehend: within the movement of the tides there is this and there is that; as Au Bala says, 'like spring tide and neap tide one is contrary to the other'. So Sis, who hasn't read books on dialectics, has always known that there is opposition in all things.

The processes of social healing that sprung the tombstone unveilings and 'the new *wauri*' in the 1930s, came to represent Islanders' dissimilarity with others. As Au Bala says, 'Making a tombstone has become our custom and we're going to treasure it'; with the 'hands of love' one may go to any Islands from Mer down to Boigu and find friends. At a fundamental level, the existence of reciprocal ties which strengthen and enlarge the two circles among the *le*, the living, and between *le* and the immortals, are signs of the living heart of the culture. The 1930s, when the Storm-Winds blew with all their might, were the very time when a metamorphosis occurred quietly through which Islanders' social life was strengthened in the 'coloured networks' which began to form.

The new syntheses are many-sided; they take in the universalist message, the promise of the All-One of the Cosmos as a fulfilment of the project of 'before', a valorisation of the circles of cosmic 'order'. When Kapin searched the heavens for a message he was seeking not only to redress the loss created by the taking of the land by singular forces, a 'this-worldly' quest, so it would seem. He was searching for a reordering of the Cosmos, an 'other-worldly' quest. Yet in his mode of awareness these are inextricably part of one Quest: the search to make sense of the 'new', which means at the same time also to integrate it within the old, which in turn may give rise to a new meaning of the old. In that comparative process lies cosmic repositioning and cosmic renewal; there lies also the possibility of a new giving through an awareness of the 'we' no longer circumscribed by the 'old cosmos' but part of and participating in a new cosmic circle. Within that new circle 'we' may give back what is now 'Island', like the acts of kindness of *wauri*, the lost part of the Gospels, which are offered as gifts within a context of the Administration and all that kills (Kebi Bala), of those who 'come with the sword and make themselves boss' (Kapin). They are offering a way of living together according to the principles of *wauri* as seen in the light of the contradiction between good teachings and evil ways. To some minds these offerings may seem mundanely this-worldly. To Islander minds of the stature of say Kapin or Au Bala, the high and the lowly, the heavenly and the earthly go together as matching halves of one another.

Sis had a vision and her father told her that the Voice she heard was that of the true God whom his family had always worshipped. In following the Voice she travelled 'like the sun rises and sets', on a cosmic path towards an ending and a re-beginning. In bringing 'the true religion that you've waited for', the Voice said, 'Your father knows Me. His father knows Me. And his father's father before him knows Me...' (Book of Islanders 1984, B106–07).

Like that of Kapin, Sis's cosmological scheme valorises the cyclical conception of the cosmos and of time; through the role of the 'I' it also transforms it. That God came to walk upon the earth as a man holds the promise of a joining of heaven and earth that was not possible before. Here is also an intimation of a move from myth into history and back again, rather like the spiral of oral tradition among the Binandere of Papua New Guinea, where the experience of 'history' is deposited in the spiral of myth after six generations. Kapin says that the *agud*, Malo, came for seven generations, 'the protean seed' until the missionaries arrived (Book of Islanders 1984, B24, B28). In Sis' father's tradition, which is reaffirmed for her in the 'true religion' which came in her vision, the gift of renewal comes in seven-yearly cycles.

NEW SYNTHESES: A DEVELOPING AWARENESS

'I did my dance' was a dramatic sign of defiance and an assertion of cultural difference; it was also an expression of possibility. Through a process of contrast and comparison, Second Meriam Man had, like Kebi Bala, become proud of his culture. He was born in 1936, a time when his parents and his grandparents were refusing the terms forced on them by Kole, sending back the luggers to TI and demanding the right to manage their own affairs on an equal footing with others.

In the 1970s the younger Meriam Man was interacting with a system undergoing major transformation. Those on the 'other side' who upheld his right to an equal footing and helped him to found the Black Community School were acting in a similar way to the white comrades whom his parents met during the Second World War and its aftermath. In assisting him they were also recognising the integrity of his cultural difference.

Between about 1901 and the outbreak of the Second World War Islanders had only an occasional chance to make reciprocal ties with white people. In varied ways those who would 'share' their knowledge, by which Islanders mean 'exchange', stand out as figures of light upon a sombre ground: 'I always remember him. I thought he was great.' Au Bala recalls with a gesture of pleasure Tom Chandler, the government teacher at Darnley Island, who both took him into another world of scientific knowledge and stuck up for him against Kole. 'We loved him; we really loved him. None of my friends were ever like Dr Don', Sis recalls the anthropologist Donald Thomson at the Lockhart River of her childhood: 'We felt he was ours'.

In the 1960s and 1970s, changes within the dominant culture itself which had led to a questioning of the old certitudes gave rise to the possibility that some of the younger generation of white teachers would walk out with Meriam Man. That transition also contributed substantially towards the possibility of a 'double-sided' school founded upon Meriam Man's cultural tradition.

Second Meriam Man's vision of a project of cultural renewal is also representative of the thinking of each of the persons here: As Au Bala says: 'I see that the knowledge that had been with the people is still thriving'.

The Stars of the Torres Strait over many generations are countless like stars in the sky; there are also special Stars, whom we have seen in this book mediating the contradictory forces of an era: for example Revs Poi (Poey) Passi, Sailor Gabey and the Island priests; 'Old M'; the dramatic narrators; and many others. As of old, through exemplification they have provided inspiration to others, by their practical political leadership, and by the depth of their wisdom and the poetry within them. They have an affinity with the priests, the poets and song composers of ancient times. Each of these people could answer Dr Haddon's question: 'Where was Malo-Bomai pointing?'

Elsewhere (1988, 77), I have referred to the new custodians of a widening tradition who 'are the centre of the creation of qualitatively new syntheses...', whose task as 'joining' people is the formidable one of making non-destructive syntheses between the key principles of their cultural traditions and traditions which come from the other side of the Great Divide between cultures. This compares with Read's characterisation of leadership among the Gahuka-Gama of Papua New Guinea. Those who have achieved a position of generalised authority have 'a fine feeling for the opinion of others', 'some detachment', 'the ability to see many different points of view at the same time', 'a breadth of vision and a degree of self-control which signifies a measure of autonomy' (1959, 435). Leadership requires a man who has some feeling for the antithesis and manifest tension between the values of 'strength' and 'equivalence', where the former concerns not primarily physical strength, but innovative creative potential (1959, 434).

Some, like First Meriam Man were called upon to play a decisive part in practical struggle: he foreshadowed by more than forty years the model of 'people's business' of the bakery at Moa, of projects like MAW (which owed an immense debt to Uncle), and of cooperative fishing projects such as that spearheaded by Crossfield Ahmat, the late Chairman of Badu Island who died in 1986. Others, such as Kapin and Kebi Bala, are more like theologians showing people the way to their own syntheses. Au Bala's creative synthesis centres around the deepening and developing meanings of Malo *wali aritarit*: we have a seed to offer the world from which through reciprocity we can harvest and so enrich our culture.

Yet he can only do this through his grounding in the truth of Malo-Bomai — in the correct version of the myth, which says that the more sacred one, Bomai, who is Malo's maternal uncle, came first.

Second Meriam Man's strength comes also from his inheritance of the Malo-Bomai tradition. It was with him when he went south 'in search of something'; it was with him when he 'did his dance' in the early 1970s; and it was with him in the Supreme Court of Queensland when he recounted his early socialisation in Malo's Law in giving evidence as first plaintiff in the *Murray Island Land* case.

Sis gives expression to a new consciousness, different to that of her grandfather or her father. She has been an inspirational person, through the breadth of her intellectual and practical wisdom, through her formidable strength in meeting troubled situations: her role was critical in the Border Action Committee's Canberra negotiations; she was the first person in the Torres Strait to call for a land case; and she has become an active advocate of political sovereignty for Torres Strait Islanders, an advocacy which for her goes hand in hand with a cultural identification aware of its own genealogy. Grandfather T is Sis' grandfather. Reverend Poi (Poey) Passi is Kebi Bala's uncle. Sis and Kebi Bala link their respective genealogies with their impelling wish to attend a land conference in Townsville in 1981 where the *Murray Island Land* case began to take concrete form.

The dissimilarity — its uniqueness — remains immersed in an 'obsession with regeneration' which is integrally associated with a belief in the Eternal Return of the Cosmos and the search for the All-Unity which joins the separate quests. In the cosmologies of Kapin or Sis the 'longing for eternity' also implies a necessary longing 'for a concrete paradise', a paradise that 'can be won *here*, on earth, and *now*, in the present moment': their 'cosmic Christianity' speaks an earthly message (Eliade 1974, 407).

Christianity held the answer to the problem of retaining reciprocity as a form of interchange and at the same time subordinating that part of its content which advocated an eye for an eye, a tooth for a tooth. For Christianity offered the most powerful mediator and hence the power of reversal; those whom one would kill might become like brothers and sisters.

Their message and that of others given 'in the original' may show forth patterns of hidden connections to others who come after. Paul Radin prefaced the publication of the four myths published under the one title, *The Culture of the Winnebago: As Described by Themselves*, with the intention to offer students 'authentic material for the study of Winnebago culture'. Many years later, Claude

Lévi-Strauss saw a deep unity at a structural level for making them the subject of one publication. This book is many books in one; it is certain that the various meanings given here do not begin to exhaust all the truths of the Stars of Tagai.

NOTES

NOTES TO PREFACE

1. On my first visit to the Torres Strait Islands in 1978, Mr Gaetano Lui Snr identified three events for me, which crystallised and gave impetus to a sense of common identity among Islanders. Two further events of major significance occurred in the 1980s.

2. AC Haddon made a valuable collection of artefacts, described by Moore as 'among the most complete and fully documented of any made among native peoples in any part of the world' (1984, 38). He wrote further: 'The only collections made anywhere in the Australasian region that can be compared with the Haddon collections' are those WE Roth acquired in his capacity as Chief Protector of Aboriginals, now in the Australian Museum, Sydney. Many other 'items' were collected by the government teachers and donated to Australian museums, particularly the Queensland Museum. One noteworthy case is the theft of the *agud* Waiet from the sacred place at Waier in 1925 by OAC Davies, government teacher at Mer (Orrell 1969, 82).

NOTES TO INTRODUCTION

1. For an analytical summary of the reciprocal process as a series of interconnected propositions, see Sharp 1984, 94–95; for a critical discussion of its contrast with commodity exchange, see 1984, 69–96.

2. Foliation (Latin *folium*, leaf) denotes a layered totality which characterises reciprocal gift-giving societies where the economy remains embedded within other social relations (Polanyi 1965a, 71; Baudrillard 1975, 75). The totality created is a cyclical, not a linear one and moments of crossing over from human to cosmic cycles — initiation, death for example — are seen as 'foliating events' (see Chapters 2 and 3).

3. This contrasts sharply with Fisk et al 1974, 42–44, whose interpretations manifest a demonstrable enthocentrism in selecting such indices of communication as letter-writing. For a critique see Sharp 1980a, 24–32; Sharp 1984, 132–33. Beckett states that they 'exaggerate the separation' between the two groupings (1987, 212).

4. In a tribute to Paul Radin, the eminent French anthropologist, Claude Lévi-Strauss discerned among his many talents 'the authentic aesthetic touch': 'This is what we call in French *flair*: the gift of singling out those facts, observations,

and documents which possess an especially rich, meaning...' (1978b, 198). In an important sense his creative perceptions and often intuitive discernment of the underlying structures foreshadow the structuralist project laid out by Lévi-Strauss in *Tristes Tropiques* in 1955 which he later systematised and formalised.

5.   Before beginning this project, I had identified three broad phases of rule (see 1980a, 1–90), and I had listed what seemed to be the major social events since encroachment and invasion became widespread in the Torres Strait region; see also 1984, 137–41 on steps in finding a language of intercultural inquiry.

6.   These relate to: contrasting life-categories; the non-written character of stored traditions; the 'hidden' character of colonial experience; and the absence of a theory of transition.

7.   Alavi 1973, 59, emphasises the complex interrelationships between class and the 'factional' or cultural mode of politics.

8.   Hurley 1924, 38, caught a glimpse of Islanders' characteristically 'invisible' socio-cultural comment on Kole during his visit to the Torres Strait Islands in the early 1920s: 'One of the most amusing [dances] witnessed by the party was a pantomine satirizing the white military authorities. In this the dancers mimicked with genuine exaggeration the stiff walk, the manners and the pomposity of the ruling white men.'

9.   See Sharp, 1984 Weaving a Two-sided Story, Vol 1, Appendix A, A1–7.

NOTES TO CHAPTER 1

1.   Flinders 1814 uses the possessive case for the name of the Strait and the islands named by Edwards and Bligh; Lewis 1836 — 'Torres Strait'; and Haddon 1904–35 — 'Torres Straits'.

2.   Tobin wrote: 'The bows are the most powerful I have yet seen in any Indians, none of our people, nor the two Otaheitans, were able to string them. They are of split bamboo, some are seven feet; the arrows are equally destructive and pointed with bone and barbed several inches from the point' (see Lee 1920, 186); see also Portlock 1920, 254).

3.   On his return to the Islands as Commander of the *Investigator*, he wrote of the Murray Islanders on 29 October 1802. 'At sunset, two of the canoes returned to Murray's Island, paddling to windward with more velocity than one of our boats could have rowed...' (1814, II, 109). The following day he wondered '...how these long canoes keep to the wind, and make such way as they do, without any after sail, I am at a loss to know' (II, 111).

In appreciating the qualities of their difference, Flinders sought 'to secure the friendship of these islanders to such vessels as might hereafter pass through Torres Strait'... (1814, II, 110). His awareness of their prowess also made him cautious: 'I did not forget the inhabitants of these islands had made an attack, upon the *Providence* and *Assistant* in 1792', he wrote on this second occasion. 'The marines were therefore kept under arms, the guns clear, and the matches lighted; and officers were stationed to watch every motion, one to each canoe, so long as they remained near the ship' (II, 109).

4.   Flinders 1814, II, 111, estimated the population of the Murray Islands from the number of men in the canoes he sighted on Saturday 30 October 1802: 'There were many Indians sitting in groups upon the shore, and the seven canoes which came off to the ship in the morning, contained from ten to twenty men each, or together, about a hundred. If we suppose these hundred men to have been one half of what belonged to the islands, and to the two hundred men, add as many women and three hundred children, the population of Murray's Isles will amount to seven hundred; of which nearly the whole must belong to the larger island.' On 15 November 1879, Pennefather mustered the inhabitants of Darnley Island, counting thirty-three men and boys, thirty-five women and twelve children; at Murray Islands he mustered 166 men and boys, 114 women and girls, ninety-four children (Captain C Pennefather, Report of a Cruise, in QSA COL/A288). Beckett 1963, 40, estimates the pre-1871 population of Darnley Island at 500, from LMS sources. His estimate of the total 'pre-contact' population of the Torres Strait Islands as 3,000 to 4,000 (1963, 66, 65) was revised to between 4,000 and 5,000 (1987, 26 including n 1).

5.   Au Bala says the Meriam went as far as Saibai where they collected the canoes which were sent along the coast of Op Deudai from Kiwai. Haddon 1908, 185, identifies two 'trade routes' to Op Deudai, but he does not mention Saibai; Au Bala also says that the Meriam went to Muri (Mt Adolphus) and to Keo Deudai (B148–49); see Kitaoji 1978, 158. Haddon 1908, 145, says that the remoteness of the Meriam virtually debarred them from intercourse with Australia; Moore 1979, Map 5, 302, shows a trade route between Dauar, one of the Murray Islands and Aurid, Paremar, Waraber and Muri.

6.   On the character and construction of the double-outrigger canoes of the sandbeach people of Cape York Peninsula, see Thomson 1952, 1–5 and map; on their seafaring prowess, see Thomson 1934, 237–62 and Plates XXIX–XXXI. Thomson 1952, 2, points out that the booms 'rest on top of the gunwale of the canoe and are then secured with light rope of *Hibiscus* fibre; they are not carried through the hull'. (See Roth 1907–10, 12ff; Haddon 1935, 311; Haddon and Hornell 1937.)

7. See Haddon 1904, 296–97; Landtman 1927, 211–15, on the trading voyages of the Kala Lagaw Ya speakers of the Western and Central Islands. Haddon 1908, 186, notes 'the giving of "presents" by the intermediaries as an anomalous feature' among the Meriam; Landtman emphasises the 'gift' character of the whole transaction (1927, 211–15).

8. The following account is summarised from 'The Coming of Bomai; The Coming of Malo', as told to me by Au Bala at Thursday Island in June 1984 (Cassette 135/AB/TI/3/84). The basic account and style do not differ from that given by Haddon 1908, 33–44; see 44–46 on the discrepancies between different versions and the significance of the myth. In the version written by *Aet* Pasi for Ray (1907, 233–39) there is only one narrative, 'The Story of Malo', which combines the two complementary narratives; see Lawrie 1970, 326–36.

9. Kapin, Book of Islanders 1984, B26, says that Malo went to the Lockhart River area. On Pai'yamo, Rainbow Serpent and I'wai, crocodile, see Thomson 1933, 453–537. There are similarities in the cultural practices of the Meriam and the Kuuku Ya'u, six clans with a common tribal centre on the upper Pascoe River, for example, mummification of the dead, which was not practised by Kala Lagaw Ya speakers.

10. An elderly Lockhart man known here as 'First Lockhart Man', whom people identified as the 'right' person to tell the myth of I'wai, sang the chant in Kuuku Ya'u and in English (Cassette 128/LRS/LR/7/83). He told me that I'wai made possible long sea voyages and exchange which were similar to *wauri*. I'wai is the 'culture hero' of the sacred Okaintä ceremonies (Thomson 1933, 473–81). See n 9 above.

11. Haddon is contradictory on the extent of the voyages, concluding that there was little contact between the two linguistic groups in the Islands (1904, 233, 296–97; 1908, 120–21, 185; 1934, 350). 'I believe', he writes, 'Murray Islanders rarely made the whole journey' to Kiwai for canoes (1908, 186). Yet the account he obtained from Mr Bruce (1908, 186–87) suggests that they did. On the voyages of the Western Islanders, see Haddon 1904, 296–97. Scholars have followed Haddon in his doubt that Islanders made the long journey to Kiwai. So for example, Moore 1979, 123, has doubted Brierly's record of evidence from Barbara Thompson that Manu of Muralag went to Saibai or Op Deudai (Daudai) in *Kie Marina*: 'Possibly Brierly misunderstood him and he was merely enumerating the places via which he had obtained the canoe' (1979, 123). Along with the canoe voyages the double-outrigger canoes soon vanished; perhaps with them went the awareness of voyagers

like Flinders who sensed the way the long slender canoes sped across the water.

12.   Haddon 1904, 38–40; Ray 1907, 248–50; Haddon 1908, 23–55; Lawrie 1970, 297–99. The people at Injinoo, Cowal Creek, Cape York Peninsula, told Rev WH MacFarlane that Gelam came from there and went to Moa because there were no wild yams (Haddon 1935, 104). Aborigines at Lockhart River believe that Gelam came from there. See Au Bala, Book of Islanders, B149; First Lockhart Man connects the myth of I'wai, alligator, with the myth of Gelam (Cassette 127/LRS/LR/6/83).

13.   'The Murray Islanders will have Murray Island to themselves', John Douglas officially reported on 6 August 1885 following a visit to Murray Island that year, during which an agreement was signed on 29 July between Douglas on behalf of the Queensland Government and representatives of the South Sea Islanders resident on Murray Island, stating that they would leave for Darnley Island within sixty days (QV&P, 1885). On the high standard of the school at Murray Island, see for example, Butcher in Torres Strait District Annual Report for 1906, Darnley Island, 4 January 1907, LMS correspondence. A further reason for focussing on the Murray Islands relates to the valuable additional information sent over the years to Haddon by John (Jack) Bruce, who resided on Mer from 1890–1923, and was government school teacher there from 1892–1923. Haddon 1908, xx, makes acknowledgements to Bruce, for example, see 192 fn 1 on his very detailed and extensive information on magic (192–240).

14.   Five reasons may be given for the apparent disappearance of beliefs and customs deriving from Malo-Bomai: the rapid and virtual total destruction of the symbols and shrines of Malo-Bomai by the LMS missionaries; the rapid and virtual complete acceptance of Christianity by Murray Islanders; the custom of secrecy central to the teachings of Malo; the way Murray Islanders were taught to regard their old beliefs as inferior and 'heathen'; and the fact that most of their continuing customs followed Malo's Law, which was simply taken for granted as unquestioned truth by Murray Islanders.

15.   Thus it would seem that *Aet* Pasi used the name Malo as a cloak for the more sacred name of Bomai, so writing only one narrative for Ray; in protecting '...the *ged kem le*, the true one of the island', the *Aet* produced a version which has sometimes been taken literally (see Lawrie 1970, 326–36).

16.   *Mabo and Others v State of Queensland and Commonwealth of Australia* (High Court of Australia, No 12 of 1982). For a historical account and analysis of two contrasting cultural perspectives on the case, see Sharp 1990b, 1–31; 1991, 78–93. See also Land Bilong Islanders, Yarra Bank Films 1990.

NOTES TO CHAPTER 2

1. Kitaoji 1982, 68, observes that such a 'cultural centre or supposed cradle of civilization' is absent among the people of the Western and Central Islands. See Eliade's discussion of the Hebrew tradition where the creation of the world is like an embryo which grows from the navel, its central point, from where it spread out in all directions (1959b, 44).

2. Haddon 1908, xvii, writes that the Eastern Islanders 'practically regard themselves as one people...'. By analysing the stratified semantic components of Meriam lexicography Kitaoji shows the way in which the formation of Meriam cultural identity proceeds by a continuing process of bifurcation. The result is a multi-layered conception of Meriam home territory with seven overlapping meanings (1982, 68).

3. The custom predates Malo, but a part of Malo's Law was said when a taboo was placed on a garden (Haddon 1935, 147). Lawrie 1970, 337–38, give the full text of Malo's Law. For a discussion of four interrelated aspects of Malo re Gelar: its valorisation of proprietary rights; its injunction to cultivate and conserve; its normative and restitutive function in a system of rights and duties; and its mediation of diversities in unity of Murray Islanders, see Sharp 1986, 2–8.

4. In their seasonal variation the Meriam may be both compared and contrasted with the Inuit (Eskimo), for whom, as Mauss has written, the imprint of the two contrasting phases of the year (summer and winter), is so sharply different 'that it almost springs to view' (1979, 79). The two great opposed seasons, which are reflected socially in contrasting times of 'social concentration' and times of almost solitary existence, stamp Eskimo character as alternately individual and collective, differences which are also expressed in norms and jural systems. In like manner, Thomson has suggested that the seasonal variation in the way of life of the Wik Mungkan of Archer River was so great that an uninformed onlooker seeing these people at different times of the year might mistake them for different groups (1939, 211–12). Their movements, wrote Thomson, form a regular and orderly annual cycle carried out systematically and with a rhythm parallel to, and in step with, the seasonal changes themselves (211).

      Among the sedentary Meriam, the people's character is stamped by seasonal variation, although, in contrast to people whose camping place varies with the seasons, they may appear to the outsider in their year-round 'sameness', rather than in their difference at different times. Among the Meriam, only the men moved to the garden houses at *arit kerker*, planting time; only the warriors undertook seafaring voyages: the *zogo le*, the old men, the women and the children remained tied to the environs of home island for the full circle of the seasons.

5. See Kitaoji's pioneering work on *lubabat* among the Meriam (1980, 1–17, and Figure 2, 8–10). The existence of *lubabat*, totems, among the Meriam, was not apparent to Haddon and the Cambridge ethnographers. Haddon 1908, 242, states that '*lu babat* is anything which is revered as belonging to an ancestor'; see Ray 1907, 151 *lu-babat*, an heirloom. Beckett 1963, 1987 makes no reference to the existence of totemism. In noting the association of persons and groups with stars and constellations, Haddon concludes that this 'is highly suggestive and may be a survival of a division of natural objects between social groups such as is found among many peoples' (1912, 220). See 1908, 174: 'One of the chief interests of the social organisation of the Miriam is the complete disappearance of all traces of a totemic system which it is almost certain must have once existed'. See also 254–56. And Durkheim and Mauss 1903, 28: '...totemism is found only in the western islands and not in those of the east'.

6. In writing of Sebeg and Ulag as *au nei*, Haddon 1908, 171, observes: 'The fact that no marriages have occurred between Keweid, Sebeg and Mad, nor between Akup and Ulag, is in favour of the view that these five villages should be regarded as two villages in the sense of *au nei*'. Similarly, Gigred as *au nei* includes three *kebi nei*, the small villages of Gigred, Begegiz and Nerugab (Haddon 1908, 169).

Elsewhere it is argued that through the mediation of language, reciprocal categories act as metaphors for one another; in doing so they create a layered system of relationships which makes for cultural depth among the Meriam (see Sharp 1989, 1–25).

7. 'Rose of the Winds' is Dr Keith Hutchinson's phrase for which I thank him. It is noteworthy that early compasses carried a rose.

8. The Meriam today confirm Haddon's observation (1912, 145) that they '...plant when they see the *kakigaba* [perennial white yam] and *ketai* [perennial climbing yam] (136) beginning to shoot out their vines', which he identifies as our spring (226). See also his brief discussion of The Seasons of the Eastern Islanders (228). Thomson's table of the Annual Cycle of Activities, based upon, and regulated by, Seasonal Changes — Wik Monkan Tribe, 1939, 214–15, 'begins' with the southeast season, the time of the great vegetable harvest.

9. See Haddon 1912, 236. The label on the *wauri* in the British Museum reads '...very valuable, worth a man or a canoe' (Haddon 1912, 236).

10. See Godelier on the Baruya of Papua New Guinea, who, like the Islanders, established contacts with neighbours, effecting 'trade-and-protection' pacts, which carried on from one generation to another (1977, 140).

11. Mauss 1970, 93, n 25, discusses the means of exchange in societies 'preceding those which minted gold bronze and silver', designating their character as 'talismans or "life-givers"'

12. Eliade 1959b, 47, writes of the archaic and widely disseminated idea of a centre at which 'the four horizons are projected in four cardinal directions'. Thus 'the Roman *mundus* was a circular trench divided into four parts; it was at once the image of the cosmos and the paradigmatic model for human habitation'.

13. 'Malo language, archaic Kala Lagaw Ya' (Ray 1907, 50), was like a 'language of devotion', not understood by most Meriam. *Zogo mir* and many of the sacred songs of the Meriam are of Western Island origin (Haddon 1908, 243).

14. The Eskimo feast of the dead embodies this unity of the temporal and the eternal. Mauss writes that according to custom the latest child to be born takes on the name of the last person who has died. At the beginning of the feast there is a request for the souls of the dead to be reincarnated for a short time in each namesake. The latter are then laden with presents, gifts exchanged among all those assembled, and the souls return to the land of the dead: '...at this time, the group not only regains its unity but sees itself re-formed, through this same ritual, as an ideal group composed of all successive generations from the earliest times' (1979, 59).

15. The Meriam believed that the sun went down under the sea at Umar Pit at the western end of Mer and passed down to Beig under the island, the resting place of the spirits of the dead on their way to and from Boigu, the homeland of *lamar*, the immortals (1908, 252).

NOTES TO CHAPTER 3

1. The 'New Law', which returned a measure of autonomy to Island Councils, resulted from the 1936 maritime strike. It was introduced immediately before the first interisland Councillors' Conference at Yorke Island in 1937. See Chapter 7 below.

2. Commenting on the 'Prologue in Heaven' of Goethe's *Faust*, Eliade writes: 'In Goethe's conception, Mephistopheles is the spirit who denies, protests, and, above all *halts* the flux of life and prevents things from being done. Mephistopheles' activity is not directed against God, but against Life' (1965, 79). *Maid le* are 'against Life'.

3. See Riesman 1955, 275–97 on the qualities of what he calls the autonomous character-type; see also Read on the Gahuka–Gama of Papua New Guinea (1959, 425–36); Radin's discussion of 'speculative philosophers' and their qualities is highly relevant here (1957, 231–36, 277, *et passim*).

4. See Gladwin 1964, 171. See also McMillan 1982, 45–47, who presents some of Gladwin's comparative observations about Trukese and European navigation in the context of a discussion of 'reason and intuitive knowledge'.

5. I am paraphrasing Geertz's words; he contrasts the religious with the scientific perspective (1966, 26–28). See Daly on the Elizabethans: 'It was easy for such minds to relate things, to consider them in a milieu, rather than isolating for analysis' (1979, 7).

6. Radin observes that among the Winnebago the 'custodians of the tribal traditions who were most careful to see that the practical aspects of the situation did not militate too markedly against success...' often '...refused their sanction' with the words: 'The spirits have not blessed you with sufficient power...' (1957, 22).

7. See Burridge's discussion of a 'developing awareness' among Tangu of New Guinea (1969, especially 458–69; 1960, 273–82), to which the following discussion on the emerging quality of individuated awareness among Islanders is especially indebted.

NOTES TO CHAPTER 4

1. The 'Quetta' memorial cathedral, the first solid concrete church in North Queensland, commemorates the disaster of the *Quetta*, which struck a rock and went down within three minutes in 1890, drowning 133 people (MacFarlane 1950, 9, 44). The foundation stone of the cathedral was laid in 1893 by John Douglas, the Government Resident at Thursday Island (Bayton 1965, 66).

2. In his Eighth Memorial to His Majesty the King of Spain Quiros cautioned speed to begin the journey across vast distances, lest 'enemies of the Roman Church should come to sow false doctrine...for there is much that is lost by each hour that is wasted, which can never be recovered' (Markham 1904, 486). The LMS missionaries perceived the Roman Catholic Church as a threat in the area. Thus Rev James Chalmers wrote in his Report on the Gulf District of New Guinea and Torres Strait that the 'Romanists', having already looked around the western stations of the LMS, had applied for land at Daru; 'I shall be sorry if they pick the fruit of our toil' (LMS Correspondence, Microfilm Box No 2 ANL, AJCP, Canberra).

3. In seeking to secure the islands on which the LMS had placed its mission stations, the Rev S McFarlane informed the Minister for Lands on 22 April 1882

that the Society had 'paid the owners no mere *nominal* sum but at the rate of at least, one pound per acre...' (LMS Correspondence).

4.   Otto 1936, 18, writes of *orgė*, the Wrath of Yahweh: '...it is patent from many passages of the Old Testament that this "Wrath" has no concern whatever with moral qualities. There is something very baffling in the way in which it "is kindled" and manifested. It is, as has been well said, "like a hidden force of nature", like stored-up electricity, discharging itself upon any one who comes too near. It is "incalculable" and "arbitrary".' See the qualities of *zogo* discussed in Chapter 3 above.

5.   The Institute was established 'to meet the peculiar wants of this mission'; wrote McFarlane, '*viz.* to assemble promising young men and boys...and there, removed from their evil surroundings and family influences teach them, making the *English language* and an *industrial school* prominent features...' (1888, 81).

6.   MacGregor commented critically on the way the system by which Murray Islanders obtained their canoes at the New Guinea coast in exchange for shell ornaments had been sundered by the customs barrier between the Commonwealth and Papua maintained in the preceding six years: 'This rupture of ancient intercourse has been much felt at Murray Island, and at other places in the Straits' (Governor of Queensland to State Secretary for Colonies, 20 July 1911, Despatch No 21).

7.   There is nothing in Rev Done's diaries to suggest that he saw the dances as either continuing or reviving the meanings of Malo-Bomai. However, his attitude appears to contrast not only with that of the LMS, but with the position first taken by the Anglican Church. According to Bishop Gilbert White, three Murray Islanders were ex-communicated for attending forbidden dances in 1915 (White 1917, 51).

8.   From the mid-1880s both the Roman Catholic and the Anglican churches established themselves at Thursday Island. See QV&P, 1889, Vol III, 222; see also Evans 1972, 94–104, on the establishment and growth of Christian churches at Thursday Island.

9.   The following words are taken from a sermon preached by Kebi Bala at Quetta cathedral, Thursday Island, on the 112th anniversary of the 'Coming of the Light', 1 July 1983, eight years after his sermon on the meaning of 'the Light', Cairns, 1976.

10.   The custom was somewhat different in the Western and Eastern Islands; in the latter the body was mummified. See Haddon 1904, 248–61; 1908, 126–60, and Au Bala, Book of Islanders, B66–67.

11.   Cohn 1970, 13, writes that millenarian sects or movements always picture salvation as collective, terrestrial, imminent, total and miraculous.

12. Andreas Lommel, Der 'Cargo Cult' in Melanesien: Ein Beitrag zur Problem de Europaisierung der Primitivien, *Zeitschrift fur Ethnologie*, LXXVIII, 1, 1953, 55, as quoted in Lanternari 1963, 186 fn, draws attention to the relationship between the cult of the dead and the arrival of cargo: 'From the cult of the dead, there derives all the traditional religious life of Melanesians. For them, it is not conceivable that the cargo comes from Europe, the existence of which they are not aware, for them the cargo comes from the world of the dead.' I have suggested a connection between a central agrarian myth in Melanesia on the return of the ancestors and the 'special conditions' of Australian rule in the emergence of 'cargo cults' on a very wide scale persisting long after the Second World War (1975, 338–39).

13. See Worsley 1970, 106, on the significance of 'German' 'as an anti-Government symbol': the leaders emphasised that they were not 'King George's Men'. Lanternari uses the term 'religions of the oppressed' to describe movements of colonial millenarianism (1963).

NOTES TO CHAPTER 5

1. The *Government Gazette* of 2 April 1904 states: 'The offices of Northern and Southern Protectors have been abolished, and the working of the Aboriginals Acts and Regulations placed under a Chief Protector for the whole State... One of the primary features for the initiation of the Acts was the doing away of the old-time dispersals and meeting the blacks in a hostile manner' (QPP 1905, 22).

2. Prior to 1918 the 'Annual Report of the Chief Protector of Aboriginals' was not listed alongside other sub-departments. 'Inmates' of Reserves under the Protection Acts were controlled by the Aboriginals Department, a sub-department of the Department of Health and Home Affairs. In 1932 the other 'inmates' so defined were the Diamatina Hospital for Chronic Diseases, Dunwich Benevolent Asylum, Eventide Home, Inebriate Institution, Queensland Industrial Institution for the Blind, Westwood Sanitorium and the Home for Epileptics. Aborigines and Islanders were frequently referred to as 'inmates' in official reports: see for example, Annual Report of the Chief Protector of Aboriginals for the Year 1913 (QPP 1914, 13), and the Report of the Local Protector at Thursday Island (QPP 1933, 11).

3. The first school in the Torres Strait was begun by the LMS at Darnley Island on 24 August 1873 (Ray 1907, 49).

4. On 7 September 1886 a code was drawn up delegating powers to a *mamus*, or 'head-man' (QV&P 1887). The Report of the Chief Protector of Aboriginals for

1904 states that John Douglas instituted this 'excellent system' to assist the *mamus* (QPP 1905, 21).

5. 'The half-caste, no matter how civilised, is rarely able to hold his own in business or the labour world...the marriage of full-blood women to whites or aliens is rigidly tabooed, half-castes of aboriginal nature are encouraged to marry back, and the superior type are assisted to uplift themselves and mate with their own kind' (QPP 1924, 7).

6. In 1922 the Chief Protector reported: 'A perusal of the statistics for the last two years, 1921 and 1922, discloses an interesting fact — that, contrary to the common belief, the natives are not dying out fast... It is not inevitable that they should die out' (QPP 1923). The Chief Protector had reported in 1913: 'As everyone is aware, the aboriginal races are slowly dying out...' (QPP 1914, 1).

7. The language of racism pervades the Chief Protector's comments on the intention and implications of the 1934 amendments relating to the possibilities of the 'quadroon and lighter types with definite European characteristics' being able to 'uplift' themselves: 'Some anxiety naturally was caused in certain quarters amongst quadroons and others exempt from the Protection Acts by the extended powers of the control provided' (QPP 1935, 10).

8. See Burridge 1960, 281–82, who interprets a cargo cult among Tangu of Papua New Guinea as 'a protest against the disnomy' of their experience.

9. This became Eastern Island hymn number 145; see Pilot (comp) nd (c1973), 56.

NOTES TO CHAPTER 6

1. See Loos 1982, especially Chapter 5. See also J Jardine to Colonial Secretary, 1 January 1872, Records of Somerset 1872–1877, 2 of 1872, Dixson Library; QV&P 1900, 583–85; QV&P 1901, 133; QV&P 1891, Vol III, 172. In the Annual Report of the Government Resident at Thursday Island for 1892–93, John Douglas writes of the unrestrained carrying off of young men and women from the area near Cape York 'as food for the fisheries' (QV&P, 1894, Vol II, 914).

2. See QV&P 1895, 13. In 1892 the remnants of the people of Tutu (Warrior Island) were resettled on Yam Island (QV&P 1899, 426); by 1900 the population of Nagir was almost wiped out (Haddon 1901, 180). By 1902, the only islands with stable or increasing populations were Murray and Darnley, the latter being mainly South Sea Islanders (QPP 1903, 26). Administrators believed that the closer Islanders or Aborigines came into contact with industrial society, the greater the ravages of disease (see Douglas, QV&P 1894, Vol II, 914).

3. Reverend FC Jagg and Mr William Kennett, who were stationed at Somerset from 1867–68, were forced to abandon the mission after eighteen months. Bayton 1965, 33–39, discusses the reasons for their departure; see also Sharp 1982a, 151–53; 1992a, Chapter 3. For an account of the 'punitive expedition' to Muralag (Prince of Wales Island) in 1869 headed by the Acting Government Resident, HM Chester, see HM Chester to Colonial Secretary, 10 August 1871, COL/A160 in QSA 71/2499; see also JM Carroll's edited and annotated version of Chester's letter, 1969, 35–42. For an overall account of destruction at Somerset see Sharp 1992a, 25–80.

4. Henry M Chester to Minister for Lands; letter headed, 'Douglas Pitt and Joseph Tucker have been in unlawful occupation of Murray Island', Thursday Island, 23 September 1882, exhibit U to the affidavit of PJ Killoran, *Murray Island Land* case (MILC, High Court of Australia, No 12 of 1982).

5. See Chester to Douglas Pitt, 11 May 1882: 'The Government of Queensland having proclaimed Murray Island as a reserve for the native inhabitants, I hereby, on behalf of the government of Queensland give you sixty days notice to remove your plant and effects and quit the island'; exhibit S to affidavit of PJ Killoran, MILC; D Pitt to Minister for Lands, Murray Island, 13 May 1882, seeking the right for himself and his family to stay after thirteen years residence during which time he had had ten houses erected on the island for his family and twenty employees (in exhibit S, MILC).

6. The occupational distribution of ethnic groups in the shelling industry at Thursday Island in 1880 was: boat-owners (European); divers, men 'in-charge' (South Sea Islanders); and boat crews (Asians, Torres Strait Islanders and Aborigines); see Evans 1972, 31.

7. By the mid-1890s the shelling industry was being carried on mainly by Japanese; see Report of the Commission on the Pearl-Shell and Bêche-de-Mer Fisheries, Queensland 1897, 1316; Royal Commission to Inquire into… 1908, QPP 1909, 442.

8. Evans 1972, 34–35, writes that over the thirty-four years between 1880 and 1914 there was a reversal in the positions of South Sea Islanders and Asians in the shelling industry, the latter tending to replace South Sea Islanders as divers and men in charge.

9. In 1937 it was revealed that the Pearlshellers' Association had approached the Islander owners of the 'Company boats', promising that if they gave them up the employers would increase their wages to four pounds per month. See O'Leary to Chief Protector, 7 September 1937 in QSA 37/9577.

10.   The stated objective of the Island Fund was 'to promote a spirit of independence...and generally make provision for the welfare of their relatives and villages without asking monetary assistance from the Government' (QPP 1914, 14). It was established in respect of each Reserve on the Islands of Torres Strait according to regulations under the Aboriginals Protection Acts 1897–1901 and approved by the Executive Council, Queensland on 19 December 1912.

11.   EB Connolly, who was a government teacher in the Islands from 1913 to 1920, wrote critically of the defrauding of Islanders by traders at Thursday Island almost under the eye of the officers of the Aboriginals Department (*Unemployed Clarion*, 27 August 1921; 3 and 17 September 1921).

12.   'Very unsatisfactory reports are received of the workings of the native-owned boats', the Chief Protector observed in 1908, '...and too much time has apparently been spent in hunting for dugong, turtle etc., and probably visiting the neighbouring islands' (QPP 1909, 24).

13.   The Chief Protector's Report for the Year 1935 states: 'The captain of this boat [*Wakaid*], Tanu Nona, is an outstanding native. Not only has he won the cup for "company" boats on every occasion it has been competed for, but he has consistently beaten the record of all other boats in the marine industry' (QPP 1936, 20).

14.   Beckett comments, 'The *Wakaid's* success was not easily won'; Tanu Nona explained to him how he got the men to work: 'If they not get much shell I not let them into the dinghy to eat dinner, midday. They got to eat their piece of damper standing on the reef. Some skippers work only half day, six in the morning till dinner time, then sail on to the next reef. That way they lose half a day. But I keep them there till six in the evening. We cook the shell and sail on to the next reef night-time' (1977, 90).

15.   Marx 1949, 42 writes: 'A commodity is therefore a mysterious thing, simply because in it the social character of men's labour appears to them as an objective character stamped upon the product of that labour. There it is a definite social relation between men, that assumes, in their eyes, the fantastic form of a relation between things.'

16.   Wolpe 1975, discusses the complexities of these contradictory processes in relation to the Bantu of South Africa: see also Hartwig 1978, in relation to Australian Aborigines. Here I am arguing that 'White Australia' acted as an (often hidden) cultural imperative in 'successful' opposition to the economic interests of capitalist enterprise. See Sharp 1975, 327–48, in relation to the 'external territories' of Papua and New Guinea.

17. Beckett 1963, 129, writes: 'Native leaders of the Ex-servicemen's movement, recalling the promises and friendliness of their white comrades during the war, put their trust in the Legion. The appearance of the Christian Co-operative aroused similar hopes.'

NOTES TO CHAPTER 7

1. See also Extra Police for Thursday Island. Result of Native Trouble, *Cairns Post*, 10 February 1936.

2. Thursday Island Trading, Minister Explains Firm's Closure, *Brisbane Courier-Mail*, 8 July 1936: 'He was being transferred in accordance with the Public Service system of limiting the period of service at isolated stations'.

3. Report by Deputy Chief Protector of Aboriginals on the Origin and Cause of Discontent amongst Torres Strait Islanders, 11 May 1936, 5, enclosed in letter of Chief Protector to Under Home Secretary, Torres Straits. Refusal of Natives to work boats — Mr O'Leary's Report, 18 May 1936, 36/4901, is enclosed with letters top numbered to 36/5997 in QSA.

4. Mr Frith had refused permission for Rev Francis Bowie to enter the village, insisting on his staying in the Mission area at Mabuiag (Report 22 February, 2).

5. On 20 April 1936, WS Munro described interisland solidarity at this time: 'The workless ones would no doubt receive gifts of flour, tobacco, etc. from their colleagues, thanks to the excellent communal spirit which exists throughout the Islands' (Report to Minister for Health and Home Affairs, Refusal of Natives to Work Boats, enclosed with 36/5997).

6. The influence of the Church on Islander opinion is emphasised in the Deputy Chief Protector's main report: 'The necessity for co-operation between Church and State is stressed when it is recognised that the Church influence in Torres Strait is particularly strong, so much so, that the opinion of the Bishop of Carpentaria on matters outside the function of the Church are [*sic*] accepted in preference to the advice of the Protector' (11 May 1936, 11).

7. In his Report on 11 May 1936, O'Leary wrote: 'The published speech [of the Bishop] was conveyed to the various Native Priests by the Captain of Aboriginal Industries lugger *Mulgrave*' (11). He, Mairu, is also reported to have transmitted 'the message' about the strike to Dauan during 1935.

8. He adds: 'There is no doubt whatever in my mind that the general strike amongst the natives was undertaken at the behest of the native priests on the Islands of Torres Strait in their endeavour to support the Bishop of Carpentaria

in his move to have the control of the aboriginals transferred from the State Government to the Commonwealth Government' (16).

9. Earlier in the report, O'Leary made explicit his move to interfere in the Church's province: 'It is considered that the Department as Protector of the Torres Strait Islanders should have some control over these Native Priests and the Bishop should be requested to immediately remove Sailor Gabey and Poey Passi from Office as such in Torres Strait or in any other Aboriginal community' (13).

10. In his Report on 11 May 1936, 14, O'Leary claims that informants at Mabuiag attributed this belief to the Darwin solicitor, Mr Fitzgerald: '...it is reasonable to assume', he continues 'that it originated from the Thursday Island Halfcaste Association who accepted the proposals of the Bishop of Carpentaria as likely to materialise'.

11. That this was no isolated event and that unrest was occurring in other islands is suggested by McLean's report of this incident: 'It was necessary to transfer one boat ("*ERUB*") under this regulation from Darnley Island to Murray Island during 1935 and threats of similar action were made at Mabuiag and Yam Islands but not proceeded with' (Report 4 March 1936, 2). George Mye states that the leader of the strike at Darnley Island was James Idagi, also known as James Williams (personal communication).

12. McLean mentions that the letter from Murray Island was written by 'Maru', whom I take to be Marou, also spelt Marau. McLean also states that a Murray Islander had told a crew member of one boat 'that Torres Strait was going to be handed over to the Commonwealth' (3).

13. See 'Copy of Minutes of Torres Strait Islanders Councillors' Conference held at Yorke Island 23 to 25 August 1937', in O'Leary to Chief Protector, 7 September 1937; Chief Protector to Under Home Secretary, summarising the conclusions of the Councillors' Conference, 29 September 1937 enclosed with 37/9577.

14. A decade later, his emphasis moved away from economic causes, although he gives no explanation for this change: 'The strike was directed specifically against the government, and the precipitating issue was the discrepancy between effort and reward on the Company boats' (1987, 52).

15. The 1979 amendments to the Act made each Island Council a corporate body being '...capable in law of suing and being sued, of acquiring, holding, leasing and otherwise dealing with property, real and personal, and of doing and suffering all such acts and things as bodies corporate may in law do and suffer'. (See Aborigines and Islanders Amendment Act 1979, 21.) Yet according to regulation 19 of the Act, all moneys raised in communities must be paid to an Island Fund which was subject to ultimate control by the DAIA.

16. 'Bio-power' is the increasing order of all realms of life under the guise of improving the welfare of the individual and the community as a whole. 'Pastoral power', the exercise of power over the individual's psyche, prizes out people's inner secrets for the sake of their salvation. For a discussion of 'bio-power', see Dreyfus and Rabinow 1982, xxii, 135; of 'pastoral power', see 213–16.

NOTES TO CHAPTER 8

1. See Sharp 1980c, Map A, Queensland Offshore Petroleum Permits, 1 July 1979. A major permit, which included the northwestern Islands, was taken out jointly by California Asiatic Oil Co and Texaco Overseas Petroleum; Gulf Interstate Overseas Ltd held the other permit in the Cape York–Torres Strait area. In February 1989, the latter permit was still retained (Q/IIP-Department of Mines, Queensland).

2. See *Wacando, Carlemo Kelly v Commonwealth of Australia and State of Queensland* (writ of summons dated 12 December 1978 in the High Court of Australia; transcript of proceedings, Sydney, 10 July 1979, 13 February 1980; Canberra, 5 and 6 May 1981, No 153 of 1978). Wacando 'claimed that Islands lying more than sixty miles from Cape York, which were annexed by Queensland, were *not* included within the boundaries of Queensland in 1901 when the Commonwealth of Australia was formed by the federation of states. In 1925 this error was rectified, but according to the legal challenge, this required a referendum which was not held' (Sharp 1980c, 3).

3. In 1980 Essington Investments had a nominal share capital of $10,000; its board of directors were Neil Ohlsson (also a director of First Northern Territory Cattle Co Ltd and of Nuclear Productions Pty Ltd) and Kevin N Norris (also a director of First Northern Territory Cattle Co Ltd).

Oil Company of Australia NL had an authorised capital of $100,000,000 in 1980. Its directors then were: Sir John Proud, also a director of Peko-Wallsend (Aust) which has a 25 per cent interest in the Ranger uranium mine in Arnhem Land, Northern Territory; Neville C Green, Lord Catto, AC Freeleagus, Sir D Hibberd and GA Weston (Stock Exchange Research Service, Sydney).

4. These events were covered by non-Queensland media; for example, the *Sydney Morning Herald, Age, Australian, Australian Financial Review.* In 1979–80 coverage of the Torres United Party's call for independence outside the Townsville-based media was the exception: see Sharp, Torres Strait Islanders Move for Independence, *National Times*, 29 December 1979, ABC Broadband, April 1980, Torres Strait Islanders: Their Quest for a Future, ABC Broadband, 1 October 1980.

5. See *Age* 27 June, 10 August 1988. At that time Essington Ltd was owned by Consolidated Press (Chairman, Mr Kerry Packer) and Bangaroo Investments (Mr Malcom Edwards's family company).

6. Originally, *Mabo and Others v State of Queensland and Commonwealth of Australia* (No 12 of 1982). AR Castan QC, B Hocking and BA Keon-Cohen, instructed by G McIntyre, appeared for the plaintiffs: Eddie Koiki Mabo, Celuia Salee, Sam Passi, Reverend Dave Passi and James Rice; Sam Passi withdrew from the case at that stage, and Celuia Salee died. In January 1992 Eddie Koiki Mabo also died; the two remaining plaintiffs were Reverend Dave Passi and James Rice. For a detailed discussion of the history of the case from 1982 to 1990 see Sharp 1990b, 1–31; 1991, 78–83; for a reflection on the judgement of the High Court, *Eddie Mabo and Others v State of Queensland*, 3 June 1992, see Sharp 1992b. On 22 November 1992 the Australian Human Rights Medal was awarded jointly to the five original Meriam plaintiffs and the Melbourne barrister Barbara Hocking (see Medal Honours Fallen Trio, *Sydney Morning Herald*, 23 November 1992; Ovation and Medal too Late for Battler, *Age*, 23 October 1992; Mabo Six Win Human Rights Award, *Torres News*, 27 November–3 December 1992.

7. Determination pursuant to reference of 27 February 1986 by the High Court of Australia to the Supreme Court of Queensland to hear and determine all issues of fact raised by the pleadings, particulars and further particulars in High Court action B12 of 1982, 16 November 1990, 11; hereafter D.

8. An excellent account of the Yolngu people at Yirrkala, Gove Peninsula, and their fight for recognition of their system of land tenure is given in Williams 1986. In two land cases in Canada brought by indigenous groups who are not sedentary cultivators, courts reached opposite conclusions to those of Judge Blackburn: *Calder v Attorney-General of British Columbia* (1970) 8 DLR (3d) 61; *Hamlet of Baker Lake v Minister of Indian Affairs and Northern Development* [1980] FCR 518 (see Sharp 1990b).

As sedentary cultivators Murray Islanders' claims may be novel: unlike the Yolngu at Yirrkala, who claimed communal title, the plaintiffs claimed specific plots of land themselves and on behalf of family groups (see Sharp 1991, 83–84). The Murray Islanders also claimed that their lands were acquired not by peaceful settlement but 'by naval act of war on or about 10 November 1879' (plaintiffs' statement of claim, 30 April 1982, 10, para 7; see also Chapter 1).

9. The above discussion on the *Murray Island Land* case draws heavily upon Sharp 1991.

10. As the *Brisbane Telegraph* stated on 12 February 1936: '...so great has become the resentful feeling of the natives that — though naturally as between island and

island they are not sympathetically disposed towards each other — they have "solidified" on the matter of their treatment by the Protection Department'.

11. Of critical importance in this process in the 1980s has been the role of educators, especially at James Cook University, and in particular the many-sided program of the Aboriginal and Islander Teacher Education Program (AITEP) begun in 1977.

12. The Aboriginal and Torres Strait Islander Commission (ATSIC), established by the Aboriginal and Torres Strait Islander Commission Act 1989, places emphasis on assisting community projects and marginalised groups: for example, women; its policy is consistent with the idea of assisting Islanders to build economic structures which will generate their own incomes. For a discussion and recommendations on Torres Strait development, see Arthur 1990.

13. Following the High court judgement in the *Murray Island Land* case in June 1992, new initiatives for united action by Islanders living at Mer (the newly announced official name of the three Murray Islands) and on the Australian mainland have been made. A meeting of the Meriam Council of Elders, formed on 11 February 1992, the Magani Malu Kes Committee and Meriam people living in Townsville, Mackay, Gladstone, Thursday Island and Darwin was held in Townsville from 7–8 August 1992. A meeting of the Council of Elders and the Murray Island (Mer) Community Council was held in Cairns with legal counsel to discuss questions of autonomy in the light of the High Court's recognition of customary title to land. The Council of Elders was formed to consider questions of traditional land, customary rules and the transmission of Meriam culture from older to younger people. See Murray Islanders to Form a Provisional Government, *Torres News*, 25 September–1 October 1992. On moves for autonomy in the Torres Strait as a whole, see *Cairns Post*, 9 October 1992. For a discussion of the issues for far northern Australian Aboriginal peoples arising from the High Court judgement, see Aboriginal Land Issues Workshop, Aboriginal and Torres Strait Islander Commission and Cape York Land Council, Cairns 27–28 August 1992; Surviving Columbus Conference, The Environment Today and Tomorrow, 30 September–2 October 1992, Report, 1–8.

     The High Court judgement has led quickly to claims by traditional owners on the mainland. These include the claiming of traditional lands north of the twelve degree parallel on Cape York Peninsula by the Injinoo Aboriginal Community Council on behalf of customary owners; major areas of land on Cape York Peninsula (see Cape York Land Council); a claim by the Northern Land Council against Nabalco Pty Ltd for mineral rights to 50,000 square kilometres in the Northern Territory (see Mabo Leaves 10 per cent of Nation's Land up for Claim for Blacks, Map of Claims, *Weekend Australian*, 5–6 December 1992; NT Aboriginal Mineral Claims Cause Uproar, *Age*, 5 December 1992).

14.   The old certitudes of the coloniser were manifest in three propositions: that the Murray Islanders are, or were, primitive people without any proprietary rights in land recognisable in British law; that the only valid evidence is the written or 'objective' (which puts a system of rights to succession in oral form outside the scope of the law); and that Islanders had made a total break with their traditional culture and were assimilated into the culture of the coloniser.

BIBLIOGRAPHY

BOOKS AND ARTICLES

Alavi, H.
    1973   Peasant Classes and Primordial Loyalties, *Journal of Peasant Studies* 1, 1 October.

Allen, J. and P. Corris (eds)
    1977   *The Journal of John Sweatman: A Nineteenth Century Surveying Voyage in North Australia and Torres Strait*, University of Queensland Press, St Lucia, Queensland.

Arthur, W.S.
    1990   (with the assistance of Victor McGrath) *Torres Strait Development Study 1989*, Australian Institute of Aboriginal Studies, Canberra.

Austin, T.
    1972   F.W. Walker and Papuan Industries Ltd, *Journal of the Papua New Guinea Society* 6(1), 38–62.

Babbage, R.
    1990   *The Strategic Significance of Torres Strait*, Strategic and Defence Studies Centre, Australian National University, Canberra.

Bach, J.
    1961   The Political Economy of Pearlshelling, *Economic History Review* 14(1), 105–14.

Bach, J.P.S.
    1961–63   The Pearlshelling Industry and the 'White Australia' Policy, *Historical Studies* 10, 37–40, 203–13.

Baudrillard, J.
    1975   *The Mirror of Production*, trans M. Poster, Telos Press, St Louis (1st French edn 1973).

Bayton, J.
    1965   *Cross over Carpentaria, being a History of the Church of England in Northern Australia from 1865–1965*, W.R. Smith & Paterson, Brisbane.

Beckett, J.R.
    1963   Politics of the Torres Strait Islands, PhD thesis, Australian National University, Canberra.

    1972   The Torres Strait Islanders. In D. Walker (ed), *Bridge and Barrier: The Natural and Cultural History of Torres Strait*, Australian National University, Canberra, 307–26.

1975   A Death in the Family: Some Torres Strait Ghost Stories. In L.R. Hiatt
            (ed), *Australian Aboriginal Mythology*, Australian Institute of
            Aboriginal Studies, Canberra, 163–81.

1977   The Torres Strait Islanders and the Pearling Industry: A Case of
            Internal Colonialism, *Aboriginal History* 1(1), 77–104.

1987   *Torres Strait Islanders: Custom and Colonialism*, Cambridge
            University Press, Cambridge.

Beckett, J. and Koiki Mabo
1992   Dancing in Torres Strait. In B. Reynolds (ed), *Material Culture
            Handbook, Northeast volume*, Crawford House Press, Bathurst.

Berndt, R.M. and C.H.
1987   *End of an Era: Aboriginal Labour in the Northern Territory*,
            Australian Institute of Aboriginal Studies, Canberra.

Bible
nd   *The Holy Bible* containing the Old and New Testaments translated
            out of the Original Tongues: and with the former translations
            diligently compared and revised by His Majesty's Special Command.
            Authorised King James version, Oxford University Press, Oxford.

Bleakley, J.W.
1961   *The Aborigines of Australia*, Methuen, Brisbane.

Book of Islanders
1984   Springs of Originality among the Torres Strait Islanders, Vol II, La
            Trobe University, Bundoora, Victoria. Based upon cassette recordings
            made by Nonie Sharp in the Torres Strait Islands and Cape York
            Peninsula 1978–84, Cassettes 001–128 as listed B167. (See Sharp 1984.)

Brierly, O.W.
1848–50   *Rattlesnake* Journals. Manuscripts, Drawings, Mitchell Library,
            Sydney. In D. Moore 1979.

1862   *Canoes in Australia*, Athenaeum, London.

Bruijn, J.V. de
1951   The Mansren Cult of Biak, *South Pacific* V(1), 1–10.

Burridge, K.
1960   *Mambu: A Melanesian Millennium*, Methuen, London.

1969   *Tangu Traditions: A Study of the Way of Life, Mythology, and
            Developing Experience of a New Guinea People*, Oxford University
            Press, Oxford.

Campbell, J.
1974   (assisted by M.J. Abadie) *The Mythic Image*, Princeton University
            Press, Princeton.

Carroll, J.M. (ed)
1969   Journey into Torres Strait, *Queensland Heritage* 2(1), 35–42.

Cass, D.
1988   Do the Torres Strait Islanders have a Valid Claim for Self-Determination at International Law?, Hons thesis, Law School, University of Melbourne.

Chinnery, E.W.P. and A.C. Haddon
1917   Five New Religious Cargo Cults in British New Guinea, *The Hibbert Journal* XV(3), 448–63.

Clune, F.
1970   *Captain Bully Hayes*, Angus & Robertson, Sydney.

Codrington, R.H.
1969   *The Melanesians: Studies in their Anthropology and Folklore*, Clarendon Press, Oxford (1st edn 1891).

Cohn, N.
1970   *The Pursuit of the Millennium: Revolutionary Millenarians and Mystical Anarchists of the Middle Ages*, Paladin, London (1st edn 1957).

Cornford, F.M.
1957   *From Religion to Philosophy: A Study in the Origins of Western Speculation*, Harper and Row, New York (1st edn c1912).

Daly, J.
1979   Cosmic Harmony and Political Thinking in Early Stuart England, *Trans Amer Philosophical Society* 69, 1–41.

Done, J. (Rev)
1915–26 Diaries and Personal Papers, manuscript in possession of his son, T.E. Done, New South Wales; see also *Wings across the Sea*, compiled by Barbara Stevenson, 1987, Boolarong Publications, Brisbane.

Douglas, J.
1899–   The Islands and Inhabitants of Torres Strait, Address to the Royal
1900   Geographical Society of Australasia, Queensland, 17 January 1900. In *Queensland Branch, Queensland Geographical Journal* XV, 25–40.

Douglas, M.
1978   *Implicit Meanings: Essays in Anthropology*, Routledge and Kegan Paul, London.

Dreyfus, H.L. and P. Rabinow
1982   *Michel Foucault: Beyond Structuralism amd Hermeneutics*, University of Chicago, Chicago.

Duncan, H.
1975   *Socio-Economic Conditions in the Torres Strait*, Vol I, *The Torres Strait Islanders*, Australian National University, Canberra.

Durkheim, E. and M. Mauss
1969   *Primitive Classification*, trans R. Needham, Cohen and West, London (1st French edn 1903).

Eliade, M.

   1959a   *Cosmos and History: The Myth of the Eternal Return*, trans W.R.
            Trask, Harper and Row, New York (1st French edn 1949).

   1959b   *The Sacred and the Profane: The Nature of Religion*, trans W.R. Trask,
            Harcourt Brace, New York (1st edn not cited).

   1965   *The Two and the One*, trans J.M. Cohen, Harvill Press, London (1st
            French edn 1962).

   1974   *Patterns in Comparative Religion*, trans R. Sheed, Meridian, New
            American Library, New York (1st English edn 1958).

Evans, G.

   1972   Thursday Island 1878–1914: A Plural Society, BA (Hons) thesis,
            University of Queensland, St Lucia, Queensland.

Evans-Pritchard, E.

   1940   *The Nuer*, Clarendon Press, Oxford.

Fisk, E.K., H. Duncan and A. Kehl

   1975   *The Islander Population in the Cairns and Townsville Area*, Vol III,
            The Torres Strait Islanders, Australian National University, Canberra.

Fisk, E.K., M. Tait, W.E. Holder and M.L. Treadgold

   1975   *The Border and Associated Problems*, Vol V, *The Torres Strait
            Islanders*, Australian National University, Canberra.

Flinders, M.

   1814   *A Voyage to Terra Australis; Undertaken...in the Years 1801, 1802,
            and 1803, in His Majesty's Ship the 'Investigator'...*, two volumes with
            atlas, G. and W. Nicol, London.

Frankfort, H., H.A. Frankfort, J.A. Wilson, T. Jacobsen and W.A. Irwin

   1946   *Before Philosophy, The Intellectual Adventure of Ancient Man: An
            Essay on Speculative Thought in the Ancient Near East*, University
            of Chicago Press, Chicago.

Geertz, C.

   1966   Religion as a Cultural System. In M. Banton (ed), *Anthropological
            Approaches to the Study of Religion*, Tavistock, London.

Gellner, E.

   1974   *Legitimation of Belief*, Cambridge University Press, Cambridge.

Gill, W.W.

   1876   *Life in the Southern Isles*, Religious Tract Society, London.

Gladwin, T.

   1964   Culture and Logical Process. In W.H. Goodenough (ed), *Explorations
            in Cultural Anthropology: Essays in Honor of George Peter Murdock*,
            McGraw Hill, New York, 167–77.

Godelier, M.

   1977   *Perspectives in Marxist Anthropology*, trans R. Brain, Cambridge
            University Press, Cambridge.

Golson, J.
1972   Land Connections, Sea Barriers and the Relationship of Australian and New Guinea Prehistory. In D. Walker, (ed), *Bridge and Barrier: The Natural and Cultural History of Torres Strait*, Australian National University Press, Canberra, 375–97.

Goody, J.
1962   *Death, Property and the Ancestors: A Study of the Mortuary Customs of the Lodagaa of West Africa*, Tavistock, London.

Graves, R.
1982   *The Greek Myths*, two volumes, Penguin, Harmondsworth (1st edn 1955).

Griffin, J.
1977   Impasse in Torres Strait, *Australian Outlook*, 31(2), 217–40.

Griffin, J. (ed)
1976   *The Torres Strait Border Issue: Consolidation, Conflict or Compromise*, Townsville College of Advanced Education, Townsville, Queensland.

Haddon, A.C.
1890   The Ethnography of the Western Tribe of Torres Straits, *Journal of the Royal Anthropological Institute* 19, 297–440.

1894   *The Decorative Art of British New Guinea: A Study in Papuan Ethnography*, Academy House, Dublin.

1901   *Headhunters, Black, White, and Brown*, Methuen, London.

Haddon, A.C. (ed)
1904–35 *Reports of the Cambridge Anthropological Expedition to Torres Straits*, Cambridge University Press, Cambridge. 1904, Vol V, *Sociology, Magic and Religion of the Western Islanders*; 1908, Vol VI, *Sociology, Magic and Religion of the Eastern Islanders*; 1912, *Arts and Crafts*; 1935, Vol I, *General Ethnography*.

Hall, R.
1980   Aborigines and the Army: The Second World War Experience, *Defence Force Journal*, 24.

Hamilton, G.
1793   *A Voyage Round the World in His Majesty's Frigate 'Pandora': Performed under the Direction of Captain Edwards in the years 1790, 1791 and 1792*, Berwick, London.

Harris, D.R.
1975   Traditional Patterns of Plant-Food Procurement in the Cape York Peninsula and Torres Strait Islands, Report on Fieldwork carried out August–November 1974, Department of Geography, University of London.

Hertz, R.
    1960   A Contribution to the Study of the Collective Representation of Death. In *Death and the Right Hand*, trans R. Needham and C. Glencoe, Free Press, Illinois, 27–86 (1st French edn 1907).

Hill, E.
    1971   *My Love Must Wait: The Story of Matthew Flinders*, Lloyd O'Neil, Hawthorn, Victoria (1st edn 1941).

Hurley, F.
    1924   *Pearls and Savages: Adventures in the Air, on Land and Sea — in New Guinea*, G.P. Putnam and Sons, New York.

Idriess, I.
    1933   *Drums of Mer*, Halstead, Sydney.

Jagg, F.C. (Rev)
    1867–68 The Jagg Reports, 1867–1868. In D. Moore 1979, 252–56.

Johannes, R.E. and J.W. MacFarlane (eds)
    1991   *Traditional Fishing in the Torres Strait Islands*, Commonwealth Scientific and Industrial Research Organisation, Division of Fisheries, Hobart, Tasmania.

Jukes, J.B.
    1847   *Narrative of the Surveying Voyage of HMS 'Fly', commanded by Captain F.P. Blackwood, during the Years 1842–1846*, two volumes, Boone, London.

Kehoe-Forutan, S.J.
    1988   Torres Strait Independence, a Chronicle of Events, Research Report No 1, Department of Geographical Sciences, University of Queensland, St Lucia, Queensland.

Kennedy, F.
    1991   Knowing Who I Am, manuscript.

Kennett, W.
    1867–68 The Kennett Report, February 1867–June 1868. In D. Moore 1979, 237–51.

King, P.P. (ed)
    1837   *Voyage to Torres Strait in Search of the Survivors of the Ship 'Charles Eaton', which was Wrecked upon the Barrier Reefs in the month of August 1834 in Her Majesty's Colonial Schooner, 'Isabella', C.M. Lewis, Commander...with a copy of Flinders Chart, and a Vocabulary of the Language of the Murray and Darnley Islanders*, Statham, Sydney.

Kirk, G.S. and J.E. Raven
    1962   *The Presocratic Philosophers: A Critical History with a Selection of Texts*, Cambridge University Press, Cambridge (1st edn 1957).

Kitaoji, H.
1977   The Myth of Bomai: Its Structure and Contemporary Significance for the Murray Islanders, Torres Strait, *Min Zoku Gaka Kenkyû (Japanese Journal of Ethnology)* 42, 209–12.

1978   Culture of the Torres Strait People, *Arena* 50, 54–63.

1980   Miriam Perceptions of Themselves and Those around Them: Cognitive Ordering after One Hundred Years of Culture Contact, paper presented to Australian Anthropological Society Conference, University of Queensland, St Lucia, Queensland.

1982   Coconut, Cross, and Pearl, manuscript.

Laade, W.
1971   *Oral Traditions and Written Documents on the History and Ethnography of the Northern Torres Strait Islands, Saiba-Dauan-Boigu*, Vol I, Franz Steiner, Wiesbaden.

Landtman, G.
1917   *The Folk-Tales of the Kiwai Papuans*, Finnish Society of Literature, Helsingfors.

1927   *The Kiwai Papuans of British New Guinea: A Nature-Born Instance of Rousseau's Ideal Community*, Macmillan, London.

Lanternari, V.
1963   *The Religions of the Oppressed: A Study of Modern Messianic Cults*, trans L. Sergio, Knopf, New York (1st edn not cited).

Lawrie, M.
1970   *Myths and Legends of Torres Strait*, University of Queensland Press, St Lucia, Queensland.

Lee, I.
1920   *Captain Bligh's Second Voyage to the South Sea*, Longmans, Green and Co, London.

Lévi-Strauss, C.
1969   *The Elementary Structures of Kinship*, trans J.H. Bell, J.R. von Sturmer, and R. Needham, Beacon Press, Boston (1st French edn 1949).

1967   *Tristes Tropiques*, trans J. Russel, Atheneum, New York (1st French edn 1955).

1978a   *Myth and Meaning*, Routledge and Kegan Paul, London (1st edn not cited).

1978b   *Structural Anthropology*, Vol 2, trans M. Layton, Penguin, Harmondsworth (1st French edn 1973).

Lewis, Captain. C.M.
1837   Voyage of the Colonial Schooner *Isabella* — In Search of the Survivors of the *Charles Eaton*, *Nautical Magazine* VI, 654–63 (with chart), 753–60, 799–806.

Lloyd, G.E.R.
  1971   *Polarity and Analogy: Two Types of Argumentation in Early Greek
          Thought*, Cambridge University Press, Cambridge (1st edn 1966).

Loos, N.
  1982   *Invasion and Resistance: Aboriginal-European Relations on the
          North Queensland Frontier*, Australian National University Press,
          Canberra.

Macdonald, G.
  1980   Adoption and Social Organization among the Saibailaig of Torres Strait,
          BA (Hons) thesis, Sociology Department, La Trobe University,
          Bundoora, Victoria.

McDougall, W.
  1912   *An Introduction to Social Psychology*, Methuen, London.

McFarlane, S.
  1888   *Among the Cannibals of New Guinea*, London Missionary Society,
          London.

MacFarlane, W.H.
  1950   The 'Quetta' Memorial, *Cummins and Campbell Monthly Magazine*
          26(9), 44.

MacGillivray, J.
  1852   *Narrative of the Voyage of H.M.S. 'Rattlesnake' Commanded by the
          late Captain Owen Stanley, during the Years 1846–1850*, two volumes,
          Boone, London.

McMillan, C.
  1982   *Women, Reason and Nature: Some Philosophical Problems with
          Feminism*, Basil Blackwell, Oxford.

Mabo, E.K.
  1982   Land Rights in the Torres Strait. In E. Olbrei (ed), *Black Australians:
          The Prospects for Change*, Students Union, James Cook University,
          Townsville, Queensland, 143–48.

Mackie, F.
  1985   *The Status of Everyday Life: A Sociological Excavation of the
          Prevailing Framework of Perception*, Routledge and Kegan Paul,
          London.

Malinowski, B.
  1961   *Argonauts of the Western Pacific: An Account of Native Enterprise
          and Adventure in the Archipelagoes of Melanesian New Guinea*,
          Dutton, New York (1st edn 1922).

Marcuse, H.
  1977   *Reason and Revolution: Hegel and the Rise of Social Theory*, Routledge
          and Kegan Paul, London.

Markham, C. (ed)
1904   *The Voyages of Pedro Fernandez de Quiros*, Vol 2, A Letter from Luis
        Vaez de Torres to His Majesty, Manilla, 12 July 1607, Hakluyt Society,
        London, 455–66.

Marwick, M.G.
1965   *Sorcery in its Social Setting: A Study of the Northern Rhodesian
        Ceûa*, Manchester University Press, Manchester.

Marx, K.
1949   *Capital: A Critical Analysis of Capital Production*, trans S. Moore
        and E. Aveling, D. Torr (ed), Allen and Unwin, London (1st German
        edn 1867).

1970   *A Contribution to the Critique of Political Economy*, trans S.W.
        Ryazanskaya, Progress Publishers, Moscow.

Mauss, M.
1970   *The Gift: Forms and Functions of Exchange in Archaic Societies*,
        trans I. Cunnison, Cohen and West, London (1st French edn 1950).

1979   *Seasonal Variations of the Eskimo: A Study in Social Morphology*,
        trans J.J. Fox, Routledge and Kegan Paul, London (1st French edn
        1950).

Melville, H.S.
1849   *Sketches in Australia and the Adjacent Islands, selected from a
        number taken during the surveying voyage of H.M. 'Fly' and
        'Bramble', under the command of Captain F.P. Blackwood, RN,
        during the years 1842–1847*, Dickenson and Co, London.

Meston, A.
1896   *Report on the Aboriginals of Queensland to the Home Secretary*, QV&P,
        Vol 4, Part 1.

Moore, D.R.
1979   *Islanders and Aborigines at Cape York: An Ethnographic
        Reconstruction based on the 1848-1850 'Rattlesnake' Journals of O.W.
        Brierly and Information He Obtained from Barbara Thompson*,
        Australian Institute of Aboriginal Studies, Canberra.

1984   *The Torres Strait Collections of A.C. Haddon: A Descriptive Catalogue*,
        British Museum, London.

Moresby, J.
1976   *Discoveries and Surveys in New Guinea and the D'Entrecasteaux
        Islands — A Cruise in Polynesia and Visits to the Pearl-Shelling
        Stations in Torres Straits in H.M.S. 'Basilisk'*, Murray, London.

Nandy, A.
1985   *The Intimate Enemy*, Oxford University Press, Bombay.

Narokobi, B.
1981   Christianity and Melanesian Cosmos, manuscript, Port Moresby.

Nelson, H.
   1972   *Papua New Guinea: Black Unity or Black Chaos?* Penguin, Ringwood,
            Victoria.

O'Dowd, B.
   1909   *Dawnward?*, Standard Publishing Company, Melbourne (bound with
            The Silent Land..., 1913) (1st edn 1903).

Olbrei, E. (ed)
   1982   *Black Australians: The Prospects for Change*, Students Union, James
            Cook University, Townsville, Queensland.

Orrell, J.
   1969   Pasi — A Story of the Islands, typescript of the manuscript by A.O.C.
            Davies edited and compiled by Orrell for Bishop H.F. Jamieson,
            Thursday Island, 1–282 plus editor's comment, i–x.

Osborne, B.
   1988   An Analysis of Takeover of Education in Torres Strait, paper presented
            to National Conference, Culture: Theory and Practice, ICPS, Griffith
            University, Nathan.

Otto, R.
   1936   *The Idea of the Holy: An Inquiry into the Non-Rational Factor in
            the Idea of the Divine and its Relation to the Rational*, trans J.W.
            Harvey, Oxford University Press, London (1st English edn 1923).

Paracelsus
   1913   *Liber Paramirum*, Paris (trans Corillot de Givry).

Peel, G.
   1947   *Isles of the Torres Straits*, Current Book Distributors, Sydney.

Pilot, B. (compiler)
   c1973   Diocese of North Queensland, *Eastern and Western Hymn Book and
            Liturgy*, Torres Strait Island Ministry, arranged by Rev Boggo Pilot,
            Townsville, Queensland.

Polanyi, K.
   1965a   Aristotle Discovers the Economy. In K. Polanyi, C.M. Arensberg and
            M.W. Pearson (eds), *Trade and Markets in the Early Empires*, The
            Free Press, New York, 64–94 (1st edn 1957).

   1965b   The Economy as Instituted Process. In K. Polanyi, C.M. Arensberg
            and M.W. Pearson (eds), *Trade and Markets in the Early Empires*,
            The Free Press, New York.

Portlock, N.
   1920   The Journal of Lieutenant Portlock. In I. Lee, *Captain Bligh's Second
            Voyage...*, London, 223–78. (See I. Lee 1920.)

Radin, P.
   1957   *Primitive Man as Philosopher*, Dover, New York (1st edn 1927).

Radin, P. (ed)
1963   *The Autobiography of a Winnebago Indian: Life—Ways, Acculturation, and the Peyote Cult*, Dover, New York (facsimile of 1st edn 1920).

Ray, S.H.
1907   *Reports of the Cambridge Anthropological Expedition to Torres Strait*, Vol III, *Linguistics*, Cambridge University Press, Cambridge.

Read, K.E.
1959   Leadership and Consensus in a New Guinea Society, *American Anthropologist* 61, 425–36.

Riesman, D.
1955   *The Lonely Crowd: A Study of the Changing American Character*, Doubleday Anchor, New York (1st edn 1950).

Rigsby, B.
1992   The Languages of Torres Strait, in B. Reynolds (ed), *Northeast volume*, Crawford House, Bathurst, New South Wales.

Roth, W.E.
1901–06   *North Queensland Ethnography Bulletins* 1–8, Government Printer, Brisbane.

1907–10   *North Queensland Ethnography Bulletins* 9–18. In *Australian Museum Records*, 6–8.

Sahlins, M.
1981   *Historical Metaphors and Mythical Realities: Structure in the Early History of the Sandwich Islands Kingdom*, University of Michigan Press, Ann Arbor (ASAO Special Publications No 1).

Scott, E.
1914   *The Life of Captain Matthew Flinders RN*, Angus & Robertson, Sydney.

Scott, J.M.
1987   Torres Strait Independence: An Historical Perspective, mimeograph, Thursday Island, 23 October, 1–15.

Segundo, J.L.
1977   *The Liberation of Theology*, Gill and Macmillan, Dublin (1st edn 1975).

Seligman, C.G.
1904–08   In *Reports of the Cambridge Anthropological Expedition to Torres Straits*, Vol V 1904; Vol III 1907; Vol VI 1908.

Sharp, G.
1989   After Development, *Arena* 87, 5–17.

Sharp, N.
1975   Millenarian Movements: Their Meaning in Melanesia, in *Festschrift Jean Martin*, Sociology Department, La Trobe University, Bundoora, Victoria, 299–359.

1979   Torres Strait Islanders Move for Independence, *National Times*, 22–29
            December.

1980a   Torres Strait Island, A Great Cultural Refusal: The Meaning of the
            Maritime Strike of 1936, Department of Sociology, La Trobe
            University, Bundoora, Victoria, mimeograph, 1–25, plus appendix,
            bibliography.

1980b   Torres Strait Islands 1897–1979: Theme for an Overview, Sociology
            Paper No 52, Sociology Department, La Trobe University, Bundoora,
            Victoria.

1980c   Torres Strait Islands, The Case for Independence: The Underlying
            Issues, mimeograph, Melbourne.

1982a   The Seafaring Peoples of the Cape York Region: Themes in a Quest
            for Homelands. In E. Olbrei (ed), *Black Australians: The Prospects
            for Change*, Students Union, James Cook University, Townsville,
            Queensland, 148–62.

1982b   Culture Clash in the Torres Strait Islands: The Maritime Strike of 1936,
            Journal of the Royal Historical Society of Queensland, 107–26.

1984   Springs of Originality among the Torres Strait Islanders, two volumes,
            PhD thesis, La Trobe University, Bundoora, Victoria.

1987   Faces of Power in the Torres Strait Islands: The 1980s and the 1930s,
            paper presented at the 57th ANZAAS Conference, James Cook
            University, Townsville, Queensland.

1988   A Melanesian Journey: New Ways in Co-operation, *Arena* 83, 50–80.

1989   The Flower of Meriam Identities, manuscript, 1–25.

1990a   A Second Invasion: Aboriginal Space at Cape York, *Arena* 92, 32–40.

1990b   Comparative Cultural Perspectives in the *Murray Island Land* Case,
            Law in Context 8(1), 1–31.

1990c   Armed Space at the Top End?, *Arena* 93, 29–33.

1991   A Landmark: The Murray Island Case, *Arena* 94, 78–93.

1992a   *Footprints along the Cape York Sandbeaches*, Aboriginal Studies Press,
            Canberra.

1992b   Scales from the Eyes of Justice, *Arena* 99/100, 55–61.

Shineberg, D.
1967   *They Came for Sandalwood: A Study of the Sandalwood Trade in
            the South-West Pacific 1830–1865*, Melbourne University Press,
            Carlton, Victoria.

Shnukal, A.
1983a   Blaikman Tok: Changing Attitudes to Torres Strait Creole, *Australian
            Aboriginal Studies* 2, 25–33.

1983b   Torres Strait Creole: The Growth of a New Torres Strait Language,
            Aboriginal History VII(2), 173–85.

1985   The Spread of Torres Strait Creole to the Central Islands of Torres Strait, *Aboriginal History* 9(1–2), 220–34.

1988   *Broken: An Introduction to the Creole Language of Torres Strait,* Pacific Linguistics, Series C107, Australian National University, Canberra.

Sohn-Rethel, A.
1978   *Intellectual and Manual Labour,* Macmillan, London.

Stanley, O.
1848–49 *Voyage of the 'Rattlesnake',* Album of Sketches, Mitchell Library, Sydney, Folio PX. C281.

Stevenson, B.
1987   See J. Done.

Sweatman, J.
1847   Journal of a Surveying Voyage to the North-east Coast of Australia and Torres Strait in H.M. Schooner *Bramble,* Lieutenant C.B. Yule, Commander, 1842–1847. Vol 2, manuscript, including illustrations by H.S. Melville, Mitchell Library, Sydney. (See J. Allen and P. Corris.)

Thaiday, W.
1981   *Under the Act,* North Queensland Black Publishing Co, Townsville, Queensland.

Thomson, D.F.
1933   The Hero Cult, Initiation and Totemism on Cape York, *Journal of the Royal Anthropological Institute of Great Britain and Ireland* LXIII, July–December, 453–537, with Plates XXVII–XXXVI.

1939   *The Seasonal Factor in Human Culture: Illustrated from the Life of a Contemporary Nomadic Group,* reprinted from the proceedings of the Prehistoric Society, paper No 10, July–December, 209–21 with plates.

1952   Notes on some Primitive Watercraft in Northern Australia, *Man* 1 (January), 1–5 with map.

van den Berghe, P.L.
1967   *Race and Racism: A Comparative Perspective,* Wiley, New York.

Vanderwal, R.L.
1973   The Torres Strait: Protohistory and Beyond, occasional paper, 2, Anthropology Museum, University of Queensland, St Lucia, Queensland, October, 157–94.

van Gennep, A.
1969   *The Rites of Passage,* trans M.G. Vizedom, University of Chicago Press, Chicago (1st French edn 1909).

Wagner, R.
1981   *The Invention of Culture,* Prentice-Hall, Englewood Cliffs.

Waiko, J.D.D.
    1982   Be Jijimo: A History according to the Tradition of the Binandere, PhD
                thesis, Australian National University, Canberra.

Walker, D.
    1972   Bridge and Barrier. In *Bridge and Barrier: The Natural and Cultural
                History of Torres Strait*, Australian National University Press,
                Canberra.

Weber, M.
    1952   *Ancient Judaism*, trans H. Gerth and D. Martindale, Free Press,
                Glencoe, Illinois (1st German edn 1921).

Webster, C.
    1980   *From Paracelsus to Newton: Magic and the Making of Modern Science*,
                Cambridge University Press, Cambridge.

Wemyss, T.
    1837   *Narrative of the Melancholy Shipwreck of the Ship 'Charles Eaton',
                and the Inhuman Massacre of the Passengers and Crew...*, Stockton.

White, G.
    1917   *Round about the Torres Straits: A Record of Australian Church
                Missions*, Central Board of Missions, London.

Wilkin, A.
    1904–08   In A.C. Haddon (ed) *Reports of the Cambridge Anthropological
                Expedition to Torres Straits*, Vol V 1904; Vol III 1907; Vol VI 1908,
                Cambridge University Press, Cambridge.

Williams, N.
    1986   *The Yolngu and their Land*, Australian Institute of Aboriginal Studies,
                Canberra.

Worsley, P.
    1970   *The Trumpet shall Sound*, Paladin, London (1st edn 1957).

Wolpe, H.
    1975   The Theory of Internal Colonialism: The South African Case. In I.
                Oxaal, T. Barnett and D. Booth, (eds), *Beyond the Sociology of
                Development*, Routledge and Kegan Paul, London.

GOVERNMENT PUBLICATIONS

QUEENSLAND

Proclamation notifying that 'Certain Islands in Torres Strait lying between the
Continent of Australia and the Island of New Guinea' are part of the Colony of
Queensland, 18 July 1879 (supplement to *Queensland Government Gazette* of 19
July 1879, XXV, 10, 21 July 1879) under provision of the Queensland Coast Islands
Act of 1879.

Aboriginals Protection and Restriction of the Sale of Opium Acts 1897–1939; Aboriginals Preservation and Protection Act of 1939, 3 Geo VI No 6; Torres Strait Islanders Act 1939, 3 Geo VI No 7; Community Services (Torrres Strait) Act 1984, No 52; Queensland Coast Islands Declaratory Act 1985; Aborigines and Torres Strait Islanders (Land Holding) Act 1985, No 41; Torres Strait Islander Land Act 1991.

Report of the Western Pacific Royal Commission, 16 October 1883, QV&P, Vol II. Report of the Royal Commission... 1908, QPP 1909.

Queensland Votes and Proceedings to year ended 31 December 1901: reports of the Government Resident at Thursday Island to the Chief Secretary: reports of the Inspector of Pearl-shell and Bêche-de-mer Fisheries.

Queensland Parliamentary Papers 1902–. Annual Reports of the Northern Protector of Aboriginals to the year ending 1903; Annual Reports of the Chief Protector of Aboriginals to the Under Secretary, Home Secretary's Department to the year ended 31 December 1917; Aboriginals/Aboriginal Department — Information Contained in Reports for the years ended 1918–39; Annual Reports of the Director of Native Affairs (DNA), of Aboriginal and Island Affairs (DAIA), of Aboriginal and Islanders Advancement (DAIA) for the years ended 1939–84, of the Department of Community Services (DCS) 1985–91.

COMMONWEALTH

The Torres Strait Boundary, Report and Appendixes, Joint Committee on Foreign Affairs and Defence, Parliamentary Paper, Canberra, No 416/1976. Treaty between Australia and the Independent State of Papua New Guinea concerning Sovereignty and Maritime Boundaries, in the area between the two Countries including the area known as Torres Strait, and Related Matters, signed at Sydney 18 December 1978, Government Printer, Canberra.

Aboriginal and Torres Strait Islander Commission Act 1989.

ARCHIVAL SOURCES

London Missionary Society Records relating to the South Seas 1796–1906. Reels M1–12, especially 11 and 12; South Seas Journals 1796–1899, Reels 1–10; Papua Journals 1872–1901, Reel 11; Papua Reports 1882–1906, Microfilm AJCP Australian National Library, Canberra (LMS Archives, Livingstone House, London).

Chester, H.M. Extracts from Letter-Books of the Police Magistrate at Somerset, Queensland, manuscript, Dixson Library, Sydney, 1869–71. Somerset Magistrate's Letter-Book, manuscript, Oxley Library, Brisbane, 1872–77.

Queensland State Archives. Aboriginal Sub-Department, Department of Health and Home Affairs, Correspondence, especially records for the years 1930–39. See especially Chief Protector, Torres Strait Is. — Refusal of Natives to work on boats, 14 January 1936, 36/1761; Chief Protector, Torres Strait Is. — *Strike* — Mr O'Leary's Preliminary Report, 22 February 1936, 36/4579; W.S. Munro, Refusal of Natives to work boats, 20 April 1936, 36/4901; Chief Protector, Torres Straits. Refusal of Natives to work boats. Mr O'Leary's Report, 18 May 1936, 36/5511; Chief Protector, Thursday Island — Protector and P.M. [Police Magistrate] — creation of separate positions, 10 June 1936, 36/5997; Chief Protector, Torres Strait Islanders. Refusal of Natives to work boats, 26 June 1936, 36/5997. Above reports and other correspondence enclosed with letters top numbered to 36/5997.

Department of Public Instruction, especially 1903–04, EDU/Z1993.

COURT RECORDS AND PROCEEDINGS

Murray Island Native Court Records, 1911–39 (incomplete).

Milirrpum v Nabalco Pty Ltd and Commonwealth of Australia (1971) 17 *Federal Law Reports* 141–253.

Wacando, Carlemo Kelly v Commonwealth of Australia and State of Queensland, writ of summons No 153 and statement of claim dated 12 December 1978 in the High Court of Australia. Transcript of proceedings, Sydney, 10 July 1979, 13 February 1980.

Mabo and Others v State of Queensland and Commonwealth of Australia, in the High Court of Australia, No 12 of 1982. Statement of claim by five Murray Island plaintiffs, 2 May 1982; affidavit of P.J. Killoran for the first defendant, 16 August 1982 with accompanying exhibits A–W; transcripts of proceedings before High Court of Australia, Supreme Court of Queensland 1984–89. *Eddie Mabo and Another v State of Queensland and Another* (1988) 166 *Commonwealth Law Reports* 186, High Court, reasons for judgement on plaintiffs' demurrer (1985), 8 December 1988. Determination pursuant to reference of 27 February 1986 by High Court to Supreme Court of Queensland to hear and determine all issues of fact raised by the pleadings, particulars and further particulars in High Court action B12 of 1982, 16 November 1990 (determination). *Eddie Mabo and Others v State of Queensland* (1992) 66 *Australian Law Journal Reports* 408 (High Court, Full Bench, 3 June 1992).

SERIALS AND NEWSPAPERS

The Carpentarian, Anglican Diocese of Carpentaria.

The Islander, Aboriginal Sub-Department, Department of Health and Home Affairs (1936–37).

Age, Australian, Australian Financial Review, Brisbane Courier-Mail, Brisbane Telegraph, Cairns Post, Canberra Times, National Times, Papua New Guinea Post-Courier, Sydney Morning Herald, Torres News, Townsville Daily Bulletin, Unemployed Clarion, Workers Weekly.

UNWRITTEN SOURCES

RECORDINGS 001–138

Cassettes 001–138 recorded between December 1978 and June 1984: Thursday Island, Badu, Murray Island, Townsville, Darnley Island, Kubin Village (Moa Island), Cowal Creek, Cairns, St Paul's Community (Moa Island), Weipa, Lockhart River, Brisbane. Recordings are mainly life-stories of Torres Strait Islanders, cultural traditions old and new, narratives of events experienced by themselves or handed down. All but four are by Islanders, Aborigines and others born in the Torres Strait or northern Cape York region. They include songs, dancing, music, chants, hymns; ninety-one cassettes are ninety minutes, forty-seven are sixty minutes (some incomplete). In the possession of the author.

Transcripts are listed in Book of Islanders, B167. Other recordings quoted in the text are cited in the notes to respective chapters; five cassettes are recordings made in July/August 1980 and form part of a series, Torres Strait Islanders: Their Quest for a Future (see below, ABC Broadband).

TORRES STRAIT/CAPE YORK COLLECTIONS

Torres Strait Collection of A.C. Haddon; W.E. Roth Collections on Torres Strait, Australian Museum, Sydney; Torres Strait Collection, Queensland Museum, Brisbane; Donald Thomson Collection, University of Melbourne, housed in the Museum of Victoria.

OTHER SOURCES

Australian Council of Churches Seminar on Torres Strait Border, Stanmore, New South Wales, 18–19 March 1977, six cassettes.

ABC Radio Recordings, The Case for Sovereignty, Torres Strait Islanders, Broadband, April 1980; Torres Strait Islanders: Their Quest for a Future, Broadband, 1 October 1980; The *Murray Island Land* Case, The Law Report, September 1986 and 19 April 1988; Sovereignty in the Torres Strait, Late Night Live, 17 March 1988.

National Film and Sound Archive, A.C. Haddon, Torres Strait, untitled 1898; Frank Hurley, Pearls and Savages 1924; The Native Problem in Queensland, Aboriginal Sub-Department, Health and Home Affairs, c1937.

Yarra Bank Films, Trevor Graham (Director), *Land Bilong Islanders*, fifty-minute documentary 1990.

GLOSSARY

Language words listed in the glossary are in Meriam Mir unless indicated otherwise. I would like to thank the late Sam Passi, Meriam authority on Meriam Mir for his valuable assistance in the compilation of this glossary.

ad giz: time of coming into being.

Adai (KLY): Cape York Peninsula.

adud wer: star in southwest as *mek* for *kipa gogob*.

Aet: *see Zogo le.*

agud: god.

aritarit: planting, garden preparation, a Malo word from *arit*, to plant.

arit kerker: time to plant.

au au nei: generic class.

au kop: sacred space facing *pelak*, Malo initiation ground.

au nar: large ships.

au nei: big name, species or generic name.

Au Sasrimsasrim: God the Almighty Power.

augud (KLY): totem, god.

bakei: west wind, with which Giar Pit people are associated.

Begegiz: headquarters of Peibre *nosik*.

beizam: tiger shark.

Beizam *boai*: the dancers in the Malo ceremonies, Shark brethren who had charge of the sacred emblems of Malo.

bid: dolphin.

biribiro: kingfisher.

boai: crew man, crew, mob, members of a fraternity.

Bomai: secret and sacred name of the god of the Meriam.

Broken: Torres Strait Creole, Blaikman, Big Thap, Pizin.

dabor: mackerel.

Dam: *mamgiz* or sacred place at which the Bomai mask is worn and kept in *pelak*.

Damut: Dalrymple Island.

dari: headdress of white crane feathers.

Dauar: one of the three Murray Islands.

deumer: Torres Strait pigeon.

deumer lub: a single Torres Strait pigeon feather worn at the back of the head by *kesi*.

dibadiba: dove.

Eip Ged: middle islands, Central Islands.

elikup: boundary marker cut from *ur sekerseker*.

Em (TSC): the singular, non-reciprocal, the wild, the 'other condition'.

emes le: person who follows behind *opole* in Malo ceremony.

eneo: wongai fruit or tree, wild plum.

Erub: Darnley, Darnley's Island.

galbol: whale.

Ganomi: ancient warrior culture hero of the Meriam.

gared: south wind with which Magaram people are associated.

gared: southern division of *sager*.

Gazir: one of the three sacred
  places at which the Bomai mask
  is worn.

ged: home-place, homeland,
  habitable island with water
  resources, womb.

ged kem le: landowner.

gedub: garden.

gedub boai: garden groupings of
  the sacred order of Malo-Bomai
  composed of easterly to southeast
  clans.

Gelam: mythical culture hero who
  travelled from Moa, highest hill
  on Mer shaped like a dugong.

gelar: taboo, prohibition, rule, law,
  commandment.

gelar tonar: law and custom.

giz: root of a tree, origin, spring.

giz ged: place of origin, beginnings.

giz le: founding person.

ikok: five sacred chants of Malo.

Injinoo: Cowal Creek.

irewed ziai: west-southwest
  division of ziai with which Eip
  Kes and Giz people are associated.

irmer wed: rain songs, chants.

Ka nali wauri: I am *wauri*, I am
  your *tebud*.

kakigaba: variety of yam with roots
  near the surface.

keber: spirit ceremonies.

kebi nei: small name, variety.

Kek (Ilwel): planet Venus.

kekuruk le: medicine people.

kemerkemer mai: a circular fretted
  pearl shell sacred ornament.

Keo Deudai: Australian mainland
  (KLY: Kie Daudai).

Keo Ged: back islands, Western
  Islands.

kerkar: fresh *kerker* denoting
  renewal, change in continuity.

kerker: seasonal time.

kesi: Malo initiates.

ketai: perennial, wild yam.

keubkeub meta: grass-thatched
  'beehive' round houses.

Kiam: one of the three sacred
  places at which the Bomai
  mask is worn and kept in *pelak*.

kipa gogob: first rains at the end
  of dry time.

Kirriri: Hammond Island.

koki: northwest wind, with which
  Komet people are associated.

koki kerker: northwest season.

kole: master, white man.

Kwoiam: culture hero in Western
  Islands.

lamar: reborn spirit of a person,
  ancestor living in the place of
  lamar, the immortals.

lar: fish.

lar boai: fish groupings of the
  sacred order of Malo-Bomai
  composed of the westerly clans.

Las: village on Mer to which Bomai
  was taken.

le: term used by two brothers or
  two sisters for one another, man,
  person, human being, *wauri
  tebud*, mortal.

lewar kar: cultivated yams, true, real, proper food.

lewer: vegetable harvest, *au nei* for vegetable food.

logab ziai: south-southwest division of *ziai* with which Ormi Teg people are associated.

lubabat: totem.

lu kem le: nameholder for family-owned land.

Magani Kes: Great North East Channel (KLY: Magani Malu).

mai: nacre of pearl shell, pearl shell in a natural state, a piece of pearl shell.

maid: malevolent magic, the power of the singular or non-reciprocal, the power of Death.

maid le: purveyors of malevolent magic.

maimai: a stage in the life-cycle of frigate bird.

malili: iron.

malo, malu (KLY): the sea.

Malo-Bomai: Meriam culture heroes.

Malo ra Gelar: Malo's Law.

Malo: *wali aritarit, sem aritarit,* Malo plants everywhere ...

mam: blood, kin.

mamgiz: springs of common blood, sacred place of *pelak*.

mamus: head man.

mar: shadow, 'double' of a person, spirit energy, ghost of a departed person not yet reborn, a grass-like scented plant from Op Deudai.

mared: easterly division of *sager* with which Piadram and Samsep people are associated.

mari (KLY): shadow, 'double' of a person, undying spirit, ghost of a departed person not yet reborn.

mariget (KLY): the in-laws who prepare the tombstone, 'spirit-hand'.

markai (KLY): reborn spirit of a person, ancestor living in the place of immortals.

Masig: Yorke Island.

Mauar: Rennel Island.

mek: sign, the rising of a star or constellation as sign of a new season.

mekek lager: fish-line rope.

Mer: largest of the three Murray Islands, the three Murray Islands.

Muralag: Prince of Wales Island.

Muri: Mount Adolphus Island.

Nagir: Mount Ernest Island.

naiger: northeast, northeast wind (KLY: *naigai*). Wind with which Mei-Zagareb people are associated.

naiger kerker: northeast season.

naiger pek: northeast side.

naiwet: brother-in-law.

nam: green turtle.

nat (KLY): a platform from which dugong are harpooned.

nener: boundary marker.

nerutonar: people with a different custom, 'another kind' of people, the hostile other.

nesur: *lavalava* (TSC), 'calico'.

nosik: clan, 'peoples' of Mer.
Nurupai: Horn Island.

olai: *zogo nei* for part of Bomai
  mask, immature female turtle.
Op Deudai: Papua New Guinea
  (KLY: Mugie Daudai).
Op Ged: face islands, Eastern
  Islands.
opole: wearer of the sacred mask of
  Malo-Bomai.
Opolera Wetpur: Eucharist, The
  Lord's Feast.

paier: platform or framework on
  which to carry the dead.
Palai: ancient warrior culture hero
  of the Meriam.
Paremar: Coconut Island.
peibre sor: mantaray.
pelak: dome-shaped *zogo* house.
pur: uncultivated land.
puripuri: sorcery.

sab: north, wind direction with
  which Meauram people are
  associated.
sager: southeast, southeast wind
  (KLY: *sager*). Wind with which
  Geauram people are associated.
sager kerker: southeast season.
sager pek: southeast side.
sai: stone fish-traps, stage in
  life-cycle of frigate bird.
sap: driftwood.
sara (KLY): platform on which the
  dead are placed.
sarup: shipwrecked, rejected by
  the sea.

sasrim a kelar: the power that
  comes from strength.
Seg: part of the constellation Tagai,
  Orion.
seker lu: bamboo pole to which
  gifts are attached in *wauri*
  exchange.
sem: yellow hibiscus.
serar: tern.
seuriseuri: star-headed stone club
  of Malo.
Sida, Sido: mythical hero from Op
  Deudai who brought a variety of
  plants, two different languages to
  the two sides of the Strait, and
  who buried *wauri* in sandbanks
  and reefs.
sirib lager: rope made from vine
  for outriggers and houses.
sorbi: red skinned, apple-like fruit
  (*Eugenia*).

tabo: snake.
Tag mauki mauki: Keep your
  hands to yourself.
Tagai (Togai): sea hero, constellation
  consisting of Scorpio, Lupus,
  Centaurus, Crux, Corvus, part of
  Hydra and one star of Ara;
  maternal uncle of Kwoiam in
  Western Islands.
Teter mauki mauki: Keep your feet
  off other people's land.
tebud-in-Malo: partners or friends
  through the mediation of Malo.
tebud le: partner in *wauri*.
ter: fringing reefs.
teter mek: footprints.

Tomog *zogo*: important divinatory shrine at Mer facing Erub.

tug: a fire lit to announce important news like the death of a *Zogo le*, the outrigger pole.

Tutu: Warrior Island.

u: coconut, coconut palms.

Ugar: Stephen Island.

ukes ziai: south-southwest division of *ziai* with which Teg people are associated.

ume le: those who may see the masks, those who know the truth, members of the Malo fraternity.

ur sekerseker: variety of ironwood.

Usiam: part of the constellation Tagai, the Pleiades, Seven Sisters.

u zogo: magical power associated with the coconut.

wada: fully grown red-throated frigate bird.

wag: wind.

Waibene: Thursday Island.

Waier: the smallest of the three Murray Islands.

Waiet: *agud* of Waier.

wali: a creeping vine.

Waraber: Sue Island.

waumer: frigate bird.

wauri: cone shell, armlet made from cone shell (KLY: *waiwi* (*conus millepunctatus*, variety *conus litteratis*).

wauri tebud: shell friends, partners.

wed le: song men of Malo, *Zagareb le*.

wet: digging stick.

wetpur: a ceremonial feast for a brother-in-law, feasting, a live coal of fire.

wewer mebgorge: west-northwest, wind direction with which Peibre *nosik* is associated.

Yata: Port Lihou at Muralag.

yumi (TSC): you and me to the exclusion of others.

Zagareb *le*: song men of Malo ceremonies.

zeub: pipe of peace.

ziai: southwest.

ziai kerker: southwest season.

zogo: a natural or artificial object of great magical potency, power to communicate with *lamar*, intentional power like cosmic energy moving in a spiral, sacred, the spirit power of Malo, 'divine wrath', holy.

Zogo le: the three *le* entitled to wear the Malo-Bomai masks, persons with sacred or divine power, person with power to discern the movement of cosmic energy.

zogo-mai: sacred ornament shaped like a crescent moon.

zogo mir: magical words, chants.

INDEX

Abednego, Jacob xvii

Aboriginal/s Department xi, xv, 182,
  183, 185, 186, 203, 219
  renamed DNA 219

Aboriginal and Islander Teacher
  Education Program 281

Aboriginal and Torres Strait Islander
  Commission 246, 281

Aboriginal and Torres Strait Islander
  Commission Act 246

Aboriginal Development Commission
  10, 245

Aboriginal Industries Board 161, 162,
  182, 200, 210
  renamed Island Industries Board
  167

Aboriginals Protection and
  Restriction of the Sale of Opium
    Act xiii, 128, 181
  amendments of 1934 133–34, 185,
    197, 274
  consolidation of Acts 273
  exemptions from 134
  Islanders placed under 204

Aborigines and Torres Strait
  Islanders (Land Holding) Act
    (see Land Holding Act)

Adai (see also Cape York Peninsula)
  138

Adam Village 140

adoption 7

Aets (see Zogo le)

Ahmat, Crossfield xvii, 259

Ahmat, Telei xvii

Ailan Man 15, 36, 37, 93, 116, 161,
  165, 166–69, 176, 177, 186, 221,
  222

Akee, James 228, 229, 230
  and Islander identity 168

All-One, All-Ways 6, 77, 113, 152
  and cosmic renewal 117–25, 253,
    257
  the Cross as symbol 124
  and Eternal Return 260
  and Malo ra Gelar 125
  and seuriseuri 125

Anglican Church 104–10
  Bishop of Carpentaria 183, 185,
    201, 277
  and revival of Malo dances
    105, 252
  Synod 183, 184

annexation of the Torres Strait
  Islands 26, 156

Appel, George 131, 184

Arthur, W.S. 281

Assemblies of God
  as 'religion of the oppressed' 225

Assistant 19, 22, 265

Au Bala xiii, 15, 20, 29, 30, 44, 50,
  51–52, 60, 67, 72, 79–84, 88,
  90–91, 93, 94, 105, 106, 113, 116,
  121, 151, 173, 174, 210, 237, 240,
  242, 251, 252, 255, 256, 257,
  258, 259, 265, 266, 267, 272

au nei and kebi nei 54, 269

Auntie 15, 129, 134–37, 151, 152,
  253
  as healer 134

Aurid 265

Austin 160, 162

autonomy, search for (see also
  sovereignty, strike against
  protection, Torres Strait
  Islanders) xi, 219, 241–44